THE
LITERATURE
OF COMMITMENT

THE
LITERATURE
OF COMMITMENT

Charles I. Glicksberg

Lewisburg
Bucknell University Press
London: Associated University Presses

Associated University Presses, Inc.
Cranbury, New Jersey 08512

Associated University Presses
108 New Bond Street
London W1Y OQX, England

Library of Congress Cataloging in Publication Data

Glicksberg, Charles Irving, 1900-
   The literature of commitment.

   Bibliography: p.
   Includes index.
   1. Politics and literature. I. Title.
PN51.G53   809'.933   75-5148
ISBN 0-8387-1685-7

The author thanks the *Arizona Quarterly* for permission to use parts of his article "The Literary Contributions of George Orwell" (vol. 10, no. 3).

PRINTED IN THE UNITED STATES OF AMERICA

To
Stephanie and Elena

Contents

Acknowledgments

I wish to acknowledge my indebtedness to a number of people who helped me in various ways while I was doing the basic research on this book. Mr. Dan L. Levy, an Administrative Assistant at the Brooklyn College Library, was an efficient and unfailing source of bibliographical data. I thank the staff at the Bloomingdale branch and the 40th Street branch of the New York Public Library for their courteous and competent assistance. I am deeply appreciative of the professional help I received from the personnel of the Graduate Center Library of the City University of New York.

My son, Mr. Paul Glicksberg, was tireless in his zeal to lighten my task at every stage of the book's progress toward completion. I owe a special vote of thanks to Mrs. Mathilde E. Finch, Editor in Chief, for her conscientious efforts to purge the manuscript of error and to improve its stylistic quality before it was turned over to the printer. One could not ask for a more gracious and capable editor. Finally, I am grateful beyond words to my wife, who gave me her unstinted moral support while I was working on this book.

Introduction

1. *The Plight of the Intellectual*

The world about us is, as it always has been, full of gross evils and appalling misery, but it is a fatal delusion and a shocking overestimation of the importance of the artist in the world, to suppose that, by making works of art, we can do anything to eradicate the one or alleviate the other. . . .Art is impotent.[1]

Insofar as he is an intellectual he must refrain from active politics, even when he is impelled to participate as a citizen.[2]

A political "solution" is never a solution, but always a temporary expedient, an attempt to achieve the possible, a *modus vivendi.*[3]

1. W. H. Auden, "The Real World," *The New Republic* 47 (December 7, 1967): 26. Influenced by Collingwood, Auden consistently voiced the belief that art is not magic. Collingwood maintains that the purpose of art as magic is to arouse emotions, which are then transferred to the concerns of practical life. "This new aesthetic consciousness involves a two-eyed stance. It regards the subject as an integral element in the work of art; it holds that, in order to appreciate any given work of art, one must be interested in its subject for its own sake, as well as in the artist's handling of it" (R.G. Collingwood, *The Principles of Art* [Oxford: Clarendon Press, 1938], p. 71). In his essay "Henry James and the Artist in America," Auden inveighs against the tendency, rampant in our age of cultural disintegration, of transforming the artist into a magician who will deploy his creative gifts to awaken in the masses the feelings and beliefs that the authorities regard as socially desirable. This constitutes a subtle but insidious temptation for the artist, for he is led to believe that he can use art to do "good," and the world promises to reward him generously for renouncing his artistic integrity (Monroe K. Spears, *The Poetry of W. H. Auden* [New York: Oxford University Press, 1963], p. 188).
2. Elémire Zolla, *The Eclipse of the Intellectual,* trans. Raymond Rosenthal (New York: Funk & Wagnalls, 1968), p. 171.
3. Neal Wood, *Communism and British Intellectuals* (New York: Columbia University Press, 1959), pp. 115-226.

11

The first epigraph, by W. H. Auden, sums up succinctly the dilemma of the writer who has ceased to believe in the sacredness and unique importance of his calling. He leads an alienated existence in a technological society that questions the value of his creative work. He is an outsider, a man without recognized status or a legitimate function, a dreamer without a foothold in reality, a nonentity, a neurotic who uses art as a form of wish-fulfillment. A romantic seeker of the ideal of perfection, he knows that he is wedded to failure. His literary productions are only tentative and flawed sketches for the masterpiece he hoped someday to write. In his will Kafka asked that all his manuscripts be destroyed after his death. Ibsen's last play, *When We Dead Awaken*, dramatizes the crushing despair of an artist who has lost faith in his art. Professor Rubek, like Ibsen himself, is not content to remain in the aesthetic stage: "all this talk about the artist's vocation and the artist's mission, and so forth, began to strike me as being very empty, and hollow, and meaningless at bottom."[4] His bitter complaint is that in his single-minded passion for art, he had failed to live his life.[5]

In order to safeguard himself against this occupational hazard, the artist is often tempted, especially during a period of social unrest and widespread economic suffering, to join a radical political party or actively support its program, to commit himself to a revolutionary movement that will promote the cause of justice and brotherhood. He will give up his dilettantish trifling with literature or, like Mayakovsky, dedicate his talent to the writing of propaganda for the Communist Party.[6] But the writer who seriously tries to politicize his art encounters difficulties he had not anticipated when he first took the vow of commitment. He can, if he so chooses, abandon completely his devotion to literature and plunge into the maelstrom of politics. He is free, like Sartre, to stop writing plays and novels and deflect his torrential flow of

---

4. Henrik Ibsen, *When We Dead Awaken*, in *The Collected Works of Henrik Ibsen* (London: William Heinemann, 1929), 11:398.
5. The paradoxical theme of the conflict between art and life appears in Thomas Mann's story "Tonio Kröger." See Charles I. Glicksberg, "The Sickness of Alienation," in *Modern Literary Perspectivism* (Dallas, Texas: Southern Methodist University Press, 1970), pp. 44-46.
6. Or, in his hour of extreme distress, the intellectual may turn to God, as a number of writers have done: W. H. Auden, John Middleton Murry, Péguy, Edwin Muir, and T. S. Eliot.

energy into journalistic channels: the authorship of virulent polemics, feuilletons, political tracts, Marxist diatribes. Who can say which is the more desirable and rewarding choice for the contemporary writer?

Once he becomes embroiled in left-wing politics, he is beset by a number of temptations that are hard to resist. He becomes so intent on gaining his political objective and on defeating the enemy, that he is guilty at times of promulgating a calculated duplicitous ideology. Like the professional politician, he is compelled by the exigencies of battle to compromise his principles. As Paul Valéry declares: "The political mind is always, in the end, forced to misrepresent."[7] Hence he concludes "that in all possible cases *politics and freedom of the mind* are mutually exclusive. The latter is the *true enemy of parties*. . . ."[8] Valéry had no faith "in *direct* political action"[9] by intellectuals. He confessed that the grotesque spectacle of the world of politics made him sick.

The pathos of the intellectual when he attempts to play a revolutionary role on the stage of history springs very often from his discovery that he is temperamentally unfit to act out this part in good faith and bear the full burden of responsibility it entails. Stemming as a rule from a bourgeois family background, he cannot, for all his ideological fervor, overcome the conditioning of his mind in the past. He is not at ease in the presence of workers whom he wishes to regard as comrades.[10] In Great Britain during the thirties, the spread of the Marxist doctrine led the intellectual to discover the existence of the working man. Many intellectuals, particularly in Great Britain, sought in all sincerity to understand the character of the proletariat, but there were others who looked upon the idealized proletarian as the new hero, the savior of society, "the chosen instrument of history."[11]

The intellectuals who joined the Communist Party were expected to function as ideologists who would arouse the re-

7. Paul Valéry, *The Outlook for Intelligence,* trans. Denise Folliot and Jackson Mathews (New York and Evanston: Harper & Row, 1962), p. 206.
8. *Ibid.,* p. 180.
9. *Ibid.,* p. 327.
10. Orwell felt keenly the social distance that separated the middle-class intellectual, despite his radicalism, and the working class. A vast gulf kept the two apart, "and that gulf he never really crossed." George Woodcock, *The Crystal Spirit: A Study of George Orwell* (New York: Minerva Press, 1966), p. 22.
11. Wood, *Communism and British Intellectuals,* p. 42.

volutionary consciousness of the proletariat, but their deficiencies as politicos soon became apparent. They were too scrupulous, too casuistic, too introspective, too prone to debate an issue or to voice their doubts when unity and immediacy of action were called for. They could not, it seems, throw off their fractious individuality. Like the existentialist hero in Sartre's fiction, they give birth to thoughts that generate further thoughts, which in turn breed a further progeny of thought *ad infinitum*.[12] Their addiction to thought becomes a virtual disease, a mania, a vice. They cherish the illusion that thought, if properly applied, can solve all problems. Then comes their rude awakening: the perception that the world of social reality is not at all or only slightly affected by their play of thought. That is why the intellectuals were not held in high esteem by the leaders or the rank-and-file members of the Communist Party.[13]

Intellectually, men like Leon Blum and Walther Rathenau who enter the arena of politics must endure, despite their generous endowment of talent and the high political office they hold, many painful frustrations and setbacks in the course of their career. That is largely because they are unable to reconcile practice with the theory of politics, refractory reality with the purity of the ideal. Once they are invested with the power of leadership, they are forced to make concessions since they must satisfy the competing demands of various classes and social groups. Their idealism must give way if they are to remain in office; they must work closely in cooperation with existing political organizations.

12. See Victor Brombert, *The Intellectual Hero: Studies in the French Novel, 1880-1955* (Philadelphia and New York: J. B. Lippincott, 1960).
13. The steady influx of intellectuals into the Communist Party created a number of difficult problems. The Party leaders looked upon them with suspicion. They were held up to ridicule and derision as flighty, unstable, irresolute, incorrigibly individualist. Some of these charges were not without substance. Intellectuals do not submit readily to group discipline. Lenin was cognizant of the negative traits of the intellectuals: their anarchistic leanings, their unwillingness to follow directives. When Stalin gained control of the Communist movement, the campaign against the feckless intellectuals was intensified. The fathers of the Revolution, the early Bolsheviks, were supplanted by a band of servile bureaucrats. Trotsky was forced to flee into exile. The intellectuals in the Soviet Union were henceforth denied access to the seats of power. It is interesting to note that Communism in China seems to be following a similar course. The correspondent for *The New York Times* reports that the Chinese masses are inculcated with a feeling of contempt for the intellectuals *(The New York Times,* November 3, 1968).

The careers of all three men [Leon Blum, Walther Rathenau, and Filippo Tomasso Marinetti] raise the question of how far a man of intelligence, or imagination, sensibility or originality, independence or scrupulousness can in fact stand up to the strain of the ruthless machine-politics of the twentieth century, and whether the intellectual in politics is not always going to be doomed to failure because of the nature of his own virtues.[14]

The warning that the intelligentsia who took up politics were doomed to failure did not deter a number of "progressive intellectuals"[15] from earnestly seeking to serve the interests of the proletariat. They emulated the example set by the narodniki and the nihilists in Russia during the last quarter of the nineteenth century. They were motivated by a quasi-religious spirit. Actuated by the highest ideal of service to mankind, many during the depression joined the Communist Party as the one militant organization that could, like the Bolsheviks in Russia, change the world. But their quixotic experiment did not last for long. Some of these intellectuals found themselves at odds with the leadership of the Communist Party, which practiced Realpolitik and, when necessary, followed the dictates of expediency. Nor could they ally themselves with an exploited class, the proletariat, which repulsed their overtures, sometimes with contempt. The intellectual remains at bottom unattached, disoriented, frustrated and confused in his effort to see life as a whole. He is the deluded victim, the Marxists complain, of abstractions that have no relation to the concrete conditions of social reality. Trained to view social and political conflicts from a variety of perspectives and dwelling as he does in an open society that believes in the ideal of boundless inquiry, the intellectual "has the characteristics of a Proteus who perennially transcends and reconstitutes himself, and whose foremost motives are renovation and reformation."[16] By scrupulously examining every doctrine for its degree of error, he is able to resist the

14. James Joll, *Three Intellectuals in Politics* (New York: Pantheon Books, 1960), p. x.
15. Zolla points out that the term *progressive intellectual* has been grossly abused, so that we are ashamed to utter the soiled adjective; we must not abandon its use and thus deny ourselves the right to judge. Elémire Zolla, *The Eclipse of the Intellectual*, pp. 171-72.
16. Karl Mannheim, *Essays on the Sociology of Culture,* ed. Ernest Manhaim and Paul Kecskemeti (New York: Oxford University Press, 1956), p. 92

lure of political absolutes. But this tendency to question everything beneath the sun, including his own motives, incapacitates him for a life of action. It holds him back from the supreme act of "commitment."

Though this sharpened critical faculty prevents him from going to rash extremes in his espousal of revolutionary romanticism, he is, in many instances, dissatisfied with this resolution of his inner conflict between detachment and commitment. Some writers are depressed if they adopt this method of strategic withdrawal from the ongoing battle of politics. To them this withdrawal into the inner fortress of the self seems like a retreat, an abdication of responsibility. The writing of popular but innocuous books in an age that is heading inexorably toward an atomic Armageddon is an unpardonable egotistic indulgence. The writers of this description are fiddling with words while Rome burns. As mere purveyors of literature, they are without power or influence, the voice of an impotent minority, whereas what they want to be, if that were possible, is a vital part of their age, instrumental in shaping the future history of the world. They are tired of possessing the negative virtues of disinterestedness, Olympian objectivity, and nonpartisanship. They seek to recapture the utopian aspirations of their youth and thus transcend the crippling discipline of doubt, but the goal of spontaneous, wholehearted commitment eludes them.

Nevertheless, the forces on the Left zealously push their campaign to recruit the services of those intellectuals who are in sympathy with the Marxist ideal. Some writers, to be sure, utterly fail to respond to the urgent Marxist calls for commitment. Valéry's inveterate distrust of ideologies and logical systems led him to spurn the life of politics. He pointed out the vagueness and, in fact recklessness characteristic of political speculation, its tendency to indulge in sweeping but unsupported generalizations. Affirming as he did the constructive function of the rational mind in modern civilization, he protested against those movements in Europe and the United States which emulated the ideal of efficient operation rightly applied to a machine and refused to tolerate those individuals who did not conform to their prescriptive ethic. He divided the body of intellectuals into two groups: *"intellectuals who serve some purpose and intellectuals who serve none.* For man's bread, clothing, and shelter, and his physical ills, neither

Dante, nor Poussin, nor Malebranche could do anything whatever."[17]

Though Valéry was greatly admired as a poet and critic, his reflections on politics of the mind did not receive from his contemporaries the attention they deserved. The intellectuals paid little or no heed to his admonitions. During the thirties, when the triumph of Fascism seemed imminent, many writers and intellectuals rediscovered the necessity for commitment and affirmed their faith in the politics of the Left.

2. The Writer and the Politics of Commitment

But whatever else he does in the service of his party, he should never write for it. He should make it clear that his writing is a thing apart.[18]

Politics in a work of literature are like a pistol-shot in the middle of a concert, something loud and vulgar and yet a thing to which it is not possible to refuse one's attention.[19]

Why write a political novel? Many writers, as well as readers, would doubt the validity of the exercise, for what can a mere book hope to *change?* What in fact do we know of the effect of politically oriented literature on a reader's political attitudes or behavior? . . . It may well be that books can bolster, but rarely subvert, already formed beliefs. But the question whether they can inculcate where only a vacuum existed before is wide open.[20]

The writer who has won recognition in his field does not suddenly announce his adherence to the truth of Marxism or

17. Paul Valéry, *The Outlook for Intelligence*, p. 84.
18. George Orwell, *Such, Such Were the Joys* (New York: Harcourt, Brace and Company, 1953), p. 71.
19. Stendhal (Marie Henri Beyle), *The Charterhouse of Parma*, trans. C. K. Scott Moncrieff (New York: Liveright Publishing Corporation, 1944), 2: 209. This is an excellent example of the political novel in the nineteenth century.
20. W. D. Redfern, *Paul Nizan: Committed Literature in a Conspiratorial World* (Princeton, N. J.: Princeton University Press, 1972), p. 119. Redfern adds this elucidative comment: "Now, if what we are invited to ally ourselves with is a political outlook, what are the problems facing the writer? What resistance must he overcome, even while trying to encourage the reader to be critical and think for himself? First, he should avoid the temptation to provide totally predigested material." *Ibid.*, p. 120.

act rashly on impulse when he decides to join the Communist Party. His political commitment is, like a religious conversion, a gradual, often a sudden, process of intellectual awakening and spiritual growth. He comes to feel that he is personally responsible for the calamitous condition of society. He condemns the evils of capitalism and, inspired by Marxist humanism, allies himself with those who are actively engaged in building the ideal City of Man. When the cause to which he has given himself is in grave danger, he puts aside his creative work and enlists in the fight against the common enemy. The outbreak of the Spanish Civil War, for example, called forth intense feelings of support for the Loyalist side on the part of the aroused intellectuals in the West, many of whom served as volunteers in the International Brigade. The vision of the Kingdom of Heaven established on earth— namely, the classless society based on justice, equality, and brotherhood—this was the shining ideal that motivated them to become loyal Communists or fellow travelers. Arthur Koestler describes the steps that led to his conversion in 1931, when, at the age of twenty-six, he became a member of the Communist Party in Germany. He had seen the light. Marxism had revealed to him the secret of life. Here was the science of dialectical materialism, which could answer every question the mind of man could ask. Thus the convert gained "inner peace,"[21] born of the conviction that history was on his side. He had been vouchsafed an interpretation of life that accounted for everything under the sun. Like the Holy Roman Church, the Party was infallible in its logic and its morality. It could not err morally, for its policies were dictated by the dialectic of history; hence all the means it used to achieve its purpose were justified. Logically, the Party was on the right track because it acted as "the vanguard of the Proletariat, and the Proletariat [was] the embodiment of the active principle in History."[22]

Silone also tells how his decision to join the Communist Party in Italy meant "a conversion, a complete dedication."[23] He ceased to believe in Catholicism and its doctrine of individual immortality. The Party took the place of the Church.

21. Richard Crossman, ed., *The God That Failed* (New York: Bantam Books, 1951), p. 22.
22. *Ibid.,* p. 33.
23. *Ibid.,* p. 99.

In his introduction to *The God That Failed,* Richard Crossman declares: "The emotional appeal of Communism lay precisely in the sacrifices—both material and spiritual—which it demanded of the convert."[24]

The writers who were converted to Communism believed that Marxism furnished a valid interpretation of all of man's interests and activities. The science of politics is not only of paramount importance, it is all-encompassing in its sweep. Everything is included within its scope, not only the ownership of property, the means of production, the distribution of wealth, the wages a worker is paid, but the totality of the superstructure as well—philosophy, religion, ethics, literature, science, and art. All of culture is thus subsumed under the rubric of politics. The writer is therefore urged on all sides to commit himself politically. He cannot afford to remain inactive and unconcerned. To do nothing is to be guilty of perpetuating the status quo.

Once the writer committed himself politically to the extent of espousing the revolutionary cause, he began to wonder what he could hope to accomplish by means of his creative imagination. Before his adoption of Marxism, he had assumed that art as propaganda possessed only limited efficacy

24. *Ibid.,* p. 6. David Caute warns of the dangers that arise in connection with the method of selecting—and heavily stressing—only one of the many complex factors that induce the intellectual to embrace Marxism and then Communism. The ex-Communist, who has freed himself from this delusive Marxist myth, is prone to fall into this species of error. He has made up his mind that since the Communist Parties pay little attention to Marxist theory and are not in the least concerned to maintain an attitude of consistency, therefore intelligent intellectuals "cannot . . . have come to communism by way of 'reason', whatever belief they hold to the contrary" (David Caute, *Communism and the French Intellectuals 1914-1960* [New York: The Macmillan Company, 1964], pp. 262-63). He is therefore wary of subscribing to the view that Communist intellectuals found in Marxism a drug to quiet their anxieties, an ersatz religion that could help them solve their personal problems. While it is unwarranted to speculate rashly about the motives that prompted intellectuals in the West to enroll in the Communist Party, it is equally unwarranted to set aside as untrustworthy the detailed confessions of such ex-Communists as Arthur Koestler and Ignazio Silone. Their reports after leaving the Party are not to be discounted as the biased reaction of disgruntled utopians. Silone, a man of unimpeachable integrity, writes that his decision to live in the city and take an active part in the workers' movement was "a sort of flight, an emergency exit from an insupportable solitude. . . . But it was not easy to reconcile my state of mental rebellion against an old and unacceptable social order with the 'scientific' requirements of a minutely codified political doctrine. For me as for many others, it was a conversion, a commitment. . . ." (Ignazio Silone, *Emergency Exit,* trans. Harvey Fergusson II [New York and London: Harper & Row, 1968], pp. 64-65).

and was ephemeral in its appeal. Who nowadays reads *Uncle Tom's Cabin* or *The Jungle?* The omnibus term *propaganda* is used cunningly and often casuistically to cover a multitude of semantic sins. In a discussion between George Orwell and Desmond Hawkins in "The Proletarian Writer,"[25] Orwell remarks that every writer is a propagandist, but he does not mean that he practices the art of political propaganda. The honest and gifted artist resists the corruption of politics, but Orwell repeats his conviction that every artist is a propagandist in that "he is trying, directly or indirectly, to impose a vision of life that seems to him desirable."[26] As I shall show in a later chapter, which examines Orwell's work in detail, his definition is so broad that it embraces all forms of imaginative writing. In the thirties, however, literature was "swamped by propaganda,"[27] most of it political in content. In a world of fearful threats and economic insecurity, the writer found it impossible to cultivate his own garden, to keep aloof while the battle against totalitarianism is being fought. He was told again and again by the spokesman of the Left that he must choose between two warring camps, Fascism and Socialism. "Literature had to become political, because anything else would have entailed mental dishonesty."[28] In a number of broadcasts and articles that reflect the tensions and pressures of the war then being fought, Orwell warned the writer of the danger he runs if he responds too zealously to an ethic of commitment. About 1939 many writers discovered "that you cannot really sacrifice your intellectual integrity for the sake of a political creed—or at least you cannot do so and remain a writer."[29] In practice, Orwell drew a distinction between various types of propaganda, among which he singled out political propaganda as the most damaging.

A number of European writers in the nineteenth century, in their desire to promote the cause of social justice, were drawn actively into the world of politics,[30] but they rep-

25. Delivered over the BBC and printed in *The Listener* in December 1940.
26. George Orwell, *My Country Right or Left 1940-1943*, in *The Collected Essays, Journalism and Letters of George Orwell*, ed. Sonia Orwell and Ian Angus (New York: Harcourt, Brace & World, 1968), 2: 41.
27. *Ibid.*, p. 123.
28. *Ibid.*, p. 126.
29. *Ibid.*, p. 126.
30. A list of names chosen at random would include such writers as Georg Büchner, Heinrich Heine, Thomas Carlyle, John Ruskin, William Morris, Emile Zola, and Charles Kingsley.

resented a variety of political opinion. They were not required to submit to Party control. Many of them were hostile
to the established order because of their alienation from the
crass commericialism of their age. As business boomed and
the prosperous middle class rose to positions of dominance,
writers voiced their detestation of the rampant spirit of
greed, the tyranny of the cash-nexus. Though they themselves stemmed from bourgeois stock, they repudiated the
ethos of their class; they despised its vulgarity, its shameless
worship of Mammon, its honorific display of the signs of
wealth. Such a society had nothing to offer the creative elite;
they saw that it was ruled by men whom they held in contempt and who had no use for the rebellious tribe of artists.
These historic changes in the class structure of society intensified the alienation of the artists at the time and adversely
affected their socioeconomic status.[31] In France, for example,

31. "An altered society had changed the nature of the literary market and the
literary trade. It had created and demanded a new view of the relation between the public and the man of letters and a new definition of the source and
function of literary work" (César Graña, *Bohemian versus Bourgeois* [New York
and London: Basic Books, 1964], p. 20). This diagnosis is amply confirmed by
Balzac in his novel *Lost Illusions*. Lucien, the hero, a young aspiring poet,
hopes that he will be able to conquer the world by means of his superior intellect, though he shrewdly suspects that "money is the fulcrum of intellect"
(Honoré de Balzac, *Lost Illusions*, trans. Kathleen Raine [New York: The Modern Library, 1967], p. 177). Lousteau, a journalist who once nursed the ambition to become a writer, discloses to Lucien the bitter truth of reality. "To
write good books, my poor boy, you must draw tenderness, vitality, the sap of
life, from your own heart's blood at every dip of the pen, and put your very
soul into the passions, sentiments, and phrases of your work. Yes, supposing
you write instead of acting, sing instead of battling with the world; supposing
you keep your wealth for your style, your money and fine clothes for your
characters, while you walk about the streets of Paris in rags, happy to think
that you have rivalled the Registrar of Births by bringing into existence an
individual called Adolphe, or Corinna, or Clarissa, or René or Manon; when
you have ruined your life and your digestion in order to give life to this creation of yours, you will see it condemned, betrayed, sold and swept into the
back quarters of oblivion by the journalists, and disregarded by your best
friends" (*ibid.*, p. 262). Lucien comes to realize that money is "the key to all
riddles" (*ibid.*, p. 283). He decides to abandon the group of intellectual friends
who, sustained by a spirit of idealism, are determined to remain poor rather
than compromise their artistic ideals. In Lucien's considered judgement they
are fools. He concludes that it is indeed difficult "to keep any illusions on any
subject in Paris. Everything is taxed, everything is for sale, and everything is
manufactured, even success!" (*ibid.*, p. 399). Small wonder that Marx and Engels greatly admired the genius of Balzac. See F. Schiller, "Marx and Engels
on Balzac," *International Literature*, no. 3 (July 1933), pp. 113-24. For a perceptive analysis of the social and political implications of Balzac's *oeuvre*, see
Harry Levin, *Gates of Horn* (New York: Oxford University Press, 1963).

some artists were convinced that their work had the power not only to transfigure the mind and heart of man but also to change the world for the better. Like the utopian socialist Proudhon, "some artists believed that art was the moral expression of societies and ought to be their guide."[32] They were imbued with a fervent sense of their "quasi-religious as well as . . . moral and social mission."[33]

Dickens in *Dombey and Son* (1848) exposed the shocking evils that were spawned by the newly emerging industrial society—the power of money to impose its uncurbed will upon the world, an economic system that reduced people to commodities and used the cant of morality to justify its business enterprises, which were measured solely in terms of profit and loss. Dickens pictured the grim realities of the class struggle and showed how they nullified all humane considerations.[34] Then in *Hard Times* (1854) Dickens made an impassioned humanitarian plea in behalf of the exploited workers in Coketown. The novel is a jeremiad, a polemic instinct with moral indignation.[35] Dickens was a social reformer, but his proposed remedy for the horrible conditions of the poor in Coketown was politically inept.[36] He had no intention of agitating for legislative measures that would abolish or greatly mitigate the evils of industrialism. He was no fire-breathing, iconoclastic critic of the existing social order, and had no desire to tear it down in order to build anew. No matter what kind of society man fashioned, Dickens believed, evil would still be active and unvanquished if human nature were not transformed. Dickens was not opposed to the prevailing system of private property; he be-

---

32. Geraldine Pelles, *Art, Artists and Society* (Englewood Cliffs, N. J.: Prentice-Hall, 1963), p. 19.
33. *Ibid.,* pp. 19-20.
34. See John Lucas, "Dickens and *Dombey and Son:* Past and Present Imperfect," in David Howard, John Lucas, and John Goode, eds., *Tradition and Tolerance in Nineteenth-Century Fiction* (New York: Barnes & Noble, 1967), pp. 99-140. See also "The Radicalism of 'Little Dorrit,'" by William Myers, in John Lucas, ed., *Literature and Politics in the Nineteenth Century* (London: Methuen & Co., 1971), pp. 77-104.
35. Friedrich Engels published his pioneering work, *The Conditions of the Working Class in England,* in 1845. In 1847 Marx and Engels wrote the *Communist Manifesto.*
36. "On every page *Hard Times* manifests its identity as a polemical work, a critique of mid-Victorian industrial society dominated by materialism, acquisitiveness, and ruthlessly competitive capitalist economics." David Lodge, *Language of Fiction* (London: Routledge and Kegan Paul, 1966), p. 145.

trayed no Socialist leanings. In fact, his sympathies were with the capitalists, at least with those who were benevolent and philanthropic. The world, he was convinced, would be a fine place to live in if mankind could be taught to behave decently. That was the heart of his moral message.[37] Though Dickens is not, *"in the accepted sense,"* a revolutionary writer, "it is not at all certain that a merely moral criticism of society may not be just as 'revolutionary'—and revolution, after all, means turning things upside down—as the politico-economic criticism which is fashionable at this moment."[38]

Dickens, like Mrs. Gaskell and Anthony Trollope, could preach to his readers without feeling that he was violating a taboo formulated by the high priests of the art of fiction in France. Flaubert's austere conception of the novel as a self-contained, autonomous universe of being in which the author remains invisible behind the scenes and scrupulously refrains from controlling the actions and utterances of his characters, did not gain many disciples until the twentieth century. Flaubert's insistence that such alien and unassimilable ingredients as politics, moral judgment, and propaganda must be excluded from the novel was adopted as an article of faith, the credo of the avant garde by those modern writers who resisted the pressure of their age to make the novel serve some extra-literary ulterior aim. Ortega, in *The Dehumanization of Art* and *Notes on the Novel*, effectively sums up the case for the novel as a pure art form. He maintains that "every novel is still-born that is laden with transcendental intentions, be they political, ideological, symbolical, or satirical, for those themes are of such a nature that they cannot be dealt with fictionally, they have meaning only in relation to the actual horizon of each individual."[39] Such ingredients destroy the illusion the work of art is meant to create. The novelist who exploits this genre as a form of magic regards himself as a reformer who wants to remake the world, but his missionary designs on the reader misfire, for the novel, Ortega asserts,

---

37. "Dickens is . . . opposed to any change in the political and economic structure of society, and places his hopes for amelioration in a change of heart, mind, and soul in those who possess power, who will then disseminate the fruits of this change over the lower echelons of society." *Ibid.*, p. 147.
38. George Orwell, *Dickens, Dali and Others* (New York: Harcourt, Brace and Company, 1946), pp. 22-23.
39. José Ortega y Gasset, *The Dehumanization of Art* and *Notes on the Novel* (New York: Peter Smith, 1951), p. 92.

"cannot propagate philosophical, political, sociological, or moral ideas; it can be nothing beyond a novel."[40]

This is not to say or even imply that there is a "law" of aesthetics that categorically forbids the imaginative writer to touch a tabooed subject like politics. There is no such "law," no such prohibition. Dramatists from Aristophanes to Dürrenmatt, Frisch, and Brecht have dealt effectively with such themes. There is no formal interdiction the writer is required to obey. He is free to write on any subject or theme within the vast range of human experience: prostitution, homosexuality, industrial strife, misogyny, the alienation of man under capitalism, moral nihilism, madness, incest, decadence. The choice of a suitable theme, however, is the least part of the writer's creative labor. What counts in the final analysis is how he handles the theme, gives it a local habitation and concrete name. What arouses the skepticism or psychic resistance of the reader is not the political theme *per se* but the simplistic propagandistic fervor of the author, as in Gorky's novel *Mother*.

There is no reason why the novelist or dramatist cannot respond to the challenge of politics and produce a work that is not ephemeral despite its concern with the issues of the day or one that is not marred by the gratuitous intrusion of the didactic or propagandistic impulse.[41] In such novels as *Under Western Eyes*, *Heart of Darkness*, and *Nostromo*, Conrad overcame his subjective urge to take sides. From Flaubert he had learned the creative wisdom of not injecting his personal bias into a work of fiction. Though he was deeply moved by the political conflicts of his age, as a novelist he steered clear of ideologies and panaceas. In *Heart of Darkness* he composed "a vehement denunciation of imperialism and racialism without damning all men who through the accident of their birth in England were committed to these public policies."[42]

There are some critics, however, who argue that the mod-

---

40. *Ibid.*, p. 94.
41. Richard Poirier complains that a number of writers seek to remove literature from the contamination of politics. "They claim to believe that literature or education or sex or violence should not be thought of in political terms." Richard Poirier, *The Performing Self* (New York: Oxford University Press, 1971), p. xi.
42. Eloise Knapp Hay, *The Political Novels of Joseph Conrad* (Chicago and London: The University of Chicago Press, 1963), p. 112.

ern writer cannot, as a matter of conscience, refuse to become actively involved in the political crises of his day.[43]

> For the modern writer politics in all its forms, as theory, as commitment, as action, has become a matter of consciousness and of conscience. Aesthetic considerations are invariably colored by social-political demands.[44]

This quotation tells us little about the character and content, the style and structure, of the political novel. It assumes, without offering any supporting evidence, that aesthetic criteria are conditioned by the historical situation, that the novelist, however "pure" his intentions, is bound to be influenced by the social and political forces of his age. What, then, is the political novel? It is not to be judged primarily or solely by its ideological content, for the abstract ideas must be given sensuous embodiment as they are defended or fiercely attacked by various protagonists. The portrayal of individualized characters in depth, with all their failings and inner flaws, must not be neglected in order to clear the ground for the emergence of "the positive hero." The difficulty the political novelist faces is

> to make ideas or ideologies come to life, to endow them with the capacity for stirring characters into passionate gestures and sacrifices, and even more, to create the illusion that they have a kind of independent motion, so that they themselves—those abstract weights of idea or ideology—seem to become active characters in the political novel.[45]

43. Angry, intemperate, accusatory, the critical voices of the New Left demand that the writer commit himself, mind, heart, and soul, to the Revolution. All those literati who do not support the revolutionary forces of the Third World are reactionaries of the worst kind. There is no mistaking the vituperative fury that informs a book like *The Mythology of Imperialism* by Jonah Raskin, which is dedicated to Ho Chi Minh. The author brands such men as T. S. Eliot, E. M. Forster, F. R. Leavis, and Lionel Trilling as "gangsters, conspirators and terrorists of the printed page" (Jonah Raskin, *The Mythology of Imperialism* [New York: Random House, 1971], p. 4). Trilling, in particular, is denounced as the prototype of the liberal anti-Communist academician. He is guilty, it seems, of the crime of making "Matthew Arnold, not Marx or Mao, the supreme dialectician" (*ibid.,* p. 8). He is damned, too, for ignoring "black culture, the art and literature of liberation" (*ibid.,* p. 10).
44. George A. Panichas, ed., *The Politics of Twentieth-Century Novelists* (New York: Hawthorn Books, 1971), p. xxii.
45. Irving Howe, *Politics and the Novel* (New York: Meridian Books, 1957), p. 21.

This concedes too much to the role of ideas and ideologies. Regardless of the position taken by such prominent Marxist literary critics as Lukács, Goldmann, and M. Lifschitz on the dialectical relationship between form and content, and their tendency to single out the world view of writers like Shakespeare, Racine, Balzac, Dickens, or Proust, it is clear that the effectiveness of the political novel does not depend on its ideological foundation. The outstanding examples of this genre—novels like *La Chartreuse de Parme, The Blithesdale Romance, The Possessed, Fathers and Sons, Nostromo, Darkness at Noon, Doctor Zhivago, The First Circle*—were not born of the overriding desire "to make ideas or ideologies come to life." That was the disastrous mistake made by many of the so-called proletarian writers of fiction during the nineteen-thirties: they endeavored to carry out with rigorous fidelity the ideological directives, cast in the optative mood, of Socialist realism. The result was that they produced edifying novels replete with Party slogans and Marxist epiphanies, but without a spark of life.

3. *Literature and Politics*

The politically committed writer on the Left (one thinks of men like Louis Aragon, Henri Barbusse, and Roger Garaudy) regards himself as a tough-minded realist. He is no Don Quixote beguiled by the rhetoric of idealism. An ardent student of Marxism, a seasoned veteran who has survived many intra-Party conflicts, he knows what he is about; he is at home in the world of power politics. Convinced that politics is the all-important, all-inclusive category, he harbors no illusions about the importance of literature. He is perfectly willing, if the need arises, to forsake literature for journalism or bring forth, in response to Party demands, a Marxist-oriented work of art, one that fulfills the requirements of Socialist realism. He has no use for the cult, sterile and dilettantish, of art for art's sake. In his censorious eyes, the pursuit of formal perfection is a bourgeois aberration, a criminal waste of energy. He feels only contempt for those misguided creatures who were followers of Mallarmé or who believed in the Revolution of the Word.[46]

46. Eugene Jolas, "Manifesto: The Revolution of the Word," *Transition Workshop,*

As a rule, it was out of idealistic motives that many gifted writers either joined the Communist Party or became devoted fellow travelers.[47] They were determined to break out of the ivory tower of aestheticism and become political activists. If they were prepared to give up the life of art, it was, basically, because they realized that in the modern world art performed no useful social function. Yet, throughout the nineteenth century the artist was assigned an exalted role as prophet, messiah, redeemer.[48]

But when the life of society is threatened by external danger, all the resources of the State are mobilized to combat and overcome the danger. In such an emergency, poets, dramatists, and even literary critics are recruited for the express purpose of arousing the fighting spirit of the people. We recall how Mayakovsky gained the title of poet laureate of the Revolution. He wrote topical, inspirational verses for the soldiers at the front and workers in the factories. A number of writers fought in the Spanish Civil War: Malraux, Orwell, Ralph Fox, Regler, John Cornford, Christopher Caudwell, Julian Bell, and Ralph Bates.

ed. Eugene Jolas (New York: The Viking Press, 1949), pp. 173-74. Some of its demands read as follows: "TIRED OF THE SPECTACLE OF SHORT STORIES, NOVELS, POEMS AND PLAYS STILL UNDER THE HEGEMONY OF THE BANAL WORD, MONOTONOUS SYNTAX, STATIC PSYCHOLOGY, DESCRIPTIVE NATURALISM, AND DESIROUS OF CRYSTALLIZING A VIEWPOINT . . . WE HEREBY DECLARE THAT: THE REVOLUTION IN THE ENGLISH LANGUAGE IS AN ACCOMPLISHED FACT. THE IMAGINATION IN SEARCH OF A FABULOUS WORLD IS AUTONOMOUS AND UNCONFINED. . . . WE ARE NOT CONCERNED WITH THE PROPAGATION OF SOCIOLOGICAL IDEAS EXCEPT TO EMANCIPATE THE CREATIVE ELEMENTS FROM THE PRESENT IDEOLOGY" (*ibid.*, pp. 173-74).

47. David Caute asserts that the Communist Party in France directed its appeal primarily to the political idealism of the intellectuals, and their response to this appeal was motivated "for the most part" by their spirit of idealism. David Caute, *Communism and the French Intellectuals 1914-1960*, p. 30.

48. "In view of the downfall of religion and the inevitable relativism of science, art was expected to take upon itself nothing less than the salvation of mankind. Art was important for two reasons: on account of its subjects which dealt with the profoundest problems of humanity, and on account of its own significance as a human pursuit from which the species derives its justification and dignity." (José Ortega y Gasset, *The Dehumanization of Art and Notes on the Novel,* pp. 49-50.) Many nineteenth-century writers were deeply troubled by the question whether their art possessed social relevance. The poets wondered whether the writing of poetry was not a frivolous preoccupation, Tennyson confronted the problem of "commitment" in "The Palace of Art." See John Lucas, "Politics and the Poet's Role," in John Lucas, ed., *Literature and Politics in the Nineteenth Century,* pp. 7-43.

There were some writers, however, who did not respond to the rallying cry of the Communist Party. Though they were deeply concerned about the fate of civilization, they did not believe that war would insure the survival of mankind. They were not carried away by the political passions of the hour to a point where they lost sight of the universal values they were resolved to support. They refused to join in the tribal chant of frenzied hatred for "the foe." Resisting the propagandistic pressure that each international crisis or threat of war generates, they would not allow themselves to be used as pawns in the game of power politics. Robinson Jeffers, for example, because he espoused the cause of isolationism during the thirties, was called a Fascist. In the thirties he published such poems as "Rearmament" and "Air-Raid Rehearsals," in which he voiced his Cassandra warning that pity would avail naught to check the deathward drive of history, the murderous manias and self-destructive rage of mankind.[49]

But during the embattled thirties, the dominant tendency among intellectuals belonging to the Left was to interpret all the crucial issues of life in political terms. When the policy of the United Front was in effect, writers were urged to enlist in the war against Fascism. The Spanish Civil War taught Francis Scarfe that human values, if they are to survive, must be fought for. He declares:

> The great tragedy of our times, and of our destiny, is not merely that "butcher-birds" in the shape of Germans, Italians, Hungarians, Roumanians, and Bulgarians are destroying civilization, but that civilized peoples are destroying each other.[50]

In "A Personal Statement" Scarfe describes his stay in Paris in 1936 and 1937; he was then engaged in writing Surrealist poetry; he decided to become a member of the Communist Party. It is not surprising that he abandoned both these movements, Surrealism and Communism, becuase of their narrowness of vision. The monolithic emphasis of Marxism on the economic factor led to an utter neglect of the spiritual element in man, his quest for transcendence.

49. Robinson Jeffers, *Such Counsel You Gave to Me and Other Poems* (New York: Random House, 1947. This volume contained the poem, "Air-Raid Rehearsals." "Rearmament" was published in *Solstice and Other Poems.* (New York: Random House, 1935.)
50. Francis Scarfe, *Auden and After* (London: Routledge, 1947), p. 173.

4. *The Function of the Writer*

Many intellectuals were attracted to Marxism because of its humanistic content, its moral appeal, its vision of a just society in which men were no longer objects to be exploited but individuals, respected as such, who worked cooperatively with their fellow men. But this vision of the ideal society could not be sustained in the face of the exigent demands the Communist Party made upon the creative elite in the West. Many would not submit to Party indoctrination and control.[51] If many of them left the revolutionary movement, it was because they could not tolerate Party discipline that called for unquestioning and unconditional obedience. The avant-garde artists, in particular, found the most congenial climate for their work in an "open" society. (Krushchev was unrestrained in his detestation of nonrepresentational or abstract art, damning it on ideological grounds as formalistic, decadent, and reactionary.[52]) Only in genuinely democratic, libertarian regimes are avant-garde artists granted the right to experiment and to express their dissenting point of view freely, without fear of punishment by the powers that be. The hypothesis—it is really only an analogy, according to Renato Poggioli—"that aesthetic radicalism and social radicalism, revolutionaries in art and revolutionaries in politics, are allied, which empirically seems valid, is theoretically and historically erroneous."[53]

Avant-garde literary movements like Expressionism, the Revolution of the Word, Dada, or Surrealism, were not at their inception inspired by leftist political aims. What were

51. Aligning himself with the left, as with the right, is only one of the numberless ways open to men of being an imbecile. . . ." José Ortega y Gasset, *History as a System,* trans. Helen Weyl (New York: W. W. Norton & Company, 1961, p. 70).

52. On December 1, 1962, Nikita Khrushchev, then holding the position of First Secretary of the Communist Party and Prime Minister of the Soviet Union, visited an exhibition of "Thirty Years of Moscow Art." It included "a small number of nonrepresentational paintings and sculpture, none of which was avant-garde by Western standards." Priscilla Johnson, *Khrushchev and the Arts,* ed., Priscilla Johnson and Leopold Labedz (Cambridge, Mass.: The M.I.T. Press, 1965), p. 101). Khrushchev could not restrain his wrath at this flagrant and irresponsible departure from the canons of genuine Soviet art. "What is hung here," he declared, "is simply anti-Soviet. It's amoral. Art should ennoble the individual and arouse him to action" *(ibid.,* p. 103).

53. Renato Poggioli, *The Theory of the Avant-Garde,* trans. Gerald Fitzgerald (Cambridge, Mass.: Harvard University Press, 1968), p. 95.

the political convictions of writers like Ezra Pound, James
Joyce, Marcel Proust, Wyndham Lewis, Virginia Woolf, T. S.
Eliot, and Alain Robbe-Grillet? Those writers and artists who
were daring innovators played no part in the outbreak and
eventual triumph of social revolutions.[54] How could it have
been otherwise? Their endowment of talent, their creative vision, their capacity for originality of design or style or insight, did not prepare them in any way to undertake the role
of political revolutionaries. Those who belong to avant-garde
movements are usually libertarians or anarchists who struggle
to preserve their individuality and freedom of expression in a
post-industrial age that in both capitalist and socialist countries is increasingly totalitarian in its demand for conformity
to the needs of technology. Whatever degree of sympathy the
avant-garde artist may feel for the professed ideals of Communism, he tends to believe first and foremost in his God-
given genius and in his exceptional, if not unique, destiny as
an artist.

The writer of imaginative literature suffers a serious loss of
spontaneity and creative power when he attempts to use his
work as a political weapon, especially if he does so at the behest of the Party or its appointed leader, for then he surren-
ders his autonomy and becomes a compliant tool of the dominant faction. At bottom, the writer wishes to be left to his
own devices and brooks no ideological interference. Herbert
Read, an outspoken, independent-minded critic, declares:

> I personally take the view, which is heterodox to most people,
> that the more consciously moral or political values are imposed
> on art, the more art suffers. Art is spontaneous, the unpremedi-
> tated act of an individual, but always innocent.[55]

T. S. Eliot advised the writer not to yield to the temptation of
uttering magisterial opinions in specialized fields where he
has no competence. The poet or novelist is not qualified to
deliver *ex cathedra* judgments on political issues. Eliot was
constantly besieged by requests that he voice his ideas on the
leading controversies and conflicts of his age. General state-

54. Donald Drew Egbert, who subscribes to the point of view enunciated by Pog-
    gioli, points out that an artist may create work that is liberal or radical in form
    or content while he is not at all interested in political or economic changes of
    a revolutionary kind. In some cases, like T. S. Eliot, he may be conservative in
    his political outlook. Donald Drew Egbert, *Social Radicalism and the Arts* (New
    York: Alfred A. Knopf, 1970), p. 59.
55. Herbert Read, *The Grass Roots of Art* (New York: Wittenborn, 1947), p. 11.

ments that support the cause of peace or deplore the evil of race discrimination—what does one achieve by supporting such appeals? Since the writer is bound by the same duties that devolve upon the ordinary citizen, Eliot signs petitions even when he is convinced that they will serve no purpose. He points out that there are a number of complex issues that the writer is unable fully to comprehend. When the Spanish Civil War raged, he felt that the situation would have improved if there had been less foreign intervention on both sides. He concluded that the duty of a writer is "essentially to protect writers like Dery and Pasternak."[56]

There were other writers besides Robinson Jeffers and T. S. Eliot who rejected the ethic of commitment. "An Attempt at Justification" is Hesse's reply to a letter by Max Brod in 1948 asking him to support the Jews on the hotly debated issue of Palestine. Hesse would not intervene. He was not, as a writer, invested with the power to affect the outcome.

For Hesse believed that such an appeal or protest or threat addressed to the powerful rulers of the earth is a pseudo-action that is spiritually harmful and one by no means to be taken. The function of the writer, he declared, is not to preach a message or to plead for the redress of grievances. Writers must come to realize that they can not exert the slightest influence on the world because of the fame they have won.[57] Hesse emphatically denied that in adopting this attitude he was shirking his responsibility as a writer and responding to the cries for help of his fellow mortals by an air of Olympian indifference. He scrupulously observed the limits placed on his creative calling. That is why he refused to sign any of the hundreds of petitions and proclamations and protests that the intellectuals sent forth "to the detriment of the humanitarian cause."[58] Is the writer to distinguish between his duties as a citizen and those he must carry out as an artist? Is he to refrain from signing noble-sounding but essentially futile petitions? Is he to avoid the political conflicts of his age and resist the pressure that bids him use his art as a vehicle for propaganda? If he resolves to act on the belief that his primary allegiance is to his art, does he become a practitioner of art for art's sake?

56. Quoted by C. L. Sulzberger in his column "Foreign Affairs," in *The New York Times*, January 5, 1965.
57. Hermann Hesse, *If the War Goes On. . .*, trans. Ralph Manheim (New York: Farrar, Straus and Giroux, 1971), p. 182.
58. *Ibid.*, pp. 183-84.

THE
LITERATURE
OF COMMITMENT

Part I
SOCIAL RESPONSIBILITY
AND LITERARY COMMITMENT

1

Literature and Social Responsibility

1. *Aestheticism*

The aesthetic aim of any fiction is the creation of a verbal world, or a significant part of such a world, alive through every order of its Being.[1]

The Aesthetic Movement was a criticism of contemporary society and often spoke of it with horror and disgust. To its adherents the whole achievement of the industrial revolution was a matter for lamentation, the idea of progress a mirage, the destruction of ancient standards the prelude to an odious uniformity.[2]

It is clear that art is useless. . . . Art tells us nothing about the world that we cannot find elsewhere and more reliably. Art does not make us better citizens, or more moral, or more honest. It may conceivably make us worse. It is easy to become addicted to art; it can be as dangerous as any drug. Art is something of a nuisance. . . . The great poetry if we take it too seriously, is capable of teaching us the most revolting nonsense.[3]

1. William H. Gass, *Fiction and the Figures of Life* (New York: Alfred A. Knopf, 1970), p. 7.
2. C. M. Bowra, *Poetry and Politics* (Cambridge, England: At the University Press, 1966), p. 37.
3. Morse Peckham, *Man's Rage for Chaos* (Philadelphia and New York: Chilton Books, 1965), pp. 313-14.

In the nineteenth century, particularly in France, many writers and artists felt cut off from their public and at odds with their world. They turned against society because it was more interested in material well-being than in art; it betrayed no genuine understanding or appreciation of their work. Furthermore, they were antagonized by the stupidity of conservative critics and the inveterate hostility of the venal press. Alienated and embittered, they resorted to more scandalous provocations, glorying in their "formlessness," their "unintelligibility," their "immorality," their diabolical genius. Gradually they created the legend of the artist as the prophet without honor in his native land, the martyred victim of philistine society.

The enemy was "the bourgeois," the stolid, hypocritical, vulgar citizen who demanded of art not that it be original but entertaining; he spurned any literary fare, however enthusiastically praised by the cognoscenti, that he found "difficult," "obscure," or "arcane." Mammon was the God he and his kind worshiped. After the fifties, the artists of the preceding century openly rebelled against a society that had run amok in an orgy of acquisitiveness. Many withdrew from a social reality that was hideously ugly, banal, and boring. In their disaffection they devoted themselves to the creation of "pure" art, divorced from the insidious pressure of economics and the contamination of politics. They gave themselves wholly to the expression of beauty. The writers for their part struggled to achieve perfection of style and produced work that was neither useful nor edifying, studiously avoiding what Poe called "the heresy of *The Didactic*."[4]

4. Edgar Allan Poe, "The Poetic Principle," in *The Complete Poems and Stories of Edgar Allan Poe*. 2 vols. (New York: Alfred A. Knopf, 1951), 2: 1025. Poe goes on to say: "It has been assumed. tacitly and avowedly, directly and indirectly, that the ultimate object of all Poetry is Truth. Every poem, it is said, should inculcate a moral, and by this moral is the poetical merit of the work to be adjudged. We Americans especially have patronized this happy idea. . . . We have taken it into our heads that to write a poem simply for the poem's sake. . . . would be to confess ourselves radically wanting in the true poetic dignity and force:—but the simple fact is that would we but permit ourselves to look into our own souls we should immediately discover there that under the sun there neither exists nor *can* exist any work more thoroughly dignified, more supremely noble, than this very poem, this poem *per se*. this poem which is a poem and nothing more, this poem written solely for the poem's sake" (*ibid.*, 2: 1025). "The Poetic Principle" was first printed in 1850. In 1857, Charles Baudelaire published his essay "New Notes on Edgar Allan Poe," which assails Victor Hugo as being guilty of introducing into his poetry "what

The writers of that time found fulfillment in their art. They despised the shoddy cultural values of the middle class; they looked upon themselves as outcasts, outsiders. Their revolt was partially held in check by the fact that they were, whether they liked it or not, an inseparable part of the bourgeois society they contemned.[5] This accounts for the ambivalence of their attitude toward society, a mixture of attachment and disgust, rebellion and dependence.[6]

The Symbolists of the nineteenth century were diehard pessimists, disillusioned with mundane reality, the tedious routine of everyday existence. They sought in poetry an avenue of escape from the commonplace and (to them) sordid world they had to live in. Contemptuous of the prizes the ruling middle class was in a position to grant, they willingly gave up their privileged place in society and cherished in private the uniqueness of their creative self. The idealism of the Symbolists, their aesthetic beliefs, the reason for their proud withdrawal into the hideout of the self, are set forth in *Axel,* written by Villiers de l'Isle-Adam and published in 1890. The hero in this poetic drama, which will be examined later on, prefers to subsist on the stuff of dreams, the fantasies born of the night. He is not a rebel; he harbors no subversive design of destroying society and of building a more desirable

Edgar Poe considered the chief modern heresy—*the heresy of the didactic"* (Charles Baudelaire, "New Notes on Edgar Allan Poe," in *Modern Literary Criticism,* ed. O. B. Harrison, Jr. [New York: Appleton-Century-Crofts, 1962], p. 173).

5. They could not deny, and the politicos on the Left, never allowed them to forget, that they did not belong to the pure proletarian breed. They were *bourgeois* intellectuals. In their education and professional training they derived incalculable benefits from the economic security and freedom of expression that bourgeois society made possible. After all, it was this society and this culture that gave them a public, however small, who read and admired their work. "The frequent emphasis on the contrast between 'artist' and 'bourgeois' must not lead to the conclusion that nineteenth-century literature had any other soil to grow in than that of the bourgeoisie. There simply was no other" (Erich Auerbach, *Mimesis,* trans. Willard R. Trask [Princeton, N. J.: Princeton University Press, 1953], p. 504).

6. "In this dilemma of instinctive aversion and necessary implication, yet at the same time amid an almost anarchic freedom in the realm of opinion, choice of possible subject matter, and development of personal idiosyncrasies in respect to forms of life and expression, those writers who were too proud and whose talents were too personally distinctive to produce the mass merchandise for which there was a general demand and a profitable sale were driven into an almost stubborn isolation in the domain of pure aesthetics and into renouncing any practical intervention in the problems of the age through their works" (*ibid.,* pp. 504-5).

social order on its ruins. He lives wholly within himself. The dream, he is convinced, is far more rewarding than anything "reality" at its best can offer.

The poet, unfortunately, could not remain shut up in his castle of dreams. As the twentieth-century world grew technologically more complex, the writer discovered that he did not know the audience for whom he wrote.[7] Society had become impersonal, specialized, and the writer could no longer say where he belonged, exactly for whom he wrote. Some writers, making a virtue out of their painful state of alienation, professed to be utterly unconcerned about the reactions of this nameless and faceless public, a statistical homunculus. They found fulfillment in their work, and that was enough to satisfy them. "Faced with the dissolution of thought and the isolation of the artist, what else could he do but declare his independence and self-sufficient supremacy both as an intellectual and an artist."[8] Painters experimented with abstractions and paid no heed to the clamor for commitment raised by "the true believers" in the field of politics.

The retreat of the artist from a society that is materialistic, corrupt, spiritually unawakened, shallow and conformist in its thinking, crude in its taste, indifferent to the meaning and magic of art—this retreat did not preclude his eventual return to communion with a public that was more enlightened. The modern writer may not know for whom he writes, but he does not create for himself alone.[9] "What is an artist but a strongly defined self that posits itself, so to speak, by opposing itself to the outside world, as well as by acting upon and within itself?"[10] If the literary critic who supports the cult of aestheticism and believes in the autonomy of art is to be considered as thoroughly confused in the values he cherishes,

7. In discussing the situation of the writer in 1947, Sartre declares that literature is a dying profession. "We no longer know—literally—for whom to write" (Jean-Paul Sartre, *What Is Literature?*, trans. Bernard Frechtman [New York: Philosophical Library, 1949], p. 241). For a Marxist-Sartrean analysis of this complex and troublesome problem, the relation of the writer to his audience, see the chapter entitled "For Whom Does One Write?" (*ibid.*, pp. 67-159).

8. Richard P. Blackmur, *Anni Mirabilis 1921-1925: Reason in the Madness of Letters* (Washington, D.C.: The Library of Congress, 1956), p. 5.

9. See "Self and Society," in Charles I. Glicksberg, *The Self in Modern Literature* (University Park, Pa.: The Pennsylvania State University Press, 1964), pp. 182-84.

10. René Huyghe, *Art and the Spirit of Man*, trans. Norbert Gutterman (New York: Harry N. Abrams, 1962), p. 43.

there is at the other extreme "the politico-ideological judge of literature who absurdly measures literary creations by degrees of their 'realism,' or, worse still, by the relative conformity or dissent of the political opinions they seem to utter or imply."[11]

2. *The Social Responsibility of the Writer*

There is little political authenticity to be found in the aesthetic sphere. Therefore, it would seem that, vis-à-vis all forms of moralizing politics, it befits the artist to remain skeptical and ironical rather than "committed."[12]

Under the insistent and aggressive pressure of Marxist ideology, the political implications of literature have received a disproportionate share of critical attention in the twentieth century. Those interested in this problem invariably brought up the related question: what is the social responsibility of the writer? There is no clear-cut answer. Various cultures in the past have defined the role of the writer in strikingly different ways. Cut off from the strenuous but superficial life of mass society and often in opposition to its collective norms, the modern artist feels alienated and embittered; he becomes an exile, a Bohemian, a rebel, a revolutionary. This opposition between the modern artist and society is to be observed not only in the social position he occupies and his relative lack of influence in the world, but also "in the character of his vision and in his form of expression, that become more and more removed from the world, the concepts and the language of his public."[13] This explains in part why many writers indulged in eccentric behavior and high jinks (like Alfred Jarry and his absurd "science" of 'Pataphysics), defiantly affirmed their individuality (like E. E. Cummings in *Eimi* (1933) with its defense of the inner self against the encroachment of the totalitarian State), and were attracted to the cult of aestheticism.

In Greece, by the time of Aristophanes, poetry was still

11. Erich Heller, "Literature and Political Responsibility," *Commentary* 51 (1971): 511.
12. *Ibid.*, p. 53.
13. Eric Kahler, *Man the Measure: A New Approach to History* (New York: Pantheon Books, 1943), p. 493.

considered the basic source of education, a model of wisdom for the young to emulate. Aristophanes composed plays that passed severe judgment on the social life and political unrest of his age. The tragedies produced during this period were deeply concerned with the social problems faced by the city-state.[14] The tendency in the fifth century was to condemn the poet if the morality of his chief characters was not above suspicion. Plato spearheaded the attack on the poets on moral grounds. He took it for granted that the poet must be animated by a moral purpose. In an excellent article, "Literature and Political Responsibility" (1971), Erich Heller traces the ideological link that connects Plato's rigorous chastisement of the poet for his moral failings with the stern aesthetic pronunciamentos issued by the Russian Communist Party against all art that fails to shoulder the burden of social responsibility. The leaders of the Soviet Union voiced their faith in and vigorously enforced the regnant dogma of Socialist realism. While they did so, to the consequent detriment of literature and art in the Soviet Union, "poets, from the Parnassians' l'art pour l'art to the Symbolists' absolutely 'pure poetry,' have been passionately intent upon making the highest artistic virtue out of precisely that which Plato regarded as the ineradicable vice of poetry: its detachment from the body politic, its unreliable ambiguities and ironies vis-á-vis the seriousness demanded by the moral life, and its helpless exposure to the seductions of fantasy, play, and pure form. . . ."[15]

The modern rebel not only turns against society because it is defective, corrupt, and degenerate, but also ventures to propose a new and more desirable order of being. "The rebel fights the way of life of his society because to him personally it is wrong, but in art, morality and religion, as more obviously in politics, the new reality he proposes is more than personal; he is offering it a new way of life."[16] Some writers will not take up the challenge of social responsibility; they

14. For a Marxist interpretation of Greek tragedy, see George Thomson, *Aeschylus and Athens* (London: Lawrence & Wishart, 1941). Thomson considers tragedy one of the distinctive functions of Athenian democracy. "In its form and its content, in its growth and its decay, it was conditioned by the evolution of the social organism to which it belonged" (*ibid.*, p. 1). Thomson sets out to portray the work of Aeschylus and the development of Greek tragedy in their relation to the class struggle.

15. Erich Heller, "Literature and Political Responsibility," p. 51.

16. Raymond Williams, *The Long Revolution* (New York: Columbia University Press, 1961), p. 89.

stand alone, resisting all efforts to enlist their talent for a cause that is alien to their personal needs. Timothy Leary's advice to the young is summed up in three terse commandments: "Turn on, tune in, drop out."[17]

Most writers, unwilling to divorce their art from life, were strongly tempted, especially during critical times, to commit themselves politically, while some held back for a variety of reasons: fear that their art would suffer, fear that they would be required to serve as propagandists for the Left. In the nineteenth century such fears were groundless. William Morris, for example, gradually became involved in the social and political conflicts of his age. The Liberal Government in power did not carry out its promises. Urgently needed reforms at home were ignored while imperialistic wars were fought without regard to cost. At this juncture, William Morris felt depressed; political radicalism was making no progress in the land. His efforts to cultivate a genuine feeling for art in the working class seemed to bear no fruit. The happiness he derived from his work as an artist deepened his sense of guilt as he observed the wretched, unrelieved drudgery to which the lower classes in England were condemned. In 1883 he became an active member of the Socialist movement and supported it for the rest of his life. He paid no heed to those who called him an apostate because he had exchanged his role of poet for that of "politician."

He prepared himself zealously for his new mission. He studied the work of Karl Marx and Robert Owen. Confident that the social revolution was imminent and that England would be the first nation to start a revolution, he lectured on Socialism before worker audiences and contributed articles to the newspaper *Justice*. His predictions were not fulfilled. By 1890 he realized that the revolution was indeed far off.

The twentieth century ushered in an age of vertiginous change and traumatic shocks: Futurism, world wars, Dada, psychoanalysis, Surrealism, the October Revolution, Fascism, concentration camps, genocide, the triumph of technology. According to statistics compiled by Unesco, the annual production over the entire earth amounted to five million books, printed in three thousand languages, not counting

17. Timothy Leary, *The Politics of Ecstasy* (New York: G. P. Putnam's Sons, 1968), p. 141.

newspapers and periodicals.[18] Literature had become a gigantic industry catering to a vast but heterogeneous audience. The State enjoyed a monopoly of political influence and control. A critic like Cyril Connolly could assert his independence: "So I have nothing to say to the masses or to the machines, to bosses or to bureaucrats, to States or statistics, to Nations or Parties."[19] The writer has forfeited his prophetic function and has ceased to exercise moral leadership. The State is steadily widening its sphere of authority. "The state dictates the total life of man; it is taking over all functions."[20] In a lecture, "The Human Crisis," delivered in the United States in 1946, Albert Camus warned, among other things, of the spread of bureaucracy in the world and the replacement of the living man by the political man. It was unfortunate, as he pointed out, that "the cult of efficiency and abstraction" was in the ascendant.[21]

The politically committed writer takes with the utmost seriousness his responsibility to society, but that responsibility cannot, he discovers, be carried out with conspicuous success. The frustrations that attend his creative efforts are born of the realistic knowledge that his books, however honestly wrought, achieve but little in helping to shape a better world. If he resorts to forthright exhortation, he defeats his own ends as an artist. He must paint life as it is, not as he would like it to be, if his work is to be stamped with the seal of authentic conviction. Yet his aroused social conscience impels him to utter his moral protest. He will not make his peace with the Establishment; he continues to cherish his right to criticize. He persists in his state of alienation, an intransigent member of the opposition.[22]

18. J. W. Saunders, *The Profession of Letters* (London: Routledge & Kegan Paul, 1964), p. 1.
19. Cyril Connolly, *The Unquiet Grave* (New York and London: Harper & Brothers, 1945), p. 107.
20. Jacques Ellul, *A Critique of New Commonplaces*, trans. Helen Weaver (New York: Alfred A. Knopf, 1968), p. 107.
21. William Wasserstrom, ed., *Civil Liberties and the Arts* (Syracuse, N.Y.: Syracuse University Press, 1965), p. 245.
22. "What they [the intellectuals] have come to fear is not so much rejection or overt hostility, with which they have learned to cope and which they have almost come to regard as their proper fate, but the loss of alienation. Many of the most spirited younger intellectuals are disturbed above all by the fear that, as they are increasingly recognized, incorporated, and used, they will begin merely to conform, and will cease to be creative and critical and truly useful" (Richard Hofstadter, *Anti-intellectualism in American Life* [New York: Alfred A.

3. *Art, Ethics, and Revolution*

Artists in general, novelists among them, tend to be viewed with suspicion by the rulers of the world, and with good reason. But revolutionaries, I think, should be wary of artists too: most revolutionaries, after all, are would-be rulers, who aren't in power yet; the rest are nihilists hating order, and art is a kind of order. Rulers dread chaos and nihilists love it; novelists, an ambidextrous breed, have no use for it.[23]

The writers who wish through their work to launch or promote a revolution are practicing, whether they know it or not, a species of magic. They believe in the function of art as propaganda and indeed set up political guidelines as criteria of excellence. Implicit in their role as dedicated Marxists is the belief that art and literature can enlighten the proletariat as to the truth of their debased condition and imbue them with the courage and determination to transcend that condition. The fundamental aim of Socialism, Marx wrote in his *Economic and Philosophical Manuscripts,* is to liberate the creative power man possesses, so that he is no longer an exploited object of labor but working cooperatively with his fellow men, at one with himself and his world. Socialism was not the end of the quest; it merely provided the conditions necessary for the fulfillment of the whole gamut of human potentialities.

Basic to this grandiose scheme for transforming the structure of society and altering the psychological attitudes of men was an ethical ideal, a *moral* commitment that enabled the revolutionary to work anonymously in the underground and endure years of imprisonment or exile without losing his faith in the ultimate triumph of Communism. Such an ideal, such a commitment, was alien to the Marxist interpretation of history. The conflicts of conscience, the spirit of sacrifice, are of no account in the outcome of the class war. The Marxist system disposes of such spurious abstractions as justice, equality, and rights; it rejects the teachings of supernaturally oriented religions. These are screeens designed to blind men to the truths of economics, the realities of exploitation. What

Knopf, 1963], p. 393). See Marcus Klein, *After Alienation: American Novels in Mid-Century* (Cleveland and New York: The World Publishing Company, 1965).

23. George P. Elliott, *Conversions* (New York: E. P. Dutton & Co., 1971), p. 35.

do Marx and Engels have to say about the ideals proclaimed by what they call the ideological superstructure?

> Engels polemicizes against " 'true love of humanity' and empty phraseology about 'justice,' " and Marx attacks the "higher ideal" type of socialism which wants "to replace its materialistic basis . . . by modern mythology with its goddesses of Justice, Freedom, Equality and Fraternity." They deny explicitly that communists preach morality and their strictures against those who inveigh against egotism or demand that we love one another are at times so vigorous that timid readers conjure visions of the anti-Christ, and the idea is critically advanced with textual support that historical materialism is not only no ethics but anti-ethical.[24]

And the logical positivists, like the Marxists, insisted that ethical concepts are pseudo-concepts expressive of desire; they are without objective validity.[25]

But the widespread use of concentration camps in which the Nazis inflicted fiendish tortures upon the inmates, the knowledge of the crematoria in which millions of Jews were put to death with genocidal efficiency—all this testified to the breakdown of Western civilization and demonstrated to the intellectuals the appalling reality of Evil.[26] The writers of the time, witnessing this outburst of homicidal fury, this upsurge of a nihilism unprecedented in the history of the human race, wondered how they could reconcile their moral relativism with their faith in a humanism that affirmed the greatness of man. "What is the relationship between morality and politics?"[27]

24. Vernon Venable, *Human Nature: The Marxian View* (New York: Alfred A. Knopf, 1946), p. 163.
25. "There cannot be such a thing as ethical science, if by ethical one means the elaboration of a 'true' system of morals" (Alfred J. Ayer, *Language, Truth and Logic* [New York: Oxford University Press, 1936], p. 168).
26. "The tragedy of our time has been that only the emergence of crimes unknown in quality and proportion and not foreseen by the Ten Commandments made us realize what the mob had known since the beginning of the century: that not only this or that form of government has become antiquated or that certain values and traditions need to be reconsidered, but that the whole of nearly three thousand years of Western civilization, as we have known it in a comparatively uninterrupted stream of tradition, has broken down; the whole structure of Western culture with all its implied beliefs, traditions, standards of judgment, has come toppling down over our heads" (Hannah Arendt, *The Origins of Totalitarianism* [New York: Harcourt, Brace and Company, 1951], p. 434).
27. Sartre, *What Is Literature?*, p. 223.

The traditional assumption of the humanist that literature and art could serve as a humanizing agency has had to be abandoned. The apocalyptic disasters that occurred in this "enlightened" scientific age brought such comforting illusions to an end. The intellectuals of Nazi Germany, the writers, the artists, the professors, took no firm stand against the political madness of their country. The German people on the whole supported Hitler. They were citizens of a highly cultured nation, but their literary studies failed to humanize them. "In a disturbing number of cases the literary imagination gave servile or ecstatic welcome to political bestiality. That bestiality was at times enforced and refined by individuals educated in the culture of traditional humanism. Knowledge of Goethe, a delight in the poetry of Rilke, seemed no bar to personal and institutionalized sadism."[28]

Faced with these terrifying disclosures about the nature of man, the intellectuals reconsidered the logic of the argument that moral judgments are merely an expression of preference and hence not to be verified. According to this relativistic outlook, anything goes. The culture into which the individual is born determines the morality to which he adheres. The ethical relativist consequently "renounces all claims to judge other people's moral standards and is rather apologetic about his own which he regards as an acquired if ineradicable prejudice."[29] Yet the historical events of the recent past have disproved the validity of such a point of view. The rise of Fascism, the brutal stamping out of the last spark of freedom in Germany and its conquered territory, the systematic extermination of "inferior races"—all this called forth a degree of moral outrage in the free world that could not easily be squared with a philosophy of ethical relativism.

The eruption of barbarism in Nazi Germany strengthened in the intellectuals on the Left, especially those who were members of the Party, their conviction that Communism was

---

28. George Steiner, *Language and Silence* (New York: Atheneum, 1967), p. 61.
29. R. E. Money-Kyrle, *Psychoanalysis and Politics: A Contribution to the Psychology of Politics and Morals* (New York: W. W. Norton & Company, 1951), p. 8. Here is a psychoanalyst who sets out to demonstrate that moral beliefs are not prejudices or mere matters of preference but beliefs that can be proved to be either true or false. He had undertaken this investigation of the problem out of a personal sense of discomfort: "the rise of fascism had left me profoundly dissatisfied with the ethical relativism which till then had seemed to me to embody the only scientific attitude to morals and politics" (*ibid.*, p. 17).

the implacable enemy of Fascism. Such fiendish crimes could not possibly happen in the Soviet Union, the homeland of the Revolution. They denied the ugly charges leveled against Stalin: these were false rumors spread by Trotskyites and the hired tools of capitalism. Anti-Semitism could not possibly exist in the Soviet Union. Then in 1952-53, nine doctors, seven of whom were Jewish, were found guilty of the murder of Zhdanov in 1948; they were said to have confessed. When Stalin died on April 4, 1953, the press revealed that these doctors were innocent; their confessions had been obtained under torture. Then in 1956 Khrushchev addressed the Twentieth Congress of C.P.S.U. and divulged some of the horrible crimes that had been committed during Stalin's reign. The intellectuals on the Left in Europe and the United States had dutifully believed these manufactured lies of the Soviet Union. The Party had denied them; therefore, they were false. The Party would never permit such a monstrous perversion of the truth. When in July 1956 the revolt in Hungary was crushed by Soviet troops and tanks, many leftist intellectuals, like Sartre, rejected all the face-saving rationalizations that the Communists had to offer.

Though a number of Communist intellectuals left the Party because of these events and disclosures, the contingent of the faithful stood fast, silenced their doubts, and intensified their revolutionary zeal. But the tactics of the Stalinist intellectuals had been discredited and repudiated.[30] And the campaign in behalf of the mystique of commitment never ceased.

---

30. The feeling spread that they could not be trusted. Their tone of righteousness, their fanatical insistence that the decisions made by the Comintern or by Stalin were irreproachable, the dialectical casuistry with which they defended the Moscow Trials and the existence of concentration camps in the Soviet Union, their demand for a dictatorial control of culture and art—all this "violated the sensibilities of a potentially sympathetic audience" (David Caute, *Communism and the French Intellectuals 1914-1960* [New York: The Macmillan Company, 1964], p. 367).

2

The Mystique
of Commitment

Naturally the artist is an enemy of the state. He cannot play politics, succumb to slogans and other simplifications, worship heroes, ally himself with any party. . . . Even when convinced of the rightness of a cause, he dedicates his skills to a movement, he cannot simplify, he cannot overlook, he cannot forget, omit, or falsify. In the end the movement must reject him or even destroy him.[1]

If sincerity is one's highest value, one will never become fully committed to anything, not to a Church or to a party, nor to a love or a friendship, not even to a particular task; for commitment always assumes that one's affirmation surpasses one's knowledge, that one believes by hearsay, that one gives up the rule of sincerity for that of responsibility. The intellectual who refuses his commitments on the pretext that his function is to see all sides is in fact contriving to live a pleasant life under the guise of obeying a vocation. He resolves to avoid all resolutions and to supply strong reasons to those weak in conviction. He who is not with me is against me. Not being a Communist is being anti-Communist. Sincerity itself is deceitful and turns into propaganda.[2]

1. William H. Gass, *Fiction and the Figures of Life* (New York: Alfred A. Knopf, 1970), pp. 287-88.
2. Maurice Merleau-Ponty, *Sense and Non-Sense*, trans. Hubert L. Dreyfus and Patricia Allen Dreyfus (Evanston,: Northwestern University Press, 1964), pp. 178-79.

In a broad sense, all literature is engaged when it says something, since it always speaks of our relations—poetic or profane—with the world and with men. At the same time, as it intends to change these relations only by virtue of expression and by means of the truth, it is in conflict with propaganda and the profane techniques of action.[3]

A committed literature of the Left remains, in one shape or another, a socialist literature.[4]

It is absurd to ask an author for "commitment": a "committed" author claims simultaneous participation in two structures, inevitably a source of deception. What we can ask of an author is that he be responsible. . .an author's true responsibility is to support literature as a failed commitment.[5]

However much "art and commitment" has been discussed over the past twenty years, political commitment and artistic commitment have rarely been found to correspond. On the whole, I do not believe that genuine art could have a political function these days for good or for evil. Or at least as far as countries belonging to the western brand of culture are concerned.[6]

The call for "commitment" in the domain of art is a distinctly twentieth-century phenomenon. I have already referred to some nineteenth-century writers who were involved in the battle of politics, but they were not required to subscribe to a single ideological doctrine as embodying the whole truth of social reality nor was pressure brought to bear upon them to join a political party that guided the revolutionary aspirations of the working class. Doctrinal orthodoxy, monolithic loyalty, was not then the *sine qua non* of political commitment. Marxism had not yet established itself as a "science of society," and the International Association that Karl Marx and Friedrich Engels had organized was struggling to stay alive. On the whole, the writers who were influential a century or so ago were not inclined to form close political alliances. Today, however, the climate of opinion has in this respect changed radically. The writer is urged to bear the full burden of social responsibility. Sartre declares with magisterial finality that "the writer's duty is to take sides against all injus-

3. Merleau-Ponty quoted in Albert Rabil, Jr., *Merleau-Ponty* (New York and London: Columbia University Press, 1967), p. 211.
4. David Caute, *The Illusion: An Essay on Politics, Theatre and the Novel* (New York and London: Harper & Row, 1971), p. 59.
5. Roland Barthes, *Critical Essays*, trans. Richard Howard. Evanston, Ill.: Northwestern University Press, 1972), p. 146.
6. Gillo Dorfles, *Kitsch* (New York: University Books, 1969), p. 113.

tices, wherever they may come from."[7] Merleau-Ponty reasons that not being a Communist is tantamount to being anti-Communist. Modern writers who adopt the rhetoric of commitment and use the term in a eulogistic sense mean one thing by it: dedication to the Marxist ideal, though this may be couched in a cryptic style or in Aesopian language. Commitment is an imperative call of conscience, a jihad in which every writer of good will is expected to join. It is a mystique that obscures the different meanings of the key term. For the truth is that every writer is "committed," even if only to the book he is working on. There are many diverse forms of commitment open to the writer; there is no reason why he must participate in the Communist crusade. He may devote his energy to the perfection of his work or decide to make his life a superb work of art. Like Yeats he may feel an inveterate indifference to politics.[8]

The war of words that has broken out over this controversial issue of "commitment" has shed more confusion than light. The impassioned cry for commitment encourages a spirit of righteousness, of intolerance, that is inimical to the organic development of literature as art. Robert Conquest analyzes the "logical" steps by means of which the writer becomes a convert to the ethic of political commitment.

(1) I am against injustice, (2) therefore I am a "socialist"; (3) because "socialism" is the way to prevent oppression it is justified, (4) including injustice.[9]

The gibe in step 4 is unfair to many writers on the Left who did not indulge in such casuistry. They were sustained by the conviction that their cause was bound to triumph, and it was incumbent on them to hasten the advent of this day of triumph.[10] They responded affirmatively to this challenge.

7. Jean-Paul Sartre, *What Is Literature?*, trans. Bernard Frechtman. (New York: Philosophical Library, 1949), p. 286.
8. See Conor Cruise O'Brien, "Passion and Cunning: The Politics of W. B. Yeats," in *Literature in Revoluion,* ed, George Abbott White and Charles Newman (New York: Holt, Rinehart and Winston, 1972), pp. 143-203. O'Brien writes: "I no longer believe Yeats' political activities to have been foolish or fundamentally inconsistent or his political attitudes to be detachable from the rest of his personality, disconnected from action, or irrelevant to his poetry." *Ibid.,* p. 143.
9. Robert Conquest, "Commitment and the Writer," *Literary Annual,* no. 1, ed. John Wain (New York: Criterion Books, 1959), p. 19.
10. On the alleged value to be derived from the act of commitment, see Henri

"We are committed; we must be committed. Nothing will be done unless we are committed."[11]

The first mild skirmish of what later grew into a furious war of words came early in the twentieth century when H. G. Wells and Henry James were embroiled in a controversy about the proper sphere and function of the novel. For Wells, the central importance of the novel lay in its power not only to observe reality but to influence the behavior of men and women. The experimental method applied to fiction would, he hoped, supplant the old reliance on abstract ethical principles. The "new" novel, he announced, "is to be the social mediator, the vehicle of understanding, the instrument of self-examination, the parade of morals and the exchange of manners, the factory of customs, the criticism of laws and institutions and of social dogmas and ideas."[12] In *Experiment in Autobiography*, Wells states that what he then had in mind came close to the propagandistic novel.

The insistent clamor for commitment that rose to a crescendo of adjuration during the thirties, gained a surprisingly large number of recruits among the intellectuals. Communism appealed to them because it promised to establish a society free of the evil of exploitation and the taint of the profit motive. But the writers who responded to this call failed to perceive that imaginative literature cannot be effectively used as an incitement to revolutionary action. Barthes dismisses as absurd the notion of commitment on the part of authors. Anthony Cronin, in conducting an aesthetic inquiry into the problem of commitment, points out some of the outstanding semantic ambiguities of this concept.

> Oddly enough we never hear of Mr. Eliot as committed, or Ezra Pound or Yeats, though the verse of all three is passionately, profoundly and fundamentally committed to the truth of certain views about the moral basis of civilisation and the importance of the kind of society we live in. These beliefs are not, however, made the occasion for boasting or hectoring, nor are they presented as if the mere holding of them were a feat deserving of great acclaim.[13]

Peyre, *Literature and Sincerity* (New Haven and London: Yale University Press, 1963), p. 341.

11. Jacques Ellul, *A Critique of the New Commonplaces*, trans. Helen Weaver (New York: Alfred A. Knopf, 1968), p. 34.

12. *Henry James and H. G. Wells*, ed. Leon Edel and Gordon N. Ray (Urbana, Ill.: University of Illinois Press, 1958), p. 154.

13. Anthony Cronin, *A Question of Modernity* (London: Secker & Warburg, 1966, pp. 30-31

The intellectual is an iconoclast who is in opposition to the enshrined values of his age. As Gass remarks, the artist is the sworn enemy of the State. He explodes sanctified dogmas and persistently questions the validity of the so-called eternal verities. The only danger he runs is that in demolishing the false gods of the past he is tempted to set up his own system of idolatry as the true religion. Hostility to the existing order of things becomes the supreme virtue. "Nobody can be a serious intellectual today unless he is an outcast."[14] The result is that the intellectual, despite all his learning, is cleverly exploited by the Party; he comes to believe that it is his sacred duty to participate in the political conflicts of his day.

There are always new, earnest recruits, especially among the young, to engage in this campaign to teach the uncommitted, or wrongly committed, writer the error of his ways. In *The Reactionaries*, which is subtitled *A Study of the Anti-Democratic Intelligentsia*, John R. Harrison examines the work of Yeats, Wyndham Lewis, Ezra Pound, T. S. Eliot, and D. H. Lawrence and endeavors to find out what motivated them to espouse "reactionary" views. Why is it, he asks, that creative artists are capable of rejecting the values basic to liberal, democratic society? The critic must work out the answer to this important question, for such culpable and aberrant political attitudes are bound to affect the quality of their work.[15] Harrison knows beforehand what political views the writers of our time should embrace. He intends to look closely into the contents of their published work for evidence of their contumelious rejection of democratic values. The writer, Harrison tells us, is not a recluse, an aesthete dwelling alone in an ivory tower. On the contrary, he is very much a part of the age he lives in. To argue that the poet is well advised to steer clear of politics, and that if he does become involved we should simply ignore that aspect of his work, results, Harrison contends, in "a one-sided view" and is "likely to lead to misinterpretation of the poetry itself."[16]

In England during the fifties and sixties, writers did not respond to the rallying cry for commitment raised by such social-minded critics as Kenneth Tynan and Raymond Williams, especially the latter. The writers were for the most part not interested in political agitation, feeling, as many of them

14. Ellul, *A Critique of the New Commonplaces*, p. 7.
15. John R. Harrison, *The Reactionaries* (New York: Schocken Books, 1967), p. 15.
16. *Ibid.*, p. 16.

did, a deep-seated mistrust of ideological categories. They questioned the wisdom of exploiting literature as a medium for achieving politically desirable results. "Commitment, not to party or formula but to truth and humanity," Robert Conquest urged, "provides a better standpoint for judging events . . . ."[17]

In France, Roger Martin du Gard decided that he was primarily a novelist, not a philosopher or sociologist. Though he was in sympathy with the ideas advocated by liberalism, he did not believe it was part of his duty as a writer to meddle in political affairs. Though in his major work, *The Thibaults,* he tried to avoid the pitfalls of ideology, he was nevertheless considered to be a politically committed writer. The truth about his fiction is more complex. He was not composing propagandist novels that sounded a call to action. A writer may be politically concerned without disclosing his partisanship or indulging in overt preachment. In his *Journal,* dated May 20, 1945, Martin du Gard records his decision to reject the solicitation of his friends that he speak out on the issues of his day. He had no desire to produce journalism. He was convinced that those writers who, out of a compelling sense of duty, become embroiled in politics turn out novels that are a mélange of current slogans and battlecries. Their art is spoiled by the cant of politics. Such writers, blinded by a false sense of duty, neglect "their true duty, which, it seems, would be to pursue their work as writers."[18] Avoiding all polemics, Martin du Gard preferred the role of spectator. The artist, no lusty trumpeter of ephemeral causes, does not take sides. He remains an individualist, cherishing the uniqueness of the human soul that collectivism was bound to stamp out.

This is enough to indicate that the omnibus term *commitment* is best with ambiguity and instinct with paradox. The militant critic on the Left, however, pays no attention to such semantic obfuscation. He persists in defining commitment in accordance with his political *parti pris.* He unfurls the banner of radicalism. "Relative to the general social situation, the literature of Commitment is radical. It is a literature of protest, not approval, of outrage, not tribulation."[19] The writer who

17. Conquest, "Commitment and the Writer," p. 17.
18. David L. Schalk, *Roger Martin du Gard* (Ithaca, N. Y.: Cornell University Press, 1967), p. 179.
19. Eric Bentley, *The Theatre of Commitment and Other Essays on Drama in Our Society* (New York: Atheneum, 1967), p. 197.

is defending a political cause does not realize that while he attempts to "influence" the reader, this "influence" does not carry over into the sphere of social action. Literature, despite the assertions of Erwin Piscator and Bertolt Brecht to the contrary, does not of itself initiate social change. "God help any regime—and God help any rebellion—that depends heavily on its artists! They are on the whole, not a dangerous lot, as Plato thought, but a useless lot."[20] Similarly, Robert Brustein is not taken in by the grandiloquent posturing of the revolutionary contingent in the theater. He is "skeptical about the radical theatre's power to affect anybody except those who are already converted. . . ."[21] The dramatic critic must be able to distinguish propaganda plays from plays that are works of art.[22] The artist is free, of course, to choose his strategy of appeal, the nature of his commitment. "In any event, an artist cannot give up regarding himself as the conscience of mankind, even if mankind pays no attention."[23]

Negro writers have developed their own kind of commitment. In their theater of commitment they unleash their intemperate polemics: plays that resound with visceral rage and murderous hatred of the whites. They use the theater as a forum that will broadcast their denunciation of racism. C. W. E. Bigsby makes the point

> that the committed writer is capable of producing valid drama only in so far as he is able to subordinate immediate social and political objectives to a concern with "the whole man." Those playwrights who in the nineteen-thirties saw in the stage a useful extension of the political platform failed to produce any significant drama precisely because they chose to replace the universal with the particular and the complexities of human relationships with utilitarian stereotypes.[24]

LeRoi Jones, the prophet of commitment for his race, for-

20. *Ibid.,* p. 123.
21. Robert Brustein, *Revolution as Theatre* (New York: Liveright, 1971), p. 129.
22. "When Sean O'Casey writes about a Communist revolution bringing sensuality to Puritan Ireland, or when Arthur Miller evokes our sympathy for the plight of the common man, we are confronted less with works of art than with political acts or social gestures, and it is by utilitarian rather than literary criteria that such acts and gestures should be judged." Robert Brustein, *The Theatre of Revolt* (Boston: Little, Brown and Company, 1964), pp. 24-25.
23. Bentley, *The Theatre of Commitment,* p. 153.
24. C. W. E. Bigsby, *Confrontation and Commitment: A Study of Contemporary American Drama, 1959-66* (Columbia, Mo.: University of Wisconsin Press, 1968), p. 120.

mulates what he considers a revolutionary aesthetic aim for the Negro writer, who should always write as a Negro. Nonviolence on the part of the American Negro perpetuates the *status quo*. Jones argues that revolutionary violence is the only road open to the Negro who is determined to win his freedom. The economic system that exploits him must be destroyed, root and branch. "The black man is the only revolutionary force in American society today, if only by default."[25] Jones goes on to say: "Left to their own devices, the masses of Negroes will finally strike back, perhaps even kill, in a vertiginous gesture of fear and despair."[26] He believes that the revolutionary theater should be used to the full as an instrument of social change. It must sound the doom of the whites, the twilight of their gods, the end of their power. "The Revolutionary Theatre," Jones proclaims, "must Accuse and Attack anything that can be accused and attacked. It must Accuse and Attack because it is a theatre of Victims."[27]

The demand for commitment never let up and continued to gain new disciples. The writer, who often feels guilty without the need for a trial because of the suspect nature of his creative calling, was bombarded with exhortations to make his work socially relevant, to politicize his art. The object of "committed literature" is to promote social reform and support revolutionary causes. "The "committed" writer wants to change the world.[28] Not for him the refinements of aesthetics or the beautification of style. Art for art's sake he condemns as a perversion, the product of rootless and irresponsible Bohemians. His belief in the axiomatic principle that all is

25. LeRoi Jones, *Home* (New York: William Morrow & Co., 1966), p. 151.
26. *Ibid.*, p. 152.
27. *Ibid.*, p. 211.
28. The politically committed writers evidently took to heart the thesis Marx propounded in *Eleven Theses on Feuerbach* (1845): "Philosophers have only *interpreted* the world, but the real task is to *alter* it" (quoted in Bertrand Russell, *A History of Western Philosophy* [New York: Simon and Schuster, 1945], p. 784). Unfortunately, they disregard the admonitions of such masters of the art of fiction as Flaubert, Chekhov, Henry James, and Thomas Mann. In a letter dated May 25, 1926, and sent to Ernst Fischer, Thomas Mann said: "To my mind an artist is not obligated to know a great deal or to solve problems, to be a teacher and leader. . . . An artist is occasionally pushed into tis role, and then he must play it as well as he can, and meet its demands. But his vocation, his nature, consists not in teaching, judging, pointing directions, but in being, doing, expressing states of the soul" (Thomas Mann, *Letters of Thomas Mann*, trans. Richard and Clara Winston [New York: Alfred A. Knopf, 1971], pp. 152-53).

politics gives rise to the corollary principle that all of literature is at bottom a form of propaganda. Adereth, an English critic who has a special fondness for the novels of veteran French Communist Louis Aragon, asserts "that in the twentieth century human destiny is decided through politics."[29] Hence Adereth exalts the committed writer and expatiates on the fruitful impact of a life of action on the writer's creative work. Adereth dwells at some length on the positive advantage the writer derives from his affirmative response to the call for commitment: through his participation in politics he gains a deeper understanding of social reality, and this understanding is a more powerful stimulus to his creative work than his private attempts to solve the metaphysical mysteries of the universe. Why should he waste his time and his precious talent trying to solve the riddle of life, to find answers for unanswerable questions, when society is still rife with injustice and oppression? He cannot send forth the piercing cry of resignation that A. E. Housman uttered in "Be Still, My Soul, Be Still":

> Ay, look: high heaven and earth ail from the prime foundation;
>   All thoughts to rive the heart are here, and all are vain:
> Horror and scorn and hate and fear and indignation—
>   Oh, why did I awake? When shall I sleep again?

The politically aroused poet does not give in to such moods of absolute despair. He believes in the mission of committed literature to achieve social salvation for mankind. Not that literature of this kind, we are told, need be prescriptive in character, nor is it compelled to exclude competing points of view.[30]

The command is given, the inspiriting call to rally around the red flag is sounded, and the committed writer is expected to take up his quarrel with the capitalist foe. The question whether he is at all qualified for such an extremely difficult and onerous assignment is not raised. After all, what business

29. M. Adereth, *Commitment in Modern French Literature: Politics and Society in Péguy, Aragon, and Sartre* (New York: Schocken Books, 1968), p. 17.
30. "Commitment does not claim to have all the answers . . . nor does it suggest there cannot be more than one answer. What it does say is that they are bound up with one's philosophy of life and that the writers and artists whose obvious right and duty is to contribute to their solution can hardly do so without taking sides in the political and moral debates of their times, in other words without committing themselves" *(ibid.,* p. 21).

has the imaginative writer offering ready-made solutions for problems that have baffled philosophers, social scientists, and psychologists for over two millennia? He has no special credentials as a political partisan. Politics—that is not his métier. As a novelist or poet or dramatist he is endowed with no knowledge or insight that would make him a trustworthy guide through the labyrinthine ways of politics. He can, of course, cash in on his fame—and his Communist sponsors are willing to do this for him—and announce his support of this or that movement, but what does he accomplish by such methods? Auden, when queried about his views on the war in Vietnam, replied that he was astounded by this widespread practice of soliciting writers for their opinion on the leading controversial political issues of their time. Why is this done? Writers are not oracles and their views carry no greater weight of authority than those of well-educated citizens who have no claim to fame. Auden remarks that the statements released by writers seem to demonstrate that on the whole there is no positive correlation between literary talent and political wisdom.[31]

The writer who struggles to safeguard his independence generally adopts a neutral stance, but the apostles of commitment assure him that it is impossible to sustain such an attitude in the modern world. The writer's vaunted freedom to write as he pleases is a pure fabricated myth; the literature he actually produces springs inevitably out of the clashes and collisions of contemporary values. "Moreover, does the idea of independence mean that an author is not accountable to anyone for what he writes because it is his privilege to be above human restrictions?"[32] This type of argument begs the question. It takes for granted that *all* literature is inescapably "political" in content, and should therefore be subject to social regulation. But if the writer has a responsibility to society, what is the exact nature of that responsibility? Is a literary work to be judged good or bad in the light of its "correct" political orientation? Adereth, however, is willing to make a number of important concessions in the name of art.[33]

31. Quoted in Gass, *Fiction and the Figures of Life*, p. 277.
32. M. Adereth, *Commitment in Modern French Literature*, p. 26.
33. " 'Literature engagée' has always emphasized that an ideology cannot be artificially introduced into a work of art. It should come from within the artist himself and be inseparable from his own personality. Although it believes that all art is a form of 'propaganda' in the sense that it is a criticism of life and

The Communist critic brooks no compromise. Christopher Caudwell analyzes the character of what he calls "capitalist" poetry and concludes that bourgeois art, under the aegis of capitalism, is skeptical, experimental, supersaturated with the acids of doubt, agitated, iconoclastic. The contradiction that bourgeois society exhibits between the unrestricted individualism of the ruling class and the virtual serfdom of the rest of the population, is reflected in the culture it produces. In bourgeois culture, freedom is synonymous with individualism, but this is merely a figure of speech. The bourgeois draws a flattering portrait of himself as a hero who, standing alone, fights gallantly in the name of freedom; he is the staunch individualist battling to throw off the social relations that restrict the natural man. Man is supposedly born free, and yet how account for the paradox that he is everywhere bound in chains?[34] But the bourgeois poet soon grows weary of this illusory freedom. As the world around him becomes more menacing, he tends to retreat from society and his poetry, emptied of meaning, falls into a feeble, valetudinarian strain, solipsistic and despairing.

In his concluding chapter, "The Future of Poetry," Caudwell reveals the revolutionary implications of his method. Bourgeois culture, he warns us, is on its last legs and will soon perish; a new society is emerging from the womb of the old. The light of Communism is dawning. The proletariat, the exploited class that can achieve its freedom only by destroying the bourgeoisie, will assume the leadership in this decisive revolutionary struggle. It will, Caudwell prophesies, create proletarian art, which will give expression to the aspirations and struggles of the proletariat. Its transcendent goal, its ultimate aim, is to end its existence as a separate class and become "coincident with society as a whole."[35]

Faced with these world-shaking convulsions, the bourgeois artist is forced to choose between the old and the new, the dead and the living. He can remain loyal to his own class and fight against the armed proletariat or he can become a fellow traveler and ally himself with the militant working

expresses a particular point of view, if propaganda is superimposed in the work of art, the artist has failed" (*ibid.*, p. 29).
34. Christopher Caudwell, *Illusion and Reality* (New York: International Publishers, 1947), p. 59.
35. *Ibid.*, p. 280.

class. Caudwell considers such an alliance unsatisfactory, since the writer retains his individuality and stands actually apart from the ranks of the workers. Because he is not a member of the Communist Party, his creative work is stillborn. The future he envisages is an amalgam of his personal aspirations for freedom. Artists of this stripe betray the "Trotsky-like element in their orientation."[36] Then Caudwell pens an astonishing doctrinaire ultimatum.

In martial tones it proclaims the ineluctable fact that the revolution is steadily advancing under the leadership of the proletariat, and this is taken to mean that these lukewarm and vacillating bourgeois artists must obey "the marching orders" of "the proletarian general staff." Otherwise, they are rendered impotent, unable to take decisive action. They must respond to the imperative call for united action, while some will perceive the necessity for their joining the Communist Party.[37] To those insecure and equivocating fellow travelers who stubbornly refuse to make their work conform to the ideological requirements formulated by the Party, Caudwell has the conscious proletariat, here personified, address this edifying message. Art grants them no refuge from the class war; it is not a privileged sanctuary. It is not a neutral world. It is fundamentally a social activity. Hence they must choose between class art and proletarian art. "There is no classless art except communist art, and that is not yet born; and class art to-day, unless it is proletarian, can only be the art of a dying class."[38] The liberal, the fellow-traveler, must finally make up his mind and choose between Communism and Fascism. Artists must rid their work of its tainted "bourgeois" content. To all bourgeois artists who sympathize with their cause and wish to share their revolutionary task of changing the world, the conscious proletariat addresses its exhortation. The demand that the creative fruit of their labor be wholly proletarian in spirit and substance is not a call for applying "dogmatic categories" and stereotyped Marxist phrases to their work. That would, in fact, represent a bourgeois compromise. "We ask that you should *really* live in the new world and not leave your soul behind in the past."[39]

36. *Ibid.,* p. 284.
37. *Ibid.,* p. 285.
38. *Ibid.,* p. 288.
39. *Ibid.,* p. 288.

There is something touching and yet naive in this identification of living art with proletarian art, which is left abstract and undefined. And classless art, like the classless society that was supposed to follow the dictatorship of the proletariat, is a dream of the ever-receding future; it does not exist. The artist is told in no uncertain terms to work within the revolutionary movement and submit to Party discipline, though Caudwell disclaims any intention of demanding that the artist should follow the commands issued by the proletarian dictatorship.[40]

Once the Soviet Union was securely established, writers outside of Russia could observe how literature and art flourished under the benevolent guidance of a Communist regime. The bubble of utopian expectation was soon punctured. Many writers were being persecuted, arrested on trumped-up charges, imprisoned, often without a trial, sent to forced labor camps. Some were shot or mysteriously disappeared. Mayakovsky, the poet laureate of the Revolution, took his own life. Why did all this happen? In the Soviet Union, the writer must conform to the dictates of the Communist Party. If his work contains ideological errors he must publicly recant his "sins." What makes matters worse, according to Stefan Heym, a novelist who lives in East Germany, is that the writer must somehow resolve the conflict raging in his own mind. The writer is not blind to the defects and deficiencies of Socialism and the humanistic ideal it strives to carry out. Thus he confronts a question of ethics: what good does he accomplish by dwelling solely on the "often cruel and crude contradictions"?[41]

40. "This leading role of the proletariat in the upheavals of our time has proved to be the Utopian element of Marxism" (Franz Borkenau, *The Communist International* [London: Faber and Faber, 1938], p. 421). "If 'scientific' socialism would only be scientific enough to regard its own doctrine as the object of psychological analysis, it would find that such notions as that of the social revolution, the dictatorship of the proletariat, or the future society, are, from the outlook of social psychology, nothing more than myths, that is to say verbal symbols of faith" (Henry de Man, *The Psychology of Socialism* [New York: Henry Holt & Co., 1927], p. 159). Georg Lukács writes: "Out of the consciousness that the proletariat is the revolutionary gravedigger of bourgeois society, the forms of the proletarian class struggle, the necessity of uniting the workers in class organizations, (trade unions, the Party), out of the class struggle itself arises the possibility for depicting the class conscious proletarian as a 'positive' hero" (Georg Lukács, "Essay on the Novel," *International Literature*, no. 5 [1936], p. 73.

41. Stefan Heym, "Involved Writers in the World," *The New York Times*, January 2, 1971.

As the intellectuals gained a deeper knowledge of the crushing handicaps under which writers in the Soviet Union labored, they did not hesitate to act. They openly disavowed the mystique of commitment. Alain Robbe-Grillet rejects all ideas decreed from above. He is a born rebel. If art is employed instrumentally, then its value is reduced to zero. The only acceptable meaning the call for "commitment" can have for the artist, Robbe-Grillet declares in *For a New Novel,* is commitment to his art. Alberto Moravia exposed the messy and intolerable contradictions that are to be found in the arbitrary aesthetic prescriptions of Socialist realism. In Communist countries, the artist is forced to produce propaganda that affirms the policy currently formulated by the Party.

> What is the artist's duty in a time of struggle, supposing he wants to take part in the struggle? In my view the artist's duty is notably different from that of other participants who contribute to the struggle with arms and political actions. The artist's first duty is to create art, for he knows that an art which is non-art can make no efficient contribution to the cause of action in which he believes. If he succeeds in creating genuine art, the question resolves itself. Indeed, it does not even arise.[42]

When the partial history of Stalin's crimes became known to the world, the writers in the West who had all along loyally defended the Soviet Union, branding as infamous propagandist lies the charges leveled against the Stalinist regime, were at first dismayed. Each year more damning and incontrovertible evidence was forthcoming. Roy A. Medvedev published his *Let History Judge: The Origins and Consequences of Stalinism.* I discuss this matter in great detail in a later chapter. Here I merely point briefly to the blighting effect of Stalinist repression on Soviet literature. Jürgen Rühle, a specialist in this field of study, sums it up incisively as follows:

> The interrelation of political and cultural factors in a totalitarian society makes the intellectual emancipation of the Soviet Union a protracted and conflict-ridden process, one which will continue as long as the Party ideology controls the arts.[43]

The Western intellectuals who belonged to the Left were at

42. Alberto Moravia, *Man as an End,* trans. Bernard Wall (New York: Farrar, Straus & Giroux, 1965), p. 123.
43. Jürgen Rühle, *Literature and Revolution,* trans. Jean Steinberg (New York and London: Frederick A. Praeger, 1969), p. 3.

first badly shaken by these damaging revelations. Though there were a number of defections, the faithful on the whole remained faithful nor was the ideal of literary commitment discarded. It may have been abused in some cases, but it was, basically, a noble objective for the writer to pursue. New converts to the weakened cause of commitment appeared on the scene. Foremost among them was the brilliant scholar and critic David Caute. In *The Illusion: An Essay on Politics, Theatre and the Novel,* he frankly states his convictions on the various controversial issues he takes up, makes known his sympathies, the writers he particularly admires, the reasons for his faith in the literature of commitment. In capitalist countries, his indictment reads, literature and art provide chiefly entertainment; they are not necessities, and as a result the writers in such a culture suffer from a feeling of alienation and ineffectuality. Their contribution is not highly regarded, and in their frustration some of them are driven to attack "the system" that supports them and resolve to put an end to it. They compose manifestos, declarations of principles, protests, impassioned appeals; they organize conferences, publish books, write indignant letters to the editor. The revolution, alas, never comes off. Their radical activities and utterances constitute no threat to "the system," and that is why they are not restrained. They are harmless, since their brave words do not lead to revolutionary action.

Caute is decidedly in favor of the ethic of commitment. His heart approves, but his critical intellect perceives the dangers that stand in the way of the committed writer: the smog of semantic confusion, the false aesthetic preconceptions, the use of the wrong strategy. First of all, Caute tells us that he does not accept the conventional belief that a book is a self-contained, autonomous entity. Second, he criticizes the shallow realism that writers on the Left practice: their use of literature as a means to an end.

Caute advances a number of heterodox ideas that he feels literature should be made to serve. He does not believe in the function of literature as an end in itself, but he is equally opposed to the use of literature as a medium for mimesis. Like Brecht, he decries the imaginative writer's reliance on verbal magic and the art of illusion. He adopts that part of the Brechtian aesthetic which seeks to banish the technique that facilitates and intensifies the feeling of empathy. Such a method is anachronistic. It is practically obsolete. Caute characterizes it as ideologically retrograde. Literature that is based upon such a method is a resounding lie. It defeats its own end. Its efforts to distinguish between "form" and "content" betray its confusion of categories and its abortive premises.[44] Here is a perceptive, outspoken critic who does not hesitate to expose the lamentable shortcomings of many works of radical literature.

Despite the flagrant mistakes the New Left had made, it has managed to achieve a great deal. It has launched a movement that is designed to appeal to the young and that repudiates the tainted Marxism that characterized the Stalinist era. Undaunted by the many failures of innovators in the past to create a viable literature of commitment, Caute tries to provide a new basis for the birth of literature rooted in political commitment (p. 30). He underlines the discouraging fact that the great majority of the unions contracted between the artistic avant-garde and the politically committed writer on the Left "resulted in crippled offspring" and the hasty dissolution of the union (p. 31). His experiences as a critic, a college teacher, and a writer of novels have helped Caute to shape his prospectus for the "new" politically committed literature he has in mind. It will be modern and experimental, but not carried away by the contemporary craze for newness. It will be rational in its approach and radical in its outlook. It will be "a dialectical literature" (pp. 32-33).

The rehabilitated image of the politically committed writer that Caute presents evokes no salvos of applause on the Western literary front. On the contrary, it is greeted with skepticism; it lends itself to satiric deflation. It gives rise to the derisory picture of the minuteman of the Revolution grimly grinding out his daily quota of "committed literature." A volunteer in this war of the classes to change the world, he tries to deploy his partisan ideological weapon with deadly effectiveness against the foe. He knows what he has to leave out in order to dispose of the enemy. Negative capability, the pluralistic vision, the recognition of human diversity, the reliance on disparate, incompatible perspectives, intimations of the ironic aspects of the human condition—these are sacrificed without compunction on the altar of commitment.

Caute is untroubled by the negative reactions the theme of

44. Caute, *The Illusion*, p. 21.

commitment arouses in the West. He does his thing. He recommends that all "public" as distinguished from "private"
writing be infused with a feeling of subjective commitment.
Caute questions the widespread assumption that literary
commitment is "a special preserve of the Left" (p. 46), but
the logic of his argument does scant justice to the forces on
the Right. He decries the commitment of the Right as lacking
in authenticity. Negative in its aims, narrow in scope, restricted in its vision of the future, it sets an example of "bad
faith." The Right "resists whatever the Left is demanding . . . and is nagged by the feeling that history is helping
the other camp (pp. 46-47). The men on the Right, Caute
reminds us, display their own brand of commitment.
Nevertheless, he admits that the idea of literary commitment
is connected with the Left. It was no accident that Sartre and
his circle of friends who developed the concept of engagement, were militant Socialists. Sartre was the influential advocate of a politically committed literature, and in the Soviet
Union bureaucrats like Zhdanov and Fadeyev urgently
preached the evangel of whole-hearted commitment on the
part of the writer, a commitment that would lead him to
utilize the constructive aspects of Socialist realism (pp. 52-53).

Caute repeats Caudwell's contention that the artist is not
free under capitalism. The "subversive" in "the democratic"
West is muzzled or clapped into prison. Art is granted a special charter of freedom only when it is demonstrably certain
that it is utterly ineffective in those spheres of activity where
the right of freedom is vigilantly safeguarded. In capitalist
society, art is able to enjoy a relative degree of freedom from
what Caute, adopting the vocabulary of Freud, calls "the reality principle," but he pays the price for this exemption. The
consequences are that he experiences "a relative impotence
within the sphere of reality" (p. 71). Caute, however, acknowledges that a direct artistic assault on the "system" achieves
nothing. It is a mistake, and a costly one, to harness literature
to a strictly limited political program. The language of art
and the various forms of imaginative writing are suitable for
the exploration of the mysterious universe and for recording
man's quest for authenticity of selfhood and his search for ultimate meaning. These aims cannot be reconciled with "the
assertive, closed, schematic and rhetorical ideas employed by
the Revolution" (p. 80).

Caute, whose declared purpose it was to defend the idea of

committed literature, spends in *The Illusion* more than half his allotted space in documenting the glaring and often ludicrous faults that crop up with annoying frequency in the literature that parades under the banner of commitment. The committed writer betrays his impatience with the artificial frippery of his art, its contrived techniques, its preoccupation with the niceties of form and the subtle harmonies of style. He is interested primarily in broadcasting his message and, through his inflammatory art, starting the fire of revolution. But experience teaches the committed writer that it is wrong of him to expect immediate results. Agitprop fails both as art and as propaganda. Caute compares agitprop to a kind of fertility dance which prepares the group for the assured victory it will gain in the world conflict that is to be fought out (p. 225). Alas, too many novels and plays that come to grips with the political theme run to extremes: they are guilty of strident explicitness, message-mongering, melodramatic epiphanies, and crude satire and caricature. Despite these methodological blunders, Caute indignantly denies that literature and politics cannot be fruitfully allied. It is only private literature that is restricted in its range. Public literature is free to reach and utilize the political motif in all its challenging complexity. Then he asks: "Where is the Brecht of the modern novel?" He replies to his own question: "I do not see him" (p. 265).

If this figure did not appear, it is because the task which Caute wished to assign him is beyond his powers. Politics and literature cannot cohabit and produce viable offspring. Where are the great politically committed novels as compared with such great nonpolitical novels as *The Brothers Karamazov, The Magic Mountain, Steppenwolf,* and *The Sleepwalkers?*

Part II
THE COUNTERCOMMITMENT
AND THE REACTIONARY CLIQUE

3

The Countercommitment in Céline

1. *The Rationale of Commitment*

The problem of a Marxist hermeneutic arises whenever we are called upon to determine the place of what we may call right-wing literature, whether it be the the traditional conservative literature of the past of a Flaubert or a Dostoyevsky, or in our time a Fascist literature of great quality, as is the case with Wyndham Lewis or Drieu, or with Céline.[1]

Soviet orthodoxy falsely pretends that literature can be produced in conformity with a predetermined political line; Western orthodoxy pretends that literature, being connected with spiritual values, can be kept out of politics, which belongs to a baser, more material sphere. Both these false doctrines are closely related to political realities in their areas of origin, because they are ways of diverting serious critical attention from these realities.[2]

The Marxist critic assumes as a matter of course that the aesthetic of commitment possesses substantive meaning and validity only when it is linked with the cause of Communism.

1. Frederic Jameson, *Marxism and Form* (Princeton, N. J.: Princeton University Press, 1971), pp. 118-19. The subtitle of the book, *Twentieth-Century Dialectical Theories of Literature,* furnishes a clue to its contents. Professor Jameson attempts to show the underlying connection between culture and the class struggle.
2. Conor Cruise O'Brien, *Writers and Politics* (New York: Pantheon Books, 1965), p. 142.

A Fascist ideal of commitment is a travesty, a fraud, just as a Fascist philosophy is a contradiction in terms, since it derives its ideological content and its pseudo-revolutionary symbols from the writings of the Left. But the shortcomings of the Marxist system of aesthetics, which stresses the primary influence of economic forces and the basic reality of the class struggle, have rarely been analyzed and acknowledged. In the twentieth century a sociology of literature, Marxist in content, was built up, which attracted a number of productive disciples.[3] Whatever compromises and concessions the Communist Party may have made in the past, it has never abandoned its faith in the need for "commitment" on the part of the writer.

The Marxist critics were quick to spell out the consequences that logically follow when a writer becomes "committed." Is it possible for a Fascist literature to emerge?

> Is it possible, for example, that a novelist who holds non-. progressive values, a conservative reactionary or even neo-Fascist, could create a genuine literature? D. H. Lawrence. for example, is usually regarded as a major novelist, yet he was strongly anti-democratic, while his conception of some kind of mystical blood bond existing between men and women and men and men is the antithesis of reason and might conceivably suggest a Fascist mentality.[4]

Sartre, too, argues that an author of right-wing views could never succeed in creating a true work of art. The forces on

---

3. Marxist literary criticism is interested primarily in tracing the influence of economic forces at a given time and in stressing the all-important motif of the class struggle. A sociology of literature, largely Marxist in its methodology, was gradually built up in the twentieth century. In assessing the achievements of this movement, Alan Swingewood writes that "the results were poor. In many cases an extremely one-sided and mechanical explanation was put forward, dogmatically defining literature as a mere epiphenomenon of the social structure" (Diana T. Laurenson and Alan Swingewood, *The Sociology of Literature* [New York: Schocken Books, 1972], pp. 40-41). This negative judgment, however justified, fails to take into account the remarkable ability of some Marxist critics to profit from the mistakes of the past, even from the sclerotic dogmas imposed by the Stalinist dictatorship. They regroup their forces and shrewdly revise their method of attack. For example, Frederic Jameson, in his introduction to *Marxist Esthetics* by Henri Arvon, declares: "With the Chinese and Cuban Revolutions, the American New Left, the events of May 1968 in France, Marxism has emerged from the arthritis of Stalinism as a freshly creative and pluralistic school of thought" (Henri Arvon, *Marxist Esthetics*. Trans. Helen R. Lane [Ithaca, N. Y.: Cornell University Press, 1973], p. vii).
4. Laurenson and Swingewood, *The Sociology of Literature,* p. 83.

the Right, he concedes, may still be in control of events in the world, but they lack the ability to understand the underlying meaning of these events. "It [the Right] has surrendered most of its old ideals and has not replaced them; it does not understand the nature of its adversaries."[5] Blind to the facts of history, it is incapable of bringing a work of art into being. "For a work of art, even if it is nonpolitical, must proceed from an understanding of one's era, it must be in harmony with the age. One can't imagine a modern play that could be at the same time right-wing and good."[6]

This sweeping generalization, an expression of Sartre's Marxist faith, cites no specific example to prove its point. It illustrates one of the leading fallacies of our time: the implicit assumption that literary value is dependent on "the correct" kind of political orientation. If that is the case, is Céline to be dismissed as a novelist because he is a psychopath, a vicious anti-Semite, a "traitor" who collaborated with the Nazis? Is the work of Knut Hamsun to be damned because of his role as a Quisling during the Second World War? Is the poetry of T. S. Eliot to be condemned on the ground that he is a Royalist, a reactionary? And what about the sensational case of Ezra Pound? Do such pejorative labels as *conservative, reactionary, right-wing,* or *Fascist* help to deepen our critical insight and heighten our power of aesthetic judgment?

Questions such as these suggest the complexity of the problem confronting the literary critic. Frederic Jameson, the author of two influential books of Marxist criticism *(Marxism and Form* and *The Prison-House of Language)* advocates a Marxist hermeneutic that classifies literature according to its ideological alignment: it is either Left-wing or Right-wing, Fascist or revolutionary. In his introduction to Henri Arvon's *Marxism Esthetics,* Jameson seems to approve of a *prescriptive* aesthetic in a socialist society or in a society struggling to establish Socialism, an aesthetic "which encourages the artists and writers themselves to produce a particular type of art for a particular political purpose."[7] One wonders what kind of "encouragement" would be used on such refractory writers as Mandelstam, Pasternak, Sinyavsky, and Solzhenitsyn?

5. Kenneth Tynan, *Tynan Right & Left* (New York: Atheneum, 1967), p. 307. Tynan interviewed Sartre.
6. *Ibid.,* p. 307.
7. Arvon, *Marxist Esthetics,* p. xi.

In the second epigraph placed at the beginning of this chapter, Conor Cruise O'Brien does not refer to the axiomatic faith that sustains those writers who have joined forces with the Left: they are wholly committed to the belief that the cause they serve is on the side of the angels; it is progressive, affirmative, life-nourishing. Communism, they are convinced, will usher in the millennium, the Kingdom of Heaven on earth. Thus committed to the quest for a scientific Utopia, these writers cannot comprehend why other members of their calling are hostile to their scheme of redemption. Such men, defenders of a dying class and a dying culture, must be guilty of "bad faith." To denounce writers of this stamp on the ground they are not "sincere" is to resort to an *ad hominem* argument. (Of course, a writer may be utterly sincere in his beliefs and still be the victim of illusion.) Was Dostoevski sincere in his attack on nihilism in *The Possessed*? Was Robinson Jeffers a Fascist because he preached his philosophy of Inhumanism and regarded war as "the best way to eradicate humanity . . . for the world must be cleansed of the stain it had received from mankind"?[8] Was Charles Péguy, born a Catholic, "sincere" when he turned to Socialism and proclaimed himself to be an atheist? Was he "sincere" when he was reconverted to the faith of his fathers? Selfless generosity, a spirit of sacrifice, a willingness to suffer obloquy for his beliefs: these characterize the man. He fought for the vindication of Dreyfus; here was a cause that offered a crucial test of virtue. It served, he felt, to separate the sheep from the goats: those who embraced *la politique* from those who believed in *la mystique*. "By *mystique* he meant an unqualified and disinterested adherence to spiritual values . . . ."[9] These values represented moral absolutes whereas *politique* called for the compromise of these absolute values. Then in 1908 Péguy suddenly recovered his faith as a Catholic. How did it happen? Why? Péguy was a man who believed passionately in the truth and was resolved that nothing would stop him from finding it. How, then, account for his return to the fold? As he wrote at the time: "It is out of good atheists and out of those who don't expect it, that good Christians are made."[10] No, the writer on the Left cannot

8. Arthur B. Coffin, *Robinson Jeffers: Poet of Inhumanism* (Madison and London: The University of Wisconsin Press, 1971), p. 14.
9. Marjorie Villiers, *Charles Péguy* (New York: Harper & Row, 1965), p. 48.
10. *Ibid.*, p. 220.

don the mantle of righteousness and accuse his opponents of insincerity.

The writers of the Catholic Revival, for example, believed in the reality of miracles and the truth of their mystical vision. They "were almost unanimous in taking an intransigent, reactionary attitude in relation to matters of both faith and politics."[11] If Marxism voiced the aims and aspirations of the Left, the Catholic Revival formulated the creed of the Right, though it was not concerned chiefly with politics. "The mistrust of science, and the fear of the positivist ideas which appeared to stem from it, led in most of the Catholic writers of the time to a rejection not merely of intellectualism but of the use of the intellect itself in religious matters."[12] They became militant anti-rationalists.

Confronting an age of rampant materialism that they were powerless to combat, the Catholics turned inward in their despair and looked backward in time for models of a society unified by faith and they found their model in an idealized version of the Middle Ages: a hierarchical order ruled by orthodoxy.

The stormy history of twentieth-century literature demonstrates that there are many different kinds of commitment. Knut Hamsun warned his countrymen against the suicidal folly of opposing the German invasion of Norway; they should give up all thoughts of resistance to the invincible power of Hitler's armed forces. His countrymen never forgave him this act of treason. *On Overgrown Paths* is the account of his arrest in 1945 and his removal to a hospital. A prisoner in his old age, he declares that his conscience is clear. In his statement before the court he insisted that what he had written for the newspapers in behalf of Nazism was not wrong. "It was right, and what I wrote was right."[13] He wanted to save his people from certain destruction if they took up arms against the invader. He had no intention of betraying his country. To the very last he continued to protest his innocence.

Hamsun's collaboration with the Nazis, Céline's call for the extermination of the Jews, Ezra Pound's broadcasts from Fas-

11. Richard Griffiths, *The Reactionary Revolution: The Catholic Revival in French Literature 1870-1914* (New York: Frederick Ungar Publishing Co., 1965), p. 4.
12. *Ibid.*, p. 7.
13. Knut Hamsun, *On Overgrown Paths*. Trans. Carl J. Anderson (New York: Paul S. Erisson, 1947), p. 142.

cist Italy attacking the United States and spreading the poison of anti-Semitism—such examples degrade the image of the writer as the conscience of mankind and make a mockery of Shelley's triumphant peroration in *A Defense of Poetry* that poets are the unacknowledged legislators of the world. There is no point in questioning the "sincerity"—or sanity— of these writers in *their* commitment to a reactionary movement. Does their political error—or aberration—vitiate the creative work they produced in the past? Are Hamsun's novels infected beyond hope of redemption? Is Céline's art as a novelist to be admired, despite his misanthropic nihilism and his venomous, unrelenting hatred of the Jews?

2. The Politics of Céline

Céline's entire work—both in theme and style—is an illustration of the view that existence is an endgame played out on a cannibal isle or in a cosmic jungle, in an irrational and vicious setting with a multiple décor of slaughterhouse, asylum, and dunghill.[14]

Not only does he refuse to attribute to literature the ability to reform existence, but he also firmly believes that the present social system is as rotten as any other, past or future. His horror and disgust go much further; the attacks are directed against life itself.[15]

I've always been an anarchist, I've never voted, I'll never vote for anything or anyone. . . . The Nazis despise me as much as the socialists or the commies, too.[16]

Céline, the enfant terrible of modern French literature, deliberately insults his readers and exaggerates his own misanthropic outlook. The bitter, uncompromising nihilist of our age, he detests the race of mankind. He is prepared to jettison all the higher values civilized people pretend to live by: these are evasions, shoddy lies, opiate illusions. This toplofty talk of aspirations, ideals, spiritual goals, transcendence, is so

---

14. Erika Ostrovsky, *Céline and His Vision* (New York: New York University Press, 1967), p. 18.
15. *Ibid.*, p. 30.
16. Allen Thiher, *Céline: The Novel as Delirium* (New Brunswick, N. J.: Rutgers University Press, 1972), p. 228.

much blague. He regarded all political schemes for the ultimate salvation of mankind—democracy, anarchism, Socialism,
Fascism, Communism—as examples of utopian folly. Food,
sleep, sexual intercourse, the preservation of one's life—these
are the gods men really worship. What arrant hypocrites men
are in kneeling before graven images that cannot prevent or
even delay the fate of death. The earth is a madhouse
crowded with inmates who are driven by a homicidal hatred
of their fellow mortals. They are cruel and murderous because they sense the nearness of death. On the field of battle,
one beholds the behavior of men at their bestial, demented
worst.

Though misanthropy does not in itself define a political attitude (Hobbes, who described life as "nasty, brutish, and
short" in a state of nature, urged the wisdom of setting up a
despotic form of government and recommended that men
should submit to authority), in Céline's case it culminated in
an apocalyptic nihilism that looked upon homo sapiens with
absolute contempt. "Céline is a nihilist by default. . . ." His
fight against the destructive powers in life bears witness to his
"thirst for affirmation and perhaps for transcendence. . . ."[17]

When war is declared, the masses are ordered to fight and
die, and the remarkable thing is that they obey orders. Céline
is unmatched in his description of the horror of war, the latent sadism that leaps forth when all civilized restraints are
removed, the orgiastic pleasure the individual soldier derives
from the sport of killing the enemy and suffering no after-
math of guilt because of it. His country rewards him with a
medal of honor if he has shown conspicuous bravery and uncommon skill in killing off the men on the opposing side.
Céline pictures the war in *Journey to the End of the Night* as a
meaningless nightmare of blood and death. To the protagonist, the unfortunate and unheroic Bardamu, the war
brings home the grotesque and hideously farcical reality of
death. Only those without imagination can possibly believe
that death does not matter. Otherwise they could not have
endured this hellish ordeal in mud-soaked trenches where
they could at any moment be blown to bits by a German
shell. Yet the combatants on both sides went ahead with this
ghastly business of killing the enemy and thus inviting their

17. *Ibid.,* p. 43.

own death. Céline's central aim in his novels is to make this truth known to the world: namely, how diabolical men can be.

Journey to the End of the Night helps us in part to understand why Céline later became a collaborationist or was accused in France of being one. What difference did it make, after all, who ruled a country so long as one was allowed to remain alive? Even if the Germans occupied France and destroyed everything in Paris and slaughtered the people in it, what would Bardamu, if he survived the holocaust, have lost? "Morals, in fact, were a dirty business."[18] To survive at all costs—that ambition was at bottom more honest and honorable than the highfalutin patriotic sentiments the citizens mouthed at home. "Lie, copulate and die. One wasn't allowed to do anything else."[19]

If the sheer horror of war drove Bardamu insane, he found some compensation in losing his reason; madness was at least a way out of this inferno. And who were the so-called sane people? Those who demanded more sacrifices of blood, more "glorious victories" in battle? Were they considered sane because they constituted the majority and held the reins of power? Céline focuses his lens on the wards of the hospital set aside for shell-shock victims, the malingerers, the psychopathic sufferers. Bardamu frequently wonders if he is not really mad. In a topsy-turvy world where one is judged to be mad if he questions why he is being led to the slaughter, "obviously it is very easy to be considered insane."[20] Bardamu does not believe in the sacredness of war. Even if the whole world condemned him for this unpatriotic attitude, he would not change his mind. What do the common soldiers who perish on the battlefield die for? For nothing! They are buried and soon forgotten. In a few thousand years, who will care one way or the other about the issues for which this war was ostensibly fought? Why should the individual soldier consent to being killed and providing food for the worms? The poor man is offered two options, two ways of dying, "either through the complete indifference of his fellow men in time

18. Louis-Ferdinand Céline, *Journey to the End of the Night*. Trans. John H. P. Marks (New York: New Directions, 1960), p. 49.
19. *Ibid.*, p. 50.
20. *Ibid.*, p. 59.

of peace or by the homicidal fury of these same fellow men when war comes."[21]

Céline's fiction is the feverish outpouring of a mind that is obsessive in its quest for a meaning and that seeks, compulsively, to explore the night of being, the metaphysical void, even if this drives the protagonist to the edge of madness and on occasion pushes him over the edge. Céline is certainly a committed writer in that he is determined to reveal the inescapable horror of existence. This is the shattering truth he has discovered, this is an integral part of his delirious vision. It is not a rationally conceived and logically developed pessimism that Céline elaborates. Reason betrays man. It abandons him in times of intense suffering or great danger.[22] Céline scorns the tribe of intellectuals with their finespun metaphysical theories, their windy abstractions, and their penchant for noble-sounding rhetoric. They close their eyes to the universal madness of war. For this world is well trained in the art of killing. And Bardamu, for his part, felt that it was downright stupid to die like all the other hapless victims. "To trust in men is itself to let oneself be killed a little."[23]

After passing through this Gehenna of war, Bardamu travels to the United States, which is a more terrifying place than the tropical jungle. Here he beholds how robots are harnessed to the machine, men who work, eat, and sleep as if nothing were wrong with the world, as if their journey would never end in the darkness of the grave. And what shall one do, where is one to turn, Bardamu, the persona of Céline, asks, when the madness subsides? "Truth is a pain which will not stop. And the truth of this world is to die."[24] Céline uncovers the hidden, intolerable truth of the human condition; his nightmarish version of the truth is unmistakably nihilistic in content. Like his protagonist Bardamu, he harbors no illusions. He is haunted by the ever-present threat of annihila-

21. *Ibid.*, p. 78.
22. Thiher interprets this extinction of the faculty of reason to mean that Céline's quest leads to the ultima Thule of madness. Céline describes the character of being by relying on his dominant and recurrent metaphor of madness. Thiher maintains that "nearly every episode in *Voyage* can be considered a manifestation of madness and hysteria." (Thiher, *Céline*, pp. 20-21.)
23. Louis-Ferdinand Céline, *Journey to the End of the Night,* p. 176.
24. *Ibid.*, p. 199.

tion, the futility of man's protest against death, the irremediable absurdity of his brief stay on earth. Céline, like Dostoevsky, is fully aware of the bestiality of the human animal, but unlike the Russian novelist he holds out no hope of salvation. His savage pessimism definitely implies that there is no possibility of improving the lot of mankind.

Bardamu returns to France and settles down to practice medicine in a foul-smelling slum section of Paris. His experience as a doctor enables him to observe how the poor spend their days: they quarrel, periodically get drunk, toil at a monotonous task for a mere pittance, contract disease, discharge whatever surplus energy they have on holidays, and then die. Fear hems them in on all sides: fear of sickness, fear of losing their job, fear of destitution, fear of the death that is soon to come. Céline is revolted by these poverty-stricken patients: their pettiness, their avarice, their outbursts of cruelty, but the medical specialists are no better than that hydra-headed monster, the People. As for the young, they betray a fretful impatience to grow old. It is better to let youth pass away, so that one can get "a glimpse of what people and things are really like."[25]

Céline harps on his favorite theme: that men possess the nature of the beast. People are so vile that it is frightening to encounter them when they are well, for then their ruling desire is to kill.[26] Only when prostrated by a serious illness are they less dangerous. *Journey to the End of the Night* is chock-full of such angry blasts at vile mankind. This harsh judgment of his fellow men is perfectly in keeping with his nihilistic reading of life. As Bardamu watches the masses having "a good time" at the Fair, he hears the pounding of his heart,

25. *Ibid.*, p. 287.
26. If Céline seems deranged at times in his compulsion to express his consistently low estimate of human nature, he represents a point of view that resembles in some respects the one held by Sigmund Freud. The latter announced that the truth, "which people are so ready to disavow, is that men are not gentle creatures who want to be loved, and who at the most can defend themselves if they are attacked; they are, on the contrary, creatures among whose instinctual endowment is to be reckoned a powerful share of aggressiveness. As a result, their neighbor is for them not only a potential helper or sexual object, but also someone who tempts them to exploit his capacity for work without compensation, to use him sexually without his consent, to seize his possessions, to humiliate him, to cause him pain, to torture and to kill him. Homo homini lupus." Sigmund Freud, *Civilization and Its Discontents.* Trans. James Strachey (New York: W. W. Norton & Company, 1961), p. 58.

knowing that one day it will grow louder and louder like thunder and burst. "Let it! One day when the inner rhythm rejoins the outside one and all your ideas spill out and run away at last to play with the stars."[27] What on earth is the use of striving? What is the good of satisfying this furious pro-creative urge, each generation of copulating beasts repeating the same meaningless cycle of existence, only to die when their time is up? "One isn't even capable of understanding death."[28] The molecules of which the body is composed want to fall apart, to lose themselves as soon as possible in the universe of matter, so that they will cease to be "mere cuckolds of the Infinite."[29] That is the biological ignominy which the human adventurer cannot transcend; poor or rich, all men finish their round of destiny by being deposited like so much ordure in the cemetery. In the midst of life we ignore this Gorgon-aspect of reality. "You only find yourself in silence, when it is too late, like dead men."[30] There is no point, however, in trying to conceal things, for there is no way out of the universal trap, the death that dooms all creatures born of the flesh. The process of dying goes on all the time within the vulnerable body, till it is rendered defenseless and ceases to resist. Plagued by this secret torment, this metaphysical obsession, Céline is indifferent to the time-bound battles of politics.

Death on the Installment Plan also furnishes a shockingly low estimate of human nature. Céline is unsurpassed in his ability to highlight the vicious, sadistic streak in the characters that people his fictional world: their spite, their rancor and resentment, their malignant hatred, their unregenerate selfishness and stupidity. Despite all they are made to suffer, they cling tenaciously to life. However desperate their condition, they dream absurdly inflated dreams of grandeur, foolish, incredible dreams of happiness. Céline is surprised by the ferocious strength of their will to survive. Even the beggars, the wounded, the cripples, fearful of dying, hold on feverishly to life. Céline describes this fearful struggle against Thanatos with a mass of sordid physiological details: the oozing pus, the gangrenes, the chancres, the syphilitic dis-

27. Céline, *Journey to the End of the Night,* p. 310.
28. *Ibid.,* p. 330.
29. *Ibid.,* p. 335.
30. *Ibid.,* p. 347.

charges, the rotting flesh, the infected blood, the smell of excrement. As in *Journey to the End of the Night,* Céline interprets life as an agonizing and futile struggle, full of pain, misfortune, and disaster.

Céline's political outlook emerges by indirection in his deliberate effort to debunk the heroic ideal, the ethic of humanitarianism. He uses the visceral language of the body, the racy slang of the gutter, to puncture the colored balloon of romanticism. Life, as he sees it, is a jungle in which the strong, the cunning, and the unscrupulous forge ahead and stay alive while the weak, the naive, and the virtuous go under. That, Céline declares fiercely, is the way things are. That is the truth of the human condition we must accept and learn to live with or else remain deluded and sooner or later suffer a calamitous collapse. We must come to grips with the politics of disillusionment and realize that the people we deal with are not saints but scoundrels. The masses are not motivated by generous or altruistic impulses; they are, without exception, concerned solely with their own selfish interests, their own advancement in the race—and the devil take the hindmost.

Death on the Installment Plan describes how the young protagonist, Bardamu, discovers that silence is the best defense against the aggressions of social hypocrisy. He distrusts all those who seek to reform his character; they will only bring misfortune upon him. His parents are a striking example of well-intentioned blunderers. They preach the sound wisdom of thrift, they believe in the virtue of hard work, they remain incorruptibly honest, and what is the net result? They become steadily poorer and poorer, their health broken in this hopeless economic struggle. Born victims, helpless innocents, they are gulled and bludgeoned into failure. Their sacrifices for their son's welfare fail to help him. If he is to keep his head above water, he must master the art of trickery and humbug. His experiences as an employee turn out badly. The men he encounters are often angry, but their sense of outrage is superficial, not the real thing.

> Real outrage comes from deeper down, it starts way back in youth, youth battered, helpless, grovelling at the grindstone. That's the true hatred—it kills. There'll be more of it, so far down that it shall spread and be everywhere, spurting out over

the world to poison and leave nothing growing on the surface of the earth but malice among men.[31]

It is the spirit of vindictive hatred, monomaniacal in its fury, that prevades the novel.

Céline, the dedicated prophet of disillusionment and disaster, has rid himself of all sentimental nonsense, religious shibboleths, and moral commandments. In *Guignol's Band,* the protagonist is a victim who has turned criminal. Céline pictures the smash-up of civilization. He makes no apology for his thoroughly negative, iconoclastic conclusions. Let the critics damn his work with opprobrious epithets; let them call it decadent, pessimistic, nihilistic, "mad." He will be read despite their calumnious attacks. He will continue to broadcast his signals of dire warning. Life is threatened. The world is dying in convulsions. The apocalyptic end of civilization is being acted out on the blood-soaked battlefields of Europe. Paris is being bombed. "We throw ourselves on our knees. . . . We beg the Virgin Mary! with his fervent sign of the cross!. . . God the Father."[32] But there is no letup in the bombardment. The plane in the sky is guided by the angel of death.

Guignol's Band was published in 1944 when France was occupied and Céline was about to flee to Germany. In this "comic" novel, Céline portrays death as a farcical event. He is able to master his frightening obsession by viewing it through this comic perspective. He is aware of the shock value to be derived from his technique of bringing death on the scene: Death, the farceur, when he appears suddenly and unexpectedly, Death the grim and grotesque joker. Céline refers in one passage to his effective technique of exploiting the comic potentialities of the theme of death. Every time he introduces the image of "fatal death," his readers roar with unrestrained laughter. Death serves, too, as an ironic and illuminating commentary on reality. This reality is arranged in a ludicrous manner. Its multitudinous details affect us more as burlesque than as tragedy, and on the surface of this reality "squirm a few billion knots of atoms that have scarcely been tied to-

---

31. Louis-Ferdinand Céline, *Death on the Installment Plan.* Trans. John H. P. Marks (New York: New Directions, 1938), p. 142.

32. Louis-Ferdinand Céline, *Guignol's Band.* Trans. Bernard Frechtman and Jack T. Nile (Norfolk, Conn.: New Directions, 1954), p. 11.

gether and having conceitedly cried out their name of man, start to come apart: is there anything that's more farcical?"[33]

Céline hurls his anathemas at a degenerate civilization that has given in to this murderous frenzy. How can one possibly survive this infernal cataclysm? He has no desire to be blown up, reduced to ashes and dust. He cries out: "Death to illusions!"[34] If one yields for a moment to the collective hysteria, he is utterly done for. *Guignol's Band* recounts the adventures of the wounded hero in flight from a war that never ends. The nightmarish memories of the past—his wound in the arm and in the head—condition his present behavior. He is afraid of being dragged back to the fighting front. Men were not meant to fight for victory but to live. Ferdinand has had enough of the fighting. "I'd had three years of it! . . . my youth knocked around in the army!"[35]

> I brought back my bones and the mortgages! holes everywhere! . . . my arm twisted! Just a hunk of flesh left. . . maybe enough for them to yank me in again! The little game wasn't over! . . . War hooks on! . . . You've got to watch out.[36]

Because of the evil reputation Céline had built up as a collaborator with the Nazis, he had to flee for his life: first, to Germany; then, when that country was systematically attacked by Allied bombers, to Denmark, where he was imprisoned and then allowed to remain there as an exile. In 1951 he was granted amnesty and allowed to return to Paris. In the last three novels he produced—the trilogy consists of *Castle to Castle, North,* and *Rigodon*—he pictures himself as the victim of the blood-lust of the French. *Castle to Castle* is a kind of confessional novel that reviews the events in Céline's political past that made him not only a *persona non grata* in his native land but a traitor, a convicted collaborationist with the Nazi regime. He does not apologize for his past deeds; instead he leaps to the attack and castigates all those responsible for his persecution, forcing him to flee from France and seek refuge in Denmark. With paranoiac vehemence he excoriates his enemies, the greed of his friends who seized his manuscripts after his precipitate flight from France, the cupidity of the relatives who took possession of his household goods and were enraged when he was at last permitted to re-

33. Thiher, *Céline,* p. 114.
34. Céline, *Guignol's Band,* p. 18.
35. *Ibid.,* p. 70.
36. *Ibid.*

turn home. He lambastes the venal critics who had hounded him with the cry of "Fascist, Nazi, collaborationist, traitor." He has never repented of his alleged crimes nor repudiated his past. Céline, as we see in *North*, was not burdened with a sense of guilt. He feels that he has been unjustly persecuted simply because he was incautious enough to voice "the wrong" political sentiments. Céline never actively collaborated with the Nazis; he joined none of the anti-Semitic organizations that existed in France before and during the Occupation. Yet the impression his published work produced was sufficient to brand him a collaborator.[37] The French government attempted to have him extradited from Denmark. While incarcerated in a Danish prison, he issued a statement calling himself an "abstentionist." Céline was, of course, guilty of giving vent to inexcusable racist hatred. He disseminated the noxious propaganda in *Bagatelles pour un massacre* that the Jews were in a conspiracy to drag a peace-loving Germany into war. Some critics maintain that Céline was provoked into composing these tirades against the Jews for fear that their attacks on Hitler might plunge France into another war. But he went far beyond this issue, caricaturing them as the source of all the evil in the world. Milton Hindus, in *The Crippled Giant*, declares that Céline was "not a collaborator in the juridical sense."[38] He did not act on his professed beliefs.[39] The central clue to his "reactionary" politics is to be found in his conception of human nature as incurably evil, bloodthirsty, unutterably vile.[40]

37. See the chapter called "Political Delirium" (Thiher, *Céline,* pp. 118-37), which is a fair-minded inquiry into the problem relating to Céline's political obsessions. In opposition to the beliefs many critics have held, Thiher delivers his verdict that Céline is not guilty as charged. The accusation brought against him seems to be groundless. "In fact, there is no reason to suppose that Céline was ever a fascist. . ." (*ibid.*, p. 119). Erika Ostrovsky declares that legally his guilt is "open to question," but his *"human* guilt cannot be so easily be passed over" (Ostrovsky, *Voyeur Voyant* [New York: Random House, 1971], p. 357).

38. Milton Hindus, *The Crippled Giant* (New York: Boar's Head Books, 1950), p. 116.

39. Céline refused "to join any political party, to become a member of any antisemitic organization, or to collaborate with the German Occupation. . ." (*ibid.*, p. 122).

40. Early in this chapter I noted the distinction that Péguy drew between "politique" and "mystique." What damaged Céline's reputation and compromised him in the eyes of his countrymen is that he went beyond the bounds of his "mystique" and soiled his hands in the polluted stream of politics. "Had he limited himself to the expression of a racist mysticism, he might have suffered little more than, say, a Montherlant who indulged himself in fantasies about the meaning of the Swastika" (Thiher, *Céline*, p. 135).

4

Wyndham Lewis: The Reactionary Artist and His Commitment

Today all thought tends to have a political implication, whether it is intended to or not.[1]

After his life is over, an artist's work as a whole can be judged fairly dispassionately in the perspective of time, but the time perspective must be long enough to enable the critic to evaluate the work in question with a sufficient measure of detachment and objectivity. The judgment we make regarding the permanent value of his contribution is not affected by his "wrong" political loyalties. But the fierce passions of controversy that writers like Céline, Wyndham Lewis, and Ezra Pound aroused have not yet cooled off. Though all three now rest in Abraham's bosom, their reactionary fulminations are still remembered and in some quarters bitterly resented. They were infected to a greater or lesser degree with the deadly virus of Fascism; they were guilty of disseminating, each in his own way, their anti-Semitic hatred. If the artist's

1. John R. Harrison, *The Reactionaries: A Study of the Anti-Democratic Intelligentsia* (New York: Schocken Books, 1967), p. 86.

84

vision is thus impaired, then what value can his creative work possess? The artist cannot, after all, be separated from the man.[2] How can a man like Ezra Pound go so far astray in his political manias and still be capable of producing authentic poetry? He was an aggressive and righteous purveyor of reactionary politics at its worst, combined with scurrilous anti-Semitic diatribes. In his book *Culture* (1936), Pound praised Lewis for his superior gift of perception in "discovering" Hitler, just as Pound had discovered Mussolini. Truculent and contentious, Lewis was drawn inevitably into the political battles of his time. Convinced like the Marxists, but for different reasons, that there was an inseverable connection between literature and politics, Lewis decided to use the arts, including the art of criticism, as a political weapon in combating what he considered the pernicious heresies and ideological follies of his age.

Wyndham Lewis stands forth as, in one respect, an exemplary figure in his commitment to the life of art. He would allow nothing to interfere with his fulfillment as an artist. In a world in which the element of the sacred had been liquidated, he continued to look upon his vocation as if it were a mandate from the gods. He was superbly endowed for this mission. In the course of his meteoric career, he found he had to justify his aesthetic beliefs against philistine scoffers and Bohemian detractors. A lusty fighter, he attacked all those who failed to agree with him.

Possessed of a venturesome and versatile mind, he engaged in polemics that revealed his vast fund of erudition and the far-ranging scope of his speculations. There is scarcely a phase of Western culture that he has not written about: sociolo-

2. See Karl Shapiro's book *In Defense of Ignorance,* which attacks T. S. Eliot as a mandarin-poet who seeks beauty and inspiration in the mystical past, who praises the anti-noetic function of the mind, and who embraces a religious outlook that has no room in it for the scientific vision. In his study *The Political Identities of Ezra Pound & T. S. Eliot,* William M. Chace shows that Eliot, like Wyndham Lewis and Pound, entered the political arena because of his desire to foster the creative individual, the genius, the man endowed with genuine artistic talent. Rossell Hope Robbins, in *The T. S. Eliot Myth,* bluntly charges that Eliot's anti-Semitism springs from a fundamental lack of love for people and a deeply rooted distrust of democracy. Eliot's anti-Semitism, he argues, is "only the surface sore of a much deeper disease. How a man looks at any one group of people must be related to how he looks at all people in the world. The ugliness of Eliot's anti-Semitism is fully understood only when his antihumanism is recognized." (Rossell Hope Robbins, *The T. S. Eliot Myth* [New York: Henry Schuman, 1951], p. 21.)

gy, anthropology, metaphysics, literature and art, history, the meaning of time, and, of course, politics. To write about these highly specialized subjects he had to do an enormous amount of reading and research. He was never daunted, always ready to take on a challenge, prepared to battle against his adversaries. His professional function, he felt, was to oppose the then rampant cult of the time-philosophies. His chosen role, and he played it with verve and distinction, was that of an intransigent dissenter, a rebellious individualist who, in sheer self-defense, is driven to wage war against the collectivist fantasies and fixations of his contemporaries. He carried the war into the enemy's quarters. An artist, a poet, a novelist, a critic, an editor of avant-garde magazines, he emerged as the anointed prophet of the creative life. He tried to keep aloof from the political quarrels of his day, but he was compelled to enter the fray by the need to refute the pernicious ideas that sought to capture and subvert the minds of men. Behind the dominant ideologies that were being preached, he detected a political bias, a streak of fanaticism, which he was resolved to destroy.

A formidable satirist, he set out to demolish the absurd notions the Western world swore allegiance to. In carrying on this campaign, he betrayed his own antipathies. He hates with unrestrained gusto. He hates the American people, democracy, Communism, the Soviet Union, Jews, the spirit of reform, the pretensions of science. He is adamantly opposed to the idolatry of modernism, the vogue of "newness," the theory of relativity, Bergson's philosophy of vitalism, the idealization of youth, and the worship of the primitive. Lewis steals the ideological thunder of the Left by arguing that, regardless of the aesthetic principles advanced by the Marxists, the artist is a "revolutionary" in the practice of his art. The genuine artist follows no fixed rules or prescriptive ideas; he has no use for abstractions. He does not belong to the Church of Science or kneel before the shrine of industrial progress. These traits of the emancipated, truly "revolutionary" artist resemble closely the features that make up Lewis's own portrait. A nonconformist to the very end, Lewis staunchly defended the maligned cause of individualism.

Lewis exerted a profoundly disturbing influence on the modern cultural scene. He has been called a reactionary and other invidious names, but he is no slavering fanatic carried away by the violence of ignorant passion. He has prepared himself thoroughly for his self-sought task of cultural decontamination. He has read the work of Karl Marx, Proudhon, Fourier, Machiavelli, Sorel, Bertrand Russell, Locke, H. S. Maine, Westermarck, Saint-Simon, Nietzsche, and a host of others. His polemics—and most of his books fall into that category—are often heavily documented. In *The Doom of Youth* (1923), he denounces the sentimental idealization of youth. Priding himself on his scientific "detachment," he begins the assault by affirming his belief in the fundamental truth of the blood-homogeneity of the race. The young, he charges, are being rapidly enslaved by the politics of Youth, the real purpose of which is to speed up and render more efficient the process of industrial production. The politicalization of youth is designed to destroy their naturalness, deprive them of their spontaneity, strip them of their vital egotism, and fit them to obey the rhythm of the machine. "Politics," Wyndham Lewis points out, "have become economics."[3] Anti-Marxist in outlook, he denies the existence of the class war. The conflict that rages today is between conservatism and "revolutionaryism," between the old and the new, the individual and the collective, the personal and the abstract. Interested exclusively in the individual, Lewis undertakes to defend the most highly gifted individuals, the creative elite, against the persecution of the mob.

He fulminates against democracy because it disinherits the individual and breeds mediocrity. Under its maleficent rule, man is molded in the image of the machine and his span of life shortened. His hatred of democracy is motivated by his rooted conviction that it is a leveler of innate distinctions of character and ability. The man of no visible talent usurps the place of genius. It is Communism, Lewis holds, that is chiefly responsible for this degradation of the standard of excellence. Communism is "a highly organized, semi-religious movement to deprive the *individual* of anything he possesses in excess. . . . Brains in *excess* would be as bad as money in *excess*."[4] What arouses his ire is this campaign to eliminate the individual. If this were successful, it would spell the death of genius, for genius is essentially nothing more than an excess

3. Wyndham Lewis, *The Doom of Youth* (New York: Robert M. McBride, 1932), p. 31.
4. *Ibid.*, p. 131.

of individuality. This is the heart of Lewis's creed. He will fight to the bitter end the menace of Communism, which is at bottom a conspiracy "to abolish that *excess* of life we call 'genius.'"[5]

Lewis is thus committed to a faith in the creative individualist, and it is this faith that leads him, in *The Art of Being Ruled,* to engage in more determined attacks on Communism. If all men are regarded as equal, then the average is set up as the norm. In the course of his philippic, he disposes not only of Karl Marx but also of Nietzsche, Sorel, Bertrand Russell, Bernard Shaw, and Bentham. He finds revolutionary politics, and particularly the revolutionary mentality, inexpressibly dull. Step by step, he refutes the empty abstractions fathered by messianic Marxism. Now that the idea of revolution has become fashionable, it is time to strike it down. Lewis thinks the resort to revolutionary violence is insane because men can be changed more effectively by other methods. Not that life is sacred; no mystical value belongs to it. "No 'moral' or ethical value can stand for a moment against the intoxication of death."[6] Violence, when judged objectively as a biological phenomenon, is no more than an outburst of excessive energy. To counter the destructive impact of violence, the aesthetic principle, when applied, proves more effective than the call for moral restraint. Since all true art opposes excess, Lewis proposes that the best way of dealing with the problem of violence is to seek for a solution along aesthetic lines "rather than moral (the police) lines, or humanitarian ones" (p. 63).

Lewis attempts to clarify the honorific but hopelessly confused notion of freedom prevalent in his day. Not every individual is entitled to freedom or freedom of the same kind. If the demand for freedom is not restrained by rational means, then each person will in effect be encouraged to develop his own egocentric universe. Carried to a logical extreme, Western democracy with its built-in defense of the rights of man, culminates in anarchy. Like the Grand Inquisitor in Ivan Karamazov's "Legend," Lewis argues that most men really don't want the gift of freedom. What the majority of people, the gregarious herd, desire most is "a disciplined, well-

5. *Ibid.,* p. 141.
6. Wyndham Lewis, *The Art of Being Ruled* (London: Chatto and Windus, 1926), p. 63.

policed, herd-life. . ." (p. 35). At this point the issue narrows down to a choice between liberal democracy and the rule of dictatorship. What is there to be feared, Lewis asks, if Fascism should triumph? Why should the bare name evoke such a feeling of horror? Fascism, he contends, is really an extreme version of Leninism "adapted to an ancient and intelligent population" (p. 69). He readily agrees that everyone today endorses the revolutionary ideas, but this need not be political in character. The revolution Lewis approves of and heartily recommends to his countrymen is a "spiritual" one that will make it possible to arrange people in a "natural" hierarchical order, an order that will guarantee that not the vast undifferentiated majority but the talented and the competent will govern. The intelligent few, the aristocracy of the intellect, should unite their forces so as to defeat the host of organizations now being formed to incite—and exploit—the passions of the ignorant multitude. The division of the population into economic classes is a taxonomic fiction. Only two different species exist: the men superbly endowed by nature, the geniuses, and the mechanical men. What Lewis hopes to achieve is not the recognition of social rank but "something like a *biological* separating-out of the chaff from the grain" (p. 139). The class-system that Marx postulated and foisted upon the consciousness of the Western world proves invaluable in that it can be used by the powers that be to regiment the masses into trained, automatically obedient units. But the man ideally free would be "the man *least* specialized, the *least* stereotyped, the *least* clamped into a system—in a word, the most individual" (p. 166).

Lewis is a destructive satirist who denounces the evils of modern civilization with unrestrained fury. As in the case of Ezra Pound, what call forth his most frenzied objurgations are those doctrines, institutions, and forms of government that are hostile to the creative life. If, like Pound again, Lewis vents his anger on the mob, it is because the mob is the enemy of art, the foe of greatness, the detractor of genius. The democratic myth fosters all those tendencies which by dint of flattery induce the mediocre to believe they are as good as other men. Equality, Lewis assures us, does not and cannot exist. All men are not born equal. The best thing for the future well-being of society would be the recognition of the biological fact that men are innately different in ability as well as intelligence. After blasting away at the swindle of democracy and the contemporary deification of the unconscious, he fires a broadside at the citadel of science. Once give the scientist (he is only a narrow-minded specialist) absolute power, and he will betray the blood-lust of the mob. Lewis arrogantly concludes that science is a pseudo-religion that is "on the side of death" and is "impregnated with the *romance of destruction*" (p. 261). All this is written by a man who professes to uphold the standards of the intellect against those who would dethrone reason in favor of some mystical creed born of intuition.

In defending the rights of genius against both Communism and Western democracy, he praises the model of centralization used by the Italian government under Mussolini. Fascism, far from being a monster of evil, is but a workable version of Socialism. "All marxian doctrine, all *étatism* or collectivism, conforms very nearly in practice to the fascist ideal" (p. 369). With unshakable self-assurance, Lewis upholds the Mussolini brand of Fascism. This is the sovereign remedy he prescribes for the socioeconomic ills of England. It is to be noted that his rough outline of a Fascist-coordinated society is based on the principle of spiritual ascendancy. In the interest of art, Lewis sought to protect the creative man, the artist, against the crass interference of politics. Thus Lewis, like Ezra Pound, based his politics on the dynamic values he derived from the world of aesthetics. It is the life of the intellect, unburdened by dogma and uninvolved in politics, that Lewis honestly believes he is extolling. The servants of the intellect, he observes, do not constitute a caste, "but [are] individuals possessing no concerted and lawless power, coming indifferently from all classes, and living simply among other people" (p. 433). They have nothing in common with the hereditary aristocrat.

In *Time and Western Man,* his most ambitious work, Lewis carries to extreme lengths his attack on the time-philosophy that is dominant in the Western world. He launches this spirited attack in order to protect the life of art against the pernicious influences that threaten to vulgarize it. He wishes to preserve the spatial sense, the beauty of the concrete, against the phantasmagoric flux of the time-bound philosophers. "I am for the physical world," he declares.[7] Time is more

    7. Wyndham Lewis, *Time and Western Man* (New York: Harcourt, Brace and Company, 1928), p. 113.

abstract than space and, as an artist, he distrusts abstractions. The new time-reality is a phantom, but it has the power to disintegrate the sensuous, solid world we know into a whirlwind of atomic ghosts. The literature and art of the twentieth century are a faithful reflection of the time-cult. To make matters worse, this philosophy has been eagerly taken over by millenarian politics. The revolutionary in particular is drawn to the philosophers of Time. "But I am entirely sick to death, like a great host of other people, of many of the forms that 'revolution' takes, in art, sociology, science and life. . . ."[8] The art that today is called "revolutionary" is inferior art, shallow, didactic in tone, self-consciously political in content. "In a period of such obsessing political controversy as the present, I believe that I am that strange animal, the individual without any 'politics' at all."[9] It is, of course, not true. What he probably means is that he would like to throw off the burden of politics because it interferes with his commitment to art.

In *Paleface* (1929) Lewis composes another slashing polemic from the point of view of genius. In the name of genius, everything is to be permitted. Social institutions, government, the machinery of economic production, work and wealth—all these things exist for the purpose of making possible the flowering of genius. He reiterates his conviction that democracy has given rise to a new type of slavery. Originally adapted to the needs of a small, compact, homogeneous group, democracy is no longer suited to our "vast, sprawling, dreamy polyp-organisms we call nations."[10] The verbal illusion of freedom has blinded the populace to their actual servile condition.

He paints a nightmarish picture of the damage wrought by science. Democracy is a gigantic hopper into which human beings, however different in brain-power and talent, are poured and ground to a cementlike uniformity. Enforced regimentation—that is the final upshot of the democratic process. As nationalism spreads across the face of the earth and the tempo of industrial production increases, the enjoyment of freedom is drastically curtailed, and life becomes more impersonal, more efficiently controlled.

8. *Ibid.*, p. 135.
9. *Ibid.*, p. 119.
10. Wyndham Lewis, *Paleface: The Philosophy of the 'Melting Pot'* (London: Chatto and Windus, 1929), p. 72.

In thus voicing his reactionary social philosophy, in aggressively opposing the democratic ideal and the gospel of Communism, he was forced to assume the role of virtual outlaw. As a member of the opposition, he was stripped of all political influence. He personally wishes that he did not have to become involved in these political fracases. Instead of making demagogic speeches or concocting propagandistic tracts, he would prefer to publish books in his field of primary interest: "my abilities, and my interests . . . do not lie in the economic or the political field at all, but in that of the arts of expression, the library and the theatre."[11]

Though Lewis admits he has no special competence in the sphere of economics or politics, the message he addresses to the world is colored by his aspirations and fears as an artist. In his book *Hitler* (1931), he openly sympathizes with the German dictator. Wearing for the occasion the mask of a skeptic, he assures the reader that he does not accept every item in the National Socialist program, but when his detestation of democracy and his hatred of its bastard progeny, Communism, reach the fever point, he tears off the mask and cheers unreservedly for the Nazi cause and its charismatic leader. As he summed up the issue then, men must choose between Communism and National Socialism, and he chooses to support Hitler. He swallows the myth of racial purity and makes it the basis for his belief in race as opposed to class. With regard to the charge that the Nazis have introduced anti-Semitism as an integral part of their scheme for world conquest, Lewis writes soothingly: "And as regards . . .the vexed question of the 'antisemitic' policy of his party, in that also I believe Hitler himself—once he had obtained power—would show increasing moderation and tolerance."[12] The experiences Lewis went through in the First World War cured him of the tendency to indulge in humanitarian nonsense. In this struggle of the white race against extinction, it is futile to rely on moral categories.

> Ever since the War, where I served on the Western front with the Artillery . . . there are certain questions I have asked of life which it would never have occurred to me to ask before. The War . . . went on and on, and these questions in the end asked

11. *Ibid.*, pp. 82-83.
12. Wyndham Lewis, *Hitler* (London: Chatto and Windus, 1931), p. 48.

themselves, as it were, with a more obstinate urgency every day.[13]

Henceforth he would believe only what produced good results. Since the Nazi ideal had performed wonders in Germany, he recommends that it be adopted by other countries that possess a similar type of culture.

He is inclined to agree that his time and energy could have been spent more profitably in creating works of art than in hammering out pamphlets for a variety of unpopular causes, but he is not at all convinced that this activity on his part did not help him in his career. He became a pamphleteer, a polemicist, he tells us in *The Diabolical Principle and the Dithyrambic Spectator,* as a necessary complement to his work as an artist. How else could he defend himself against his enemies? As an outsider, not belonging to a political party or member of some clique, he had no alternative than to turn pamphleteer. Hence, if he publishes a novel, he has to protect his opus, his *"Corona* rattling away like a machine-gun"[14] against the malevolent sniping of the critics. That is how he clears the ground of ideological rubbish and enables his work to make some headway. Nor is he wasting his precious time by any manner of means, for "a personal system of ideas requires defending as much as an individual work-of-art requires it" (p. ix). That is how he manages to educate his public. If he singles out doctrinaire revolutionaries for chastisement, it is because the gospel of Communism they preach so rabidly leads them eventually to betray the cause of art. It is the revolution they believe in with fanatical intensity, and for its sake they are prepared to sacrifice everything. Art is but an epiphenomenon, a part of the superstructure. Lewis considers it his fundamental right "to act and to think non-politically in everything. . . . I am an artist and my *mind,* at least, is free" (p. 37). He takes his stand against the ruling idea of his day, the belief that all aspects of existence were in essence political in nature. The political infection has spread fast and some of the best artists in the English-speaking world have been seduced by the siren songs of revolutionary propaganda. Lewis takes it upon himself to purge the body

13. *Ibid.,* p. 128.
14. Wyndham Lewis, *The Diabolical Principle and the Dithyrambic Spectator* (London: Chatto and Windus, 1931), p. viii.

of art of this lethal poison of political fanaticism: "for the freedom of art, like that of science, depends entirely upon its objectivity and non-practical, non-partisan passion" (p. 40).

In his denunciation of the various literary and artistic trends of his time, which Lewis regarded as fraudulent and harmful, he zeroed in on Surrealism as the prime offender. Against its aesthetic pretensions and its investment in radical politics, he directed his most deadly fire. He flatly rejected its key doctrine that dream and reality must be fused so as to achieve a super-reality. This synthesis of external and internal reality culminates in the art of infantilism. The founders of this cult of "super-reality" hoped to endow every man and woman with the creative faculty. The popular life would thus be enormously enriched and the interests of democracy be served. "It is merely a picturesque phase of the democratization of the artistic intelligence and the creative faculty" (pp. 66-67).

Lewis spared no pains in his effort to expose the presumptuous folly of this quest for "super-reality." Faithfully carried out, this movement would reach the climax of its development in its fatuous apotheosis of the unconscious. What he objects to in the experimental projects initiated by Surrealism is its aim to use art as a way of transforming reality. The art to which it gave birth was "a feverish, untrue, dehumanized, exceedingly artificial art" (p. 68). What he utterly despises is the charlatanry, the fake acting, the philistinism of the professional Surrealist. As he sees it, this is an intensely political movement, spouting pernicious nonsense, and it has given rise to "the *political artist*, or, better, the *politician* as artist" (p. 121).

Lewis devised a strategy of attack designed to put an end to this ethico-utilitarian conception of art. "The *politicalization* of art is a human catastrophe of the same order as the politicalization of science" (p. 122). The politicalization of art follows one of two divergent roads: the ethical puritanism advocated by Tolstoy in *What Is Art?* and the cult of diabolism, the deification of the satanic principle, which cultivates hatred as a creative force. Political revolt must be complemented by spiritual revolt (p. 125), but that is decidedly the wrong way in which to approach the arts. At this point he takes the trouble to state his own political position. It is a curious definition, seemingly confused in its eclecticism, but characteristic of the man. His political beliefs, he remarks, are in part Communist and in part Fascist—a strange coupling of antinomies. When he announces that "a distinct streak of monarchism" (p. 126) is mixed with his Marxism, we begin to wonder what is behind this paradoxical alliance of incompatible elements. The last part of his political confession resolves the contradictions that appear in it: at bottom he favors anarchism, though he qualifies his anarchism by stressing the need for order.

Communism, he suspects, is bound to triumph. It is therefore vitally important not to run with the pack but to side with the gifted minority and try to move them in the right direction. The only thing left to criticize is "the revolutionary machine" (p. 148). The artist, Lewis reiterates, is a born revolutionary. The costly mistake made by the Communist critic who believed in the doctrine of revolution for revolution's sake sprang from his inability to perceive that "art can effect more, even politically . . . than any pure propaganda or popular sociological moralist religion" (p. 151).

In *Left Wings Over Europe* (1936), Lewis reveals his Fascist leanings at their worst. He gained a measure of notoriety by his idealized portrait of Hitler. There is no danger of attack from Germany, he writes, that would justify the unholy military alliances being formed against her. Germany is completely surrounded by foes; she will not take the suicidal step of declaring war. Though Lewis, as in *The Lion and the Fox,* prides himself on being a devoted student of Machiavelli's *The Prince,* he naively places his trust in the demagogic promises of Der Führer. Hitler is his God, Stalin is a son of the Devil.

Blasting and Bombardiering (1937) is an autobiography that deals with his experiences as an artillery officer in World War I; he does not indulge in self-pity or moral indignation. He is interested exclusively in furthering his career as an artist. Self-centered, impelled by a remarkable tenacity of purpose, he tends to look upon war, death, economic rivalry, and political conflicts as affording him the nuclear material for his artistic creations. The writers of the war generation, "the Men of 1914," had endeavored to rely on the technique of classical restraint to avoid the trap of propaganda, but they failed miserably. Lewis considers it a calamity that native literature and art were harnessed to the chariot of politics.

In *Blasting and Bombardiering* he is truculent in defending his life as an artist. Versatile in his endowment of talent, gifted as a painter, sculptor, critic, novelist, journalist, essayist, and polemicist, he represents the modern version of Renaissance man. There is nothing falsely modest about Wyndham Lewis. He states that his life during the period he is writing about, the years from 1914 to 1926, was not immersed in politics. This was at a time when all controversial issues were reduced to an elemental conflict between Communism and Fascism. "I am not one of those who believe that either 'communism' or 'fascism' are in themselves solutions of anything."[15] As a young painter just starting his career, he was primarily concerned with color, line, form, not with the abstractions of politics.

During the thirties, however, it was impossible not to heed the call of commitment. The stance of neutrality was out of the question. Lewis suddenly changed his mind about the war that seemed to be imminent and plunged into the thick of the fray. Like Harold Laski (a strange comrade-in-arms for Lewis to support), he urges the English Government to draw up a document that will state plainly "for what object this war was to be fought—if to retain the empire, what share in that empire the common man was to have: if to punish a foreign criminal, that such criminal practices should no more be indulged in by ourselves: if for some unavowable reason, and the rank and file were to be mercenaries merely, that their blood-money at least should be adequate."[16] Lewis refuses to be hoodwinked by political promises that will not be kept after the war is won. A realist, he starts with the premise that all wars are wrong. He knows full well that politics is a dirty business. It is not conducted in accordance with ethical rules. Why must England play the part of Sir Galahad in quest of the Holy Grail? Wars are generally fought for power or the acquisition of territory. Is England fighting for some purpose other than this? The Englishman who fights in this war will feel that he is called upon to defend "a principle—liberty, a more rational life, or however it may be expressed" and "not to defend an Anglo-Saxon hegemony—as against a Teuton hegemony."[17] Lewis had reached a point in his intellectual

15. Wyndham Lewis, *Blasting and Bombardiering* (London: Eyre and Spottiswoode, 1937), p. 16.
16. Wyndham Lewis, *The Hitler Cult* (London: J. M. Dent & Sons, 1939), p. 185.
17. *Ibid.,* p. 202.

development where he realized the need for a world order. He had apparently undergone a change of heart. Only three years ago he scornfully rejected the idea of an international merger. Now he is in favor of federated world unity under a common Parliament.

> More every day I am convinced that to isolate any part of that Whole is impracticable. We should let the whole thing rip. Our instincts as men born to a great tradition of human freedom is to hold back what we can from the political merger. The monster business is "soulless," we say; the monster state must be the same. But monstrous and "soulless" wars to stop the merger—to stop *Earth Ltd* coming into being—are no solution.[18]

What conclusions are we warranted in drawing from this farrago of splenetic egotism, contentious theories, and political obtuseness? Lewis was without question a splendidly gifted artist who believed it was his duty to rescue the men of genius from the crude and contumelious hostility of the philistines, the untutored, gullible mob and its unchallenged power in a democratic country, and the malicious derision of the Communist intellectuals. He is totally committed to his work as a creative artist. He is not only anti-Communist but also anti-democratic. There are times when, proudly unfurling the banner of the genius who becomes a rebel because the world does not recognize him at his true worth, he cries out that he is beyond good and evil. Belonging as he does to the unique brotherhood of genius, he resists all attempts to make him join a political party or become a part of a movement. Lewis, however, will not surrender his identity.

His apotheosis of genius marks the last stand of beleaguered and discredited individualism. Lewis, the implacable enemy of collectivism, sees no reason why the will of the majority should prevail. A righteous—and eloquent—reactionary, Lewis gave his commitment to the politics of genius at a time when public opinion was strongly opposed to the hero-worship of the artist. Lewis was not one to concede defeat. He continued to defend the freedom of the artist and thus inevitably found himself "in conflict with the inveterate prepossessions of his age and country. . . ."[19] He realized the importance of politics and accepted the patent fact that some

18. *Ibid.,* p. 241.
19. Wyndham Lewis, *Rude Assignment* (London and New York: Hutchinson & Co., 1951), p. 10.

form of government is indispensable. "What 'politics' are, then, is anything to do with that burdensome machinery by means of which man maintains himself as social being" (p. 59). When he decided to undertake a penetrating study of the State, its structure, function, and style of operation, its *modus operandi,* he did so with a definite purpose in mind: he was urged to carry out this task by "a wish to find out under what kind of system learning and the arts were likely to fare best" (p. 64). He saw that politics "was for the Twentieth Century what Religion was for the Sixteenth and Seventeenth" (p. 69). Politics now constitutes the central reality of life. "They [politics] outweigh, in any average scale, all other matters. . ." (p. 105). He protested in vain against the neglect and abuse of the arts—"debased, vulgarized, brought to the level of an unintelligent pastime" (p. 189). In a letter of 1940 he sums up his credo, the character of his countercommitment.

> My trade is painting. Many of my books are merely a protest against Anglo-Saxon civilization, which puts so many obstacles in the way of the artist.—I really do believe in music, pictures, and books: that is a completely authentic obsession of mine. The politician and the religionist mean very little to me, except in relation to these activities.[20]

In retrospect, we can see that Wyndham Lewis was led as-

20. *Letters of Wyndham Lewis,* ed. W. K. Rose (London: Methuen & Co., 1963), p. 275. It is not at all surprising that in his fiction Lewis betrays the same pattern of preoccupation: his celebration of the creative miracles wrought by genius and his cruel caricature of the Bohemian, the pseudo-artist; his anti-Semitism; his fulminations against Marxism. In *The Apes of God,* first published in 1930, he treats with brutal derision those pseudo-artists who are voluptuaries, vulgar seekers after a good time. The bane of the creative life, these Bohemian hangers-on look upon art as only an excuse for throwing off all restraints. Interlopers, they cash in on the respect the artist calls forth in the public mind. Lewis identifies the apes of God as "those prosperous mountebanks who alternately imitate and mock at and traduce those figures they at once admire and hate" (Wyndham Lewis, *The Apes of God* [Baltimore, Md.: Penguin Books, 1965], p. 131). In *Self Condemned* René Harding, a heretical professor of history, shrewdly analyzes the ideological contradictions of Marxism. "The class-war is as dear to the Marxist as is nationalist war to the Christian. No improvement, no spectacular evolutionary development, in the species for which it legislates, enters into the program of Marxism. Indeed, such an idea is entirely alien to it. The type of improvement with which it is concerned is in the bread-and-butter situation of men-in-general and great amelioration in the conditions at work. Man is envisaged as a *Workman,* not, more inclusively, as a human being" (Wyndham Lewis, *Self Condemned* [Chicago: Henry Regnery Company, 1955], p. 82).

tray by his decision to participate in the hurly-burly of politics. The role he assumed as the Enemy, the aggressive spokesman for those who believed in and supported the backlash of the countercommitment, the feuds he engaged in, used up energy that he might have applied to his quest for creative fulfillment as an artist. As a politician defending the cause of reaction, he was out of his element. His political activities achieved very little except to earn him a reputation for eccentricity and arrogance. He wielded little influence on the literature of his time, he attracted no followers; he had no desire to hold office; he was not interested in competing for the universally coveted prize of power. If he had followed the promptings of his inner self, he would not have set aside his literary and artistic pursuits; he would have refused to take part in those political brawls which posterity soon consigns to oblivion. After all, what induced him to attack Marxist ideology was the overriding need he felt to safeguard the prerogatives of genius, to create a cultural ambience that would enable the artist to create his work without the hindrance of "the mob" or the demagoguery of the Left.

Lewis was unquestionably "sincere" in the reactionary faith he espoused. He never sold out or compromised his convictions. He did not use politics as a means to advance his career. A man of courage and integrity, he stuck loyally to his sense of commitment. Unlike Céline and Ezra Pound, he was not accused of treason by his countrymen when the war broke out.

In retrospect, we can see clearly that the role he chose to play as "the Enemy" of all the progressive forces we associate with the modern age was a pathetic one. He himself had to admit that as a political spokesman defending the cause of reaction he achieved very little except a reputation for eccentricity and quarrelsomeness. If he had followed the deeper prompting of his artistic nature, he would have stuck to his creative calling and not engaged in these ephemeral political brawls that brought no luster to his fame. After all, what induced him to attack the then dominant ideology of the Left was his overriding need to preserve the rights and safeguard the prerogatives of genius against the leveling passions of the mob.

5

Ezra Pound and the Commitment to Fascism

Politicism, the attempt of the artist to interpret his position in the light of social values, to integrate himself externally within the body of society, is an attempt to avoid the responsibility of inward creativeness by placing the origin of value in the social collective. In the last resort this means that instead of the artist being a creator of values, this function is delegated to the politician, who sets the standard by which the artist has to work.... Art can only be impoverished when its pattern is cut according to the requirements of the politician.[1]

The difference between Yeats and the Communist poets of the 1930s is not that they were interested in society while he was not; he was. The difference is that they had committed themselves to a political party and were interested mainly in social conditions, while Yeats, Lewis, Pound and Eliot were really interested in society only in so far as it would allow the arts to flourish.[2]

When he first started out on his career, Pound, the poet, the Bohemian egotist, inspired by his mission to bring the uni-

1. D. S. Savage, *The Personal Principle* (London: Routledge, 1944), p. 53.
2. John R. Harrison, *The Reactionaries* (New York: Schocken Books, 1967), p. 197.

que gift of art and the rare prize of beauty to a benighted world of philistines, evinced no interest in the machinations of politics. He was too busily engaged in the task of composing poetry, formulating his critical standards. and discovering the original work of his contemporaries who possessed the vital spark of genius. He believed in the sacred function of art, he lived the Bohemian life with zest, and he spread his gospel of art. As an expatriate, cut off from his native land, he regarded its crude homespun culture with a mixture of dismay and contempt. Ensconced in London or Paris or Rapallo, there was the inimitable Ezra sending in various contributions to magazines, writing his eccentric and at times pontifical letters of adjuration and advice to a host of the creative figures of his time: T. S. Eliot, Wyndham Lewis, William Carlos Williams, Gaudier-Brzeska, and Robert Frost. He recommended to editors and collectors of art the productions of those writers and artists whom he took under his wing. He offered his services gratuitously. He recognized the genius of Gaudier, who sculpted the head of Pound in 1913. Impressed by Lewis's vitality, he became his staunch friend. Though his chief ambition was to become a poet, he poured out his energy in a number of different directions: translations, book reviews, critical articles, editorial assistance to friends, appeals to magazines and publishers to appreciate the merits of the new art emerging. From the time of his arrogant youth to his old age, he remained the teacher. At the very end he fell into silence, but he had in the past sixty years "spoken several million didactic words."[3] His persona assumed a multitude of guises as he sought to define himself and his vocation.

Toplofty and cocksure, he damned all and sundry who stood in his way. He was not a man of ideas. His lifelong commitment to the art of poetry reveals the man at his best, eager to produce poetry of his own that the world would not readily let die and zealous in his efforts to call forth the best in the work of his contemporaries. If original poetry was to survive and ultimately triumph, then the monopoly of the second-rate, he insisted, must be broken, and he was the man to do it. With exuberant confidence in his own powers, he

3. Hugh Kenner, *The Pound Era* (Berkeley and Los Angeles: University of California Press, 1971), p. 266.

played a leading part in the cultural life of his time. Whatever faults of character he possessed, he never betrayed or
compromised the creative ideal of excellence he lived by. He
never sold out.[4]

He espoused lost causes with a vigor, an enthusiasm, born
of deep conviction. He was proud as Lucifer and as rebellious. He had the Bohemian artist's contempt for the
bourgeoisie and their sordid obsession with money. Though
he owned little of the world's goods, he shared what he had
with all kindred spirits who were deserving of his largess,
small as it was. He was a preceptor, propagandist, preacher,
spreading the new aesthetic gospel according to Ezra as well
as setting an example by means of his published work. That
is what he was at bottom: a creatively gifted poet, a connois-
seur of the arts. As a poet he inaugurated a new style. At the
age of twenty-five he had visited Ford Madox Ford, to whom
he wanted to show five poems he had written in Provençal
forms. Ford rudely ended his tendency to indulge in aureate
diction. He was cured, and he became an exemplary modern
poet: "the revolutionary."[5] Ford had insisted on the use of
natural speech, the vernacular. Pound never forgot this lesson.

But his real trouble arose from the fact that while he resolutely stressed the need to maintain the highest standards,
he somehow managed to antagonize a number of people. If
they did not subscribe to his views, he impugned their motives and questioned their degree of intelligence. In the
kingdom of art he would fraternize only with his peers. To
Amy Lowell he wrote in 1917: "There is no democracy in the
arts."[6] He was convinced that there can be no question of
compromise where great art is concerned. Art, he believed,
was fundamentally aristocratic in spirit. This explains why
when a fellow poet, a T. S. Eliot or a Marianne Moore,
sought his help, he gave most generously of himself, reading
their manuscripts with close critical attention and suggesting

4. Archibald MacLeish calls attention to the love of craft that Pound exemplified,
his steadfast commitment to the art of poetry that began when he was an un-
dergraduate at Hamilton College. "A true commitment long before he had
written a line worth remembering, but it shaped and mastered his whole life"
(Archibald MacLeish, "The Most Compelling Acts of Love to Touch My Life,"
Today's Health 51 [February 1973]: 40).
5. Kenner, The Pound Era, p. 81.
6. Ezra Pound, The Letters of Ezra Pound, ed. D. D. Paige (New York: Harcourt,
Brace and Co., 1950), p. 122.

a number of what he regarded as essential revisions. This was his métier, his true calling. He went to extreme lengths to help T. S. Eliot so that he could give up his job in a bank and devote all his time and energy to his proper work as a poet. Eliot was in a sense a test case. If he could not get enough people to subsidize Eliot's future, then Western culture was doomed to mediocrity. The only feasible solution, Pound pleaded, was to make it possible for a few superbly gifted individuals, the creative elite, to survive. The artist should be granted the leisure he requires in order to create. Art provides the precious principle of leadership. "Humanity is malleable mud, and the arts set the mould it is later cast into."[7]

Later, in the thirties and forties, Pound became intensely interested in the problem of money and usury and bombarded practically all his correspondents with his recently acquired theories of economic salvation. He desired to act on his beliefs. He could not reconcile himself to living in a world that applied no rational method of control. His sense of responsibility impelled him to search for a solution. Once he was convinced that the reform of the monetary system offered an effective cure for the recurrent ills of the social order, he could not rest until he had converted the whole world or at least the most influential men in the world. It was this obsession with the evil of usury that transformed Pound from a poet and critic into a political polemicist. He had begun to feel the need for participating in or initiating some form of direct action. "Certain things needed doing in order to make the world a better place for the arts to exist in, and only the dullness, or the mendacity, of some leaders and vested interests stood in the way."[8] Like Wyndham Lewis, it was the depth of Pound's commitment to poetry and art that led him to engage in the frenzied political battles of his day.[9]

Then came his introduction to the work of Major C. H.

7. *Ibid.*, p. 181.
8. Noel Stock, *Poet in Exile* (Manchester, England: Manchester University Press, 1964), p. 162. For a detailed study of Pound's political ideas and his activities in support of these ideas, see William M. Chace, *The Political Identities of Ezra Pound & T.S. Eliot* (Stanford, Calif.: Stanford University Press, 1973), pp. 3-105. This work adds little that is new to the reader's understanding of Ezra Pound. He points out that Pound and Eliot were not the only writers who were opposed to the political philosophy of liberalism. The two were not eccentric and anomalous figures in their age, though "in the general context" they can be regarded as special cases. "They were more than interested in politics; they were entangled in, even obsessed by, politics" (*ibid.*, p. xvii).
9. Kenner, *The Pound Era*, p. 316.

Douglas, who was, like Pound, a contributor to the periodical the *New Age*, edited by A. R. Orage. He found the ideas of Douglas, a foe of capitalism, altogether convincing. Once he saw the light he became a disciple and proclaimed the unique virtues of Social Credit. Here was a movement that genuinely appreciated the contributions of the artist, whereas capitalism in a democratic country like the United States scornfully neglected the artist and made no provisions for his needs. To Pound, Social Credit "seemed . . . not one man's panacea but a time's culmination: an ordered view of what mankind is doing. For the next 40 years its Pisgah-sights were never out of his mind."[10]

He was gaining a deeper understanding of the structure and function of society and the complexities of the political struggle for power. His absorption in the game of politics did not separate him from his work as a poet and literary critic. His political diatribes were largely theoretical and abstract. Though he voiced his faith in Italian Fascism, he did not advocate that it be established in the United States. As Noel Stock correctly points out, Pound's politics "are a bundle of contradictions."[11] An extreme individualist, he went the whole hog. In the thirties he started the practice of dating his letters as well as his books Fascist style. He talked intemperately only about politics; nothing else seemed to matter. He vilified the character of practically all contemporary statesmen except Mussolini and Hitler. In his Cantos he gave free rein to his anti-Semitic mania. He never retracted his conception of the Jew as "Disease Incarnate." The war, he charged, was engineered not by Hitler or Mussolini but by the wicked usurers of the world, the Jews. During the Second World War, his broadcasts over the Rome Radio were full of resounding Fascist slogans and scurrilous condemnation of the United States as the arsenal of "judeocracy." In the spring of 1945 he was captured and kept a prisoner for some months. Then he was brought to the United States, where, as a psychiatric case, he was later transferred from prison to St. Elizabeth's Hosptial in Washington, D.C.

How account for this pathetic denouement, this humiliating anticlimax to a once-brilliant career? He suffered from

10. Stock, *Poet in Exile*, pp. 175-76.
11. Eustace Mullins, *The Difficult Individual, Ezra Pound* (New York: Fleet Publishing Corporation, 1961), p. 90.

delusions of grandeur and delusions of persecution. The original source of his disaffection lay in his unbridled individualism. We have seen that he was impressed by the dynamic personality of Wyndham Lewis and greeted his work with lavish praise. In *The Egoist* (the issue of June 15, 1914) he gave expression to ideas that Wyndham Lewis was sure to applaud. "The rabble and the bureaucracy have built a god in their own image and that god is mediocrity. The great mass of mankind are mediocre, that is axiomatic, it is a definition of the word mediocre."[12] Pound, like Lewis, believed fervently in the cult of genius. He confidently predicted that after the collapse of the old aristocracy of birth and blood, the new aristocrats of the spirit, the artists, would assume control of society.

In all his restless wandering through Europe, from London to Paris to Venice, Pound was wrestling with the question of his identity. England, he soon decided, was not for him. What did he hope to find in other places? A solution to his personal problem, an answer to the enigma of his own being, peace of mind? Paris in the early twenties was a place of enchantment. There Pound found an outlet for his creative visions. He was the coryphaeus of modernism, the acknowledged leader of the avant garde, the herald of a glorious renaissance in the near future. He encouraged the group of younger writers, and he himself set them an example of bold pioneering in the composition of poetry. He bestirred himself in behalf of the indigent Joyce, and we know now the extent to which he helped T. S. Eliot in shaping the final form of *The Waste Land.* He was never idle, never without a literary cause to ballyhoo, founding magazines, writing articles, publishing his own influential work. Then in 1924 he is back in Italy and by 1925 he is settled in Rapallo.

After Pound left his native land and became an exile, his eccentricities, which formerly had been charitably excused as the excesses of a Bohemian temperament, became more marked. They turned into incipient aberrations. In a magazine he launched, *The Exile,* he published his tirades against the land of his birth. He had by this time arrived at the conclusion that the Constitution was being perverted, that all monotheistic Jews were damnable, and that Christianity

12. Ezra Pound, *Jefferson and/or Mussolini* (New York: Liveright, 1936), p. 70.

was dying. Yeats looked upon Pound's political obsessions as incredibly confused. Whereas he was a penetrating critic of literature, sure of his ground, he was absurdly prejudiced in his political outlook. When he presumes to speak magisterially on extraliterary subjects such as economics or politics, he presents a pitiful example of what happens to the litterateur when he speculates on matters outside his sphere of competence. His *ABC of Economics,* like his *Jefferson and/or Mussolini,* is a fantastic jumble of ideas, but Pound delivers them as if they were newly discovered and redemptive truths. "In a hide-bound Italy," he announces, "fascism meant at the start DIRECT action, cut the cackle, if a man is a mere s.o.b. don't argue."[12] To hell with talk and theory; long live the dynamism of action! No wonder Pound was impressed by some of the innovations in literature, art, and culture proposed by Marinetti, the Futurist.

Pound worshiped the great man as the director of destiny. Since the masses are composed of morons, they must be guided through life by a gifted leader. Strangely enough, Pound detects a fundamental likeness between Jefferson and Mussolini. Both men, he solemnly assures us, were geniuses. What is equally strange is that Pound saw Mussolini not as a demagogue or administrator but primarily as an artist. These are the irrational judgments that Pound wishes us to take as a serious contribution to political science.

But Pound and other American spokesmen on the extreme Right were not allowed to spread their anti-democratic propaganda unchallenged. When in 1940 the German armies were winning victory after victory on the field of battle, a number of writers, especially those who belonged to "the lost generation," were berated for their failure to halt the spread of Fascism. Archibald MacLeish accused them of preaching and practicing a type of isolationism that was decidedly harmful in its effect. What had they said or done that was "irresponsible"? MacLeish does not mention Ezra Pound as one of the chief offenders.

The prosecution of the war placed the writer in a dilemma. Drawn irresistibly into this demented dance of blood and death, he felt compelled, despite his former indifference to and distaste for politics, to see this war through to the end. Thomas Mann, for example, was not concerned about politics during the twenties. In 1928 he said: "Nor do I have much leaning toward politics by nature, nor do I subscribe to any party doctrine."[13] He called himself an unpolitical man. But a series of traumatic events in the thirties forced him into exile. Now he felt that he had to speak out, even if it meant interrupting his work as a novelist.[14] In writing to Hermann Hesse, who had come out against the 'politicalization' of Mind,"[15] Mann declared: "It seems to me that nowadays nothing alive escapes politics. Refusal is politics, too; it is a political act on the side of the evil cause."[16] Hatred of the Nazis called forth a surprising unity of response among the literati. Writers during the period of the war could be roughly divided into four categories: those who, like Thomas Mann, gave freely of their time and talent so that the world might know the ghastly truth about Nazi barbarism; those who served on the far-flung fighting front; those who were connected in an official or unofficial capacity with some branch of the armed forces, and those who, for various reasons, went on with their literary work.

There were, of course, writers and intellectuals who did not properly fall within these categories. Communists and fellow-travelers violently opposed the war until the Soviet Union was attacked. An expatriate like Pound disseminated Fascist propaganda over the Italian radio. War furnishes a publicly approved outlet for pent-up impulses of aggression against the foe. After the war was over, the ideological hatred persisted. Those in France who had collaborated with the Nazis were brutally hunted down. Pound, too, was severely punished for his Fascist "sins."

He was arrested and imprisoned in an outdoor cage. These cages were prepared for the incorrigibles, but the bearded Ezra, a man without rank, was locked up in one of these

13. Thomas Mann, *Letters of Thomas Mann,* trans. Richard and Clara Winston (New York: Alfred A. Knopf, 1971), p. 165.
14. In 1934, Thomas Mann wrote that his conscience gave him no rest. "It is becoming more and more impossible for me to continue the, it may be, sublime game of novelwriting until I have 'rendered an accounting' and unburdened my heart of its concern, its perceptions, its pain, as well as its freight of hatred and contempt" *(ibid.,* p. 224). Wayne Andrews attempts to revise the generally high estimate of Thomas Mann, the novelist. He pictures him as cold, aloof, pompous, concerned solely with spreading his fame. Thomas Mann supported Germany during the First World War, despised the culture of France, and believed in the advent of the Great Man. Andrews charges that he did not like Jews. See Wayne Andrews, *Siegfried's Curse* (New York: Atheneum, 1972).
15. Thomas Mann, *Letters of Thomas Mann,* p. 471.
16. *Ibid.,* pp. 470-71.

cages as a dangerous criminal. In the eyes of the military authorities he was an extremely dangerous prisoner. He was
not permitted to leave the cage and exercise his body. "By
night a special reflector poured light on his cage alone, so he
kept his head under the blanket. There were always two
guards, with strict orders not to speak to him. Everyone, including the incorrigibles, had orders not to speak to him."[17]
He was then sixty years old and there were times when he
was tempted to end his life. Though he was later granted
four extra blankets and a military cot, he could not stand the
strain and broke down in three weeks, suffering from "claus-
trophobia, partial amnesia, bouts of hysteria and terror."[18]
He was transferred to the Medical Compound.

In his book *The Pound Era,* Hugh Kenner reviews the
course of Pound's life: his trip to London, his stay in Paris,
how at fifty he settled down in Rapallo. At sixty he was a captive in the Detention Training Center in Pisa, at seventy he
was still confined in a psychiatric ward in the U.S. Finally released in 1958 from his virtual imprisonment in a mental
hospital, he set sail for Italy. There he set to work on the last
sections of the Cantos, and then he lapsed into silence. In the
past he had been sustained by his faith in the liberating effect
and didactic function of poetry, but now that faith was being
challenged. Now he brooded in silence on his past. He must
have regretted the years when his hubristic self, with its
polemic harshness, was in command. Like Wyndham Lewis,
he had held himself to be vastly superior to the general run
of mankind. His downfall was the consequence of his uncurbed individualism, his arrogant belief that genius could
with impunity go beyond good and evil, his defiant self,
which exalted Mussolini as the hero of the modern world.[19]

17. Kenner, *The Pound Era,* pp. 461-62.
18. *Ibid.,* pp. 462-63.
19. In any essay on Bertolt Brecht, Hannah Arendt compares the German playwright to Ezra Pound, whose sins of commission cannot charitably be passed
over as the madcap folly of Bohemianism. "In his vicious radio broadcasts, he
went far beyond Mussolini's worst speeches, doing Hitler's business and prov-
ing to be one of the worst Jew-baiters among the intellectuals on either side of
the Atlantic. To be sure, he had disliked Jews before the war and has disliked
them since, and this dislike is his private affair, of hardly any political importance. It is quite another matter to trumpet this kind of aversion to the world
at a moment when Jews are being killed by the millions" (Hannah Arendt,
Men in Dark Times [New York: Harcourt, Brace & World, 1968], p. 212). Stock
writes: "It is clear from Pound's letters and writings that he did not want the
world to become Fascist, in the sense that he did not want it to adopt Fascist

As we look back on the extraordinary career of this man, we are not inclined to pass judgment on his acts of treason. His Fascist interlude can be forgotten. An eloquent and well-balanced tribute was penned by Charles Norman at the end of his study of Ezra Pound.

> Such was Ezra Pound, endowed at birth with extraordinary ability, and great goodness of heart; a man who had befriended all whom he ever met, never hesitating to share what he had, even when he had little, whether of money or clothes, shelter or books, and by putting their books before his own, helping many to deserved renown; with a sure judgment of art in all its forms, yet without judgment about himself, or the issues which have perplexed mankind, and at length undone by a mixture of vanity, flattery, cocksureness, and too-long involvement with ideas which were clear neither when he adopted them nor after he began to expound them. . . . But what was noble in his nature will not be forgotten, and what is truly great in his work will surely endure.[20]

Pound demonstrates that writers who, out of the best motives, dabble in politics often bring disaster on themselves. It is not their function to become political messiahs. One critic rejects this interpretation. The writer, he argues, is not a recluse dwelling in an ivory tower. He is very much a part of the world he lives in, and his social and political commitment

uniforms or other mere paraphernalia of Fascist government; in the case of the United States, and, I think, of England, he was in favour of democracy, but he believed that some Fascist ideas, which were above party politics and could be applied universally, were part of the future and he did not want to be left behind" (Noel Stock, *The Life of Ezra Pound* [New York: Pantheon Books, 1970], pp. 349-350). Ezra Pound is Karl Shapiro's *bête noire*. It is Pound the irresponsible Bohemian, the megalomaniac, the Fascist crackpot, whom he assails unmercifully in his book *In Defense of Ignorance*. He accuses Pound of being an unscrupulous propagandist in his poetry, strident in his didactic pronouncements, infantile in the political remedies he recommends. Whether or not he is insane when judged by clinical psychiatric standards, his poetry is not "mad." It is, if anything, too rational in content, too argumentative in tone, lacking in originality. Pound is the poet who, posing as a mandarin, parades his ideas at secondhand. When Pound was awarded the Bollingen prize for *The Pisan Cantos*, a storm of protest arose. Shapiro, who was a member of the committee that granted this prize to Pound, voted against him. As a Jew he would not support this move to honor a notorious anti-Semite. His second reason for voting against Pound was his belief "that the poet's political and moral philosophy ultimately vitiates his poetry and lowers its standards as a literary work" (*A Casebook on Ezra Pound*, ed. William Van O'Connor and Edward Stone [New York: Thomas Y. Crowell Company, 1950], p. 61).

20. Charles Norman, *Ezra Pound* (New York: The Macmillan Company, 1960), p. 466.

shapes the fabric of his literary testament. "To say that a poet is not to meddle in politics, and that if he does we ought to ignore that part of his work, is bound to produce a one-sided view, and likely to lead to misrepresentation of the poetry itself."[21] To what extent is this proposition true? Is it possible for a writer to remain uncommitted to the politics of the Left or the Right, to be thoroughly uninterested in the political realities of his age?

21. Harrison, *The Reactionaries*, p. 15.

PART III
NONPOLITICAL AND
UNCOMMITTED LITERATURE

6

The Unpolitical Writer

Every person finds his holy of Holies where he may: in Scientific Truth, Evolution, the State, Democracy, *Kultur,* or some metaphysical word like "the All" or "the Spiritual." Human life in our age is so changed and diversified that people cannot share a few, historic, "charged" symbols that have about the same wealth of meaning for everybody. This loss of old universal symbols endangers our safe unconscious orientation.[1]

Man, for these writers [modern bourgeois writers], is by nature solitary, asocial, unable to enter into relationships with other human beings.[2]

Central to a dialectical-materialist aesthetics must be a recognition that the work of art is dialectically related to the world outside it—including the perceiver and the work.[3]

1. Susanne K. Langer, *Philosophy in a New Key* (New York: Penguin Books, 1948), p. 234.
2. Georg Lukács, *The Meaning of Contemporary Realism,* trans. John and Necke Mander (London: Merlin Press, 1962), p. 20.
3. Jeremy Hawthorn, *Identity and Relationship: A Contribution to Marxist Theory of Literary Criticism* (London: Lawrence & Wishart, 1973), p. 20. Hawthorn adds that this provides the firm basis "for arguing that a work of art can never be discussed ahistorically, in 'purely aeathetic' terms, but must always be discussed in a defined context" (*ibid.,* p. 20). He remarks that the fundamental feature of Marxist literary criticism "is that to be fully understood the work of literature must be seen in the context of its socio-economic origins" (*ibid.,* p. 17).

1. *The Symbolists and Axel's Castle*

Suzanne K. Langer stresses the point that modern man, however keenly developed his intellect, finds himself in a painfully difficult situation, alienated from God, deprived of faith in life and, above all, lacking faith in himself. His high-powered intellect fails to satisfy his spiritual needs; "it lacks metaphysical myth, régime, and ritual expression."[4] According to Georg Lukács, who has survived many hotly fought ideological battles on the constantly shifting front of Marxist aesthetics, modern bourgeois writers are guilty of creating in their work an image of man that negates the vital, all-important principle of social existence. The protagonist they present is invariably alone, cut off from communion with other human beings. He is not only alone, he is trapped, without hope of ever getting out, in the hermetically sealed cave of his own self. He has no roots in the historical past, no attachment to society or the state. He is a *Luftmensch,* devoid of a sense of social responsibility. In his attack, Lukács charges that modern bourgeois realism reveals the progressive disintegration of the human personality. This loss of the centrality of self is accompanied by a frightening disintegration of outer reality. The world outside is seen as incomprehensible and hostile. Thus the work of these writers discloses, as in Kafka,[5] the cumulative nightmarish effects of alienation. The whole conception of human nature is badly distorted. In this version, man becomes an unfathomable mystery, so that his erratic behavior offers no clue to his character. Under capitalism, Lukács contends, literature of this type becomes obsessed with psychopathology. But this compulsive plunge into the turbid depths of mental disease achieves no positive results. In life as in literature, the modern bourgeois intellectual suffers acutely from subjectivism, a subjectivism so extreme that it is incapable of grasping *the truth of reality.*

"The truth of reality"—there we have a catchall phrase that can accommodate itself to a host of diverse and disparate

4. Langer, *Philosophy in a New Key,* p. 234.
5. "All those parables really set out to say merely that the incomprehensible is incomprehensible, and we know that already." Kafka, "On Parables," quoted in Ihab Hassan, *The Dismemberment of Orpheus: Toward a Postmodern Literature* (New York: Oxford University Press, 1971), p. 110.

meanings. Chernyshevski believed he knew the exact truth of reality and interpreted it for his readers in the novel *What Is To Be Done?* Dostoevski's Underground Man represents a violent protest against the restrictive categories of rationalism that Chernyshevski and other radical critics of the time so warmly defended. Dostoevski's anti-heroic protagonist flies in the face of logic and heatedly defends the life of unreason. He knows himself to be a wretched, ridiculous creature, but he stubbornly refuses to accept the arbitrary assumption that two times two makes, and must make, four. Why not make two times two equal five? The irrational but impassioned exponent of voluntarism, he argues that "reason is nothing but reason and satisfies only the rational side of man's nature, while will is a manifestation of the whole life, that is, of the whole human life including reason and all the impulses."[6] Man is a strange, unpredictable, and perverse creature.

> Shower upon him every earthly blessing, drown him in a sea of happiness, so that nothing but bubbles of bliss can be seen on the surface; give him economic prosperity, such that he should have nothing else to do but sleep, live on cakes and ale and busy himself with the continuation of his species, and even then, out of sheer ingratitude, sheer spite, man would play some nasty trick. He would even risk his cakes and ale and would deliberately desire the most fatal rubbish, the most uneconomical absurdity, simply to introduce into all this positive good sense his fatal fantastic element.[7]

Such a revolt against the tyranny of the rational and the utilitarian led a number of writers to exalt the "truths" born of the creative imagination above the rigorous "laws" of science. Placing their trust in intuition, they explored the dark labyrinths of the unconscious and heeded the revelation of their dreams. By means of introspection and introversion they were able to project a satisfying image of their authentic self. Some of them decided to withdraw from the ugliness and unrelieved boredom of everyday existence and sought in solitude the secret that would make it possible for them to preserve the purity of their spiritual being. They regarded the practical demands of life—the brutal economic struggle, the political battle for power—as too heavy and demeaning a

6. Fedor Mikhailovich Dostoyevsky, *Notes from Underground,* in *Short Novels of the Masters,* ed. Charles Neider (New York: Rinehart & Company, 1948), p. 143.
7. *Ibid.,* p. 145.

burden to bear. In taking this momentous step, they did not feel that they were betraying the human race.[8] They resisted the fate of being submerged, their individuality annulled, in the proliferating mass movements of their age. Resolved to keep their integrity clean, they obeyed only the urgently voiced mandate of their conscience.

Disillusioned with the humdrum and banal routine of so-called normal life, the Symbolists turned to poetry as an avenue of escape from the hideous middle-class world they despised. They would not kneel in worship before the idols of the bourgeoisie—success, riches, power. Fleeing from a world that was grossly materialistic, they cultivated the private garden of the self in solitude. They preferred the pure pleasures of the imagination, the victories of art, to the tainted material rewards an acquisitive society bestows on the winners in the mad scramble for success.

The members of the Symbolist movement looked upon art as a religion and the poet as "the priest revealing the mystery of life."[9] The word *symbolism* "stands for belief in a world of ideal beauty and the conviction that it can be realised through art."[10] Whereas the romantics were eager to taste all of life in its plenitude and variety, to experiment with all types of experience, not excluding the ugly, the sinister, the abnormal,[11] the Symbolists felt that

all this exploration of life was vain, the only possible field of exploration was art or dream, the rest was vulgar, below the poet's dignity, for his field of activity ought to be imagination and, in the end, non-being. The romantic despised society, the symbolist ignored it as being part of a reality which, with its transiency and vulgar agitations, is not worth the thought of the poet or the Symbolist hero.[12]

8. The story is told of a saintly scholar that he wept on his deathbed, confessing the one sin he had committed in the past: his refusal to serve as a judge. *A Rabbinic Anthology*, which contains this story, ends it on an edifying note that clearly endorses the ethic of social responsibility. "A Man who retires to his house and says, 'What have I to do with the burden of the community . . . why should I listen to their voice? Peace to thee, O my soul'—such a one destroys the world." Mortimer Ostow and Ben-Ami Scharfstein, *The Need to Believe* (New York: International University Press, 1969), p. 101.

9. Joseph Chiari, *Symbolism from Poe to Mallarmé* (New York: Gordian Press, 1970), p. 46.

10. *Ibid.*, p. 47.

11. See Mario Praz, *The Romantic Agony*, trans. Angus Davidson (New York: Meridian Books, 1956).

12. Chiari, *Symbolism from Poe to Mallarmé*, p. 51.

Mallarmé is a striking example of the poet who stands aloof from the hurly-burly of politics. He concentrated all his creative energy on the making of poems out of a radically purified language. He turned against religion as a pernicious source of illusion and affirmed his belief that art could supplant metaphysics and religion in satisfying the spiritual needs of mankind. Committed to the principle of art for art's sake, he rejected the utilitarian notion that art should extend the scope of its appeal to the widest possible audience. On the other hand, he declared that the greater the work of art, the smaller the group who are capable of understanding it.[13] But Mallarmé was not content to invoke the magic of aesthetics as a way of resolving the spiritual crisis through which he was passing. He had gazed into the infinite dark of being and perceived "a cosmic Néant."[14]

Mallarmé discovered to his cost that his austere commitment to the religion of art could not protect him against the terrifying vision of the void, the perception of the cosmic Néant. Other Symbolists, undaunted by their glimpse of the *horror vacui,* take up with zest the burden of their commitment to art. *Axel* (1890), by Villiers de l'Isle-Adam, epitomizes the hopes and aspirations of the Symbolists in their ardent search for the Absolute, their quest for the secret of the mysterious universe. Like Mallarmé, they evinced an aristocratic disdain for the commonplace. Inevitably their esoteric idealism was defeated when it encountered the recalcitrance of social reality. The play was a defiant declaration of aesthetic principles that would be caviar to the general public, a manifesto in lofty, sonorous language that voiced the faith that informs this dramatic poem.[15] Villiers, a devotee of Wagner, Edgar Allan Poe, and Eliphas Lévi, was opposed to the positivistic tendencies of his age. His love of the occult was succeeded by his acceptance of idealism. Finally, he returned to Catholicism, just as Péguy, a fervent free-thinking

---

13. Mallarmé's poetic theory upheld the ideal of "purity" "in the primary sense that it made no concession to the non-artistic values of truth and morality. It was centered in the concept of a Beauty that was by definition detached from life or dependent on a specifically artistic way of envisaging it." D. J. Mossop, *Pure Poetry: Studies in French Poetic Theory 1740-1945* (Oxford: At the Clarendon Press, 1971), p. 111.
14. *Ibid.*, p. 130.
15. Yeats attended a performance of *Axel* (it took five hours) and was deeply moved by its esoteric insights.

Socialist for a number of years, rejoined the Mother Church, and Hugo Ball, one of the enterprising Dadaists in Zurich who founded the Cabaret Voltaire, where he organized and participated in the productions designed to bait and shock the bourgeoisie—this Hugo Ball "ended his life as a staunch and even saintly Catholic. . . ."[16] Villiers builds a dramatic framework within which he holds up for our aesthetic contemplation the various life-styles, the different forms of commitment, open to the Symbolist: the life of asceticism, the occult, the ideal love that is consummated in death rather than in the erogenous flesh. Though the narrative pace of this poetic drama is intolerably slow, clogged as it is with expository material, its structure, when viewed as a whole, unfolds a complex and ambitious theoretical design. Part I is called "The Religious World," Part II "The Tragic World," Part III "The Occult World," and Part IV "The Passional World."

In *Axel* Sara foils the intention of her captors to ordain her as a nun. At the moment when her locks are to be shorn and she is about to forswear the pleasures of the flesh and achieve ineffable blessedness as the bride of Christ, she uncovers her face and refuses to take the vow. The Archdeacon threatens her with dire punishment. A pawn of the Devil, a victim of the powers of Hell, she will not be allowed to leave the convent. The Church is supreme; it is not to be vanquished. Its authority, derived from God, is not to be overthrown by sacrilegious man. To rescue her from the clutches of the infernal Tempter, he is prepared to use force, for her physical beauty is dangerous. But she outwits him and it is he who is immured in the sepulcher. Renouncing the austerities of conventual life, Sara sets out to find the treasure hidden in Axel's castle. Shielded by a rose, the Rosicrucian emblem, she arrives at the castle in the Black Forest.

In the second act, Axel, the Symbolist hero, represents the quester for the ideal; he is ascetic in his habits, indifferent to the giddy, hedonistic pleasures of youth. He is a student of ancient mysteries, a lover of silence, but he is also a superb hunter and possesses extraordinary strength. He is shown as patiently enduring the presence of his cousin, Commander Auersperg, who tries to tempt him with the promise of erotic

16. C. W. E. Bigsby, *Dada & Surrealism* (London: Methuen & Co., 1972), p. 10.

adventures in the court, the sensual allurements of aristocratic society. Commander Auersperg, while exploring the castle, is impressed by the faithful old men who serve Axel. He muses: ". . .my young squire is becoming a prey to Hermeticism, Kabbalism, and the rigmarole of the Black Mass. It must be this Master Janus who is breathing these notions in his head, instilling in him these befuddling superstitions . . . ."[17] The Commander is determined to tear Axel away from this dreary and abnormal type of existence. When Axel divines that Herr Zacharias has divulged the secret of the hidden treasure to the Commander, he decides that the latter must not leave the castle alive. Before he kills him in a duel, he tells him with what unspeakable contempt he had listened to his vulgar proposals.

The third act brings Master Janus on the scene. Skilled in magic, he urges Axel to undertake the quest for ultimate reality. Axel, however, decides to give up the world of the occult; he hears—and responds to—the call of life. He knows that the one who wishes to be all-powerful must overcome his passions and suppress his humanity, but such a conquest of self is bought at too high a price. He has begun to doubt the supreme importance of the quest for ultimate meaning. For death will come and his identity will be destroyed. Janus bids him cultivate the art of meditation and learn how to curb his restless will and free himself from the tedious oppression of time. He must cast off the illusion that he exists as a separate and autonomous self. Axel complains that thus far he has subsisted on the ethereal food of dreams. He has not lived. He now looks upon Janus as a stranger. He broods: "Science states but does not explain. She is the eldest daughter of chimera."[18]

In the last act, Axel encounters Sara in the family vault, and he falls instantly in love with her just as she does with him, but he will not respond to her passionate endearments. This love is not to be consummated. After listening to Sara's enticing vision of the exotic, far-off places they can visit and all the dreams they can bring to fruition, Axel asks: "Why realize them?"[19] The dreams, together with the hopes they

17. Villiers de l'Isle-Adam, *Axel,* trans. Marilyn Gaddis Rose (Dublin: Dolmen Press, 1970), p. 57.
18. *Ibid.,* p. 137.
19. Edmund Wilson, *Axel's Castle* (New York: Charles Scribner's Sons, 1931), p. 262.

cherished, will fade in the common light of day. "Live?" he asks, and then replies with aristocratic scorn: "our servants will do that for us."[20] Spurning her "trivial" suggestion that they enjoy at least one night of love, he proposes that they commit suicide at once. Finally he succeeds in persuading her that this is the only way out and they both drain the cup of poison.

The peerless Symbolist hero relinquishes the paltry erotic experience that reality has to offer and chooses instead the enchantment of dreams, the fantasies born of the night and nourished in solitude. He prefers the peace of death to indulgence in the sensual passion of love that will prove a cheat and a disappointment on the morrow. Axel, unlike Maldoror, is not a rebel; he does not revolt against society. Indifferent to the world around him, he lives wholly within himself. He rejects the, for him, alien sphere of politics.[21] Like one of Huysmans's heroes, he finds that the dream is far more rewarding than anything reality can provide.

2. *Aestheticism and the Phenomenology of Decadence*

The Symbolist novel that appeared in France in the decade from 1885 to 1895 was influenced in its treatment of the problematic self by a pressing need to refute the naturalistic doctrine, advocated by Taine and Zola, which asserted that the self is shaped for good or evil by its social and economic environment. The anti-naturalist reaction emphasized the sovereign unity of the self, its metaphysical dimensions, its spiritual longings. The Symbolist novelists discovered in Schopenhauer's philosophy confirmation of their deepest intuitions. The world as idea encouraged the act of contemplation, but it was a form of contemplation turned inward, focused upon the interior self. Though Schopenhauer set forth his fundamental belief that the mind, like the body, is at the disposal of the all-conquering Will, he nevertheless maintained, in defiance of logic, that the contemplative mind, as

20. *Ibid.,* p. 263.
21. "In a sense, all the poets with Romantic-Symbolist attitudes have been non-political, in as much as their values have sprung from the imagination, and the imagination is too radical and utopian to adjust to political issues proper." Michael Hamburger, *The Truth of Poetry* (New York: Harcourt, Brace & World, 1969), p. 83.

embodied in works of art, can defeat the tyranny of the biological Will. Art is exalted as a kind of religion, a surrogate for Nirvana. There is the primary source of contradiction. On the one hand, Nature in all its ramifications represents the devouring, ubiquitous principle of the Will, which is not affected by the resistance of finite reason or the persistent and utterly irrational human demand for ultimate meaning. And yet Schopenhauer takes great pains to explain the method whereby the despotic biological Will can be overcome. Out of the engulfing murk of despair shines a beacon of hope; out of the universal darkness emerges a glimmer of salvational light; faith is born anew in the passage through the night of nothingness; the mediation of art makes possible the renunciation of the self and therefore liberates the artist from the accursed clutch of the Will. The Will both exploits the individual for its own incomprehensible ends and at the same time, through the triumph of art, frees the mind from the thralldom of the Will. Through the perspective of the creative imagination, man beholds life as it is, in all its hideous aspects and atrocious truth.

> To be undeceived into deception, disillusioned into illusion, to despise the will and yet be most energetic in creation, to have "done with the world" and yet "redeem" it . . . it is such contradictory wishes that find their philosophical guardian in Schopenhauer.[22]

Schopenhauer pictures a universe drained of meaning. Man, an alien, stands apart from nature; existence is not sustained by a cosmic sense of purpose. Schopenhauer thus anticipates the modern *Weltanschauung* that is voiced by the Symbolists, by Melville, Thomas Hardy, James Joyce, Kafka, and Thomas Mann. The art of music opens the gates of salvation for man.

> It takes man out of the snare of practical concerns with which the Will fools him into doing its bidding, and it unmasks the senseless struggle for existence which both logic and morality serve by seeking to regulate it instead of doing away with it and makes us behold the truth—the pulse-beat of the Will throbbing through Eternity. But in the very process of revealing the meaninglessness of Reality, music creates form and meaning. It captures the

22. Erich Heller, *The Ironic German* (Boston and Toronto: Little, Brown and Company, 1958), p. 51.

formless Will in man-made forms. . . . Music becomes man's salvation . . . because it liberates man from delusion, initiates him into knowledge, and creates meaning in a meaningless universe.[23]

This is the heart of the aesthetic philosophy as it was formulated by Baudelaire, Mallarmé, and the French Symbolists. Throughout his *magnum opus, The World as Will and Idea,* Schopenhauer is concerned with elaborating the theme of deliverance from the Will, and he maintained that art is the most complete way of gaining redemption.

> If we lose ourselves in the contemplation of the infinite greatness of the universe in space and time, meditate on the thousands of years that are past or to come, or if the heavens at night actually bring before our eyes innumerable worlds and so force upon our consciousness the immensity of the universe, we feel ourselves dwindled to nothing; as individuals, as living bodies, as transient phenomena of will, we feel ourselves pass away and pass into nothing, like drops in the ocean. But at once there rises against such lying impossibility, the immediate consciousness that all these worlds exist only as our idea, only as modifications of the external subject of pure knowing, which we find ourselves to be as soon as we forget our individuality, which is the necessary supporter of all worlds and at all times the condition of their possibility. The vastness of the world which disquieted us before, rests now in us.[24]

The Schopenhauerian philosophy emphasized the degree to which perception shaped and colored our vision of reality. Thus interest in the phenomenology of the inner life was heightened. "The fact that the world is seen as dependent insofar as it is 'meaningful' upon perceptions originating in the Self radically determines the orientation of the new novel."[25] As in Villiers's *Axel,* the Symbolist hero is alone and dwells in a subjectivized universe of dreams, fantasies, and drugged sensations. Like Huysmans's protagonist, des Esseintes, in *Against the Grain,* he seeks to know himself.[26]

23. Walter N. Sokel, *The Writer in Extremis* (Stanford, Calif.: Stanford University Press, 1959), pp. 24-25.
24. Arthur Schopenhauer, *The World as Will and Idea,* trans. R. B. Haldane and J. Kemp. 3 vols. (London: Kegan Paul, Trench, Trübner & Co., 1906), 1:266.
25. Karl D. Uitti, *The Concept of the Self in the Symbolist Novel* ('S-Gravenhage: Mouton & Co., 1961), p. 38.
26. The Symbolist novel resembles the lyrical novel in which the characters emerge as personae for the self of the novelist-poet. The lyrical novel offers an expressive medium for the revelation of the interior world of the self. See

Huysmans (1848-1907) is a rebel against God who, from the beginning to almost the end of his literary career, struggled pridefully against the need to believe. By temperament he was repelled by the world of his time, its materialistic values, its uncritical faith in rationalism, its idolatrous faith in mechanical progress. Though his position in the French ministry of the interior compelled him to lead a bourgeois type of existence, his novels represented an aesthetic revolt so extreme that it deliberately ignored the social reality of his time. Huysmans, like Proust, was not at all interested in the passion of politics. He was absorbed completely in himself and his creative work, which was largely autobiographical in content. Sensitive to an abnormal degree, he withdrew as much as possible from contaminating contact with the madding crowd and shunned what he considered the deadly abominations of his age. His quivering sensibility was upset by the slightest discord in his environment. The roar of traffic and the cacophany of the streets were too much for him to endure. He craved solitude and peace, and yet his imagination was drawn magnetically to the depiction of the horrors of life. What fascinated him in particular was the subject of vice.

Though he began his novelistic career as a professed disciple of naturalism, he is the least "objective" of writers. Everything his pen produced dealt with himself. He was his own hero, the center and circumference of an intensely introverted world. In *Against the Grain,* he let his imagination go. His protagonist is the saint of the Decadent movement, its most representative figure. In des Esseintes Huysmans paints the portrait of a man who seeks to cut himself off from the vulgar reality of his day in order to escape from its appalling ugliness. This is the cult of aestheticism that Huysmans carried to fanatical lengths.

Though Huysmans, in creating his main character, used some details based on an eccentric figure of his time, the Comte de Montesquiou-Fezensac, he was chiefly concerned with narrating the story of his own spiritual conflicts. A nervously constituted aristocrat, des Esseintes, Huysmans's persona, is at odds with his social environment and dissatisfied with the life he is leading. He knows his Latin, is in-

Ralph Freedman, *The Lyrical Novel* (Princeton, N. J.: Princeton University Press, 1963), pp. 18-22.

terested in theology, and hates science. When he comes into possession of the fortune his family left him, he finds that the pursuit of sensual pleasure no longer affords him any satisfaction. He is bent on fulfilling his dream of aesthetic solitude. He plans to build a retreat to which he can flee from the tawdry follies of his age. Purchasing a house not far from Paris, he proceeds to furnish it and decorate it according to his extravagant but finicky taste. The house will be the quintessence of the artificial. Huysmans takes special delight in the portrayal of the monstrous and the sadistic. Later in life, after his conversion to the Church, he composed the preface to *Against the Grain*. In it he defines sadism as the bastard product of Catholicism. It presupposes, as he says,

> a religion to be violated. It consists above all in a sacrilegious practice, in a moral rebellion, in a spiritual debauch, in an aberration which is completely ideal, entirely Christian. . . . The power of sadism, the attraction which it offers, resides entirely in the prohibited pleasure of transferring to Satan the homage and the prayers which are due to God; it resides therefore in the non-observance of the Catholic precepts, or even in observing them in reverse (the key word *á rebours*), by committing, in order the more to spurn Christ, the sins he has expressly cursed: the pollution of the cult and the carnal orgy.[27]

Published in 1884, *Against the Grain* epitomizes the aesthetics of decadence. Bohemianism was approved because of its defiance of conventional moral standards. Like Baudelaire, a number of writers wished to put a halt to the pernicious practice of applying ulterior criteria, moral or religious or political, to the autonomous work of art, whose sole aim is the creation of beauty. Art struggled to free itself from utilitarian prescriptions and the exploitative demands of the social order. But the aestheticism that flourished toward the end of the nineteenth century evinced a morbid interest in sickness and decay and in the phenomenology of evil. *Against the Grain* introduces a neurotic hero who tries to flee from the distractions and frivolities of the life all around him. A complex, introverted character, he suffers from the syndrome of ennui. Not even the feverish delights of sensuality can make him forget the deep-rooted antipathy he feels for the life of his time. He has engaged in riotous and exhaust-

27. James Laver, *The First Decadent* (New York: Citadel Press, 1955), p. 86.

ing sexual excesses, possessed numerous actresses and sing-
ers, and kept a variety of mistresses. Finally, weary of these
habitual caresses that have ceased to give him pleasure, he
explores the lowest depths of degrading vice, hoping in this
manner to revitalize "his deadened senses."[28]

Nothing, alas, can relieve him of the deadly oppression of
boredom, though he persists in bouts of orgiastic sensuality
until his health breaks down. Forced to flee from the enervating tensions of city life, he retires to his ivory tower, a house
so constructed that he can enjoy illusion more thoroughly
than those pleasures that can be bought at a price in the
material world. Illusion, artifice, and fantasy are infinitely to
be preferred to mundane reality. The paintings hanging on
the walls of des Esseintes's retreat are precisely those that will
not remind him of contemporary existence. He had chosen
with great care those works of art which have introduced him
to an unfamiliar but fascinating world, which have revealed
to him new possibilities of making the nervous system respond to his delirious fantasies of erotic fulfillment and his
"complicated nightmares" of desire (p. 90).

There are times, however, when artifice and illusion begin
to pall upon him, when he is overcome by acedia, when his
mind fails to respond to the stimuli he has provided for its
delectation. At such times thoughts of his wasteful past—a
past devoted to gambling, dissipation, and promiscuous
love-making—overwhelm him. He can not remain in his present wretched state without trying to come to terms with himself. How will he resolve this conflict raging within him between vice and asceticism, between the insidious lure of
beauty and the insistent call of religious faith? What appeals
to him strongly in Catholicism is the aesthetic aspect of the
Church. He still lacks the capacity for unquestioning faith,
but his veneer of skepticism is beginning to wear thin. His
early religious training had undoubtedly left its imprint upon
him. Suddenly he breaks off this disturbing train of thought.
He must safeguard himself against the danger of succumbing
to "the disease" of faith. He is haunted by morbid images; his
mind is busy with thorny theological speculations; he
examines contradictory interpretations of religious dogma
and heresies relating to the Virgin birth; he broods upon the

28. J. K. Huysmans, *Against the Grain,* trans. John Howard (New York: Albert and
Charles Boni, 1930), p. 24.

nature of Christ, whether Christ alone or the Trinity was bound to the cross. He recalls the quarrels of bishops in the past and retraces the impressive history of the Church through the ages, the pageantry, the pomp, the persecution, the sacrifices that had to be made. Despite this retrospective fixation on theology, the Church, and the character of Christ, he has no intention of yielding to the seduction of religious faith: he is simply filled with a feeling of veneration. Then his diabolical spirit of rebelliousness reasserts itself. The artistic sense, de Esseintes realizes, is deeply moved by the beauty of Church ceremonial, of age-old Catholic ritual. The memory of these scenes drawn out of the historic past are enough to quicken his sensibility and set his imagination on fire, but then a perverse mood of revolt seizes him and he becomes the prey of images of monstrous depravity. He pictures the confrontation between omnipotent God and the Devil; he thinks of the sinister glory that is bound to result from a hideous crime committed in church by a believer who is determined to utter filthy profanities, to blaspheme. His imagination conjures up "the madnesses of magic, of the black mass, of the witches' revels. . ." (p. 126). He lacks the courage required for "the consummation of frightful and deliberate sins" (p. 127). Needless to say, the mind of an aesthete thus tormented by secret inner longings to embrace the true faith, which he nevertheless resists by imagining monstrous blasphemies, demonic acts of sacrilege, will not be disturbed by the socioeconomic crises of the world or the rise and fall of empires and political institutions. Such a man is hounded by more pressing spiritual problems.

Throughout the novel des Esseintes betrays his secret longing for the true faith. What holds him back is that he cannot get himself to believe in the promise of immortality. Schopenhauer, he feels, is closer to the truth. His pessimistic philosophy and the doctrine of the Church had much in common. He, too, emphasized the wickedness of the world. Like the German monk, Thomas a Kempis, author of *Imitation of Christ,* he revealed the misery and suffering man must endure in his life on earth. He "preached the nothingness of life, the advantages of solitude, and warned humanity that no matter what it does . . . it must remain wretched. . . " (p. 128). Unlike the Church, Schopenhauer had no panacea to offer, no cure for the inescapable evils of existence. Des Esseintes continues in this vein to extol the radical pessimism of Schopenhauer as vastly superior to the tenets of Christianity. The German philosopher did not accept the repugnant dogma of original sin. Nor did he defend the goodness and supreme wisdom of a God who snuffs out the life of a child, punishes the innocent, and protects the scoundrel. He bitterly condemned the ways of Providence, which made man the target of senseless and atrocious suffering. Unlike the Church, Schopenhauer had no need to justify as absolutely necessary the cruel suffering God had wantonly imposed on the miserable race of man. In an outburst of pity, he cried out: "If a God has made this world, I should not wish to be that God" (p. 128).

Des Esseintes now feels inwardly relieved. Schopenhauer's superior wisdom has calmed the tumult of his mind, but he continues to be tormented by religious yearnings. He is plagued by recurrent nightmares. He can no longer control his nervous malady. In his despair he tries various expedients to distract his attention. He reads Charles Dickens's novels but that author's exaltation of virtue exasperates des Esseintes and drives him to think of passionate, sinful love. He is seized by a powerful craving to commit the sins that religion abhors. Erotically aroused, he dwells nostalgically on his old sexual experiences: the women he has seduced, the women he has possessed, the women who exhausted him physically. He is a living paradox. In his case, religion had the power to inflame his sensual imagination and make him long for illegitimate and licentious sources of pleasure. "Licentious and mystical obsessions haunted his brain. . ." (p. 165).

A Rebours is the fictional study of a neurasthenic hero who, after spending a period of time in aesthetic solitude, can endure the silence no longer and longs for the sound of a human voice. He decides to travel, to be on the move. He will take a trip to England, but he never gets there. Eating in an English restaurant is enough to satisfy his imagination, and he returns home to Fontenay. There he can delight in Baudelaire's poetry to his heart's content. Baudelaire is a kindred spirit, an intrepid explorer of the underworld of disease, perversions, and criminal passions. Des Esseintes is interested only in books that appeal to his enfeebled organism and decadent taste, works that deal with sadism and diabolism. The condition of mind that leads the blasphemer to surrender to the Devil and even kneel before him cannot, as Huysmans points out, exist in the soul of an unbeliever. Nor is it an adventure in sexual excesses coupled with fiendish blasphemies, for then it would be little more than an orgiastic feast of the flesh, an outbreak of satyriasis. Above all, "it consists in sacrilegious practice, in moral rebellion, in spiritual debauchery . . . and in this it is exemplarily Christian" (p. 240).

What the Satanist enjoys most is the pleasure to be derived from doing what is expressly forbidden. He enjoys violating sacred taboos. Huysmans goes on to say that if sadism did not involve acts of sacrilege it would have no excuse for being. And he is right in contending that the man who is not a believer cannot get much satisfaction from committing sacrilegious acts. What, then, is the singular attraction sadism holds out? It consists wholly, Huysmans says, "in the forbidden pleasure of transferring to Satan the homages and prayers we owe to God. . ." (p. 240).[29] In fact, the Marquis de Sade invented nothing new in describing his perversions and uttering his horrible blasphemies. They are as old as the history of the Church. The witches' sabbath, des Esseintes observed, contained all the ingredients to be found in sadism: the obscene rituals and the foul mouthing of blasphemies.

> Over and above the unclean orgies dear to the Evil one, nights consecrated successively to lawless and un-natural coition, nights befouled by the bloody bestialities of rutting animals, he [des Esseintes] found repeated the same parodies of Church procession, the same standing insults and defiances against God, the same ceremonies of devotion to his Rival, when he was celebrated, with curses in lieu of blessings on the bread and wine, the Black Mass on the back of a woman crouching on all fours, whose rump, naked and polluted again and again, served for altar table, and the congregation communicated, in derision, with a black host on the face of which a he-goat was impressed.[30]

29. The Marquis de Sade addressed God in a manner designed to provoke God's wrath; it was as if he dared God do his worst. Morse Peckham, in the final chapter of his stimulating book, *Victorian Revolutionaries* (New York: George Braziller, 1970), pp. 235-305, shows how de Sade challenged and endeavored to demolish the basic beliefs promulgated by Christianity. He repeats his favorite argument that the ways of God are irrational, cruel, and without justification, for he enjoys inflicting suffering on mankind. If he is interested in the human creatures on earth, it is *"Because* they can suffer, and that is why He created them. Since He is all-powerful, He could easily have created a world without suffering" (*ibid.*, p. 236).

30. Joris Karl Huysmans, *A Rebours* (London: The Fortune Press, n.d.), pp. 133-

This is substantially the same kind of debauch, spiced with sacrilegious profanities, that the Marquis de Sade indulged in when he defied God, called him vile names, seeking to provoke a Deity "who he prayed might damn him, the while he declared, to defy Him the more, that He did not exist."[31]

Des Esseintes's experiment in seclusion fails. His condition grows progressively worse. What is he to do with himself? The house he has provided for his refined pleasures now holds him virtually a prisoner. The books he had so carefully selected for his enjoyment now bore him. His adventure in solitude comes to an abrupt end; he has to give up his solitary existence at Fontenay and return to Paris. Either that or he will lapse into insanity. He finally realizes the nature of the problem that oppresses him: the need to believe. He wishes he could force himself to achieve the beatitude of faith, but he cannot silence his skeptical intellect. He does not give up the struggle. He realizes at last that the logic of pessimism has brought him no relief, "that impossible faith in a future life alone would pacify him."[32] Since he is denied that hope, everything seems over for him. The bourgeoisie were enjoying themselves under the ruins of the Church, and the Church itself was being defiled. Despair descends upon him and in the extremity of his despair he prays for relief: "O Lord, pity the Christian who doubts, the sceptic who would believe. . . ."[33]

To sum up: the hero of *Against the Grain* is an aesthete who craves solitude and the stimulation to be derived from artifice, illusions, and drugs; a spiritual outcast, a sensualist, a satanic sinner, he grows weary of his artificial paradise, his experiments in evil, and his practice of diabolism. He is a Decadent who utters abominable blasphemies and commits revolting acts of sacrilege because he is at heart desperately hungry for the bread of faith. His gods have been Baudelaire, Mallarmé, Poe, Verlaine, especially Mallarmé. His energies are dissipated in this struggle to believe, to overcome his infernal doubts. Like his begetter, des Esseintes is neither aware of nor interested in the political controversies

34. This translation of the passage was chosen because it is stylistically superior to the version as given by John Howard on p. 241.
31. Huysmans, *Against the Grain,* trans. John Howard, p. 241.
32. *Ibid.,* p. 330.
33. *Ibid.,* p. 331.

and crises of his age. He has isolated himself from the contemporary world, from society, from the realities of economics. He is, despite his dealings with the Devil, a pilgrim of eternity, the seeker of salvation who is completely unconcerned about the vicissitudes of history.

If I selected the work of Huysmans for discussion and analyzed his persona as an example of nonpolitical literature, I did so without passing adverse judgment on literature of this kind. My object was to show that not all of life is to be legitimately included under the rubric of politics. It is the Marxist critic who self-righteously proscribes this literature of abnormality, its flight into disease or madness, its rejection of "reality," its reflection of social psychopathology. In his desperation, so the indictment reads, the alienated writer of the West resorts to distortion, sensationalism, stylistic extravagance, utilizing extremes of technical virtuosity that border on the unintelligible. Lukács insists that such decadent writing reflects the truth of life under capitalism, which deforms the character of man.[34]

I did not dismiss the Symbolist novel by Huysmans as representing a psychopathological trend expressive of capitalism in its final stage of dissolution. The aestheticism of decadence was, however, short-lived. The movement was bound to fail. Symbolists like Mallarmé and Huysmans demonstrated that art inspires types of commitment that do not fall within the categories prescribed by the Marxist aesthetic.

34. See Georg Lukács, *Realism in Our Time,* trans. Necke Mander (New York: Harper & Row, 1964), pp. 30-33.

7

Artaud and Metaphysical Madness

In his egotism and imbalance, recognizing as realities only his own truths, he developed, outside the shape of normal society—and in maturity, in his twenties—creative gifts so isolated that he became within his limits, one of the so-called *maudits,* or informal creators, in French poetic thinking, of whom the last great disturbing figures had been Baudelaire and Rimbaud.[1]

Rimbaud knew the fascination of pure hallucination. A visionary like Blake, he could see "quite frankly a mosque in place of a factory, a school of drummers made up of angels, carriages on roads in the sky, a parlor at the bottom of the lake; monsters, mysteries."[2] This was the creative magic he practiced with words. "At the end I looked on the disorder of my mind as sacred."[3] But he was soon disillusioned with these hallucinations and the specious magic of words. After

1. Naomi Greene, *Antonin Artaud: Poet Without Words* (New York: Simon and Schuster, 1970), p. 9.
2. Arthur Rimbaud, *Complete Works, Selected Letters,* trans. Wallace Fowlie (Chicago and London: The University of Chicago Press, 1966), p. 195.
3. *Ibid.*

131

the age of nineteen he deliberately ended his poetic career and lapsed into silence.

Antonin Artaud, like Rimbaud, was not interested in radical politics as a means of attaining a secular type of salvation. In Artaud, the categorical imperative of Marxist doctrine and its urgent call for commitment was countered by the metaphysical vision that his recurrent states of madness accentuated. He recognized that there are limits beyond which no revolution, regardless of its degree of "success," can go. No matter what sweeping reforms are instituted in the form of government and in the equitable distribution of wealth, man's fate still remains ineluctably tragic. No political or economic panaceas can save him from the ultimate effects of the human condition. This perception of the inexorable limits that the revolutionary must perforce acknowledge and abide by, despite all his brave efforts to change the world closer to the heart's desire, serves in some cases to weaken his will and to shake his faith.

Other writers had caught intimations of this metaphysical vision. In *Danton's Death*, Büchner, who was active in the revolutionary movement of his time (he died in 1837 at the age of twenty-three), includes in his play a glimpse of the nullity of man's struggle to build the Kingdom of Heaven on earth. Dostoevski, after his release from five years of exile in Siberia, attacked the revolutionary mystique that affirms the myth of the political apocalypse.[4] Hermann Hesse used the novel as a vehicle for communicating the meaning and intrinsic purpose of his spiritual quest. He had started this search for integral selfhood with *Demian*, which reveals his reaction to the First World War. He became convinced at this period of his life of the basic irrationality of human behavior. Soci-

4. Dostoevski, after his return home from Siberia (he was then thirty-four years old), participated actively in the ideological battles of his age, but his political outlook had undergone a profound change. He was now a fiery "reactionary" writer. As a devout religious believer, he felt it was his mission in life to stamp out the noxious seeds of secular humanism that flourished in a soil and climate of atheism. Dostoevski was uncompromising in his opposition to Socialism. The revolutionary intelligentsia had fed on the writings of Belinsky, Bakunin, Chernyshevski, and Dobrolyubov. They were materialists, they were atheists, they were Socialists: they represented the cause of progress. As the perfervid agents of the Enlightenment, they plotted the downfall of the Czar. For Dostoevski, they were the unregenerate sons of the Devil, the enemy to be fought without mercy until he is overcome. See Ellis Sandoz, *Political Apocalypse: A Study of Dostoevskey's Grand Inquisitor* (Baton Rouge, La.: Louisiana State University Press, 1971).

ety could be saved and its destructive conflicts eliminated not by political means but only through the mediation of personal insight. He questioned the value of reforms externally imposed.

> In the last resort the crises of politics were for Hesse (and always remained) only pointers to the ultimate issues in the inner world of man. He feels that he cannot really be engaged in a political cause, at most in a moral one; poets and artists were always, in his view, essentially *Aussenwelter* (outsiders). *Littérature engagée* distorts their nature. . . . His was the revolt of a religious, not a political conscience; he knew very well that intellectuals and artists could have little hope of influencing men of power.[5]

A confident believer in the myth of Prometheus,[6] the Communist asserts that such reactionary views as Hesse propounds are typical of the encapsulated self of the bourgeois writer, who retreats into a mysticism that shields him from the disturbing challenge of social reality. Promethean man can conquer his environment and become the architect of his destiny. The thought of death does not frighten him. He can shape the laws of heredity and determine the process of sexual selection. No longer the slave of instinct, he will learn how to defeat those forces which seal his doom as a mortal creature. Leon Trotsky, in *Literature and Revolution,* said: "Emancipated man will want to attain a greater equilibrium in the work of his organs and a more proportional developing and wearing out of his tissue, in order to reduce the fear of death to a rational reaction of the organism toward death."[7] The morbid fear of death, Trotsky prophesies, will be gradually reduced so that mankind will no longer be tempted to nourish "stupid and humiliating fantasies about life after death."[8]

5. Mark Boulby, *Hermann Hesse* (Ithaca, N. Y.: Cornell University Press, 1967), pp. 82-83.
6. In his doctoral dissertation of 1841, Marx declared that man, not God, was the supreme reality. In the Foreword to Marx's thesis, *The Difference between the Natural Philosophy of Democritus and the Natural Philosophy of Epicurus,* there appears this passage: "Philosophy makes no secret of it. Prometheus's admission 'I hate all gods' is its own admission, its own motto against all gods, heavenly and earthly, the consciousness of man as the supreme divinity." Quoted in Patrick Masterson, *Atheism and Alienation* (Notre Dame, Ind.: Notre Dame University Press, 1971), p. 179.
7. Leon Trotsky, *Literature and Revolution* (New York: Russell & Russell, 1957), p. 255.
8. *Ibid.*

Marxism has never been able to give a satisfying answer to the haunting question of death. I. Kataev, in speaking of the man of the future, knows that he will be happy since he will inherit the benefits of Socialism. Kataev then asks:

> How will he sense the space of the universe, time, the cosmos, his own existence, the approach of death? Will he retain the will to change himself and the world around him, to aim at distant, faintly flickering ends?[9]

Soviet literature has never tackled this problem. Solzhenitsyn, in *Cancer Ward,* does not deal with this archetypal theme, and yet it cannot be passed over in silence. Daniel Bell believes that as faith in the religious absolute collapsed, the "fear of death as total annihiliation, unconsciously expressed, has probably increased."[10] Even the dedicated Communist cannot free himself at times from this metaphysical obsession. For Paul Nizan the thought that one day his consciousness would be extinguished for all eternity was unbearable. When he was in the grip of such a mood he drank steadily to drown the pain of this realization.

> He had asked himself whether the Socialist creed might not somehow help him to exorcise it [the thought of annihilation that would last forever] and felt quite optimistic as to prospects; but his lengthy interrogation of young Russian Communists concerning this topic had elicited a unanimous reply—in the face of death, comradeship and solidarity were no help at all, and they were all scared of death themselves. . . . It had been a great blow to him to discover that, in Russia as in France, the individual was alone when he died, and knew it.[11]

Those writers who were not drawn to the Marxist evangel and saw no reason for submitting to a code of commitment that demanded their abdication of individual freedom of judgment and their willingness to accept the dictates of the Communist Party—such writers had to depend on their own inner resources to survive. They knew full well the impurity

---

9. I. Kataev, "Art on the Threshold of Socialism," *International Literature,* no. 1 (April 1934), p. 85.
10. Daniel Bell, *The End of Ideology* (Glencoe, Ill.: The Free Press, 1960), p. 371.
11. Simone de Beauvoir, *The Prime of Life,* trans. Peter Green (Cleveland and New York: The World Publishing Company. 1960), p. 166. Quoted in Elaine Marks, *Simone de Beauvoir: Encounters with Death* (New Brunswick, N.J.: Rutgers University Press, 1973), p. 86.

and impotence of the medium they worked in. Language was an imprecise and treacherous instrument. Hence in their quest for authenticity they decided to create "aliterature": writing that would seek to rid itself of the artifices and stifling conventions of the past. The apostles of "aliterature" took no pride in their new venture; they were secretly ashamed of their continued dependence on words, words, words, but in their worst moments of despair they kept on writing.

The high priest of "aliterature" was Antonin Artaud, who describes with anguish the loss of his sense of identity; he does not know what he is thinking; he cannot put his house of thought in order. He has no control over the tumultuous flow of thought—thoughts that cause him to fall into the dementia of incoherence, but he stubbornly persists in his search for the undiscovered Absolute. He tries to picture for us the civil war that rages on the confused battlefield of his mind, the progressive disintegration of his ego. "There is something that is destroying my thinking, something that does not prevent me from being whatever I shall be able to be, but that leaves me, so to speak, in suspense."[12] Artaud suffered from recurrent attacks of an acute anxiety neurosis.

But the onset of madness led him to create what was virtually a new literary genre. Mental illness made it possible for him to gain deeper insights into the meaning of life and the strange mutations of the self than the method of rational inquiry affords. In his painful attempts to set down the truth about his condition, he writes about the feverish inner conflicts that made him feel that he was not himself. He struggled hard to become a writer, to establish communion with the world of men, even though he frankly acknowledged the preposterous folly of harboring such an ambition. "This is my particular weakness and my absurdity, to want to write at any price and express myself."[13] That is why he was so desperately preoccupied with the disorder of his mind; he was driven by the need to find out, if he could, the cause of his accursed mental affliction. Claude Mauriac remarks: "Artaud's dementia reveals the dementia of all living men who think . . . it is not so much insanity as the impossibility of be-

12. Claude Mauriac, *The New Literature*, trans. Samuel I. Stone (New York: George Braziller, 1959), p. 36.
13. *Ibid.*, p. 38.

ing, the horror of essential solitude."[14] Artaud experimented with peyote, a drug that induces dreams and projects images dredged from the primordial depths of the unconscious. He is fascinated by the esoteric art of weaving spells and reciting magic incantations; he is trying to master the difficult, unprecedented technique of using these fits of insanity for a creative purpose. He is aware of the fact that he is striving to create the literature of madness. There are times, in fact, when he enjoys the euphoria brought on by madness. He seeks to reach God through the medium of peyote, but he learns that drugs cannot call forth this ineffable vision of God.[15]

Artaud gives expression to the supreme craving of alienated twentieth-century man to discover a truth that is commensurate with the whole truth of life. That "truth," Artaud realizes, resists conceptual formulation. Life comes first; it must be lived; only later does there arise the compelling need to understand and, above all, to believe in the "force" that makes us want to live. For life, as Artaud apprehends it, is more than the biological organization of matter; it is an abiding mystery, a perpetual source of magic. The old, dying forms must be interred so that modern man can reestablish contact with the fountainhead of being: partake of the elixir that will bestow on him the gift of timeless spontaneity, restore his faith in the reality of magic, and enable him to recover the pristine purity of perception that is the mark of the true poet. To experience all this and give it adequate expression, a new language must be forged. The revitalized theater Artaud envisaged must break through the barriers of lan-

14. *Ibid.,* p. 40.
15. In the modern world, the madman, whatever diagnostic label is used against him, is disenfranchised; he is a nonperson. He is deprived of all his rights; he may be regarded as an object of pity, but the severity of the medical treatment he receives is not mitigated. The psychotic, the schizophrenic, finds that he is denied any role that affords him safety and security. The psychotic is guilty of having ventured beyond the frontiers fixed by the powerful guarians of the "normal." Dwelling as he does in the hinterland of the imagination, he has lost his former confidence in external reality. He sees into the heart of things and often beholds the ubiquitous image of the Absurd. He feels he has gone beyond the limits of space and time. But even in his worst moments of confusion, he experiences the sense of the numinous. "An exile from the scene of being as we know it, he [the person who goes mad] is an alien, a stranger signaling to us from the void in which he is foundering, a void which may be peopled by presences that we do not even dream of." R. D. Laing, *The Politics of Experience* (New York: Ballantine Books, 1971), p. 133.

guage and liberate the power of dreams. Modern man must root himself once again in the primordial matrix of the great myths of the race and build the new theater on a foundation of archetypal conflicts. Concretely, what Artaud wishes the theater to recapture is the language of action and gesture, the ritual of the dance, the organic function of music in the drama. He does not want the theater to concern itself with the essentially sterile task of psychological analysis. He sounds a call for a theater that will release the untapped potentialities of the metaphysical vision.

Unlike Brecht, Artaud took no interest in the propagandist type of "proletarian" drama that Piscator was experimenting with in Berlin. According to Artaud, the object of the new theater he hoped to found was not to mirror reality but to come to grips with a reality that transcends the restricted sphere of the human. Artaud rejected the shallow technique of realism in order to concentrate his energy on depicting spiritual states in an expressive language of gesture. Words, he pointed out, are ambiguous and even treacherous conveyors of meaning. The effort to capture the life of feeling in words and communicate it on the stage often fails because feeling is essentially untranslatable. To express true feeling "is to betray it. But to translate it is *to dissimulate it.*"[16]

In his First Manifesto on "The Theater of Cruelty," Artaud formulates the general aesthetic principles that would guide him; he calls for the creation of a unique language of gesture that would supplant the printed text used in the past. By "cruelty" Artaud means the lucid recognition of necessity. Unlike the Marxists with their conception of the omnipotent factor of economic necessity, Artaud provides this singular definition of cruelty:

> death is cruelty, resurrection is cruelty, transfiguration is cruelty, since nowhere in a circular and closed world is there room for true death, since ascension is a rending, since closed space is fed with lives (p. 103).

The Theater of Cruelty affirms that life is conflict, contradiction, strife, irrational suffering, and gratuitous cruelty. In these dramatically presented affirmations, the importance of

---

16. Antonin Artaud, *The Theater and Its Double,* trans. Mary Caroline Richards (New York: Grove Press, 1958), p. 71.

the Word steadily diminishes. "Renouncing psychological man, with his well-dissected character and feelings, and social man, submissive to laws and misshapen by religions and precepts, the Theater of Cruelty will address itself only to total man" (p. 123).

Before total man could come to life on the stage, the fragmentary man, torn by internecine psychological conflicts, would have to acquire a sense of identity and learn how to master the language he must use in the interminable debates conducted by the inner self. This language was shadowy, unreal, phantasmal. Who, after all, is involved in the process of thinking? What is consciousness? How determine the identity of the various contentious voices that speak in its name? Words are elusive, protean creatures to work with; they seem to have a will of their own and willfully distort the meaning of what the writer is trying to say. Suffering from the disintegration of his sense of reality and the loss of self, Artaud observed how his language deteriorated into frozen ciphers.

> I suffer from a fearful mental disease. My ideas abandon me at every stage, from the mere fact of thought itself to the exterior phenomenon of its materialization in words. Words, the forms of sentences, inner directions of thought, the mind's simplest reactions:—I am in constant pursuit of my intellectual being (p. 148).

Artaud, at this point no longer concerned with that which can be expressed, leaves behind him the realm of literature and plunges into the unknown world of myth and the oceanic depths of the ineffable. In this ultima Thule, words utterly fail him; language exists only for what has already been said, not for that which he is now experiencing for the first time. He is, as it were, cut off from himself; a lost monad floating in the space-time continuum, he is nevertheless passionately in search of unity of being; he breaks down all barriers in his determined quest for the Absolute.

Artaud explores the negative pole of mysticism; he is cut off from the mundane plane of existence but he has no assurance that he has gained admittance to a higher or lower world of the spirit. All he knows and can declare with the utmost conviction is that the language of literature is pretentious nonsense. "All writing," he says, "is rubbish" (p. 151). That which can be caught in the net of words is not worth putting down on paper. The damning charge he hurls against the writers of his time is that they repeat the obvious. He dismisses the entire literary tribe as "a pack of rubbish-mongers, especially today" (p. 151). Artaud bids farewell to the fossilized fund of language preserved in a literary tradition.

Artaud rebelled against this effete, anachronistic tradition. The modern writer, he insisted, must have the courage to face his naked self and reveal the civil war raging within him. Artaud sought to orient himself in a reality that is spectral, unknown, undefined, and indefinable. He realizes that he is creating a literature born of mental illness. He is tensely aware that the road he has taken leads to suicide or madness. He refuses to yield to the insidious power of madness just as he had resisted the siren song of death. Day after day he fights this battle inside the locked cage of his mind. He feels the throbbing pain of consciousness, the unrelenting pressure of his phobias and obsessions, the fear born of his nameless anxieties and his solipsist fixation. Yet he does not look upon his abnormality as a threat. In order not to become the slave of conventional social reality, he turned to the experimental theater and endeavored to bring forth drama that is elemental in content and cosmic in scope, drama that faithfully reflects the implacable cruelty of existence. Artaud singled out Heliogabulus as the hero of the absurd. In his "Letter on Lautréamont" he voiced his admiration of this remarkable poet and his work. Isidore Ducasse, he declares, is neither a madman nor a visionary but a daring explorer of the unconscious. He pays an even more lavish tribute to the genius of Van Gogh, who belongs to the race of genuine lunatics, as Artaud calls them. A genuine lunatic he defines as one "who prefers to go mad in the social sense of the word, rather than forfeit a certain higher idea of honor."[17] Society persecutes and shuts up in asylums those who refuse to play the game of adjustment according to the prescribed rules, those who persist in their effort to proclaim a number of intolerable truths.

Artaud collaborated with the Surrealists, but with them, too, he felt misunderstood. They loved life while he despised

---

17. Antonin Artaud, *Anthology,* ed. Jack Hirschman (San Francisco, Calif.: City Lights Books, 1965), p. 137.

it. There was also the troublesome matter of political commitment that divided them. He could not endorse their eager acceptance of Marxism nor their decision to join the Communist Party. Communism, he felt, was not a panacea for the spiritual suffering of mankind. Politics was a distraction, a snare. Those among the Surrealists who did not believe in the cause of Communism were drummed out of the movement. Artaud was one of those who did not fit into this doctrinaire scheme of political salvation. He was accused of pursuing literature as an isolated activity, instead of devoting his talent to the supreme task of changing the world. He was *persona non grata* because he continued to dwell in the hermetic fastness of the mind, lost in a world of dreams. Artaud replied to these charges by rejecting the simplistic view that political revolution in and of itself could transform the nature of man.

> He berated the Surrealists for deriding him "when I speak of a metamorphosis of the soul's inner state, as if I imagined the soul in the same odious way as they do. Or, as if, from an absolute viewpoint, it could be of the slightest interest to see the social structure of the world changed, or to see power go from the hands of the bourgeoisie into those of the proletariat."[18]

The growing alienation of the artist in the twentieth century, the emphasis he placed on the dialectic of negation, his revolt against the dominant cult of rationalism, all this was brought to a head largely by the outbreak of the First World War. Pragmatism, instrumentalism, logical positivism, dialectical materialism, scientific rationalism—these were later assailed as grossly falsifying the character of man and his relation to "reality." One social critic says that "progress and idealism are two of my *bêtes noires,* because I see in them perhaps the two greatest sins of the last two centuries, the two greatest forms of irresponsibility."[19] Long before Ortega spoke out, the Dadaists battled against all that was stultifying, artificial, decadent, and downright false in the culture of their time.

18. Naomi Green, *Antonin Artaud,* pp. 24-25.
19. José Ortega y Gasset, "The Self and the Other," *Partisan Review* 19 (July-August 1952): 396.

8
Dada: To Hell with Culture and Art

[Neo-dada] has tended to reject the conception of commitment so fundamental to Sartre's existentialism, as well as to Marxism.[1]

THE ONLY TRUE DADAISTS ARE THE DADAISTS OF SPIEGELGASSE beware of imitations[2]

Alfred Jarry's *King Ubu* was produced in Paris in 1896. A mixture of madcap fantasy and scatological satire, it heralded the revolt that broke out in the twentieth century against intellectualism, naturalism, and the grotesque absurdity of politics. The play is a provocation. Bizarre, truculent, and iconoclastic, it exploits with effrontery the resources of invective, buffoonery, burlesque, obscenity, and farce in order to poke fun mercilessly at the self-serving ethic of the merchant class. It repudiates with scurrilous contempt the world as it is. "The avant-garde drama is the comedy of nihilism and despair."[3]

1. Donald Drew Egbert, *Social Radicalism and the Arts* (New York: Alfred A. Knopf, 1970), p. 366.
2. Jean Arp, *Arp on Arp: Poems, Essays, Memories,* ed. Marcel Jean; trans. Joachim Neugroschel (New York: The Viking Press, 1972), p. 7.
3. George E. Wellwarth, *The Theater of Protest and Paradox* (New York: New York University Press, 1964), p. 16.

If the Dadaists behaved at times like madmen, there was a method in their madness. Though they were specialists in the difficult art of negation, their violent protest against the destructive manias of their age was motivated by a desire to salvage and reinstate a number of positive values they believed in. For one thing, they were intransigently opposed to the war. Nor would they swear allegiance to the State, which was the instigator and breeding-ground of war. Dada defiantly announced, and not without a touch of pride, that it was completely nihilistic in its outlook. The Dadaists were resolved to abolish the evil cultural heritage that had led to a world war. Anarchists at heart, subversive in their pranks and provocations, they embodied, Marcel Duchamp declared, "the nonconformist spirit which has existed in every century, every period since man is man."[4]

The devotees of Dada, especially during the early years of the movement when their fervor was at its height, went even further than Jarry in cultivating anti-realistic techniques and in vigorously attacking the delusional system of politics. Despising all that the culture of the past had venerated, thrusting it aside as useless and irrelevant, the Dadaists unleashed a minor revolution in the kingdom of aesthetics. Unafraid to violate the canons of logic, they placed their trust in the cult of the unintelligible. They mocked the rule of reason and perversely worshiped the Great God Whim. Jean Arp gives us this apt definition of Dada: "Dada aimed to destroy the reasonable deceptions of man and recover the natural and unreasonable order. Dada wanted to replace the logical nonsense of the men of today by the illogically senseless."[5]

If Dada opted for the senseless, which was not to be equated with non-sense, it was because it valued nature higher than art. The creative spirit that originally gave birth to Dada persisted in later years. As Donald Drew Egbert points out, Neo-dada resolutely adopted a spirit of anarchistic nonconformity in matters of art. Its proponents did not care if they were fiercely condemned for their nihilistic outlook. Unlike the original founders of the movement, they did not make the costly mistake of assuming that the success of

4. Quoted in C. W. E. Bigsby, *Dada & Surrealism* (London: Methuen & Co., 1972), p. 11.
5. Jean Arp, *Arp on Arp,* p. 238.

the October Revolution in the Soviet Union would usher in a renaissance of revolutionary art.

Dada, at any rate, carried the spirit of skepticism to extreme lengths and culminated in a furious campaign designed to strip the human animal of his megalomania, his studied pose of idealism. Recognizing no moral absolutes, Dada harped insistently on the theme that truth is an illusion. The adherents of Dada were convinced, and did not hesitate to say so, that art is a pointless activity. Not that they were uncompromisingly opposed to art *per se*.[6] While millions of men were being slaughtered on the European field of battle, they felt that art, like life, was a hideous joke. And the dirty game of power politics that caused this world war was the worst joke of all.[7]

Since the bourgeoisie paid no heed to their arguments, the Dadaists changed their method of attack; henceforth they decided to employ the deadly weapon of satire against these blind leaders of the blind; they laughed at the blatant hypocrisy of the rulers of the world, their fake piety, their mask of righteousness, their official oratory that consisted chiefly of expedient lies. The battlecry of the Dadaists voiced their total disillusionment: to hell with culture and its pernicious, life-negating myths! Down with literature and art! To hell with

6. This does not imply that Dada was dedicated solely to the cause of anti-art. While vehemently denying the autonomy of art, the Dadaists pursued as their major objective the art of administering successive shocks to the public in order to make them realize the self-destructive, death-dealing character of the civilization they professed to admire. "In dada there was an oscillation between sheer iconoclastic parody and a constructively creative spontaneity of the individual self, not merely for art's sake but for the very sake of human survival." Egbert, *Social Radicalism and the Arts,* p. 296.

7. The *Manifeste Dada 1918,* which Tzara composed, contains these revealing statements: "But seeing that life is a sorry farce ... and because we feel that we should get out of it the best way we can, washing our hands of the affair, we have proclaimed one basis of understanding: art. ... Art is a private affair, the artist produces it for himself; a comprehensible work is a journalistic product" *(The European Caravan,* ed. Samuel Putnam [New York: Harcourt, Brace and Company, 1931], p. 96). Despite all their disclaimers and their intensive exploitation of the comic and satiric vein, there can be no doubt that the Dadaists took themselves and their creative work seriously. "Perhaps it is a puritan strain in human nature that finds it difficult to accept that play and seriousness, fun and art, can go together" (R. W. Last, *Hans Arp: The Poet of Dadaism* [Chester Springs, Pa.: Dufour Editions, 1969], p. 31). "Those who only describe the farcical and fantastic side of Dada, and do not penetrate into its heart, its transcendent reality, offer only a worthless fragment. Dada was no childish romp" *(ibid.,* p. 78).

everything! This is how Hugo Ball, one of the brilliant leaders of the movement, describes the attitude of Dada in "Dada Fragment (1916-1917)": "The Dadaist loves the extraordinary, the absurd, even. . . . Every kind of mask is therefore welcome to him, every play at hide and seek in which there is an inherent power of deception."[8]

Tristan Tzara, the leading spirit behind Dada, composed manifestos that displayed his virtuosity in the fine art of debunking. To laugh in derision at the pronouncements of idealism, to hold up sanctified dogmas to ridicule, to expose the fatuity of the idolatry of Art and the meaninglessness of the highfalutin talk about Culture: this was the specific task of demolition the Dadaists sought to accomplish.[9] Beyond that they did not attempt to go. It is therefore absurd, in one sense, to speak of a Dada aesthetic. Tzara's manifestos are scatalogical insults aimed, one presumes, at deluded mankind.[10] He proclaims that "Dada remains within the European frame of weakness it's shit after all but from now on we mean to shit in assorted colors. . . ."[11] In his *Manifeste Dada 1918,* Tzara wrote: "I am against action; for continuous contradiction, for affirmation too. . ." (p. 76). Tzara places his cards, face up, on the table. He shows us the hand he is playing. He doesn't believe in principles, just as he doesn't believe in manifestos. In fact, he lets it be known that he believes in nothing, but if that is so then how can he speak out? That seeming contradiction constitutes a difficulty only for those who adhere to the discredited Aristotelian law of identity, the

8. Robert Motherwell, *The Dada Painters and Poetry* (New York: Wittenborn, Schultz, 1951), p. 51.
9. Louis Aragon had, early in his youth, won a gratifying measure of success as a poet and novelist. Yet he told Matthew Josephson that poetry and the novel were dead. Like Rimbaud, he intended to give up the practice of literature. The literary group with which he was then associated "proposed to devote their time to waging war upon society, as agitators and propagandists—for Dadaism! Their literature was to be an *action,* action designed to subvert men's minds by laughter and ridicule, by generating a mood of disgust everywhere." Matthew Josephson, *Life Among the Surrealists* (New York: Holt, Rinehart and Winston, 1962), p. 114.
10. Edmund Wilson refers to the kind of comic nonsense the Dadaists contributed. He regards their jokes as silly or in bad taste. They reacted to the spiritual and moral bankruptcy of the world during and after the war by an outburst of unrestrained cynicism (Edmund Wilson, *Axel's Castle* [New York: Charles Scribner's Sons, 1931], pp. 253-56). See "Memoirs of Dadaism" by Tristan Tzara, in *ibid.,* pp. 304-11.
11. Robert Motherwell, *The Dada Painters and Poets,* p. 73.

old laws of logic based on a simplistic black-and-white dualism. The prophet of Dada obeys the prompting of his creative madness though he is not mad, and if contradictions emerge as a result he is not at all troubled. He is neither for nor against.

All this was damned as the tantrums of an infantile sect, a deliberate exercise in folly, a stupendous hoax, a manifestation of decadence. But Tzara can, on occasion, strike a serious note. For example, he questions whether there exists a psychic base common to all mankind. How, he asks, "can one expect to put order into chaos that constitutes that infinite and shapeless variation: man?" (p. 77). Thus the aim of Dada is not only to destroy; it also affirms the need for creative freedom.

Despite its boldly professed nihilism, Dada believed in art, but it was an art that transcended fixed categories, formulated principles, moral ideas, psychological analyses. Appearing as it did during the years when Europe was drawn into the demented dance of death called war, Dada emphasized its role as the enemy of civilization, the destroyer. *"We are a furious wind, tearing the dirty linen of clouds and prayers, preparing the great spectacle of disaster, fire, decomposition"* (p. 78). In short, Dada was committed to the Herculean task of cleaning up the foul mess Western civilization had caused. Progress, law, morality, culture, religion—these, the Dadaists declared, stink in their nostrils. "Logic imprisoned by the senses is an organic disease" (p. 79). We have seen how Tzara defended his hatred of systems. The most acceptable system, he maintained, "is on principle to have none" (p. 79).

Dada did not lapse into desuetude. Its nonconformist spirit is very much alive today, though it may operate under another name. In retrospect, we can see that Dada actually represented a revolt against a culture that was corrupt. Dada was animated by a vital ethical impulse which, in the early stages of its development, took a negative turn and in some cases led to a militant nihilism. "The new ethic took sometimes a positive, sometimes a negative form, often appearing as art and then again as the negation of art, at times deeply moral and at other times totally amoral."[12]

---

12. Hans Richter, *Dada: Art and Anti-Art* (New York and Toronto: McGraw-Hill Book Company, n.d.), p. 9.

Dada cannot be neatly classified and accorded its rightful "nosological" place in the history of literature and art. It was a complex, tumultuous outbreak of energy, instinct with contradictions. The Dadaists staged violent demonstrations, they availed themselves of every opportunity to insult the bourgeoisie, they devised new ways of shocking the public. In support of the contention that the sphere of politics is all-embracing, including even those cultural manifestations that are given over to destruction, it should be pointed out that the Dadaists, like the Surrealists who appeared later on the scene, engaged in what they considered to be "political" actions, actions meant to disturb the complacent slumber of the world. They staged "readings" of poetry that aroused in the audience the rage born of sheer frustration. While the poet read from his manuscript, other performers were busy ringing cowbells or blowing whistles. Amidst this deafening bedlam of noise, the voice of the reader is drowned out. One wonders what results such "negative actions" were supposed to bring about.

It is difficult in many cases to draw a sharp distinction between political and nonpolitical art. A movement like Dada, which indulged in mystification, tomfoolery, scandalous behavior, and frenzied, irrational attacks on everything under the sun, would not seem to be a fitting candidate to wear the honorific badge of "commitment." It is illogical, "unprincipled," and seemingly "irresponsible." But not all Dadaists were agreed on fundamental issues. The Dada movement had spread to other cities, in the United States, Belgium, Spain, Czechoslovakia, and Rumania. Evidently it fulfilled a need that other alienated and embittered artists also felt. Dada made its debut in Zurich and Berlin. The Berlin group, hit hard by the economic privations of their defeated country, defended the Spartacist cause. ". . . The Berlin Dadas' brief involvement with the practical aspects of revolution in 1918 and 1919 changed the tone of their movement. With a new burst of energy, the group began publishing a series of new magazines—*Der Dada, Everyman His Own Football, Bankrupt, Adversary,* and *Deadly Earnest.*"[13] *Der Dada* was interested in social revolution but it is doubtful if the members of this group supported the program advocated by the Spartacists. Some

13. Manuel L. Grossman, *Dada* (New York: Pegasus, 1971), p. 71.

critics hold that the Dadaists in Berlin believed in revolutionary activism and, because of their absorption in the strenuous game of politics, lost their identity as Dadaists. Other critics insist that this was not the case. No Berlin Dadaists joined the Communist Party. The young Berlin Dadaists, for all their extremist talk, were of no consequence as political agitators. As Grosz pointed out in 1925, "the Dadas had discovered the relationship between art and the class struggle, but had failed to really explore art as a revolutionary weapon."[14]

The Dadaists were far more enthralled by their method of creatively exploiting the world of chance, a method the Surrealists later adopted. Here was what seemed to its devotees "a magical procedure by which one could transcend the barriers of causality and conscious volition. . . ."[15] What happened when the Dadaists abandoned the restraints of rationality? Were the gates thrown wide open to the invasion of the goblins and gargoyles of caprice, the succubi and incubi of nightmares, the delirious fantasies of the unconscious, the howling demons of unreason? Hans Richter maintained that the impulse to end the sovereignty of the rational was

> meaningful, necessary and life-giving. The official belief in the infallibility of reason, logic and causality seemed to us senseless—as senseless as the destruction of the world and the systematic elimination of every particle of human feeling.[16]

Chance, the Dadaists felt, would redeem them from a world gone berserk in its deification of scientific rationalism. "The realization that reason and anti-reason, sense and nonsense, design and chance, consciousness and unconsciousness, belong together as necessary parts of a whole—this was the central message of Dada."[17]

Some of the men associated with Dada were highly gifted

14. *Ibid.*, p. 80.
15. Richter, *Dada*, p. 57. "Early Dadaists created found poems by cutting words from newspapers, shuffling them in a bag, and drawing them out blindly one by one. Sequences seldom made much sense, of course, so usually they were intelligently shuffled into some sort of grammatical form. This spoiled the purity of the random method, to be sure, but at least it could be said that whatever the resulting poem says did not *originate* in anyone's imagination or intent." Louis Mink, "Art without Artists," in *Liberations*, ed. Ihab Hassan (Middletown, Conn.: Wesleyan University Press, 1971), p. 78.
16. Richter, *Dada*, p. 58.
17. *Ibid.*, p. 64.

artists but they were skeptical of the value commonly attached to works of art. They did not believe that life had any meaning and therefore concluded that neither art nor politics was worth a tinker's damn. Picabia, a confirmed nihilist, was too deeply infected with the virus of skepticism to place his faith in life, the world, and the productions of art to which the world paid such reverential lip-service. If life was devoid of ultimate meaning, then art as the celebration of life was an empty illusion. Marcel Duchamp was also a man without faith. A complex personality, he demonstrated his extraordinary ability as a painter. Then, suddenly, he gave it all up. He was revolted by the frantic struggle for fame, the shameless competitive scramble for recognition. Giving up his early dream of glory, he withdrew into himself, dropped his painting, and managed to obtain a job. He debunked the supposedly sacred nature of art; he painted Mona Lisa with a mustache. He not only contributed a great deal to Dada but remained a Dadaist till the end.[18]

But Dada could not last.

> Born of an impulse toward liberation and life, conscious of the strength and weakness of the human mind, it had understood that it could work only toward its own ruin. It was aware of its bankruptcy and did not fight it.[19]

Surrealism took its place. Tristan Tzara did not fade into the background once Dada lost its *raison d'être*. He became one of the leading Surrealist poets, but later he broke away from this movement and announced his conversion to Marxism. Tzara had been the driving force of energy behind Dada. Consistently he let it be known that Dada had no importance whatsoever. Art was but a game, after all, a child's toy, not to be taken too seriously. "When Tzara says art is a game, he is decrying the uselessness of purely technical virtuosity, of cleverly assembling words with 'une sonnerie à la fin.' "[20]

18. See Robert Lebel, *Marcel Duchamp,* trans. George Heard Hamilton (New York: Grove Press, 1959).
19. Motherwell, *The Dada Painters and Poets,* p. 120.
20. Elmer Peterson, *Tristan Tzara* (New Brunswick, N. J.: Rutgers University Press, 1971), p. 20. Tzara was prolific throughout his literary career, writing peotry, plays, essays, and an autobiographical novel. In his essay on Tzara, J. H. Matthews deals with his efforts to write plays for the theater (J. H. Matthews, *Theatre in Dada and Surrealism* [Syracuse, N. Y.: Syracuse university Press, 1974], pp. 17-43). Mary Ann Caws, in her evaluation of Tzara's work, says:

The pronouncement that Dada was dead was premature. Dada broke loose again in 1968. It springs to life again whenever conditions become intolerable. In May 1968 the young rebels used Dada to articulate their revolt. In the events that occurred in France during that month, some observers discerned an underlying connection between politics and culture. Alfred Willener, in *The Action-Image of Society*, perceives a relationship between the happenings of May and such movements in the past as Dada and Surrealism. This French sociologist detects many striking parallels between the "actions" and "utterances" of Dada and those that were noted in May 1968.

> The same verbal and gestural violence, the same systematic practice of provocation, are found again, in May 1968, combined with a certain audacity in the use of violence if necessary. A few quotations from Dadaist authors or direct reference on the walls, a tract of avowedly Dadaist inspiration, the same peremptory insolence: such similarities are obvious enough.[21]

What conclusion is one warranted in drawing from these sociological observations and interpretations by Willener? That life imitates art? That Dada and Surrealism, like the Living Theater and avant-garde cinema, though their methods have nothing in common, serve as a catalytic agent in triggering the release of revolutionary energy in the young? Dada, at the height of its subversive activity, took no part in politics, and Neo-dada has carried on this tradition in rejecting the conception of commitment. Tristan Tzara, while he was the animating spirit of the Dadaist movement, eschewed all forms of political involvement. The Dadaists' anarchist nihilism prevented them from yielding to such a futile and ridiculous temptation. It was the Surrealists, many of whom had been Dadaists, who made the effort to unite art and life by joining the Communist Party.

"Of the Dadaists Tzara expressed most convincingly the essential Dada revolution against the sentimentality of previous literary movements" (Tristan Tzara, *"Approximate Man" and Other Writings*, trans. Mary Ann Caws [Detroit, Mich.: Wayne State University Press, 1973], p. 18).

21. Alfred Willener, *The Action-Image of Society*, trans. A.M. Sheridan (New York: Pantheon Books, 1970), p. 199.

9

From Surrealism to Communism

In rational association images are controlled by a social experience of reality—the consciousness of necessity. In free association the images are controlled by the iron hand of the unconscious instincts—and it is therefore no more free than the "thinking" of the ant.[1]

Surrealism in fact started from a collective effort, as yet never attempted, of revolution on the level of the mind. It was obliged, in order to make its first steps, to abandon this level and to fling itself into the political melée. The adherence to the political Revolution required the deployment of all the surrealist forces, and consequently the abandonment of the particular philosophy which had constituted the movement's very being at its origin. Was surrealism going to consent to its own suicide?[2]

It is only too certain that an activity, such as ours, owing to its particularization, cannot be pursued within the limits of any one of the existing revolutionary organizations: it would be forced to come to a halt on the very threshold of that organization.[3]

1. Christopher Caudwell, *Illusion and Reality* (New York: International Publishers, 1947), p. 110.
2. Maurice Nadeau, *The History of Surrealism,* trans. Richard Howard (New York: The Macmillan Company, 1965), p. 203.
3. André Breton, *What Is Surrealism?* trans. David Gascoyne (London: Faber, 1936), p. 89.

Surrealism was in the beginning grounded in the depths of subjectivity. The subliminal universe of the mind was more full of wonderful surprises than the external world. That was how to change the world of reality, by exploring the oceanic realms of the unconscious and by surrendering to the spontaneous call of desire. The Surrealist believed in the power of the imagination to put an end to his alienation and enable him to establish new, vital relations with the world of men. The daring experiments the Surrealists conducted by enlisting the aid of the unconscious in their production of painting, poetry, and fiction did not change the world; social reality resisted their best efforts; the converts they hoped to win among the avant garde did not respond to the call of the Surrealist revolution. They then decided to ally themselves with the Communists, but the attempted collaboration turned out to be a miserable failure. The Surrealists were not interested in that anachronistic abstraction The Economic Man. Nor were they willing to sacrifice their individuality and obey unconditionally the dictates of the Communist Party.

In the early stages of their growth, the Surrealists were utterly indifferent to the challenge posed by the life of politics. Like the Symbolists and the Dadaists, they distrusted the dominant tendency of their age to rely on rational methods of inquiry. They believed it was the unconscious that best revealed the essential but hidden features of reality. In its revolt against the cult of reason, in its repudiation of the certitudes of the established social order, Surrealism carried on the anarchic spirit of defiance which characterized Dada. "The systematic stupidity of the Dadaist productions had an intention, if not a meaning: its aim was to convey the feeling that absolutely everything is idiotic and senseless."[4] Whereas Dada negated "all possible moral or artistic doctrines,"[5] Surrealism derived its major insights and, in part, its creative method from the pioneering discoveries of psychoanalysis. It drew inspiration from a number of other sources: the Dionysian philosophy of Nietzsche, the work of Schopenhauer, the vitalism of Henri Bergson, the distortions to be found in primitive art,[6] and the revelations of madness.

4. Georges E. Lemaitre, *From Cubism to Surrealism in French Literature* (Cambridge, Mass.: Harvard University Press, 1941), p. 170.

5. *Ibid.*, p. 176.

6. The world of primitive man "is full of demons and devils, of black magic and

In its espousal of the irrational and in its willingness to heed the oracular voice of dreams and the dictates of the unconscious, Surrealism in effect shut out the world of logic and common sense and rejected the value-assumptions on which this world was based. The new science lent support to their daring aesthetic venture. In physics the principle of indeterminacy prevailed in the infrahuman universe. The rigid conceptual framework of science had to be scrapped as obsolete to accommodate the new version of energy. The electron seemed to behave in an unpredictable manner. Reality, thus transformed, took on wonderfully strange, unprecedented patterns. Modern man confronted the startling spectacle of the absurd.[7] In this fantastic universe, "the most improbable happenings seem normal, the critical spirit is abolished, and constraints vanish. This enchanted world is truly that of Surreality."[8]

We have seen how the movement of revolt began soon after the outbreak of the First World War. Dada turned against the culture of the West and denounced the honorific values of civilization as blatant lies, but the art of negation for its own sake proved to be an exercise in futility, sterile and stultifying in the long run. The nihilism the Dadaists adopted as their battle-cry helped to clear the way, but then the creative mind had to find a body of vital values to believe in and affirm. The Surrealists took over, utilizing the discoveries of Freud to support their faith in the potentialities of the dream. Dada, the glorification of nonsense, thus culminated in the search for a transfigured reality, the search for the infinite in the heart of the particular, the quest for superreality: absolute reality. For the dream did away with clocks, the chronology of public time, just as it transcended the principle of causality.

sorcery, and an endless series of taboos and rituals is needed as protection against these influences." Hanns Sachs, The *Creative Unconscious* (Cambridge, Mass.: Sci-Art, 1942), pp. 179-80.

7. "Man's tremendous effort over the centuries to elucidate the mystery of the universe, to make the human condition ever less and less absurd, has ended in failure. Man is defeated by the very forces he has set up to subdue. Both in his actual life and in his scientific investigations, he meets and verifies absurdity, and, today, the intellect bows before it. Abjectly, he acknowledges his own absurdity in philosophy, in literature, and in art." René Huyghe, *The Spirit of Man,* trans. Norbert Guterman (New York: Harry N. Abrams, 1962), p. 477.

8. Yves Duplessis, *Surrealism,* trans. Paul Capon (New York: Walker and Company, 1962), p. 125.

The dream was exploited creatively in the service of literature and art. Surrealist poetry was divorced from its damaging preoccupation with ideas and abstractions. Now it could devote its energy to the task of creating images that were independent of logical categories. Through the image the abstract can be mediated in the vestments of the concrete. Breton's poetry is replete with such examples of mediation: "eternity incorporated in a wrist watch, life in a virgin passport, thought becoming a white curve on a dark background, lightness shaking upon our roofs her angel's hair."[9] Reason is left behind, logical connections and analogies are not only avoided but leaped over, so that the most fantastically dissimilar objects can be brought together in a violent juxtaposition as in Lautréamont's image: "Beautiful like the fortuitous meeting, on a dissection table, of a sewing machine and an umbrella."[10]

Surrealism, as the name suggests, represents an effort of the creative imagination to get beyond, to rise above, a "reality" that is conceptualized and restricted. The Surrealist artist endeavors to capture the shapes and shadows of the dream. Dream and object, self and landscape interfuse. The Surrealist strives to achieve communion with the infinite, to translate into hypnotic poetry the experience of the ineffable, to pierce the veil of the unknown, to reach a state of cosmic consciousness. In this quest for the absolute, in their conviction that madness opens wide the gates of vision, in their demand that chimeras must be born, the Surrealists were not affected by the economic misery of the masses. It aroused in them no sense of outrage, no stirring of compassion, because they did not see it. Mesmerized wanderers in the enchanted forest of the imagination, wih its fabulous flora and fauna, they took no interest in the problems of the working class nor were they believers in the Marxist doctrine of secular salvation. Neo-romantic and nonpolitical in outlook, they labored to reveal a new beauty, unspoiled, dream-conditioned. Breton demanded "that he who still refuses, for instance, to *see* a horse galloping on a tomato should be looked upon as a cretin."[11]

In his essay "What Is Surrealism?," Breton describes the di-

9. Anna Balakian, *Surrealism* (New York: The Noonday Press, 1959), p. 125.
10. *Ibid.*, p. 154.
11. Breton, *What Is Surrealism?*, p. 25.

lemma in which the Surrealists found themselves. Though petite bourgeoisie in origin, they were artists who were strongly tempted to intervene, through their art, in the political struggle of their time. They were handicapped by their lack of experience and expertise in the field of politics; they were on the whole ill-informed. Besides, they were engaged in an all-out campaign of repudiation and had no time for taking up issues that were extraneous to their creative calling. Hostile to the world of acquisitive greed and profit-making, they refused to compromise with economic necessity. Their revolt was directed

> against the whole series of intellectual, moral and social obligations that continually and from all sides weigh down upon man and crush him.[12]

Their revulsion was aroused specifically by vulgar rationalism and superficial logic, which Breton believed caused the outbreak of war and the murderous passions that civilization approved and even rewarded. The Surrealists protested against the imposition of civic duties as moral imperatives; they questioned the sanctity of the family unit. Like the beat generation in the fifties, they rejected the social ethic of work. The only thing worth saving as civilization was being destroyed in the Gehenna of war is the creative ideal, the love of poetry and art.

"Manifesto of Surrealism" (1924) defended the autonomy of the artist and formulated the aesthetic aims of the movement. "I believe," Breton wrote, "in the future resolution of these two states, dream and reality, which are seemingly so contradictory, into a kind of absolute reality, a *surreality*. . . ."[13] Breton had discovered the method that would make it possible for him to give free rein to his fantasies and to compose monologues that sprang spontaneously from the unconscious, without interference on his part. Together with Soupault, he developed a technique for tapping the unconscious.[14] He defined Surrealism as follows:

12. *Ibid.,* pp. 45-46.
13. André Breton, *Manifestoes of Surrealism,* trans. Richard Seaver and Helen R. Lane (Ann Arbor, Mich.: The University of Michigan Press, 1969), p. 14.
14. See the essay on "André Breton and Philippe Soupault," in J. H. Matthews, *Theatre in Dada and Surrealism,* p. 26.

Psychic automatism in its pure state, by which one proposes to express—verbally, by means of the written word, or in any other manner—the actual functioning of thought.[15]

Then came the startling, unexpected announcement that the Surrealists had joined the Communist Party. This marriage of incompatibles did not last long. The "Second Manifesto of Surrealism" (1930) reaffirmed the aesthetic principles on which Surrealism was based and, like the magazines *La Révolution surréaliste* and *Le Surréalisme au service de la révolution,* retained its new faith in Marx without disclaiming the immense debt it owed Freud. "Everything tends to make us believe," the Manifesto read, "that there exists a certain point of the mind at which life and death, the real and the imagined, past and future, the communicable and the incommunicable, high and low, cease to be perceived as contradictions" (p. 123). Surrealism endeavors to transcend the distinction "between the beautiful and the ugly, true and false, good and evil" (p. 125). Committed to a philosophy "of total revolt, of sabotage according to rule," Surrealism proclaimed that "it still expects nothing save from violence" (p. 125). While exalting the potentialities of the dream, it continued to fire broadsides at the trinity worshiped by the members of the Establishment: the family, country, and religion. The "Second Manifesto" argued that the method of dialectical materialism did not invalidate the original contributions made by the Surrealists. They were willing to accept the doctrine of historical materialism, but they insisted on including one proviso: "provided that communism does not look upon us merely as so many strange animals intended to be exhibited strolling about and gaping suspiciously in its ranks" (p. 142). If they were treated as comrades, there would be no question of their loyalty to the Revolution. But their experience with the Communist Party was thoroughly disillusioning. Breton was subjected to a series of intensive interrogations. He was forced to defend Surrealism against the absurd charge that "it was essentially a political movement with a strong anticommunist and counter-revolutionary orientation" (p. 142). The professional Communists regarded Breton as the least desirable intellectual

15. Breton, *Manifestoes of Surrealism;* p. 26.

to be recruited to the revolutionary cause. He was required, of all things, to prepare a statistical report on the Italian situation, the volume of steel and coal being produced. He was sternly warned not to get involved in ideological disputes. Breton reacted in a predictable manner: *"I couldn't do it"* (p. 123). Those Surrealists who had followed Breton's example and joined the Communist Party could not restrain their indignation when their freedom as poets and artists was arbitrarily revoked; they were under secret orders. They were supposed to obey.

Despite the rebuffs they had to endure at the hands of the Party bureaucracy in France, the Surrealists did not precipitately abandon their political commitment, but at the same time they stubbornly held their ground when the question of Surrealism vis-à-vis Marxism arose. Under prodding and pressure from "the comrades," they displayed no inclination to change their mind about the intrinsic character and accomplishments of Surrealism. They were proud of its amazing achievement. The spread of the movement throughout the cultural centers of the world testified to its universal appeal and assured its ultimate worth. In response to questions put to him in 1928, Breton said that he did not believe it was possible at present to create a literature or art that would give expression to the aspirations of the working class. In "Political Position of Surrealism" (1935), he denounces a decree that compels the revolutionary to submit to the judgment of the cadre of Party leaders in the Soviet Union. Breton lashed out mercilessly at the servile cult of Stalinism. In "Political Position of Today's Art," a lecture he delivered in Prague in 1935, he protested vigorously against the regimentation of the arts in the Soviet Union under the baleful dictatorship of Stalin. There is considerable evidence to support the contention that "the political expression would appear to be anarchism. . . . And Breton links the exercise of the imagination not with order or harmony but with anarchy."[16]

In 1936 Breton defended the rightness of the steps he had taken in the mid-twenties in allying Surrealism with the Communist movement, even though it turned out badly. The Surrealists refused to renounce their faith in the omnipotence of the dream or to forgo their experimental use of the

16. Eugene Goodheart, *Culture and the Radical Conscience* (Cambridge, Mass.: Harvard University Press, 1973), p. 134.

method of psychic automatism. They could not swallow the Marxist doctrine of universal determinism and they would not conform to the ideological prescriptions of the Party. Breton scornfully rebutted the vulgar, utilitarian argument that poetry, like all art, should become an instrument of propaganda. As Goodheart remarks:

> The fact is that the imagination to which the surrealists were honestly committed is profoundly antipathetic to the political ideals they upheld as Bolsheviks: the liberation of the proletariat and the creation of a new communal life.[17]

The Surrealists retained their faith in inspiration and the alchemy of dreams, and this faith was diametrically opposed to a Marxist system of thought that was rational and deterministic in content. As Breton says: "It is only too certain that an activity such as ours, owing to its particularizations, cannot be pursued within the limits of any one of the existing revolutionary organizations. . . ."[18]

The contradiction between the aesthetic ideals of the Surrealists and their political commitment to a Party that demanded *total* compliance on the part of its members—that contradiction was not resolved. It could not be resolved so long as the Surrealists persisted in their avant-garde, anarchistic heresies, and they had no intention of giving up their creative mission as Surrealists. In the first issue of *La Révolution surréaliste* (dated December 1, 1925), this statement appeared: "Now that 'knowledge' has been brought to trial and condemned, and 'intelligence' is at a discount, the dream and the dream alone can provide the freedom that is man's due."[19]

When the Kharkov Conference officially adopted the principles of Socialist realism, the Surrealists sharply attacked this doctrine on the ground that it endorsed a narrow and restrictive conception of reality. There was surely a place and legitimate function for poetry even if it did not concern itself with the class struggle. Communism based itself on reason and the scientific method, whereas Surrealism glorified the irrational and the Dionysian voices of the unconscious.[20]

17. *Ibid.*, p. 136.
18. Breton, *What Is Surrealism?*, p. 89.
19. Quoted in Patrick Waldberg, *Surrealism*, trans. Stuart Gilbert (Geneva, Switzerland: Albert Skirra, 1962), p. 18.
20. "Because he proclaims that life is art and that life-as-a-work-of art is its own justification, the consistent surrealist must of necessity oppose society's [or the

There were a number of damaging defections from the ranks of the Surrealists. Tristan Tzara in 1935 gave up his adherence to the Surrealist aesthetic and pledged his full allegiance to the revolutionary movement. "He is no longer the exponent of a dadaist, anarcho-revolutionary protest."[21] He went so far as to say that "nothing can be valuable except that which can be put into the context of Marxism."[22] Now he believed in direct action that would transcend the limits of the creative life. He must do his share to change the world and join in the triumphant march of progress. Even before Tzara made his move, Louis Aragon deserted the Surrealist camp for good and announced his return to "reality" as interpreted by dialectical materialism.

> Surrealism, inasmuch as it had legitimacy, was a desperate attempt to pass beyond the negation of Dada and to reconstruct, beyond it, a new reality. An idealistic attitude which went towards reality instead of departing therefrom and which contained its own condemnation: the surrealists themselves pronounced it the day they declared themselves materialists. This meant putting the surrealist, Hegelian dialectic on its feet. They were not able to accept Marxism except with their lips; they did not in any way change their methods. More than that, they claimed to add to Marxism . . . the theories of Freud."[23]

Aragon, in the fervor inspired by his political conversion, blamed the surrealists for their incapacity to become full-fledged logical materialists. He bids them break with the dead past and urges them to emulate the example set by Mayakovsky, the agitator and propagandist of the Russian Revolution. and he then hails with joy "the slogan of Soviet literature: Socialist realism."[24]

Communist critics at the time concentrated their fire on the Surrealist renegades. Paul Nizan in 1934 denounced their reactionary ideas and literary method. Those realists who still

Communist Party's] demands for conformity, which implies the acceptance of a discipline imposed from without and denies the uniqueness of the work of art that each individual, whether consciously or otherwise, is in the process of acting out." Herbert S. Gershman, *The Surrealist Revolution in France* (Ann Arbor, Mich.: The University of Michigan Press, 1969), p. 10.

21. Elmer Peterson, *Tristan Tzara* (New Brunswick, N. J.: Rutgers University Press, 1971), p. 132.

22. *Ibid.*, p. 132.

23. Louis Aragon, "The Return to Reality," *International Literature* no. 1 (1936), p. 103.

24. *Ibid.*, p. 105.

possess some remnant of common sense and respond to the call of conscience are repenting the romantic follies of their past and lending their support to the embattled proletariat.

Others continue their sterile pleasures, their dreams and the analysis of their dreams. They cut themselves off more and more from the real world where war and Fascism threaten. They allow the reactionary elements within themselves to take the lead, elements which sur-realism, final form of bourgeois poetics always had latent within it. They lose themselves in the world of fancy.[25]

The Surrealists are stigmatized as saboteurs who play into the hands of the enemy; decadent bourgeois intellectuals, they are ripe for the ideological infection of Fascism.[26] Sartre castigates the Surrealists as irresponsible Bohemians who represented the pole of absolute negation.[27]

Through all the vicissitudes of his stormy career, André Breton kept his integrity; he would not yield to the pressure of economic necessity nor choose the lesser of two evils. He rebelled against a social system that forced a man to devote the major part of his life to the dull routine of work. He had passed through a difficult period of self-doubt when he questioned the *raison d'être* of art. During the First World War he had met Jacques Vaché in a military hospital where the latter lay wounded:

wounded in mind more than in body, Vaché was, in his rebellion against society, the embodiment of Lautréamont and the Marquis de Sade combined, and in his escape through absinthe he brought back Alfred Jarry.... Although Breton was born too late to meet Jarry in person, he had a substitute image in Vaché.[28]

25. Paul Nizan, "French Literature Today," *International Literature* no. 5 (1934), p. 142.
26. Paul Nizan, who had been a member of the Communist Party for twelve years, sent in his resignation in September 1939, after the Hitler-Stalin pact had been signed. Because of his apostasy, the Communists were resolved to consign his name to oblivion. He was killed by a shell in the war, but his death was not enough to silence his enemies. The Communists accused him of having sold out and called him a traitor. See Jean-Paul Sartre, "Paul Nizan," *Situations*, trans. Benita Eisler (Greenwich, Conn.: Fawcett Publications, 1966), pp. 82-83. See also W. D. Redfern, *Paul Nizan: Committed Literature in a Conspirational World* (Princeton, N. J.: Princeton University Press, 1972).
27. "For Sartre, literature can have only one function, to serve in the war of liberation against social injustice and class oppression, and only one attitude, total responsible commitment to the revolution." Gershman, *The Surrealist Revolution in France*, p. 118.
28. Anna Balakian, *André Breton* (New York: Oxford University Press, 1971), p. 23.

Vaché was a liberator, an iconoclast, a rebel who held in contempt all that society held sacred: success, wealth, power. He laughed in derision at the spectacle that civilized life presented: the unmitigated absurdity of a whole world engaged in mass slaughter. He scorned the profession of poetry and relied on the counter-defense of "black humor." Breton, who still cherished a number of illusions, was impressed by Vaché's utter rejection of literature.[29] Vaché committed suicide in 1919; his death was as absurd as the life he had lived.[30] He taught Breton that the writer must not become a captive of the essentially false notion that literature is more important than life.

Breton became involved in politics early in his career. No literary movement, however arcane its aesthetic philosophy, is completely untouched by the world of politics, and Surrealism is no exception. The Surrealists, unlike the Dadaists, did not give free vent to their anarchistic impulses. Not motivated by Dada's destructive rage against all social institutions, the Surrealists engaged in specific acts of protest against injustice. They condemned the evils of colonialism and criticized the war being fought in Morocco. Breton believed in the teaching of Marxism but registered a number of reservations. What would the workers stand to gain if in the end they were better fed but their minds were allowed to stagnate? Why assume that matter must of necessity take precedence over idealism? Breton heartily approved of the struggle Communism waged to eliminate the curse of poverty, but there was no justification for restricting the individual to economic matters alone and neglecting his existential needs,

29. "Breton himself acknowledged that Vaché influenced him profoundly. "It little matters that Vaché may have been a juvenile dandy, a foppish. Anglophile, a frustrated painter. His alibis became archetypal virtues. As Breton would have it, Vaché promoted life beyond its conventions by means of masks, confounding theater with life itself, like Jarry's Ubu, whose very improbability keeps him alive. Being an outright marionette, he thus dodges the traps of illusion and verisimilitude. Vaché was the first to insist on the importance of acts,' wrote Breton. Jerking from 'act' to 'act' like some human non sequitir, he acted out his instincts, whose only law was their absolute lack of law. In other words. Vaché, supremely the actor, became apotheosized as a nature god, a *force de la nature* whose manifold guises and apparent illogic ultimately signify his glorious self-coincidence." Frederick Brown, "Creation versus Literature: Breton and the Surrealist movement," in *Modern French Criticism*, ed. John K. Simon (Chicago and London: The University of Chicago Press, 1972), pp. 124-25.
30. Balakian, *André Breton*, p. 25.

his spiritual and creative aspirations. As Anna Balakian points out:

> Breton wanted to make it clear that in opposing committed literature he was at the same time equally adverse to the art for art's sake philosophy. He repudiated an attitude of withdrawal on the part of the artist from the scene of political action, but the role of the artist within the political arena should not be, in his opinion, the same as that of the political man.[31]

Such a critical and indeed intransigent attitude was bound to antagonize the Communists. Breton never regretted his decision to leave the Communist Party, but this did not mean that he lost interest in the sphere of politics. Between 1935 and 1946 his political activities increased. What went on in the Soviet Union, the terrorism unleashed in the name of Communism, called forth his unqualified censure. He was particularly aroused by the precarious situation of the writer in Russia, his loss of freedom and the right to dissent under the dictatorship set up by Stalin. He was hostile to Stalinism. He was not fooled by the fake Moscow trials. He saw that the Revolution had become corrupted. He continued to stress his belief that the artist must not become the tool of a political system or political party. The artist must not allow his creative gift to be exploited for political ends.

The Surrealists had no aptitude for politics. Their experiment in collaborating with the Communists failed dismally.[32] They did not change the course of events and they contributed virtually nothing to political theory.[33] They were rebels who wished, as a matter of conscience, to participate in the revolutionary movement, and their brief commitment to Communism seemed to give "some positive justification to an

31. *Ibid.,* pp. 82-83.
32. "There was much, indeed, to prevent the merging of Surrealist revolt with Marxist Revolution: the Surrealists' intense individualism; their scorn for material reality and its laws in the exploration of the *surréalite;* their contempt for the cult of work; their essentially artistic temperament; and so forth." Clifford Browder, *André Breton* (Geneva, Switzerland: Librarie Droz, 1967), p. 119.
33. Maurice Nadeau points out that the writer, the poet, the painter "succeed" by virtue of the works they produce, but, alas, their creative achievement changed nothing in the world around them. What they do achieve is "a personal adventure, often dramatic, sometimes tragic. . . . Whether it finds its end in itself or leads to silence, on the essential point it is sealed by defeat. . . . There is no great writer . . . who does not die in despair." Nadeau, *The History of Surrealism,* p. 226.

idealistic revolt which had been turning in a vacuum, propelled only by the energy and passion it consumed."[34] They had little to contribute that the Communists could use. "Surrealist pamphleteering was predominantly destructive because Surrealist politics remained what they had been from the beginning: the politics of protest. Satire and insult were its weapons. It proceeded by contradiction and not by argument. . . ."[35] They had little in common with professional Communists. For them art came first, the political commitment second. The Communist Party in France distrusted them from the start.[36] Christopher Caudwell branded the Surrealist as "the final bourgeois."[37]

Though their involvement in the Communist movement taught the Surrealists a valuable lesson in disillusionment, they did not give up the political struggle.[38] Breton later gave his support to Trotsky and the Fourth International. The Surrealists were impelled to act by a vision and a faith that exalted life above literature and art. They did not want to escape from reality or avoid the challenge of life.[39]

34. *The Left-Wing Intellectuals Between the Wars, 1919-1939*, ed. Walter Laquer and George L. Mosse (New York: Harper & Row, 1966), p. 9.
35. *Ibid.*, p. 13.
36. The Surrealists in England were not under Breton's influence or control; they followed their own path in their approach to radical politics. See Paul C. Ray, *The Surrealist Movement in England* (Ithaca, N. Y. and London: Cornell University Press, 1971).
37. Caudwell, *Illusion and Reality*, p. 253.
38. For a fully detailed account of the Surrealist venture into politics, see the chapter entitled "In the Arena: Surrealism and Politics," in Herbert S. Gershman, *The Surrealist Revolution in France*, pp. 80-116.
39. "When the Surrealists turn to dreams for inspiration, theirs is not an act of withdrawal from life. The prestige attributed to dreaming has in Surrealism nothing to do with escape. Nor is it indicative of nostalgia. Evasion is quite foreign to Surrealism, which has as its purpose to come to terms with life, not to turn away from it." J. H. Matthews, *An Introduction to Surrealism* (University Park, Pa.: The Pennsylvania State University Press, 1965), p. 65.

10

The Politics of Madness

1. *The Semantics of Madness*

It is not without significance, as I indicated at the end of chapter 8, that in France the events of May 1968 were reminiscent or imitative of the provocations initiated by the Dadaists a half century ago. The madness of Dada was methodical, deliberate, a series of shock tactics administered to the complacent bourgeois audiences in a time of war. Today it is assumed that such an outbreak of insanity is caused in the main by a society that is mechanized, technologically efficent, indifferent to human values, barbarously repressive in its efforts to coerce its citizens to conform to its mandates. Viewed in this light, insanity represents a reaction against an intolerable situation; it brings into the open the criminal nature of modern society, its emphasis on the ethic of conformity. The madman is then looked upon with sympathy as the victim of repression; actually he is the exponent of sanity and reason, whereas society is the source of the irrational, of unreason at its worst.

Though Trilling sharply attacks the cult that reveres the madman and exposes the fallaciousness of the belief that "insanity is a state of human existence which is to be esteemed for its commanding authenticity,"[1] a number of writers in our time have preferred to regard society and the State as the villain in the melodrama of collective dementia. It is social reality, they charge, that is dehumanized and hypocritical in its insistence on obedience to its utilitarian business standards. Hence the hipster espouses and at times acts out a method of revolt that the authorities denounce as sheer madness. He lets himself go the limit, he retreats to the underworld of the Negro, where he is able to release his instincts and satisfy his sexual needs. He turns to drugs as a means of intensifying and enriching his sense of life. He opts for madness as a way out of the wasteland and the kind of death-in-life existence it offers him. Like Alfred Jarry in France, Carl Solomon was venerated in the United States as a culture hero, for he had crossed over the border that separates the sane from the insane. In his "Report from the Asylum" he describes his experiences as a patient in a psychiatric hospital, where he was given shock therapy. For him, insanity

> is the ultimate retreat, more insulating than heroin, weed or bop. In a world where the "upward and onward" assurance of positivism always rings false, madness is the most sure way (next to death) of breaking the clock, stopping time, and splintering life into a stream of acutely felt sensations that impose no demands and bring no consciousness of guilt.[2]

That is how Carl Solomon leaves behind him the rat race of the competitive world of business and industry and enters a hallucinated world of madness. He identifies himself with the character K. in Kafka's fiction. The insulin treatment to which he is subjected marks a radical departure from the Kafka plot, for here, in the hospital wards, the authorities in power are not malign but benevolent. Solomon pictures for us the visions he beholds, the coma that was brought on by the insulin, the terrifying sense that he was an inhabitant of the void. The uncanny transformations wrought in him by shock therapy led him to believe in miracles. Solomon quotes Artaud, who also was given shock therapy while confined in an

1. Lionel Trilling, *Sincerity and Authenticity* (Cambridge, Mass.: Harvard University Press, 1972), p. 168.
2. *The Beat Generation and the Angry Young Men,* ed. Gene Feldman and Max Gartenberg (New York: Dell Publishing Co., 1958), p. 171.

asylum. In an essay on Van Gogh, Artaud remarks that a lunatic "is a man who has preferred to become what is socially understood as mad rather than forfeit a certain superior idea of human honor. . . ."[3]

The members of the beat generation did not glorify the extreme cases of madness. They knew that the best minds of their generation were destroyed by madness. If Allen Ginsberg dedicated *Howl* to Solomon, it was to pay homage to this man: his extraordinary courage, his exploration of the luridly lighted nether world of hallucinations, his journey through the inferno of madness. Jack Kerouac and Allen Ginsberg, William S. Burroughs and Ken Kesey were aware of the destructive, life-negating power of unrestrained madness. The schizophrenic retreats into mutism; he welcomes the silence that cuts him off from the unprovoked aggression of the world of men. If some writers composed a hymn in praise of madness, what they had in mind was its creative potential. In a number of instances, the mask of madness they put on was causally related to their obsession with the oppressive mystery of time, their fear of nuclear annihilation, their vision of the absurd. "Like Samuel Beckett they create their work in a void of silence. Their madness, in brief, is metaphysical in character."[4] Unlike Dostoevski and Nietzsche, these alienated writers deliberately exploit their "madness" for creative purposes. "The 'madness' of the lost writers of our time voices the despair they feel in a world abandoned by God."[5]

In the past, when Western culture regarded madness as a dangerous outbreak of the irrational, reason was held to be the sanctified, unassailable norm. In exalting madness as the Muse of the modern age, the plenary source of Dionysian inspiration, the writer as rebel failed to consider madness as a psychotic affliction. He did not stop to inquire whether madness could shape a genuine work of art. Madness, like neurosis, was not conducive to creative fulfillment. Even if a writer manages to produce a work of art while suffering

3. *Ibid.,* p. 180.
4. Charles I. Glicksberg, "Forms of Madness," *Arizona Quarterly* 17 (Spring 1961): 53.
5. *Ibid.* See "The Lure of Madness," in Charles I. Glicksberg, *Modern Literary Perspectivism* (Dallas, Tex.: Southern Methodist University Press, 1970), pp. 46-50. Seel also "Revolt and Madness," in Charles I. Glicksberg, *Literature and Society* (The Hague, Netherlands: Martinus Nijhoff, 1972), pp. 57-71.

from madness, it does not follow that madness was the decisive factor. The madman is at the mercy of his hallucinations and is in too disoriented a condition to achieve the order and unity required of a work of art. The fact that "from the time of Hölderlin and Nerval," the number of writers "who have 'succumbed' to madness has increased"[6] proves nothing. The artist stricken by madness struggles desperately against this fate, for his madness, as it grows in severity, incapacitates him totally for the creative task. Indeed, madness, as it extends its range of power, results in the supersession of art. As Foucault emphatically declares: *"where there is a work of art, there is no madness. . . ."*[7] Nevertheless, the phenomenology of madness, when it is integrated within a work of art, brings the world into question, for it confronts the mystery of being with the specter of nonbeing.

The medical concept of mental illness has consistently distorted the character of "the madman." He evokes a feeling of horror and encounters not only incomprehension but ridicule and persecution. He is laughed at because of his irrational behavior. Laing declares:

> The "committed" person labeled as patient, and specifically as "schizophrenic," is degraded from full existential and legal status as a human agent and responsible person to someone no longer in possession of his own definition of himself, unable to retain his own possessions, precluded from the exercise of his discretion as to whom he meets, what he does.[8]

Many psychiatrists, as Laing maintained, were blind to the inner meaning of mental illness, and their patients reacted to their ministrations with mistrust and resentment. In the essay on Van Gogh from which I quoted Artaud's definition of the lunatic, Artaud goes on to attack both psychiatry and psychiatrists. He wrote that "a vicious society has invented psychiatry to defend itself from the investigations of certain superior lucid minds whose intuitive powers were disturbing it," and that "every psychiatrist is a low-down son-of-a-bitch."[9] The psychiatrists did not comprehend the crucial role anxiety

6. Michel Foucault, *Madness and Civilization*, trans. Richard Howard (New York: Random House, 1965), p. 286.
7. *Ibid.*, pp. 188-89.
8. R. D. Laing, *The Politics of Experience* (New York: Ballantine Books, 1971), p. 122.
9. *The Beat Generation and the Angry Young Men*, p. 180.

plays in the etiology of madness. Anxiety is not in itself a psychopathological symptom. It is all a matter of degree. Anxiety arises in man when his encounter with the world fills him with a presentiment he cannot shake off that he is in the presence of danger. He begins to fear that he is threatened with extinction. He faces the gulf of nothingness, what Ludwig Binswanger describes as "the intolerable, dreadful, 'naked horror.' "[10] Existential analysis, which drew its leading insights from the writings of Kierkegaard, Kafka, Dostoevski, Nietzsche, and Heidegger, interprets mental illness as a meaningful effort to deal constructively with the world of time; the patient struggles to overcome the dread reality of nothingness.

Both the madman and the neurotic search for a way out of this appalling dilemma. They try to commit themselves to a cause, an ideal, a movement, that will save them from the nihilistic conclusion that vertical transcendence is sheer illusion, for then they are tempted to end it all. Each can cross the frontier that leads to madness or take his own life. Before he will consent to let the curtain fall on the last act of his life (what shall he call it: tragedy, comedy, farce?), he will continue his anguished quest for a solution. Unfortunately, in his feverish desire to save himself before it is too late, he chooses an ideal he cannot hope to reach. If he is defeated, he retires precipitately within the fastness of the self, where no one can do him harm. When he is at last ensconced behind the locked doors of his psychic hideout, the self ceases to exist and is replaced by schizophrenic autism.[11]

We have seen how Artaud persisted in his creative efforts, despite the unremitting pain he had to endure and the besetting fear that he was going insane. He was determined to wrest the secret from the dark primordial depths of being, to discover the magic formula that would enable him to comprehend the hieroglyphic intimations of the Absolute. The poetry he wrote testifies to the exhausting intensity of his inner struggle. What gave him the courage and the stamina to survive this ordeal was the knowledge that this siege of mad-

10. Rollo May, Ernest Angel, and Henri F. Ellenberg, eds., *Existence* (New York: Basic Books, 1958), p. 205.
11. "Where man merely shuts himself off from the world, where he just retreats in grudge and anger, suspicion or scorn, he still exists—as a grudging, laughing, distrustful, or scornful self." Ludwig Binswanger, *Being-in-the-World*, trans. Jacob Neddleman (New York and London: Basic Books, 1963), p. 288.

ness would somehow shape his destiny. He wanted to paint the fantastic landscape of "the reality" he beheld, to give an account of the sea-monsters he grappled with in the sea of his unconscious.

Unlike the Surrealists, Kafka, who was "mad" in his own inimitable way, did not rely on psychic automatism to provide inspirational material or experiment with methods to set his creative unconscious in motion. He did not simply transcribe the dreams that acted out their confused drama of desire on the night-shrouded stage of his mind. He was critical of the psychoanalysts and their mechanical dissection of the symbols that bob up on the surface of the dream. Nor did he have much faith in the therapeutic power of the Freudians.

> He did not share the view of psychoanalytically oriented physicians and poets that man's inner life could be altogether clarified by means of dream analysis, and that a radical cure of emotional and psychic disease could thereby be effected. For him all physical and psychological disease had in turn its basis in a single disease that has its exemplar in the "nature" of man whose "predicament" consists of his being unable to find absolute certainty everywhere; in the last analysis, herein lies the origin of his flight into neurosis.[12]

The world that Kafka depicts is not only surrealistically distorted but incomprehensible. It is not only incomprehensible but "insane." This distortion that projects images of the grotesque and the absurd, this disconcerting vision of a reality that baffles human understanding, this "madness" that lies at the heart of being, is not the psychological creation of the protagonist. It is the world around him that is insane. Kafka uses the technique of distortion in order to reveal types of madness that people accept as normal. By skillfully exploiting this method of portraying his fantastically distorted world as normal, Kafka succeeds in communicating "his sense of the even madder fact that madness itself is not recognized."[13]

2. *The Psychopath as Savior*

The dominant tendency today is to subsume all things beneath the sun, the ridiculous as well as the sublime, under

---

12. Wilhelm Emrich, *Franz Kofka,* trans. Sheema Zeben Buehne (New York: Frederick Ungar Publishing Co., 1968), p. 34.
13. Gunther Anders, *Kafka,* trans. A. Steer and A. K. Thorlby (London: Nowes & Bowes, 1960), p. 9.

the all-inclusive heading of politics. If it is true that all human activities are connected somehow with the sphere of politics, then the life of "the madman," whether confined in a mental hospital or left free to pursue his mythomanias, must be considered of little or no importance. He makes no impact on the world, even when he assumes the guise of Savior. His commitment to the ethos of the psychopath is without consequences.

Undeterred by such negative strictures, Alan Harrington undertakes to rehabilitate the ambiguous and disturbing figure of the psychopath. Like Norman Mailer, he is opposed to the honorific values of the Establishment. In his novel *The Revelations of Doctor Modesto,* he satirizes the incredibly inane and ugly side of American life and describes the state of satori that can be achieved through the purifying experience of madness. In *The Immortalist,* Harrington rejects with a blast of Promethean defiance the fate of death that overwhelms all mortal creatures. It contains his proposed solution: a guaranteed system of immortality. Now, in *Psychopaths,* he argues that the best way to break free of the pernicious influence of a sick civilization is to cultivate a form of madness that will help the individual to attain a measure of freedom. The psychopath can be recognized by his downright refusal to obey the laws of a bureaucratic hierarchy that seeks to crush his spirit and abolish his individuality. He yields to the impulse of the moment. He is capable of giving way to a mood of violence. He will even commit murder when the occasion calls for it.

In "The White Negro," Mailer enthusiastically espouses the cause of the rebel, the hipster, who welcomes the psychopathic streak in his nature, since it liberates him from a society in love with death. That is how he manages to affirm life even if, in order to achieve this end, he must go underground and turn criminal. Mailer defines the hipster as the man who has taken over the code of the black man. Mailer attempts to justify the psychopathic character of the hipster and defends his acts of violence. It is the hipster's quest for the good orgasm that transforms him into a sexual outlaw. That is how he can remain physically healthy, free to condemn and avoid those ideals and institutions which demand that he suppress and sublimate his sexual energy. It was the lowly and despised Negro who explored different ways of defying or circumventing the sexual taboos of puritanical America. The hipster, who is in full rapport with the imperatives of his unconscious, is not to be hindered in his craving for sexual freedom.

Harrington, like Mailer, questions whether the psychopath's behavior is really abnormal. Not when it is viewed as a reaction against a society that is in the grip of anomie. His revolt against the gods and goals of such a decadent social order is an expression of his moral health. In some radical quarters, this transvaluation of values has been adopted as a viable creed. (For example, Lenny Pincus, the picaresque hero of *American Mischief,* admires the psychopath and wishes to emulate his behavior. He has made up his mind to kill Norman Mailer, whose *Advertisements for Myself* he has read.) The hipster, the psychopath without God, believes only in the reality of the present moment. Amoral, unconscionable, irreligious, the psychopath has become the paradigmatic anti-hero of our time, the savior of society. Harrington pictures the age as calling for redemption by such charismatic and disreputable leaders. The times are searching for an idealistic embodiment of the psychopath as savior. It is possible that we may come to regard the neurotic inhibitions of the middle class as obsolete, "and abrupt, unrestrained, and conscienceless behavior as a means to mental health."[14] To be sure, some dismiss all this as meaningless nonsense. The psychopath, after all, suffers from a serious illness and is not to be set up as a spiritual model.

What this seems to stress is that today psychopathic behavior cannot be judged fairly as a predetermined case of mental disease. Such types of behavior are not restricted to juvenile delinquents, sexual deviants, and confirmed criminals such as Genet portrays in his plays and novels. The hedonism of the psychopath is not in the least affected by the disapproval of society. He will not restrain his impulses. These psychopathic rebels, Harrington speculates, may, in their single-minded quest for paradisal pleasures, well be the ones to save us from the fate of annihilation. Thus the unconscious wisdom of the race manifests itself in nihilistic outbreaks of violence, in behavior that flouts the law of the land and is opposed to the cult of sublimation or the spirit of rational control. Harrington theorizes that the psychopaths

14. Alan Harrington, *Psychopaths* (New York: Simon and Schuster, 1972), p. 37.

spawned by the evolutionary process may be able to prevent the destruction of mankind by atomic fallout and the lethal pollution of the earth, the atmosphere, and the seven seas. "Could our mind," Harrington asks, "be passing through a plague of the spirit that, destructive as it may seem, might purge the overcrowded, gassed, smog-stricken society and somehow make it better?"[15]

The beat generation drew its followers largely from the lunatic fringe: they consisted for the most part of nonconformists, anarchists, libertarians, drug addicts, homosexuals, Lesbians, and drop-outs from school or society. They flaunted their defiance of American mores by sporting a beard, wearing sandals, dispensing with neckties, smoking marijuana, attending jazz sessions, and choosing to live a life of poverty. They feel alienated from a society that used the atom bomb against the civilian population of Hiroshima and Nagasaki, a society interested primarily in gratifying the acquisitive instinct. The beat writers were not a new breed of Bohemians; they gave expression to their deeply rooted individuality. Though the members of the beat generation adhered to no fixed body of principles, they evinced as a group a distrust of collectivism. "They share no common platform, believe in no social or political panaceas. What concerns them most is how best to live." They wish to live "at the highest pitch of intensity and self-awareness."[16] Their nonconformity is frequently passive in character, reflecting a nihilism that negates the thrust of ambition and debunks the national myth of success. It is futile, many of them are convinced, to put forth any effort.

If the Marxist is correct in his assumption that no one can throw off the responsibility of participating in the political issues of his time, that each person is implicated in one way or another in the socioeconomic struggle regardless of his wishes, then the withdrawal of the beat writers from the conflicts of their day, their indifference to politics, were essentially political actions, though negatively so. The Marxist consistently argues that to remain aloof from the life of society, unconcerned and uncommitted, is in effect to support the status quo. But the apolitical stance of the beat writers was

15. *Ibid.*, p. 200.
16. John Clellon Holmes, *Nothing More to Declare* (New York: E. P. Dutton & Co., 1967), p. 110.

perfectly in keeping with their world outlook. Under no conceivable circumstances can we picture writers like Ken Kesey, Kerouac, Clellon Holmes, and Allen Ginsberg deciding to work for the Revolution. They had no desire to overthrow society. And the psychopathic "heroes" they honored kept faith with the beat vision of life; they refused to let themselves be used up in the demented race for status and success. The legendary figure of Cassady is the prototype on whom Dean Moriarty, in Kerouac's novel *On the Road,* is based. Cassady, like his fictional incarnation, qualifies "as a complete psychopath. . . ."[17] Kerouac portrays Dean as the rebel who will not bear the galling yoke of social conformity. What matters most to him is to experience as often as he can the peak moments of ecstasy that sex, drugs, and jazz make possible. Unfortunately, these ineffable states of euphoria do not last, and when the ecstasy has left the beat rebel, he is the victim of excruciating boredom. The disenchanting truth is that the beats, "always living in the present, were much of the time catastrophically bored."[18]

Cassady is the psychopath, or saint, who is the chronic prey of boredom. To save himself from such a fate, he keeps constantly on the go. Despite his sophistication as a hipster, he invariably makes a costly mistake that lands him in jail. "The glamor of living by the moment, digging only the moment, impaired his judgment."[19]

In *On the Road,* Dean Moriarty, who appears under different names in other novels by Kerouac, is an idealized romantic who lives solely for the sake of sex. He wanders restlessly over the face of the United States, speeding in stolen cars, determined to dig all of life, to capture the essence of time. Kerouac describes him as "simply a youth tremendously excited with life, and though he was a con-man, he was only conning because he wanted so much to live. . . ."[20] He is the mystic, the mad one, the possessed, filled with the need to live fully, to be "saved." He has been sentenced to serve time in prison and spent years in poolrooms and in libraries, but his past has not made him bitter. He steals cars not for profit, only for the joyrides; there is no taint of viciousness in his

17. Harrington, *Psychopaths,* p. 241.
18. *Ibid.,* p. 242.
19. *Ibid.,* p. 243.
20. Jack Kerouac, *On the Road* (New York: The Viking Press, 1959), p. 6.

criminal acts. Here, Kerouac says admiringly, is "a new kind of American saint."[21]

One Flew Over the Cuckoo's Nest, by Ken Kesey, is a scathing protest against the bureaucratic despotism that prevails in many mental hospitals and the strict code of obedience these hospitals demand of the inmates. Any show of resistance on the part of the patient is punished by a variety of means: by shock therapy or by solitary confinement. The story is told from the point of view of the Indian who, for his own protection, pretends to be deaf and dumb. It is he who reveals the incredible cruelties inflicted upon the patients. This half-breed, named Bromden, points out the supreme power of the Combine, which can compel the inmates to obey by subjecting the recalcitrant ones to the "benefits" of intensive shock therapy. Kesey's theme in this novel is that the individual is helpless when pitted against "the machine," which is today everywhere in control.

Then Randle Patrick McMurphy arrives, and disturbing, unprecedented things begin to happen. He had wangled his way out of a work farm and been transferred to this hospital, where the food is of superior quality and where no back-breaking work is required of the inmates. He has been diagnosed as a psychopath because he gets involved in too many fights, and demands that his sexual needs be gratified. Miss Ratched, the Big Nurse, the institutional tyrant, immediately senses that he is a trouble-maker. McMurphy is a rebel who questions the professed ideals of the therapeutic community; he is skeptical of the need to learn how to adjust to the group as a preliminary requirement for being released as cured. He sees what is going on behind the scenes: the Big Nurse is castrating these patients in order to break their will. They are aware of what is being done to them but they are afraid to revolt. They tell McMurphy what the penalty is for not obeying orders: the offender is strapped to a table and then tortured by successive charges of the electro-shock therapy! Given enough of these "treatments," the refractory person becomes disoriented, a mindless idiot, a vegetable. The electricity shot through the skull of the recalcitrant patient is allegedly employed for his own good. Kesey effectively communicates his meaning:

21. *Ibid.,* p. 39.

the true madness, the real dry root of the waste land is not the patient's irrationality, but the deadly order, system, and rationality of the institution. What is normal is perverted and reason becomes madness, while some small hope for salvation lies in the nonrational if not the downright irrational.[22]

Timothy Leary confirms the basic truth of Kesey's indictment: "Today, fifty years after Freud, the average mental hospital in the United States is a Kafkaesque, Orwellian, prison camp. . . ."[23] It is actually more terrifying than Auschwitz or Dachau, because the captors play the role of healers.

Ken Kesey became the acknowledged leader of the hippies. He was more influential than Leary in shaping the hippie culture. He had attended Stanford University in 1960 and was hired as an aide in the psychiatric ward of the Veterans Administration Hospital near the campus. He volunteered to serve as a subject for tests on the use of psychedelic drugs for therapeutic purposes. In the course of these experiments he imbibed a variety of drugs, including mescaline, and psilocybin, and these taught him the secret he was looking for.

Indirectly, that is how he came to write *One Flew Over the Cuckoo's Nest* (1962). After publishing *Sometimes a Great Notion* (1964), he gave up his writing career and became the leader of a group of psychedelic nomads who adopted the name of the Merry Pranksters. In *The Electric Kool-Aid Acid Test,* Tom Wolfe relates the sensational story of Kesey's career as guru of the drug movement. The action begins when Kesey buys a school bus with the proceeds of his first novel, and the Merry Pranksters convert it—wire it for sound, cut a hole in the roof, and paint it in psychedelic colors. Neal Cassady, the number-two Prankster, is the driver of the bus. On the trips they take, each Prankster is free to do his "thing." There are no restrictions. Kesey preaches no religious or moral precepts. "There was no goal of an improved moral order in the world or an improved social order, nothing about salvation and certainly nothing about immortality or the life hereaf-

22. Raymond M. Olderman, *Beyond the Waste Land: A Study of the American Novel in the Nineteen-Sixties* (New Haven and London: Yale University Press, 1972), pp. 39-40.
23. Timothy Leary, *The Politics of Ecstasy* (New York: G. P. Putnam's Sons, 1968), p. 38.

ter."[24] In 1965, the Merry Pranksters rented an old ballroom, the Fillmore, and invited the Haight-Ashbury crowd to join in the acid test. The punch was spiked with LSD. "What Kesey did was to turn the whole district on to LSD."[25]

3. *The Politics of Drugged Ecstasy*

If LSD can help eliminate guilt, hang-ups, hatred, why be upset if a legion of mutants . . . may be taking over and drastically changing our present scene, which, after all, appears in many respects quite sick?[26]

Whether or not the psychedelic revolution would have happened just as it did without him [Timothy Leary] is open to doubt. . . . Dr. Leary had so many qualities that made him just the right man for the moment. He was, among other things, a respected research psychologist and a man unafraid to break the rules and buck the establishment; he was an apostate Catholic who through most of his life nursed an unsatisfied desire to play the role of messiah; he was, in his own way, quite modest, yet willing to do almost anything to publicize his cause and win converts to it; he was utterly sincere and at the same time a bit of a charlatan.[27]

Leary describes in *High Priest* the excitement of discovery that he felt, the sense that his theories and beliefs were confirmed, when he first read Aldous Huxley's *The Doors of Perception* and *Heaven and Hell*. "It was all there," he reported. "All my vision. And more too."[28] He met Huxley and they discussed "how to study and use the consciousness-expanding drugs. . . ."[29] Huxley has not received full credit as a pioneer and propagandist of the psychedelic movement. It was Huxley's work that made Leary realize the potentialities of LSD as a new type of "religion." Huxley disclosed the mystical properties of "mescalin." Taken under the proper circumstances,

24. Tom Wolfe, *The Electric Kool-Aid Acid Test* (New York: Farrar, Straus and Giroux, 1968), p. 127.
25. Bruce Cook, *The Beat Generation* (New York: Charles Scribner's Sons, 1971), p. 200.
26. Harrington, *Psychopaths*, p. 262.
27. Cook, *The Beat Generation*, p. 188.
28. Timothy Leary, *High Priest* (New York: College Notes & Texts, 1968), p. 85.
29. *Ibid.*, p. 65.

this drug is capable of breaking down our ordinary method of perception. Though he warns of the possible undesirable consequences of the mescaline experience, he assures the reader that "the reasonably healthy person knows in advance that . . . mescalin is completely innocuous. . . ."[30] Here, by means of mescaline, the initiate finds it possible to gain the blessed transcendental experience.[31]

Among the members of the beat generation, an important part of the ritual of sex was the use of marijuana, which made them feel intensely alive. Here is a drug, sufficiently mild, that can break down the walls of reserve in those who participate in this social rite; once they get "high" they lose their self-consciousness; their tongue is unloosed, and they achieve authentic communion.

> The Eros is felt in the magic circle of marijuana with far great-er force, as a unifying principle in human relationships, than at any other time except, perhaps, in the mutual metaphysical or-gasm. The magical circle is, in fact, a symbol of and preparation for the metaphysical orgasm.[32]

When "the charge" induced by the ingestion of marijuana courses through his system, the beat feels that he has discov-ered the secret of the universe. Some beat writers say they have composed spontaneous poetry and original prose when they were under the influence of marijuana,[33] though it is

30. Aldous Huxley, *The Doors of Perception* and *Heaven and Hell* (New York: Harper & Row, 1963), p. 54.
31. A nonconformist even in his eclecticism, Aldous Huxley fused in the crucible of his imagination such different and disparate faiths as Buddhism, Yoga, Tao, and the mysticism of the Church, to which he added the "peak-experience" induced by consciousness-expanding drugs (see Aldous Huxley, *The Perennial Philosophy* [New York and London: Harper & Brothers, 1945]). In *Island,* a novel published in 1962, Huxley envisions a utopia that is the ne-gation of the typical scientific or technological utopia. An ideal community has been established, and life in Pala is incredibly good. The Palanese use "the moksha-medicine, the reality-revealer, the truth-and-beauty pill" (Aldous Hux-ley, *Island* [New York and Evanston: Harper & Row, 1962], p. 157). This pill enables even beginners to catch glimpses of the world as it is seen by those freed from the trammels of the ego. The experience they pass through, a genuine mystical revelation, is real and is accompanied by an ineffable sense of joy.
32. Lawrence Lipton, *The Holy Barbarians* (New York: Julian Messner, 1959), p. 171.
33. Those writers who belonged to the beat generation were with few exceptions romantic in their reliance on drugs to keep the flame of "inspiration" burning

fairly obvious that drugs in themselves offer no guarantee of increased creativity.

> There is no guarantee that hallucination, whether induced by trance or drugs, will "bring up" anything more than platitudes and clichés, no matter how "dissociated" or "far-out" the artist may be, unless he possesses an original mind, a great gift and a knowledge of his craft.[34]

William S. Burroughs does not share the belief that the visions called forth by drugs can be used as the germinal stuff of art. He decries the tendency to place writing done under the influence of drugs into a separate and special category.

> I have often heard it said that what is written under the influence of drugs seems to the writer of great worth at the time, whereas examined after the drug wears off it is pretentious nonsense. The same is true of any writing.[35]

Harrington, who was turned on by Timothy Leary and Dick Alpert, who gave him what he felt was a gigantic dose of LSD, passed through a difficult but unforgettable experience. It was like dying and then being reborn. He recalls the quasi-religious spirit of dedication that inspired the early experimenters with LSD. Taking the drug was then a sacramental rite. But these "holy trips" had unfortunate consequences in a number of cases: they resulted in broken mar-

---

brightly. Not heeding Burroughs's warning that "turning on" was not the open sesame to the magical intensification and enrichment of the creative process, they sought to rise above their rational, common-sense self to a supernal state of transcendence that would activate the unconscious to bring forth images of dazzling originality and allow the language to flow with magical spontaneity from the typewriter. Kerouac, the king of the beats, depended on drugs to help him achieve the heights of the creative vision. In the course of his writing career, he consumed benzedrene, marijuana, heroin, cocaine, LSD, and endless quantities of alcohol. He used benzedrene—or "bennies," as they were called—and "enjoyed the kick from bennies so much he got high as often as he could" (Ann Charters, *Kerouac: A Biography* [San Francisco: Straight Arrow Books, 1973], p. 59). This was the beginning of his dependence on drugs. He was using marijuana steadily. His consumption of drugs did not let up. "Each of Kerouac's books was written on something and each of the books has something of the feel of what he was on most as he wrote it" (*ibid.*, p. 166).

34. Lipton, *The Holy Barbarians,* p. 254.
35. Daniel Odier, *The Job: Interviews with William S. Burroughs* (New York: Grove Press, 1970), p. 153.

riages, disrupted careers, neglect of the family, and the imperious rise of new sex cravings. The leaders of the movement were not shaken in their faith; they were convinced the spiritual revolution would manifest itself in time, and "Godless America would become religious again. . . ."[36] The supposedly secure foundations of capitalism would be shaken as the employees of business and industry secretly turned on, and Harrington declares that this is what is actually happening.

In the early sixties Leary and Alpert were confident that these drugs would radically change the nature of man and greatly enhance man's potentialities for growth. Their daring prediction, Harrington assures us, came true. "The psychedelic drugs have *permanently* changed millions of heads—and there isn't any question that they helped to produce a number of the multiple revolutions now sweeping the old world away."[37] Leary and Alpert were fired from Harvard, but their crusading zeal did not lessen. Harrington asserts that Leary freed a whole generation from the curse of conformity. Now Harrington was able to understand the true meaning of "psychopath." These devotees of the drug were driven by a purposive madness to change the world.

Leary was their anointed prophet, a new type of mystic and visionary who preached the gospel of redemption to the American people, but they reacted to his blasphemous appeal with incredulity and indignation. They were outraged by his rash presumption in prescribing these dangerous drugs as the open road to salvation. But Leary was not the kind of man who would be deterred from going ahead with his mission by the threat of imprisonment. The experience of taking the drug, which occurred in August 1960, changed the whole course of his life. He was turned on for good. Come what might, he was determined to make his extraordinary discoveries known to his fellow men so that they, too, might be saved. This "sacramental ritual" of "turning on," which he has undergone (according to his count) several hundred times, yielded "religious revelations as shattering as the first experience."[38] The LSD experiences enables man to gain a deep sense of his identity. Like the beat rebels, Leary rejects

36. Harrington, *Psychopaths*, p. 257.
37. *Ibid.*, p. 258.
38. Leary, *The Politics of Ecstasy*, p. 14.

Freudian therapy as basically a method of brainwashing. Psychoanalysis aims to make the patient "adjust" to his environment. Not only psychoanalysts but their patients as well, Leary remarks, are "unbearably 'dead' and juiceless. . . ." (p. 37). Most patients under treatment resent and resist the analyst's advice to conform.

Leary is a guru who teaches his followers that life is an illusion and that death is equally illusory. The desire to escape from the trap of life is as pointless as the desire to hang on to life at all costs. Leary is certain of only one thing: that the politics of ecstasy will overcome all opposition. The drug scene has led to a religious renaissance. The LSD "kick trip" is a source of spiritual ecstasy and is at the same time "a religious pilgrimage" (p. 353). Leary's "Sermon on the Mount" to the American people is given in the following commandment: If they play the game of life seriously, then they must "turn on, tune in and drop out" (p. 353).

When Leary passed through his first psychedelic experience, he had reached the middle of his life's journey (he was then thirty-nine) and was resigned to the years ahead that would witness his steady decline and, finally, his death. But LSD was for him the Resurrection and the Life, and he set out on his quest to convert a skeptical and even hostile world. Only the young, he felt, had any comprehension of what he was trying to do. His colleagues at Harvard considered him a freak. The academic community was fearful of drugs and drew back in horror from his experiments in the use of drugs. These timid professors were too old to change. The young, however, would not heed the dire warnings of their elders. Many of them knew from firsthand experience what the drug had done for them, and they spread the word. For the psychedelic trip meant "ecstasy, sensual and unfolding, religious experience, revelation, illumination, contact with nature" (p. 123). It was not long before Leary attracted a militant band of disciples drawn chiefly from the younger generation. Of them he wrote: He hails the present younger generation as "the wisest and holiest generation that the human race has ever seen" (p. 123).

Leary earnestly recommends LSD as a means of vastly expanding the range of human consciousness; he also describes what this drug can do in revitalizing the *vita sexualis*. In fact, it was the alleged power of LSD to intensify the sexual experience that drew the young like a magnet. Leary had told them that "LSD is the most powerful aphrodisiac ever discovered by man."[39] Compared with the apocalyptic orgasm one achieved under the influence of LSD, "the way you've been making love . . . is like making love to a department-store window dummy."[40] Leary boldly broadcast the exciting news of the new sexual dispensation:

> The three inevitable goals of the LSD sessions are to discover and make love with God, to discover and make love with yourself, and to discover and make love to a woman.[41]

Every session with LSD, if it is to be complete, involves sexual union. The more widely the one who partakes of LSD expands his consciousness, the more meaningful and prolonged is his sexual response. In a truly loving, carefully prepared LSD session, Leary announced, "a woman can have several hundred orgasms."[42]

This sensational report was enough to arouse nationwide interest in the drug culture. When Leary was asked why he had now disclosed what he had until then kept a closely guarded secret, he replied that in the past he knew full well that it was not only dangerous but suicidal to make disclosures to the general public, but now he had nothing to lose. He had been indicted on the charge of possession of drugs and if found guilty he would have to spend the rest of his life in jail. He now let it be known that the LSD craze among the younger generation was caused directly by their discovery of sexual ecstasy.[43]

39. *Ibid.*, p. 127. Dr. Sidney Cohen questions the truth of the statement that LSD is the most powerful aphrodisiac ever discovered by man. It is only partially true. Dr. Cohen agrees with Leary "that sexual ecstasy is the basic reason for the LSD boom. It is superior to alcohol for releasing inhibitions when used in this context" (Sidney Cohen, *The Beyond Within: The LSD Story* [New York: Atheneum, 1970], p. 252). Dr. Louria is a physician who insists that these drugs cause serious harm. He argues that the claims made for LSD are not only greatly exaggerated but downright false. It does not heighten creativity nor is it a potent aphrodisiac, though it does increase mental eroticism. See Donald B. Louria, *The Drug Scene* (New York and London: McGraw-Hill Book Company, 1968).

40. Leary, *The Politics of Ecstasy*, p. 127.

41. *Ibid.*, p. 128.

42. *Ibid.*, p. 129.

43. Leary was at first not aware of the sexual potential of LSD. He confessed: "I was awed and confused by the sexual power. It was too easy. I was too much an Irish Catholic, too prudish to deal with it. Too Western Christian to realize

Such sex-aroused devotees, like the women of Thebes who, in *The Bacchantes* by Euripides, followed the leadership of Dionysus, were not in the least interested in the world of politics. In adopting the drug culture as their life-style, they betrayed their disillusionment with American society. Their apolitical attitude was strengthened by their decision to embrace the anarchist tradition. In their quest for Utopia, they are not held back by the conventions and compromises of practical politics. Those who belong to the psychedelic Left are utterly unlike the militant activists of the New Left, who believe that they can topple the power structure of capitalism by revolutionary means. The hippie, who carries on the tradition of beat Bohemianism, hopes to effect a change of heart, a transformation of consciousness.

> For the hippie, all works, all attempts to act effectively, are corrupt. Only right consciousness can avail. The activist accuses the hippies of futile sentimentalism, of becoming preoccupied with personal needs and hang-ups, of allowing the growth of an inhuman power structure. The hippie replies that the militants are on a "power trip," that their human relations are corrupted in the very act of revolution, that they are involved in a self-defeating pattern of escalating violence.[44]

The hippies believed their guru or high priest when he advised them to cop out. They turned their vital energy to the pursuit of sex and the search for the orgasmic ecstasy that they could experience through the use of LSD. They responded to Leary's urgent cry: "Turn on, tune in, drop out."[45] In "Hormonal Politics: The Menopausal Left-Right and the Seed Center," Leary predicts that by 1980 the dirty game of politics will cease to interest the young. The crucial question that every candidate for public office will then be asked is: "How much time did you spend making love last week?"[46]

The novitiates who join the hippie movement and who have benefited from a number of psychedelic trips, exhibit

that God and Sex are one, that God for a man is woman, that the direct path to God is through the divine union of male-female" (Timothy Leary, *High Priest,* p. 154).

44. Keith Melville, *Communes in the Counter-Culture* (New York: William Morrow & Company, 1972), pp. 54-55.
45. Leary, *The Politics of Ecstasy,* p. 141.
46. *Ibid.,* p. 168.

traits of character that identify them as psychopaths. Even those who smoke pot regularly behave in a way that reveals their psychopathic characteristics. Their recourse to drugs as a method of achieving the peace of Nirvana is a desperate expedient, an experiment that may turn out badly. A number of hippies are emotionally disturbed characters, acutely so, who find shelter and protection in the hippie community and are thus saved from confinement in a mental hospital.[47] The hippie aspirant is gambling recklessly with the dice of destiny. His search for salvation, his quest for the miracle of rebirth, by means of deliberately courting the fate of madness is, Harrington admits, "a cruel and nutty solution" to the problem of survival without the support of faith as he confronts the void. Harrington speaks out forcefully on this bedeviled issue. Who knows but that in the present fearful crisis of consciousness man is justified in turning to psychopathy as a way of escaping the consequences of the old, outworn conception of sanity, which is incapable of facing the gulf of nothingness. If he succumbs to the insidious pressure of the social norm, he is exposed to the danger of "fragmentation without rebirth (splitting before terror and meaningless)."[48]

The hippies in San Francisco organized resident communes that sought to abide by the spirit of participatory democracy. They planned to live in keeping with their ethic of individual freedom. They were encouraged to take this bold step by Norman Mailer's expressed approval of psychopathy. As hippies, they would act upon their spontaneous impulses; they would strive to fulfill themselves creatively. Each member of the commune would be encouraged to do his thing. This was the anarchistic creed they believed in and tried to practice. Their impelling desire was to get close to nature, to live in peace, to partake of LSD and enjoy the supreme felicity of sexual intercourse.

Dr. David E. Smith, one of the authors of *Love Needs Care*, established a medical center for these young people. Then came the Summer of Love, which created a serious problem in the hippie community. After the intensive publicity accorded this event before it took place, thousands of people, the curious, the prurient, the sensation-seekers, flocked to

47. Lewis Yablonsky, *The Hippie Trip* (New York: Pegasus, 1968), p. 34.
48. Harrington, *Psychopaths*, p. 278.

this Garden of Eden, where free, unrestricted sexuality was available. Thousands of hippies, wearing flowers, arrived to celebrate the occasion, but they became the helpless prey of the hoods. They were beaten and robbed, and the girls raped. The area soon degenerated into a foul slum seething with corruption and crime. Violence was rampant. In the Haight-Ashbury district in 1967 "seventeen murders, one hundred rapes, two hundred and ninety cases of assault and over three thousand burglaries were reported at the Park Police Station by the end of the year. . . ."[49]

What happened to the hippie inhabitants of Haight-Ashbury sounds like an invented tale of Gothic horror, American style. We are told of the behavior of these acid-heads, the rapes committed, the breakdown of many on drugs, those who died because they took an overdose of the drug, those who were infected by some form of sexual disease, the pitiful condition of the undernourished and neglected babies in the hippie community. There were doctors and nurses, motivated by humanitarian feeling, who came to the rescue when they beheld the ravages of disease, the widespread suffering, the outbreak of madness. These afflicted young people badly needed medical help if they were to survive.

The peace-loving hippies finally decided to leave the Haight-Ashbury area and live in self-contained rural communes that could provide some measure of protection for its members. Unfortunately, they were not prepared to endure the vicissitudes of life in the country; they were stricken with contagious diseases, they suffered from food poisoning, strep infections, hepatitis, and venereal disease. Most of these hippies were psychologically integrated persons but they were deficient in one important respect—they could not get along with others. They were loners, rebels who led erratic and eccentric lives. Their hang-ups grew out of their inner state of hostility against the world. They turned to art as a therapeutic means of overcoming their loneliness. Convinced that civilization stood in imminent danger of being destroyed in an atomic cataclysm, they lived feverishly in an eternal now.

49. David E. Smith and John Luce, *Love Needs Care* (Boston and Toronto: Little, Brown and Company, 1971), p. 251.

4. *The Literature of the Psychopath*

William S. Burroughs, the disciple of Wilhelm Reich, the defender of the individual and his autonomy in a world that seeks to achieve the maximum degree of efficiency, defies classification. Here is a gifted rebel with a cause, a prophet who delivers a heartening message of liberation. Literary success finally came to Burroughs after he published *Naked Lunch,* which describes in detail how he broke free of the drug-habit he had formed. His views on the subject of drug-addiction are forthright. He does not romanticize the drug addict, and therefore does not consider him a fit model for the portrait of the contemporary hero. Unlike Timothy Leary, he declares that the hallucinogens and the psychedelic drugs are "extremely dangerous."[50]

Naked Lunch records the horror of the life Burroughs led under drugs. To offset this picture of abject surrender to the hallucinations induced by the drug, Burroughs vividly depicts the ugliness and unrelieved uniformity of life in the United States: the deadness of soul, the manipulation of the mind of the masses, the brutal assaults by the State to rob the citizen of his personal identity. Burroughs singles out the police state as enemy number one, since it attempts to regulate the behavior of its citizens by means of thought control. In *Naked Lunch,* Dr. Benway says: "The study of thinking machines teaches us more about the brain than we can learn by introspective methods. Western man is externalizing himself in the form of gadgets."[51]

Burroughs is at home amid the whirling nebulae of fantasies that stream from his unconscious. He sets down his free, floating hallucinations, the disordered and incoherent projections of a drug addict's mind, and in *Nova Express* these lurid projections serve to suggest the paranoid terror that oppresses the protagonist, his fear of the loss of self. Burroughs portrays the drug addict as a rebel against the totalitarian tyranny of the State. With the aid of hallucinogenic drugs he is able to resist the official lies that poison the atmosphere, and is unwilling to accept an adjunct to the conventional version of reality:

50. Conrad Knickerbocker, "William Burroughs," in *Writers at Work.* The Paris Interviews, 3d ser. (New York: The Viking Press, 1967), p. 146.
51. William S. Burroughs, *Naked Lunch* (New York: Grove Press, 1966), p. 24.

There is no true or real "reality"—"Reality" is simply a more or less scanning pattern—The scanning pattern we accept as "reality" has been imposed by the controlling power on this planet, a power primarily oriented towards total control—[52]

Burroughs's conception of "reality" has been judged by some critics as mechanical and restrictive. One critic goes so far as to call Burroughs's novels diabolical maps; crisscrossed with conflicting and confused directions, they are "unreadable; they are maps of hell."[53] Perhaps this contrived infernal nightmare is the result of the cut-up method of composition Burroughs has adopted. A piece of printed matter is cut up and six or seven words or phrases are moved around at random and then combined. Brion Gysin had called this "chance" method to his attention. Is not this so-called method a confession of bankruptcy, an acknowledgment of virtual impotence, an inability to direct and control the creative process? When he is at a standstill, the writer seeks inspiration by playing the game of objective hazard. As John Vernon points out: "This is the final condition of realism: schizophrenic atomism, living in pieces, in a world of pieces."[54]

Burroughs does not deny that there are contradictions in his make-up, but he is fairly consistent in his rejections. He has never changed his belief that the writer should not commit himself politically, and he cites good reasons for taking such a stand. Overcommitment to political objectives, he maintains,

definitely does limit one's creative capacity; you tend to become a polemicist rather than a writer. Being very dubious of politics myself, and against the whole concept of a nation, which politics presupposes, it does seem to me something of a dead end, at least for myself.[55]

The New Left was, of course, not at all put out by the defection of the hippie or psychopath from the ranks of radicalism. Such decadent, psychotic types are not the stuff out of which committed Marxists or positive heroes, Soviet style, are made.

52. William S. Burroughs, *Nova Express* (New York: Grove Press, 1964), p. 61.
53. John Vernon, *The Garden and the Map: Schizophrenia in Twentieth-Century Literature and Culture* (Urbana, Ill.: University of Illinois Press, 1973), p. 108.
54. *Ibid.*, p. 109.
55. Odier, *The Job*, p. 47.

11

The Politics of the Absurd

Ionesco has held himself aloof from the taint of any political commitment or indeed of any external commitment whatsoever, but in so doing he has remained a prisoner of his own obsessions to such an extent that he cannot rise above them.[1]

Though politics is today generally defined as affecting *all* spheres of life—religion, sex, women's liberation from the chauvinistic domination of the male, the family (R. D. Laing in 1971 published a book with the title *The Politics of the Family and Other Essays*), drug addiction, morals, and what have you, there is one area of experience, man's encounter with the absurd, that has been uncontaminated by the foul breath of politics. The absurdist writer is not interested in dealing with the pressing political conflicts of the day, though he may, like Adamov, decide to abandon his absurdist position and throw in his lot with the Communists. Few absurdists have made such a shift in their world outlook. No one familiar with their work would seriously ask whether Beckett or Ionesco belonged by rights in the liberal or radical or conservative camp. Such loose, time-worn labels do not fit their

1. Julian H. Wulbern, *Brecht and Ionesco: Commitment in Context* (Urbana and London: University of Illinois Press, 1971), p. 235.

186

case. Their productions clearly show that their envisagement of the human condition transcends the values and the motives implicit in the vocabulary of politics that move men to act. Ionesco's plays, for example, point up the futility of all human striving. His characters find it impossible to justify their existence. His metaphysical drama of the absurd "reveals existence as having no reason to exist and the unjustified as existing in superabundance. In short, the world is superfluous."[2] Ionesco's plays breathe a spirit of utter disillusionment with all terrestrial affairs. They entertain no possibility of hope through the agency of politics and sound no evangel of redemption.

In his efforts to go beyond the frontiers of reality established by the rational mind, Ionesco reminds us at times of the Surrealists: their exploration of the *terra incognita* of the unconscious, their creative use of objective hazard and the illogic of the dream. But this seeming pattern of resemblance is misleading. Though he admires Breton, Ionesco is no Surrealist.[3] He belongs, in fact, to no school. It is not likely that a genuine believer in the absurd will be a follower of some literary movement. The literature of the absurd is, by definition, *sui generis*. Unlike Surrealism, it does not surrender the principle of control or deny the need for form. Spontaneity is essential, but the energy that streams forth from the cornucopia of the unconscious must be expressed with lucidity. The work of art, be it Surrealist or absurdist in inspiration, calls for selectivity, the imposition of order and form.

Apolitical in his *Weltanschauung*, Ionesco is not the type of writer who can be dragooned into espousing a set of abstract ideas, noble causes, utopian projects. He will not march in military formation in the ranks of the Left or the Right. Ultraliberal critics try to make him see the light so that he will tackle in his plays the urgent social and economic problems of his age, but he dismisses their tendentious appeals as

2. Jacques Guicharnaud, *Modern French Theatre* (New Haven, Conn.: Yale University Press, 1961), p. 182.
3. He pays a stirring tribute to the genius of André Breton, who was loved not only because he had rejuvenated the art of poetry but because of the nobility of his character. Though Breton fought under the banner of the irrational, he was the soul of lucidity. "The standard bearer of Revolution, he realized very early what tyranny, what censorship, what constraint, what 'realistic' mediocrity were hidden beneath the name of contemporary revolutions." Eugène Ionesco, *Present Past, Past Present,* trans. Helen R. Lane (New York: Grove Press, 1971), p. 148.

simplistic. He has no intention of converting the theater into a political forum, a sounding board for ideologies. He despises both the formal theater and the theater of ideas. Realism, especially Socialist realism, furnishes only a truncated, impoverished version of reality. He believes in the truth revealed by the heart of desire, the truth of dreams. In his diatribe against the theater of ideas and the thesis drama, he warns of the danger of allowing the theater to be perverted to political ends. Though he does not deny that all drama is "social" in content, this is not tantamount to saying that it must be Socialist in its orientation. The art of the drama at its best gives expression to moments of luminous insight, intuitions and epiphanies that reach far beyond the temporal plane or the exigencies of the historical situation. It holds up a vision of the fate that befalls all mankind: all human beings, without exception, must die.

Ionesco is intransigent in his opposition to the politically committed theater. He draws an important distinction between being "social" and being politically partisan. He is no admirer of Brecht's propagandistic plays or his gallery of exemplary "heroes." Ionesco proceeds to unmask the true character of "Brechtian man," who is one-dimensional. The politically committed playwright furnishes a distorted and fundamentally false picture of a given historical period because his ideology restricts his field of vision. This is the purblindness common to ideologists and people "stunted by fanaticism."[4] Metaphysical in his perception of "realities" that transcend the categories of time and the pleasures of history, Ionesco seeks to capture intimations of the universal. The great plays of the past convey this sense of the inevitability of death. Empires perish, kings are hurled from their thrones. Nothing endures. It is this haunting, inescapable experience of mortality, when contrasted with man's obdurate and irrational longing for eternity, that gives rise to the tragic vision. The only type of play that defrauds the audience is the one "with a thesis to prove, an ideological, committed play, a play that is bogus and not true profoundly and poetically, as only poetry and tragedy can be true."[5]

Ionesco is severely censured by those critics who favor the

4. Eugène Ionesco, *Notes and Counter Notes,* trans. Donald Watson (New York: Grove Press, 1964), p. 29.
5. *Ibid.,* p. 32.

committed drama created by Bertolt Brecht. In his study *Brecht and Ionesco,* Wulbern declares flatly that "he [Ionesco] remains socially and politically nihilistic. . . ."[6] Ionesco sees "death as the ultimate absurdity in an otherwise totally absurd universe."[7] Wulbern discusses in detail the gist of Ionesco's objections to Brecht's politically committed theater. Helen Weigel, Brecht's wife, disposed of these criticisms as emanating from Ionesco's blind and obsessive hatred of Marxism, and therefore rooted in the noxious soil of prejudice. Though others present at this discussion believed that Ionesco represented a significant and desirable trend in opposition to didacticism in the drama, Wulbern was impressed by Helen Weigel's remarks, "for my own reading of *Notes et contre-notes* had long led me to suspect that Ionesco had had little direct experience with or deep perception of Brecht's works."[8]

Ionesco is not moved by such partisan criticism. He regards as deluded those fanatics—he is thinking primarily of Brecht—who think they can write plays that will save the world. Kenneth Tynan, the English dramatic critic, writing in *The Observer* on July 6, 1958, tried to rebut Ionesco's aesthetic beliefs. Tynan acknowledged that he wants drama "to realize that it is a part of politics, in the sense that every human activity, even buying a pack of cigarettes, has social and political repercussions."[9] Ionesco is not taken in by the specious argument that everything under the sun is affected by politics. He insists that the distinction between ideology and reality, propaganda and art, must be reinstated. The economic society that the revolutionary activists hope to establish moves us in the direction of social conformism and "the world of alienation."[10] Just as Valéry waged a bitter, lifelong campaign

6. Wulbern, *Brecht and Ionesco,* p. 226.
7. *Ibid.*
8. *Ibid.,* p. 4. Helen Weigel presented her views at a meeting on July 28, 1965, of the Brecht Ensemble held in the Ensemble's rehearsal theater in East Berlin. Its object was to prepare the members of that troupe for their guest performance of Brecht's plays in London. Wulbern was present at that meeting and records the discussion generated by the reading of selected passages from Ionesco's *Argument gegen Argument,* the recently issued translation of Ionesco's *Notes et contre-notes.* Brecht's widow, Wulbern observes, treated Ionesco's dramaturgic ideas with scant respect, but she was the only one who did so (*ibid.,* pp. 3-4).
9. Ionesco, *Notes and Counter Notes,* p. 94.
10. Eugène Ionesco, *Fragments of a Journal,* trans. Jean Stewart. New York: Grove Press, 1964), p. 35.

against the mystagogic ideas of Pascal, so does Ionesco concentrate his attack on the dramaturgic theories of Brecht, especially the theory of *Entfremdung* that Brecht attempted to apply to his later plays. Brecht sternly forbids—and endeavors to prevent—any emotional participation on the part of the audience. The spectator is denied the pleasure of empathy; he is not allowed to identify himself with the characters Brecht presents.

> [Brecht] wants us to understand them. . . . In fact, it is his thought, his ideology that becomes the magical element."[11]

The so-called "committed" play, as often as not resorts to melodrama in order to produce the intended ideological effect on the audience.

Ionesco is the antithesis of the didactic writer. For him as a playwright, political and economic problems are of secondary importance. Why should he be preoccupied with them since he knows: "(1) that we are going to die, (2) that revolution saves us neither from life nor from death, (3) that I cannot imagine a finite universe, an infinite universe, nor yet a universe that is neither finite nor infinite."[12] Since everything in the world seems to him arbitrary, contingent, absurd, he eschews the partisan spirit. Too many ideologies are at bottom rationalizations of hidden aggressions, outlets for the destructive instinct. "The saviors of mankind have founded inquisitions, invented concentrations camps, constructed crematory ovens, established tyrannies."[13] To call for "commitment" on the part of the writer is, in effect, to deprive him of his creative freedom. As Ionesco remarks apropos *Rhinoceros,* which some critics interpreted as a political polemic:

> I've been criticized not for saying in *Rhinoceros* that totalitarianism and collectivization are evil, but for not offering a solution. But I never meant to offer a solution. I simply meant to show how a mutation is possible in collective thought, to show how it came about. I was quite simply, phenomenologically, describing the process of collective transformation.[14]

11. *Ibid.,* p. 17.
12. *Ibid.,* p. 25.
13. *Ibid.,* p. 161.
14. Claude Bonnefoy, *Conversations with Ionesco* trans. Jan Dawson (New York and Chicago: Holt, Rinehart and Winston, 1971), p. 70.

An anarchist as well as absurdist at heart, Ionesco resists the aggressive designs of the professional revolutionaries, who demand that the artist, to save his soul, give unconditional obedience to the Cause, the anointed Leader, the Party. He has repeatedly stated that he has no faith at all in the Revolution. Today, Ionesco contends, it is the Left that provides the most shocking example of ideological tyranny.

Revolutions break out in order to overthrow the established form of government, which is condemned as evil, despotic, and corrupt. Once the revolution succeeds, it becomes in its turn a source of injustice. Ionesco interprets Communism as a secularized version of the ancient and universal myth of paradise: the dream of freedom. The Communist revolution represents an ambitious but cruel and painful attempt to change the world, to liberate its constructive energies, to transform the nature of society. The cruelty is present and also the suffering because, Ionesco says, Communism is a failure. Hence the tragic element that enters in, for the miracle that the Communists wished for did not come to pass. They had believed that they could transfigure the world by technical means, just as Stalinist Russia adopted the biological theories of Lysenko, which were "mutation-oriented. Faith in mutation is the sign that there is an emotional awareness of miracle."[15]

If Ionesco was never tempted by the Marxist promise of miracles, it is because from the time of his youth until today he despised and resented the official symbols of authority. He is in many respects a philosophical anarchist, though he would be the first to repudiate such a label. He revolted against his father, who respected the State regardless of what it stood for. Ionesco declared: "I detested the State" (p. 18). In fact, he resents all infringements on his personal freedom. He derides those pundits who dogmatically declare that individualist literature is obsolete and anachronistic in our progressive, technological age and that the writer must henceforth create a species of collectivist art "in order to express the nationalist or Communist or Nazi world or some other" (p. 42).

What Ionesco finds singularly lacking in this age of political fanaticism is the metaphysical vision, the hunger for the

15. Ionesco, *Present Past, Past Present,* p. 159.

absolute. It is unfortunate that the fever of contemporary politics has supplanted the archetypal quest of man for the absolute.

> When man no longer bothers about the problems of ultimate ends . . . when the great metaphysical problems no longer cause man to suffer and leave him indifferent, humanity is degraded and becomes bestial. (pp. 43-44).

It is unutterably stupid to sell one's life for the sake of a political party. We must be on our guard against the calculated lies that define the political as the locus of the spiritual or pretend that politics gives us the answer to our metaphysical questions.

Politics in our time is a form of destructive madness, a compulsion to tear down, to sow the seeds of confusion, to unleash the whirlwind of revolutionary violence. For Ionesco the supremely ironic fact that we shall soon turn to dust renders everything else in the world insignificant by comparison. Why burst into a frenzy of anger, resentment, and vindictive hatred? Why not fall into silence? For the convictions we so passionately defend—all this will be utterly forgotten in the grave. How account for the thanatophobic upsurge that leads twentieth-century man to indulge in idolatry of the State, the Nation? Why should anyone worship the State, which is only an abstraction, an administrative system? It is not God but an idol made of clay. It is a spurious entity. But this abstraction is endowed with the attributes of the sacred and invested with the power of dispensing justice, or what it mistakes for justice. As Ionesco demonstrated with trenchant dramatic force in his play *Rhinoceros,* for those who were transformed into rhinoceroses "the State has become God" (p. 79). It is these pernicious abstractions, the hypnotic mumbo jumbo of politics, that are chiefly responsible for the alienation of the modern self.

It is the knowledge that all men are doomed to die that fills Ionesco with a nameless but oppressive anxiety. This obsession will not let him go. How can it be, he wonders, that he is still afraid of death, how can it be that he does not "fervently desire it?" (p. 40). He cannot reason his way out of these painful existential dilemmas. He is perfectly aware of the ludicrous situation in which he finds himself trapped. The absurdity of his position overwhelms him, but this is no laughing matter. He knows full well that the human condition is not to be borne, yet he holds on to existence with a desperation born of sheer animal terror and keeps on "complaining that one is going to lose what is unbearable" (p. 81). Though he realizes that there is no answer to the tormenting enigma of existence, Ionesco will never stop asking the same question: why? This is the type of non-sense question that the logical positivists have proscribed. Ionesco interrogates the universe of death. Precisely because there are no answers does man persist in asking this question. "We are here. We don't know what that means" (p. 94). A dreamer thus obsessed will not be duped by the collective manias of his age. Ionesco will not respond to the organized and efficient efforts of the bureaucratic State to condition him politically so that he will be transformed into a willing and obedient servant of the State. He is resolved to resist to the end the plan to change civilization into a model ant colony, just as he is deaf to the call for commitment that would enroll him in some political crusade.

Part IV

VARIOUS TYPES OF COMMITMENT

A. In France
B. In England
C. In Germany

A. IN FRANCE

12

Gide and the Rationale
of Commitment

we cannot possibly do politically engaged writers the favor of taking their political tendencies, intentions, self-interpretations, and manifestoes as seriously as they expect us to—unless, that is, we intend to compromise them. What will remain twenty years after the death of Heinrich Mann, Knut Hamsun, Sartre, Brecht, Ezra Pound, and others will not be their "political" partisanship and escapades, but solely the artistic value of their work. They are to be honored according to this criterion and no other.[1]

1. *Prefatory Remarks*

Literature, we generally like to assume when we are giving voice to the optative mood, leaves its mark upon the life of man; otherwise why would writers suffer this expense of spirit in a waste of words? And if literature does leave its ennobling mark upon the life of man, then we are justified in concluding that, by expanding his power of imagination, it helps to transform his character. These are bold generaliza-

1. Emil Mühlmann, "Tradition and Revolution in Literature," in *Literary Criticism and Sociology.* Yearbook of Comparative Criticism. vol. 5. Ed. Joseph P. Strelka (University Park: Pennsylvania State University Press, 1973), p. 141.

tions, to be sure, difficult to prove empirically. Perhaps they are an expression of faith. After Auschwitz, a number of critics sharply challenged the truth of this theory. Literature, like art, does not teach us anything about how to live. The best the writers can do is to confront the problem and persist in questioning the Sphinx. They have no solutions, no final answer, to offer. Why did the German people succumb to the poisonous propaganda preached by Hitler and the Nazis? Nurtured on the cultural heritage of Goethe, Schiller, and Lessing, why did they consent, by their prudent silence or hysterical support of the regime, to Hitler's genocidal campaign?

Literature is obviously designed to serve the needs of man. In its efforts to limn the bafflingly complex and elusive nature of reality, it is influenced for good or evil by the *Zeitgeist*, the historical situation, the emergent forces of social existence, though precisely how this process works has never been convincingly demonstrated.[2] Literary historians consider the epic as best suited to embody the heroic values of an aristocratic society, whereas the novel catered to the needs of the rising middle class in the eighteenth century. Literary genres undergo substantive and strategic changes as they respond to the urgent needs of the times.

2. The Political Commitment of the Writer

Late in the nineteenth century a number of influential writers in France took up the cause of radicalism. Zola became a Socialist. So did that genial skeptic and unregenerate sensualist, Anatole France. Though France continued to believe that the life of man on earth fulfills no ultimate purpose, his perception of what later was called the myth of the absurd did not prevent him from responding to the call of his aroused social conscience and joining the forces of the Left. Despite his nihilistic philosophy, he felt that it is incumbent on the human adventurer on earth to affirm a humanistic ethic and bear the burden of responsibility such an ethic

2. See Malcolm Bradbury, *The Social Context of Modern English Literature* (New York: Schocken Books, 1971). See also *Sociology of Literature and Drama*, ed. Elizabeth and Tom Burns (Harmondsworth, Middlesex, England: Penguin Books, 1973).

entails. Anatole France's career ran the gamut from conservatism through hedonistic nihilism to Socialism. His political values began to change as he became aware of the privations and oppressions of the poor. Not that he immediately espoused a revolutionary outlook. Dwelling as he does in the Garden of Epicurus, the hedonist is loath to sacrifice his accustomed round of pleasures.

In 1893, in the preface to *Les Opinions de Jerome Coignard,* he first gave tentative expression to his Socialist beliefs, though at that time his attitude was that of a reformist. Gradually, after 1898, he acquired a deeper understanding of the vital role that politics played in the modern world. When Zola's letter on the Dreyfus Affair was published in 1908, he joined the Dreyfusards and openly embraced the cause of Socialism. Even though he was then a sexagenarian, he took part in the social struggles of his time. He delivered speeches before audiences of workers and called them "comrades." By the beginning of 1900, according to one scholar, "he was a socialist, formally or not, and he soon made his adhesion official."[3] He now publicly declared that he was opposed to the institution of private property and a society based on the class war. "As a socialist, France presided at party meetings, exhorted the proletariat, fought for various liberal causes, signed petitions, and wrote propaganda."[4] After the First World War, he became convinced that only world revolution would insure the blessing of lasting peace. He became a Communist, without ever joining the Party or echoing its militant slogans. He had displayed exceptional moral courage in speaking out in the Dreyfus case. At the funeral of Zola, he delivered an address generously extolling the writer and the man whom he had cruelly reviled in the past. But the insurgent younger generation of French writers did not forget—or forgive—"the sins" of this amorist who had been the spokesman of a philosophy of skepticism. When he died in 1924, the Surrealists published a pamphlet entitled *Un Cadaver,* in which they dissected the work he had produced in order to demonstrate that his writing, like its begetter, deserved to be buried and forgotten.

But it was not until the Communist critics proclaimed that

3. Carter Jefferson, *Anatole France: The Politics of Skepticism* (New Brunswick, N. J.: Rutgers University Press, 1965), p. 115.
4. *Ibid.,* p. 116.

it was the duty of the writer to join the Party or, in the thirties, to become a fellow traveler in the United Front, that the ethic of commitment was regarded as a categorical imperative. Because of the prestige accorded them by the general public, writers and artists were assiduously wooed by the Communist Party. Once the writer became a *bona fide* member of the Party, he was subjected to all kinds of ideological pressure. Though he was ostensibly free to sever this tie if it proved too onerous, he preferred as a rule to remain within the Party. For the Communist Party stood for the cause of political idealism, and the intellectual elite supported it chiefly because of their devotion to the ideal. The Party was eager to recruit such eminent intellectuals and artists as Picasso, Louis Aragon, Rolland, and Sartre, though Sartre never joined it. Such famous men could be induced to engage in political journalism or in projects designed to enlighten the masses. The Party was proud to announce that such illustrious figures as Henri Barbusse, Anatole France, and Romain Rolland had become members. Despite this propaganda, not all was smooth sailing for the Party in France. The surface appearance of unity and harmony was broken by the resentment a number of writers voiced at the ideological control the leaders of the Party sought to impose. Rolland on occasion criticized the arbitrary exercise of authority in the Soviet Union.

Why, then, did intellectuals, especially during the thirties, join the Party or agree to support its objectives? Were they prompted primarily by emotional rather than rational factors? This problem of motivation is highly complex and cannot be discussed in abstract terms. The widely held belief that the intellectuals on the Left were the victims of an illusion, that they found in Marxism a drug that would rid them of their personal frustrations and their metaphysical malaise, does not hold water. In *Communism and the French Intellectuals,* David Caute attempts to refute the widespread belief that Marxism is the opium of the Communist intellectuals, that it offers them a way out of their distressing personal problems, and that it serves as a surrogate for the loss of the religious Absolute, but this refutation is based on a premise that runs counter to Marxist doctrine. Caute assumes that the economic forces, which are supposed to be primary factors in governing human behavior, function in this manner only "in a limited degree apart from a sense of purpose" and "a sense of what is morally desirable. . . ."[5]

Raymond Aron presents a strikingly different interpretation of the character of the Marxist intellectuals and the complex of motives that led them to choose Communism as the Way and the Life. Assuming the role of prophets, Jeremiahs fiercely denouncing all the man-made, and therefore remediable, evils in the world, they were originally converted to Marxism by the force of this moral passion. "How many intellectuals have come to the revolutionary party via the path of moral indignation, only to connive ultimately at terror and autocracy?"[6] In an age when faith in God is dead, the ideology of Communism serves as a substitute faith that guarantees to feed their spiritual hunger. "The intellectual who no longer feels attached to anything is not satisfied with **opinions merely; he wants certainty,** he wants a system. The Revolution provides him with his opium."[7]

3. *The Case of André Gide*

It seems to me that today the social question must come first, and that it must first be decided in order to permit man to give all that he is worthy of giving. The great mistake is to come to the USSR and say "It is monstrous. You heed of none but material questions!" "No, material questions are not exactly the most important, but they are the *first,* the most important in *time:* that is to say, they are determining."[8]

During the troubled thirties Gide was won over to a belief in the necessity of world revolution, but his zeal as a fellow traveler did not weaken his faith in the essential importance of art for mankind nor did it affect the quality of his imaginative writing. The traumatic shock of the First World War, the appalling evidence of the evils of colonialism he had gathered on his second trip to Africa, the brutal facts that highlighted an inhuman system of economic exploitation, the

5. David Caute, *Communism and the French Intellectuals* (New York: The Macmillan Company, 1964), p. 263.
6. Raymond Aron, *The Opium of the Intellectuals,* trans. Terence Kilmartin (Garden City, N. Y.: Doubleday & Company, 1957), pp. 211-12.
7. *Ibid.,* p. 257.
8. Louis Aragon, "André Gide and Our Times." *International Literature,* no. 2 (February 1936), p. 102. Aragon quotes a passage spoken by Gide.

miserable suffering of the poor, these made him feel that he could no longer stand aside from the realities of the political conflict. Like a number of other writers—Paul Nizan,[9] Louis Aragon, and Romain Rolland—he could not devote himself solely to the art of literature while the masses were caught in the trap of unemployment and economic distress.

At first Gide found it extremely difficult to "commit" himself politically. The emotional pull of Communism was not strong enough to keep him ideologically in line. He was in full sympathy with the Communist *ideal* and he considered himself to be a Communist at heart. Only when explicit demands were made upon him that he conform to this or that Party directive did he rebel. What, he asked himself, did literature and art have to do with political and socioeconomic issues? In his *Journal* he wrote that he preferred to remain silent rather than adapt his work "to utilitarian ends."[10] That is why he finally decided to break away from Communism. He saw that Communism represented a new secular religion; it had its own expressive mythology, its pantheon, its legendary heroes and inspiring leaders, its sacred texts and binding symbols, its ritual and liturgy and presiding high priests, all of which appealed strongly to the young. Gide observed the paradoxical phenomenon "that 'mysticism' today is on the side of those who profess atheism and irreligion."[11] Communism was the new collectivist religious faith that now aroused the enthusiasm of the young. Communism is supposed to lay the foundation for the establishment of the Kingdom of Heaven on earth, and for the sake of achieving this universal ideal in the future, the true believers are willing to make all sorts of sacrifices. If Communism is in effect a secular religion, then the cadre of Party leaders makes up a virtual priesthood, which prescribes the dogmas set forth in scriptural writings and interprets their meaning for the benefit of their followers. This was too much for Gide, who hated all forms of authoritarianism, to swallow. If he supported the masses, he did so because he was governed by "reasons" of the heart, not by Marxist commandments. This

9. See Paul Nizan, "André Gide Comes to Revolution." *International Literature*, no. 3 (1934), pp. 138-47.

10. André Gide, *The Journals of André Gide*, trans. Justin O'Brien (New York: Alfred A. Knopf, 1949), 3: 252.

11. *Ibid.*, 3: 281.

is how Gide formulated his basic objection to orthodox Marxism:

> Whether the text invoked be by Marx or Lenin, I cannot abide by it unless my heart and reason approve it. I did not escape from the authority of Aristotle or St. Paul to fall under theirs.[12]

His Christian conscience had induced him to become a Communist sympathizer. His rejection of dogmatic Christianity opened his eyes to the deplorable fact that many, perhaps most, of the ills of the world are man-made. And if that is the case, if man and not God is the responsible agent, then "one can no longer resign oneself to anything."[13] Gide became increasingly involved in left-wing politics but at no time did he surrender or compromise his integrity as an artist. He would not yield an iota of his intellectual independence, though he shrewdly suspected that his preoccupation with social and political issues resulted in a marked decline of his creative power. Though there was much in Marxism that he could endorse, he deplored the righteous fanaticism of professional Communists and their rigid "class" interpretation of literature and art. He was repelled by the negative, purely destructive rage that animated these zealots as they revaluated the cultural heritage of the past and decided to get rid of everything that was not useful to "the Cause." Though he sided with Communism and cherished the hope that the Soviet Union would succeed in its social experiment, he was not one to harbor and become infected with the vicious virus of class hatred. He admitted that his fund of political knowledge was deficient. That did not matter. Fundamentally it was not Marx but the teachings of the Gospels, the example set by Christ, that had brought him to Communism.

In 1937, after his return from a trip to the Soviet Union, he decided that he had had enough of Marxism. The Russian people were still saddled with a ruthless dictatorship and an all-powerful bureaucracy. There was no point in glossing over or concealing these unsavory developments in the proletarian paradise. Gide had forced himself, out of a sense of duty, to read *Das Kapital,* but it did not enlighten him; it was full of dreary theories and statistical data. He did not react in

12. *Ibid.*
13. *Ibid.*, 3: 181.

the manner of the impressionable and ideologically impassioned Brecht who, after reading the *Communist Manifesto,* tried to turn it into poetry. Gide was made of different clay. He had by this time thrown off the spell cast by dialectical materialism and he no longer cared if his writings failed to be in accord with or flagrantly violated the enshrined principles of Marxism. He had at first been so fearful at the time of commiting some grievous error in his interpretation of pure Marxism that he had "no longer dared to write. . . . But now I am free of that."[14] This confession speaks for itself. We can hear Gide breathe an audible sigh of relief as he frees himself from this ideological yoke. He had practiced a self-imposed censorship lest he offend the canon of orthodoxy. This was enough to show him what was clearly lacking in Communism.

His commitment to Communism was ended. Unlike Romain Rolland, he had never been a Party member. Gide was quintessentially the artist, with all the handicaps and advantages such a role entailed, while Rolland conscientiously participated in the sociopolitical conflicts of the times. Though they both supported a common cause when Communism triumphed in Russia, they were once more at odds when Gide criticized the shortcomings of the Communist regime he had noted on a visit to the Soviet Union. Rolland believed that modern art was decadent, since the artists lived apart from the masses and had no awareness of the suffering the common folk had to endure. Rolland was not attracted by the cult of symbolism and he rejected out of hand what he considered the false theory of art for art's sake. Gide, however, never forsook his devotion to art. Rolland was too closely identified with political causes sponsored by the Left to regard art as of great importance in the life of man.[15]

Gide for his part now understood full well why the Communists insisted on ideological conformity. They had no use for the autonomous individual. A heretic in both religious and political matters, he would not subscribe to the orthodox tenets of either Communism or Christianity. Boldly he proclaimed his conviction that today wisdom begins with the conquest of fear, "that it begins with the revolt of Prometheus."[16]

14. *Ibid.,* 3: 376.
15. See Frederick John Harris, *André Gide and Romain Rolland* (New Brunswick, N. J.: Rutgers University Press, 1973), pp. 110-65.
16. Gide, *The Journals of André Gide,* 3: 290.

He urged his prospective readers not to accept the injunction that it is essential first to believe and then everything else will follow. "It is first essential to doubt."[17] On February 7, 1940, he wrote that when he thought he was a Communist he was actually a Christian, "if it may be that one can be a Christian without 'believing.' "[18]

In politics as in religion, Gide remained true to himself. As he remarked in 1940: "The social question! . . . if I had encountered that great trap at the beginning of my career, I should never have written anything worth while."[19] He was not filled with regret because of his past actions; he tried hard to carry out his duties as a Communist sympathizer, but his embroilment in politics used up his time and interfered with his creative work. In the beginning he had felt an overwhelming love for this unique experiment in cooperative living that the Soviet Union was conducting. For the first time in the history of the world, man was struggling to rise above the kingdom of necessity. Here was the embodiment of all the ideals he had believed in as a Christian. Here was a collective movement for the sake of which man would be justified in renouncing his fractious individuality.

His trip to Russia made him realize that he had been nursing an illusion. Though he was willing to grant that the period of transition from the old order to the new might necessitate unparalleled hardships and costly sacrifices for some groups, he could not overlook the shocking evils he beheld: the bureaucratic centralization of power, the stifling of dissent on the cultural and political front, the tyrannical manner in which all opposition was crushed. Gide was resolved to bear witness to the truth, even if, by speaking out, he incurred the obloquy of Communists the world over. The Stalinist State was a dictatorship that did not differ in essence from the corporate Fascist State. In one sense, Russian totalitarianism was more despicable, because it masqueraded under the cloak of humanistic idealism.

Gide did not hesitate when he weighed his loyalty to the Soviet Union, the Fatherland of the Proletariat, against his obligation as a writer not to conceal or pervert the truth. He had to safeguard the future of humanity. What shocked him

17. *Ibid.*
18. André Gide, *The Journals of André Gide*, trans. Justin O'Brien (New York: Alfred A. Knopf, 1951), 4: 11.
19. *Ibid.*, 4: 20.

was the glaring evidence that privileged groups still flourished in the Soviet Union. He was aghast when he learned that no negative criticism was allowed to be published or uttered in public. Even when spoken in private, the dissident might be betrayed to the secret police by informers who remained anonymous. Each citizen had to accept the Party platform. Such autocratic rule spread fear throughout the land and fostered the cancer of corruption. Distressed by these symptoms of degeneracy in the Socialist Fatherland, he came to the conclusion that "man cannot be reformed from the outside—a change of heart is necessary. . . ."[20] He deplored the tendency he observed in the Soviet Union: the revival of bourgeois instincts and the restoration of the old social structure, which favored a privileged group of bureaucrats who could be readily identified by their spirit of conformity. What has the worker in Russia gained as the result of his victorious revolutionary struggle? Nothing but the oppressive dictatorship of Stalin. "What he [Gide] rejected was not so much communism as he thought it might and should be, but rather what Russia had made of it."[21] Since there were no free elections, the workers are powerless to defend their interests against the despot who ruled the land and its people with an iron hand. "The workers are cheated, muzzled, and bound hand and foot, so that resistance has become well-nigh impossible."[22] Gide was personally not afraid to speak out. In this vast nation ostensibly dedicated to the cause of Communism, the mind and spirit of its people were arbitrarily oppressed; the Russian folk were the victims of a reign of terror that surpassed the conditions that existed in Nazi Germany.[23]

Moreover, the artist in the Soviet Union was as bad off as the workers. He was not allowed to belong to an opposition group—there was no opposition. He was not free to criticize existing conditions. If the writer in the Soviet Union wished to survive, he must produce ideologically "pure" work that the Party functionaries would approve. He must perforce obey or face the frightening penalties the ruler might inflict

20. *The God That Failed,* ed. Richard Crossman (New York: Bantam Books, 1951), p. 185.
21. Harris, *André Gide and Romain Rolland,* p. 164.
22. *The God That Failed,* p. 186.
23. *Ibid.,* p. 189.

on him. Gide spread the disheartening news that the Revolution had been betrayed. The ardent hopes of intellectuals the world over were cruelly disappointed. The Revolution had failed to live up to the expectations it had aroused. "The same old capitalist society has been re-established, a new and terrible despotism crushing and exploiting man, with all the abject and servile mentality of serfdom."[24]

24. *Ibid.*, p. 197.

13

André Malraux: Tragic Humanism and the Political Imperative

Malraux has become a legend in his lifetime, an exemplary creative figure who, despite his age, did not retire in moral despair from the life of action. Multitalented, many-sided in his interests and activities, he is the modern incarnation of the versatile Renaissance man of honor. Unlike older writers like Paul Valéry, Roger Martin du Gard, and André Gide (his brief period of collaboration with the Communists does not count), who did not participate in the political battles of their age, Malraux, at the very start of his career, became involved in left-wing politics. Aestheticism did not appeal to him; he had no desire to dwell in Axel's castle. He was no camp follower, no propagandist. His fiction, when it deals with a revolutionary theme, is not marred by its adoption of a militant ideology. The political idea in his novels is not allowed to dominate the action and grow out of all proportion; it is presented and developed from different points of view as interpreted by the leading characters in the course of the action.[1]

1. The novels that deal with politics "can succeed by transcending politics, by postulating, and developing around, a criticism of politics. The best political

Malraux's striking success in constructing his political novels is due largely to his controlling vision of human destiny. In handling the political motif he does not lose sight of the metaphysical dimension. When Leon Trotsky criticized *The Conquerors* on the ground that Malraux's sympathy for the Chinese masses was "corrupted" by excesses of individualism and of esthetic caprice"[2] and pointed out that the novelist could have avoided such mistakes by "a solid inoculation of Marxism,"[3] the latter replied that he was writing a novel in which "the main stress is placed on the relationship between individual and collective action, not on collective action alone."[4] *The Conquerors* is primarily a protest against the human condition. Malraux achieves this complexity by his awareness of the specter of the absurd. Tutored by such men as Dostoevski and Nietzsche, he does not apply rational categories in his delineation of character. Malraux, like Orwell, never drew up a systematized account of his political attitudes; these must be derived from a close study of his novels, his autobiography, and his books on art. Alienated from bourgeois society and at odds with European culture as a whole, he was early attracted to the ideology of the Left. He sympathized with the victims of colonialism. In China he worked closely with the Kuomintang. He was opposed to Fascism during the thirties and supported the Communists when the United Front was formed. In the Spanish Civil War he flew sixty-five missions, but he did not join the Communist Party nor accept its philosophy. He was no Marxist. When he wrote *Man's Hope,* he declared that he had no intention of using the novel as a vehicle for radical propaganda. He knows there are values, aspirations, and needs that go beyond the limited horizon of politics. In brief, he views the realm of politics as only one aspect of man's ceaseless struggle to justify his existence.

Such soaring metaphysical insights, such a courageous confrontation of the void, did not blind him to the crises and conflicts of his age. The record of his adventurous life shows

novel may be, in fact, a criticism of the political novel." Catharine Savage, *Malraux, Sartre, and Aragon.* University of Florida Monographs, Humanities, no. 17, 1964 (Gainesville, Fla.: University of Florida Press, 1965), p. 5.
2. Leon Trotsky, "The Strangled Revolution," in *Malraux,* ed. R. W. B. Lewis (Englewood Cliffs, N. J.: Prentice-Hall, 1964), p. 13.
3. *Ibid.,* p. 15.
4. André Malraux, "Reply to Trotsky," in *Malraux,* p. 21.

most convincingly that he acted out his political faith in accordance with the dictates of his social conscience, despite his knowledge that civilizations die and are fogotten. He realized, too, that mankind may be utterly wiped out. Life was a perpetual battle against extinction. Thus he assumed a number of responsible and heroic roles: the student of ancient art and archaeology exploring the ruined temples along the "Royal Way" in Cambodia, the revolutionary in Indochina and then in China, the brilliant novelist, the interpreter of the history of art, his service in Spain where he joined the Loyalists, his appointment as the Minister of Culture under de Gaulle. Unlike the sectarians of the Left, he beheld the trouble and traumas of his age from the perspective of a timeless past. Disregarding the dogmas preached by the cult of Socialist realism, he portrayed the important part the individual played in the historical process. Long before Samuel Beckett and Eugène Ionesco had created their plays and fiction to highlight the pervasive presence of the absurd, he referred in *La Tentation de l'Occident* (1926) to the myth of the absurd. Ling, a Chinese intellectual, advances the idea that the universe is basically unpredictable: *"at the core of European man, ruling the important movements of his life, is a basic absurdity."*[5] This oppressive sense of the absurd appears in his later novels not as a ghostly philosophical abstraction but as a living force that works havoc with the plans of mice and men. Malraux's protagonists plunge into action and try to shape their destiny, but their quest is equivocal and ends, for all their courage and resolution, in failure. They cannot blot out their consciousness of a universe that is indifferent, if not downright inimical, to their spiritual longings and of a fate that will abruptly terminate their lease on life, just as it will, ultimately, all things human.

Malraux depicts heroes who, though definitely committed to a life of action, are not, at times, inwardly convinced that the end sought is worth the sacrifices they must make in order to reach it. Man must act in order to invest his life with meaning, but it is meaning that he has himself imposed on Nature. Human power is strictly limited. Human existence is finite, precarious, gratuitous, without reason. Death nullifies all that man strives to attain. It is not, however, the specific

5. André Malraux, *The Temptation of the West*, trans. Robert Hollander (New York: Vintage Books, 1961), p. 40.

achievement that counts. Though Malraux's heroes are foiled in their quest—the uprising of the workers is brutally put down, the plan miscarries—but their defeat bears witness to their greatness of spirit. They fail, they perish, but their persistence in the struggle in rising above the human condition represents a spiritual triumph.

The Malrauvian hero reveals himself principally by his actions, not by his thoughts. He is what he does with his life. But the collapse of the religious absolute profoundly altered man's conception of himself. "Malraux was one of the first to see that the 'death of God' involves that of man. God understood not only as the Deity, but as any principle purporting to render the universe intelligible. . . ."[6] That is why man revolts against the tyranny of the absurd by creating his own life plan, his own sense of purpose. Men make history by the strength of their commitment to action. They know that their suffering on earth, their enslavement to death, serve no purpose. Hence they invent myths designed to fill their life with the light of meaning, but when these *ad hoc* myths grow old and die they are left defenseless in the infinite dark, overcome by the feeling of dread, alienation, and despair. They must then give birth to new myths that will celebrate the miracle of life. Malraux enlarged the idea of myth and brought it close to the Sorelian conception of myth.[7]

When he broke his connections, such as they were, with Communism, the critics on the Left attacked him unmercifully. He had become a reactionary, a Fascist. But even at the height of his popularity as a novelist, the Communists regarded him as ideologically suspect. He did not develop his themes in such a way as to endear him to the apostles of Socialist realism. He portrayed no "positive heroes," only protagonists who are tragic figures, obsessed by the thought of death and the irremediable absurdity of life.

6. Everett W. Knight, *Literature Considered as Philosophy* (London: Routledge & Kegan Paul, 1957), p. 134.
7. "The fifteen years from 1928 to 1943, in which Malraux published six novels, mark a movement in his thought from directionless political thought through a form of Marxism to a humanistic political philosophy. Metaphysical criticism and speculation give way to the representation of a concrete reality that re-creates this abstract speculation and examines its political implications. Malraux turns from the essay to the novel, from consideration of the Absurd as a feature of a culture to expression of the Absurd as a feature of individual experience." David Wilkinson, *Malraux: An Essay in Political Criticism* (Cambridge, Mass.: Harvard University Press, 1967), p. 31.

Malraux's fiction, even though it concerns itself with the revolutionary struggle, is essentially metaphysical in content. The revolutionary urge is countered by the realization that all the causes to which men commit themselves are doomed in the end to failure. The tragic hero combats this enervating sense of the absurd, though his consciousness refuses to deny the truth of this confrontation. Malraux's early fiction demonstrates the inescapable absurdity of the human condition, but it also reveals the energy resident in man that enables him to resist and transcend this negative conclusion. *The Conquerors* elaborates this basic theme, which is viewed against the background of the Orient. It is the West that is the source of this infection by metaphysical despair. It is the European revolutionaries, rootless middle-class intellectuals, who seek in revolutionary action an anodyne for the painful disease of thought. Garine is the metaphysical rebel who resorts to action as a means of silencing his inner demon. *The Conquerors* explores the complex, tangled motives that led both rebels and revolutionaries to leap into action.[8]

With incisive strokes Malraux moves the plot toward the destructive denouement. The novel, which opens immediately before the fighting breaks out, attempts to do two things: to narrate the revolutionary events in the making and to delineate the characters involved in these events. The first

8. "What distinguishes the chronically indignant rebel from the earnest revolutionary is that the former is capable of changing causes, the latter not. The rebel turns his indignation now against this injustice, now against another; the revolutionary is a consistent hater who has invested all his powers of hatred in one object. The rebel always has a touch of the quixotic; the revolutionary is a bureaucrat of Utopia. The rebel is an enthusiast; the revolutionary a fanatic" (Arthur Koestler, *Arrow in the Blue* [New York: The Macmillan Company, 1952], p. 272). Raymond Aron, in examining the concept of revolt, points out the difference between the revolutionary and the rebel, though the two may at times agree to join forces and make common cause. The revolutionary is dedicated to the mystique of action because he believes in the messianic future. He will drive the chariot of history on its appointed course. Sartre aligns himself with the revolutionary, Camus with the rebel. Aron writes:
"He who protests against the fate meted out to mankind by a meaningless universe sometimes finds himself in sympathy with the revolutionaries. . . . The party of the Revolution pours scorn on the descendants of Kierkegaard, Nietzsche or Kafka as the intellectual jeremiahs of a bourgeoisie which cannot console itself for the death of God because it is so conscious of its own death: the revolutionary, not the rebel, holds the key to transcendence and meaning—the historic future." (Raymond Aron, *The Opium of the Intellectuals*, trans. Terence Kilmartin [Garden City, N.Y.: Doubleday & Company, 1957], pp. 48-49).

aim is achieved by means of tight narrative economy, by the use of wireless reports, by mesages from men who work for Garine, and by personal on-the-spot observation. But the difficulty for Malraux was how to individualize his characters, to make them human and credible, and how to reveal in dramatically effective terms the motives that impelled the revolutionary to subjugate his personal self and discipline himself to act solely in the interests of the Party.

Men like Borodin and Garine, the one a seasoned revolutionary and the other a rebel by nature, represent two contrasting types. There is no room in the revolutionary movement, with its hierarchical structure and its insistence on obedience, for a character like Garine. He is an intellectual, and that is enough for the Communist to look upon him with suspicion. What is even worse is that he is haunted by his perception of the absurdity of life. If he yields to the mythomania of action, it is in order to face the Absurd with some measure of lucidity. He has little patience for the subtleties and equivocations of theory-mongering. He craves the intoxication of power.

Even though he fights in behalf of the revolutionary cause, Garine is not particularly interested in the results to be achieved. He does not believe in the myth of the proletariat as the liberators and saviors of society. Nevertheless, he is completely devoted to his job as the head of propaganda. Then the irrational and the absurd take over. By sheer force of will Garine keeps his illness at bay; he will not permit malaria and dysentery to defeat his purpose. But the illness steadily gains ground. In growing fever he is obsessed by the specter of the absurd. What, he asks himself, has he accomplished after all? The despair that now assails him is not to be driven off. Garine had joined the Revolution as a way of exorcizing the demons of the Absurd, but his plan miscarried. Men of his stamp did not belong in the revolutionary ranks.[9]

Malraux's experience in Indochina shaped his attitude toward politics. He returned to France, but soon went back to Indochina to launch a newspaper, *Indochine Enchaînée.* The

9. "The characters are primarily types, defined by their attitude toward life and politics. Borodin is the man who has submerged his individuality in the Revolution. Hong is the Terrorist. . . . The fact that they are also men emerges very slowly, even in the case of Garine." W. M. Frohock, *André Malraux and the Tragic Imagination* (Stanford, Calif.: Stanford University Press, 1952), p. 41.

venture failed. Despite all their efforts, he and his partner could not keep it going; the odds against them were too great. The paper was poorly printed; their muck-raking campaign against the government was ineffectual; their financial resources were exhausted. Malraux tried his hand at politics, organizing a revolutionary party of his own, "Young Annam," but it was powerless to affect the course of events in Indochina. He decided to return home and in France advocate the cause of the people of Indochina and thus oust the corrupt colonial government in power. His last editorial in *Indochine Enchainée* on December 26, 1925, announced his intention of undertaking this task. He realized that the people of Indochina would not be free until they expelled the French. His stay in Indochina transformed him from a superbly talented littérateur into a militant fighter for social justice. He had witnessed the aggrandizement of white administrators, their unconscionable appropriation of public funds, their use of force against the helpless natives. Appalled by these flagrant evils, Malraux became convinced that the rampant materialism of the West and its cult of individualism were doomed. The intellectuals in the West suffered from the death of the soul. In his fully documented study *André Malraux: The Indochina Adventure,* Walter G. Langlois maintains that Malraux's experience in Indochina during the early twenties had a decisive effect on his development as a writer and as a man, transforming the young dilettante "into a deeply commited anti-authoritarian agitator."[10]

Man's Fate in 1933 won the Goncourt prize. Now Malraux was in the limelight, courted by the Russians, though he was never an orthodox Marxist or a member of the Communist Party. It was his insistence on following an independent line of action that laid him open to suspicion. Indeed, some Communist critics accused him of being a Trotskyite. And *Man's Fate* did not satisfy the Marxist pundits. The revolutionary cause is defeated. Kyo does not fit into the picture of the subservient Party member. The policy of the International is not painted as infallible but as ruled by the principle of expediency. The Party is hungry for power, regardless of the fate that overtakes its individual leaders.[11]

10. Walter G. Langlois, *André Malraux: The Indochina Adventure* (New York and London: Frederick A. Praeger, 1966), p. 229.
11. "Malraux himself is, of course, the most outstanding embodiment of the mys-

In *Man's Fate* (1933), a varied group of characters play their part, each one wrestling in his own way with the challenge of the Absurd. Some pretend it does not exist. Some surrender to it. Others try to conquer it. Each person, as Malraux puts it, is the victim of his own mythomania. Kyo, in fighting for the dignity of man, be he a coolie or an "untouchable," has found a meaning and purpose in life. The characters and the actions in which they are involved in *Man's Fate* are meant to suggest universal implications. The novel, as its French title *(La Condition Humaine)* implies, deals not merely with the civil war that broke out in Shanghai in 1927 but with the human condition as a whole. "This means that the novel is primarily 'metaphysical' rather than political, despite first appearances. The characters' antagonist is still destiny; and not all of them are revolutionary."[12] Though Malraux at this stage of his development as a writer warmly supported the Communist cause, he did not allow his political commitment to dictate his method of portraying character.

> If there is a political lesson in the novel it is surely that the social condition mirrors the human condition, that revolutionary action is politically futile, since the revolutionaries gain none of their political aims and merely bring about their own destruction.[13]

During the thirties, when the rise of Fascism menaced the freedom of the whole world, Malraux, like many other intellectuals in France, cooperated with the policy formulated by the United Front. When he was asked in 1934 why so many French writers, formerly indifferent or opposed to the revolutionary struggle, were now willing to join the proletariat in the fight to achieve Socialism and defend the Soviet Union against its enemies, Malraux pointed to the socioeconomic crisis gripping the world as responsible for making them see the light of truth. The economic breakdown turned them in this direction, that and the threat of Fascism. He was convinced, he then stated, that "the most characteristic trait of

tique of revolutionary action. His very concept of man as being what he *does* (and not what he hides), as well as his romantic belief that man's true fatherland is courage, would account for his expressed notion that everything that falls short of revolution is worse than revolution." Victor Brombert, *The Intellectual Hero: Studies in the French Novel, 1880-1955* (Philadelphia and New York: J. B. Lippincott Company, 1961), p. 150.
12. Denis Boak, *André Malraux* (London: Oxford University Press, 1968), p. 63.
13. *Ibid.,* p. 90.

the present state of mind in the West is the *perishing of individualism* in its established bourgeois form."[14] He went on to say:

> The assertion that the artist is entirely subject to the world surrounding him—is a meaningless assertion. The world by itself is formless and the first task of the artist is to find a form, select the material he needs. This selection is determined by his ideology which, in this case, plays the role of spectacles through which the artist sees.[15]

In the preface to *Days of Wrath* (1935), Malraux points out that the artist is not driven by the need to prove a thesis. It is the emotional and imaginative impact of a literary work on the sensibility of the reader that is more important than the propagandistic message the work is supposed to carry. The hero of the novel, a Communist named Kassner, is imprisoned by the Nazis and struggles to retain his sanity. The words tapped out by a prisoner in another cell give him the courage to endure his lot. An intellectual enlisted in the revolutionary cause, Kassner affirms the redemptive theme of brotherhood over the countervailing theme of the Absurd.

When civil war broke out in Spain, Malraux flew sixty-five missions for the Loyalists. He wrote *Man's Hope* (1937) at a time when he believed that the victory of the Republican forces was assured. He organized an International Air Squadron. By 1937 he was no longer involved in the fighting, but there were other important tasks he was assigned. He made speeches in behalf of the Republican cause, raised funds, and worked on his novel. He played a leading role in the Writers' Congress held in Madrid. He wrote the novel in great haste, hoping that its publication might influence the outcome of the struggle.

Man's Hope is a revolutionary novel that develops the central theme of brotherhood, but the propagandistic intention interferes with the logical development of the plot. The characters reveal themselves in relation to the crucial events in which they participate. Malraux uses the technique of reportage and furnishes terse, vivid accounts of battles fought, but the power of the narrative resides principally in its depiction of the conflict that takes place within the mind and heart

14. "An Interview with André Malraux." *International Literature*, no. 5 (November 1934), p. 144.
15. *Ibid.*, p. 146.

of the characters themselves. In this war, enthusiasm or idealism is not enough to defeat the enemy. The anarchists are brave to the point of foolhardiness; they are prepared to sacrifice their life for the cause, but their impetuous bravery wins no battles; they are simply killed off. It is the Communists who take charge of things and impose the order and discipline needed if the Loyalist army is to be at all effective against Franco's mechanized troops. The Communist as a man of action, objective, ruthless, is contrasted with the romantic anarchist, beguiled by theory, who is interested solely in fulfilling his individual desires. Malraux shows how individualism conflicts with the urgent need of achieving Party discipline. Malraux emphasizes that the realistic attitude of the Communists must prevail if the Revolution in Spain is to triumph. Only thus can the victory of the masses be assured.

Malraux reveals the price that must be paid if the war is to be won. He introduces characters who refuse to submit to Communist control; they will not compromise their ideals in order to satisfy the demands of military action. They are implacable foes of Fascism but this does not induce them to approve of Communist leadership. The Revolution generates a rising, powerful tide of idealism; unfortunately, the Revolution is not a cure-all for the ills of mankind. The Communists are the only ones capable of organizing and leading an army, but they demand the abandonment of the vision that nerved these anarchists to fight against Franco. Hernandez suffers because he cannot resolve this internal conflict; he refuses to allow others, whatever their aim may be, to use him as an instrument in the prosecution of the war; his conscience protests against the indignity of being used for such a purpose. He is obsessed by the thought of death. He is too sensitive a person to survive and the Revolution destroys him, whereas others somehow make their peace with Communism. *Man's Hope* celebrates the capacity of men to achieve communion on the battlefield, but the propagandistic stress mars the aesthetic value of the novel. One critic, however, contends that "the novel remains—in my judgment—not only the finest *roman engagé* of the century, but indeed the only one which is fully satisfactory on both the intellectual and emotional planes."[16]

After the debacle in Spain, Malraux perceived the basic

16. Boak, *André Malraux,* p. 134.

flaw in the act of political commitment for the writer. Not that he had to live down his past. A free spirit, he was not chained to the political orthodoxy of the Left. He followed at all times the prompting of his own beliefs. He had never joined the Communist Party nor faithfully echoed its ideological pronunciamentos. He did not hesitate to speak out for fear of harming the cause of Communism. Through all the vicissitudes of the thirties and forties he affirmed a tragic humanism that summed up the values he believed in.

> Malraux's concern has always been with man's relationship with death and his reaction in the face of destiny. His writings reflect this preoccupation. *"Le destin, c'est la politique."* The work of Malraux as novelist is political in the same high sense in which Napoleon considered destiny to be political.[17]

The Walnut Trees of Altenburg (1943), the last of Malraux's novels to be published, gives voice to a universal humanism. In it Malraux projects a poignant image of the conflicts raging in his own mind. Möllberg, an ethnologist, had been seeking to prove that the conception of man follows a line of historical continuity, but his trip to Mesopotamia and Africa worked havoc with this idea, and he tore his manuscript, *Civilization as a Conquest and Destiny,* to bits and left them scattered over the wilds of Africa. His studies convinced him that man is the product of chance and that the world is destined for oblivion. He reiterates the theme of the Absurd: man is headed for the ultimate fate of nothingness. Möllberg is the devil's advocate, the convert to a despairing nihilism.[18]

What issues from this colloquium, as Malraux describes it, is the fearful suspicion that man is an accident in a biological universe—a thesis recently confirmed scientifically by Jacques Monod in *Chance and Necessity.*[19] Civilization is doomed to

17. Pierre Galante, *Malraux,* trans. Haakon Chevalier (New York: Cowles Book Company, 1971), p. x.
18. "Möllberg himself is the 'nihilistic will' in scientific dress. He proposes a ground for the felt dilemma of the colloquium, that the notion of man has been eroded by science and history." William Righter, *The Rhetorical Hero* (London: Routledge and Kegan Paul, 1964), p. 17.
19. According to Monod, the essential message of modern science "subverts every one of the mythical or philosophical ontogenies upon which the animist tradition . . . has made all ethics rest: values, duties, rights, prohibitions" (Jacques Monod, *Chance and Necessity,* trans. Austryn Wainhouse [New York: Alfred A. Knopf, 1971], p. 172). The dream of the millennium must be discarded. Man must come to realize at last that he is alone in the universe, "a world that is deaf to his music, just as indifferent to his hopes as it is to his suffering or his crimes" *(ibid.,* p. 173).

perish sooner or later; the human adventure is without an ultimate aim or purpose. Malraux seems to suggest that the realm of art enables man to transcend the human condition. The artist as rebel humanizes the world. Written in the midst of World War II, *The Walnut Trees of Altenburg* marks the end of Malraux's career as a novelist.

For fifteen years he had withstood the greatest temptation that besets the writer of good will who is liberal or radical in his sympathies: the temptation to exploit his creative power for political ends. Many a writer gives in to this temptation and commits himself to a political cause. How can he keep silent and remain unconcerned while the wretched of the earth are robbed of their heritage, oppressed, and enslaved? How can he go ahead with his literary career as if there were nothing seriously wrong with the world? Out of a frustrated feeling of justice, impelled by an outraged conscience and motives of humanitarian compassion, he allies himself with the Communist Party in his country or becomes part of a movement designed to abolish a particular evil: war or racism or capital punishment.

At times, however, the writer wonders what he, *as a writer,* can hope to accomplish with his pen? He can, of course, adopt a number of face-saving, conscience-salving expedients: writer letters to influential newspapers protesting a gross miscarriage of justice or intolerable living conditions in his land or abroad, sign petitions, compose manifestos, engage in polemics, but even these efforts will consume valuable time and interfere with his creative work. Or he can try, as some have done, though not with conspicuous success, to exploit the different forms of literature as a vehicle for social protest and reform. Or, in a time of great peril to the future of mankind, he can abandon his pursuits as a writer and do what he can to defeat the common enemy.

Now, the novel lends itself admirably to the expression of political ideas, but it is questionable whether the political novel at its best exerts any influence on the course of history. The examples usually cited as proof positive that such an influence has been at work in the past are *Uncle Tom's Cabin, Hard Times, The Jungle*—and then one stops, at a loss for further impressive illustrations. What is more to the point is the fact that the novelist as a rule has not been trained in the field of political science. He has not formulated a systematic and comprehensive body of political ideas.

Malraux presents a test case of the politically committed writer during the thirties who rejected the beliefs of liberalism and democracy in favor of the revolutionary outlook. He was not interested in the intrigues of politicians or the maneuvers of political parties in their jockeying for power. The aesthetic stance of his early fiction was, as we have seen, colored by his political convictions at the time. He was part of the rebellious postwar younger generation that experienced the metaphysical despair born of extreme disillusionment—a degree of disillusionment that in some quarters reached the nadir of nihilism. He was a member of the generation that began to question the traditional conception of "reality" and came face to face with the myth of the Absurd. In *Man's Fate,* Malraux made it clear that it was not the class war that incites the workers to take revolutionary action but the need to affirm their dignity as men, their fight against alienation. When he enlisted under the banner of de Gaulle, his attitude toward Communism underwent a marked change and the critics on the Left denounced him as a traitor or Fascist. As Wilkinson remarks, Malraux "was always a spiritual fascist, or at least a nihilist: he has never surpassed his initial perception of the world's absurdity, for all his principal characters are nihilists and all their lives are empty cycles of struggle and death. . . ."[20]

In "The Death Mask of André Malraux," Garaudy performs a savage autopsy on the work of this novelist, once the darling of Communist critics. Now he is condemned on the ground that he is narrowly subjective in his insights and that his novels betray infallible symptoms of Fascist decay. Garaudy brings to light what he regards as the unmistakable symptoms of Fascist decay present in the man and his fiction; he is the recorder of the decadence of an age and the decadence of a class: the bourgeoisie. He is accused of being an existentialist philosopher who delights in scenes of carnage, but one who remains far removed from the thick of battle. The victim of metaphysical despair, he is the bankrupt author of a ravaged Europe, the effete representative of a dying culture. That is why he characteristically creates heroes who are alone, trapped in a solitude from which they cannot escape. His revolutionary themes fail to hit the mark. Even

20. David Wilkinson, *Malraux,* p. 120n.

his Communist characters are reactionaries. Malraux's crime is that he advances an ideology that is unable to inspire the proletariat and is adopted by reactionary circles. In every historical crisis, the best the Malrauvian protagonist can do is to contemplate his Narcissus-like image in the mirror. Malraux's ingrained individualism is counterrevolutionary. Garaudy charges that Malraux's work "is never rooted in real, historic oppression; nor does it ever attain a triumphant climax."[21] Instead of portraying physical man situated in his social environment, Malraux fixes his attention on the metaphysical dimension. This metaphysical approach, Garaudy insists, "leads quite naturally to an aristocratic and reactionary conception of social life."[22] Since Malraux is no longer in sympathy with the aims and ideals of the proletariat, he pictures a world that is morally defunct. Obsessed with death, he has become the lugubrious voice of defeatism.

Garaudy's vicious attack does not alter the fact that Malraux played a vital role in the political life of his time. If he never joined the Communist Party, "it seems impossible to deny that he worked for the Communist cause as actively, and with as good cause . . . for the better part of twenty years. And by now he has worked well over twenty years against it."[23] The story of his political commitment reveals the character of the man, but it will have no bearing on his reputation as an artist.

21. Roger Garaudy, *The Literature of the Graveyard,* trans. Joseph M. Bernstein (New York: International Publishers, 1948), p. 28.
22. *Ibid.,* p. 30.
23. Boak, *André Malraux,* p. 9.

14

Jean-Paul Sartre: From Existentialism to Communism

What he [Sartre] is trying to do is in some way to construct a society from metaphysically defined individuals, to construct history from the non-temporal, an historical materialism without matter.[1]

In the post-war world one needed to make carefully balanced protests against tyranny in Spain and tyranny in Czechoslovakia, race discrimination in America and forced labour in the Soviet Union, executions in Persia and executions in Budapest, in order to preserve a clear conscience and one's own intellectual equilibrium which was constantly subjected to new threats. The intellect, which had been set up as the conscience of the world, became so problematic to itself that it could see all other problems only in relation to itself; in the end the only theme of the *littérature engagée* became itself and the *engagement* ended in solipsism. Jean-Paul Sartre above all, even in his polemical writing and in

1. Roger Garaudy, *Marxism in the Twentieth Century*, trans. René Hague [New York: Charles Scribner's Sons, 1970), p. 92. Garaudy attacks the philosophy of Existentialism presented in *Being and Nothingness*. The publication of the *Critique of Dialectical Reason* did not cause him to change his mind about the value of Sartre's work. He accuses Sartre of overemphasizing subjectivity. Though he now declares that he endorses Marxism as the supreme truth of our time, his conception of Marxism, Garaudy insists, "is still metaphysical . . . and fundamentally individualist" *(ibid.,* p. 204).

his plays, never dealt with any other subject and never had any other conversational partner than himself.[2]

One of the astounding blunders of Marxist aesthetics in the twentieth century was its determined effort, especially when the rallying cry of commitment was raised, to transform literature into an instrument of ideological coordination, preferably under the auspices of the Communist Party. The writer was portrayed as the articulate conscience of the historical process, the prophet and midwife of the "ideal" collectivistic society to be ushered in. He was given an important social function, a responsible mission to carry out, a redemptive purpose to fulfill. It was incumbent upon him to reject the regnant literary tradition, the tainted heritage of a feudal and bourgeois past, and pave the way for or himself create the work instinct with the revolutionary message that will rouse the proletariat from their slumber. He was called upon to preach the gospel of Communism as a secular religion whose eschatological vision of Kingdom Come, as embodied in the Soviet Union, is to be realized on earth and in the near future. In the beginning, many writers were inspired by the Marxist evangel. They were animated by an altruistic desire to join in the fight for the liberation of the oppressed working class.

Unfortunately, the relationship between the artists in the Soviet Union and the Party leaders who ruled the country with an iron hand was not a happy one. In the early years after the October Revolution, writers and painters enjoyed a glorious period of uninhibited freedom to experiment with new forms. It was not long, however, before controls were instituted. The Stalinist regime demanded that all artists in Russia abide by the principles of Socialist realism. If the writer complained that the ideological restrictions imposed by the Party bureaucrats deprived him of his creative freedom, it was pointed out to him that he enjoyed a number of advantages denied to his professional counterparts in the

2. Francis Bondy, "Jean-Paul Sartre," in Maurice Cranston, ed., *The New Left* (New York: The Library Press, 1971), p. 58n. Bondy quotes this passage from Herbert Lüthy, "Frankreichs heimatlose Linke," in *Nach dem Untergang des Abendlandes* (Cologne, 1965).

capitalist West. He was informed that he was an integral part of an unprecedented epic undertaking to transform the character of man and shape the destiny of the human race. He was encouraged to participate in this grandiose historic movement. Unlike the artist in the West who must sell his wares in the commercial market, he was honorably employed and rewarded by the State.

> All that is asked of him in return is just one sacrifice: to say yes to the regime, to say yes to its day-to-day interpretation—an inescapable concession which yet carries the germ of a total corruption.[3]

The left-wing writer outside the Soviet Union is expected to take his stand, to align himself with the embattled proletariat the world over. He is exhorted by the leading Marxist spokesman to become involved in the social struggles of his day, and a number of writers in France have done so— Romain Rolland, Barbusse, Gide, Malraux, Louis Aragon, de Beauvoir, and Sartre. Their sense of "commitment" led them to address workers' meetings, to draft petitions, sign protests, lead demonstrations for peace, denounce Fascism, lend their support to the United Front. The result was that they had little time or energy left for the practice of their art. If they decided to withdraw from such time-consuming activities and devote themselves wholly to their creative work, their guilty conscience led them at times to inject propagandistic material into a context where it clearly does not belong. This was particularly true of those writers, like Aragon and Barbusse, who were Party members. Conditioned by the teachings of the Party, their minds frequently responded to its unspoken demands.[4] They glorified the role of the proletariat, exalting the workers by picturing them as the saviors of the world, despite the incontrovertible fact that the workers do not constitute an identifiable type and are not united by a common cause.

Writers in France who were not Party members but were

3. Raymond Aron, *The Opium of the Intellectuals*, trans. Terence Kilmartin (Garden City, N. Y.: Doubleday & Company, 1957), p. 300.
4. "The intellectual who is in a responsible position in the Communist Party mobilizes the masses. . . . A prisoner of the pitiless servitude of the régime, he is obliged to exalt the leaders of the State, to follow the meanderings of a line sanctified by the future kingdom of God." *Ibid.*, p. 303.

sympathetic to the Communist cause generally resisted the pressure of the authoritarian ideology promulgated by the Comintern. Even as fellow travelers they would not allow their political sympathies to weaken their adherence to the truth. Sartre struggled hard for a time to reconcile Marxism with his existentialist aesthetic. He believed in the validity and value of a "committed" literature. The difficulty he faced was that, as the founder of atheistic existentialism, he was bound to reject the philosophy of determinism basic to the Marxist system of thought. A rebel at heart, Sartre shied away from joining the Party. He wished to retain his independence, his freedom to criticize the Communist Party and the Soviet Union, should the need arise. He believed in the ethic of commitment and urged all writers on the Left to help create a committed literature, but committed to what? What are the canons of commitment?[5]

Sartre quarreled with Camus over the issue of Communism[6] and endeavored to collaborate with the Communists. In 1952 he attended the World Congress for Peace. He sought to demonstrate that he could work out an agreement with the Communists without sacrificing his independence of judgment, that he was being true to his "commitment." He castigated Camus for not being in rapport with the workers. He was at fault for not giving mankind a reason

5. "Is the work nothing but a means to some further end? the propagation of an idea, philosophical, economic, social, or political? If so, the author never escapes his propagandist guise, even if his work shows all the stylistic excellence of a lifetime masterpiece" (Eugene F. Kaelin, *An Existentialist Aesthetic*. Madison, Wis.: The University of Wisconsin Press, 1962), p. 121.) Professor Kaelin questions whether Sartre was guilty of insinuating propaganda into his imaginative writings. A prolific writer of feuilletons, philosophical essays, polemics, political journalism, Sartre produced novels and plays in which his ideas are artistically embodied. Though his novels, after the publication of *Nausea*, give expression to his philosophical and political concerns, they are not to be judged, Professor Kaelin argues, by the ideas they present but as works of fiction. The philosophy the various characters set forth in *Les Chemins de la liberté (Roads to Freedom)*, be it Marxist or Existentialist, is of secondary importance. See the chapter on "Sartre's Politics" in Anthony Manser, *Sartre* (London: The Athlone Press, 1966), pp. 189-205, which describes the shift in Sartre's political thought after the end of the Second World War. "Sartre has stuck to his own principles and has not hesitated to condemn the Party when it appears to have acted wrongly" (*ibid.*, p. 13).

6. See "Reply to Camus," in Jean-Paul Sartre, *Situations*, trans. Benita Eisler (Greenwich, Conn.: Fawcett Publications, 1966), pp. 54-78. See also Bernard Murchland, "Sartre and Camus: The Anatomy of a Quarrel," in Michel-Antoine Burnier, *Choice of Action*, trans. Bernard Murchland (New York: Vintage Books, 1969), pp. 175-96.

for living. In his "Reply to Camus," Sartre denounced the
ethic of irresponsibility that a number of French writers supported. He was fed up with idealistic aims. He condemned
The Rebel because it specialized in metaphysical categories and
moral injunctions. Sartre reiterated his belief that mankind is
the architect of history. "At that time, for the committed writer to give meaning to history meant to prevent the
threatened end of mankind, to fight for peace side by side
with the Communists."[7] He bitterly reproached the intellectuals for clinging to their fragile dreams. He urged them to
accept the leadership of the Communists. "Why? Because the
future of democracy is in the hands of the working man and
the Communist Party is the party of the working class."[8] In
proclaiming such views, Sartre could not avoid a clash with
Camus, who was opposed to Communism.[9]

Sartre also offers an impressive example of the committed
writer who is concerned not with the fulfillment of his literary career but primarily with the full utilization of his intellectual resources so that he can help to achieve the social,
economic, and political salvation of mankind. And he interprets "salvation" in Marxist rather than mystagogic terms.
The humiliation of defeat and the occupation of France, the
internment of Frenchmen and Jews in concentration
camps—all this convinced Sartre that the old remedies would
no longer suffice. Out of this experience of abjection, the
hopelessness that gripped the soul of France during the
period of the Occupation, the imprisonment and torture of
those who resisted the Nazi foe, his countrymen would have
to learn the need for solidarity in a world given over to the
power of evil. That is why Sartre, like Brecht before him,
urged his fellow men to discard the pernicious illusion that
they could cultivate their private garden (their talent or their
sensibility) and reach out to capture the bluebird of happiness while the earth is the battleground of the class war.

Though Sartre at this time was ambiguous in his attitude
toward the Communist Party, he did not hesitate to define

7. Burnier, *Choice of Action,* p. 80.
8. *Ibid.,* p. 83.
9. Simone de Beauvoir writes: "While Sartre believed in the truth of socialism,
   Camus became a more and more resolute champion of bourgeois values; *The
   Rebel* was a statement of his solidarity with them." Simone de Beauvoir, *Force
   of Circumstance,* trans. Richard Howard (New York: G. P. Putnam's Sons,
   1965), p. 260.

his position as being that of a Marxist. He is not, however, and never has been, what we call an "orthodox" Marxist. What he has in common with Marxism, with dialectical materialism, is its rejection of the supernatural; what he cannot accept is its conception of man as an object among objects. In the final analysis, as Sartre is aware, Marxism formulates a revolutionary myth that must be taken on faith, since this aroused faith is a powerful generator of revolutionary action. It is a myth that is capable of energizing the will. But a materialist universe logically entails the supersession of the human will. Marxism teaches that man must submit to the ineluctable mandate of history. In effect, it denies the creative role of the individual. The Communists were thus guilty of "bad faith." Sartre agrees that social classes exist and that these are the end product of the interaction of economic forces, but he does not believe that the classless society will eliminate all sources of frustration and conflict.

Sartre's remarkable career as philosopher, novelist, dramatist, literary critic, journalist, polemicist, and Marxist shows how at each stage of his development he strove to transcend himself. Though he is an avowed atheist, he evinces a quasi-religious passion in his quest for a cause to which he can give himself wholeheartedly, a cause that will justify his existence. Though he never repudiated his belief in the absurdity of existence, he went beyond the Existentialist philosophy expounded in *Being and Nothingness*. He identified himself with the working class and supported the Communist Party, which represented the interests of the workers.

The Existentialists were at first not interested in politics. Though they were in sympathy with the struggle waged by the Left, they did not subscribe to a definite political program. As a group they opposed the capitalist system, they tended to idealize the character of the proletariat, and they were impressed by the achievements of the Soviet Union, but they kept aloof from political activism, since they cherished the virtue of disinterested abstract speculation. They were intellectuals possessing all the traits that characterized them as a group. Bourgeois in their origins, bourgeois in their profession of neutrality, they were, as the Communists had suspected all along, incapacitated for the life of action. Sartre was an utter stranger to the proletariat he later glorified.

Sartre never voted (even for the election of the Popular Front) and only reluctantly accepted a union card. He and Simone de Beauvoir sometimes attended demonstrations of the United Left after 1934, but it never occurred to them "to parade, sing or shout with the others."[10]

The Existentialists were essentially spectators. In fact, Sartre felt only disdain at that time for those intellectuals who were embroiled in politics; for their interminable wordy debates, their proclamations, their abuse of the hated foe. Their opposition, Sartre then felt, counted for naught.

Gradually he turned to Marxism, which had the power to shake him out of his stance of detachment. Sartre and de Beauvoir were not content with their role as rootless intellectuals. The threat of war forced them to face the implications of the historical situation into which they had been thrust. They could no longer engage, as in the carefree past, in irrelevant aesthetic pursuits. They awoke to the reality of politics, and Sartre describes this awakening in his trilogy, *Roads to Freedom.*[11] Renouncing his role of privileged, passive observer, Sartre responded to the call for commitment. He chose politics above literature.

In *Les Temps Modernes,* Sartre harped on the theme that the writer cannot afford to stand above the battle. He attempted to formulate a political ethic that would supplant his ontology. In affirming the truth of the class conflict, he spoke not as an individual but as the representative of a class that would inherit the future. Sartre and Merleau-Ponty announced that in the event of war they would side with the Soviet Union. Though Sartre defended Marxism as a revolutionary discipline, the Communists centered their attack

10. Michel-Antoine Burnier, *Choice of Action,* p. 5.
11. By means of a series of sharp contrasts, Sartre develops the theme of commitment. Mathieu is troubled by a feeling of guilt because he had not gone to Spain to fight on the side of the Loyalists. His friend Gomez, the artist, left for Spain on hearing that Irun was captured by Franco's troops. Gomez leaves his unfinished canvases behind him. "Gomez's action was decisive, virile, and in total opposition to the ineffective procrastination of Mathieu" (George Howard Bauer, *Sartre and the Artist* [Chicago and London: The Unviersity of Chicago Press, 1969], p. 67). All Mathieu can do is to debate the issue with himself: "Why am I caught in this loathsome world of noises, surgical instruments, furtive taxi-rides, in this world where Spain does not exist? Why am I not in the thick of it, with Gomez, with Brunet? Why haven't I wanted to go and fight?" (Jean-Paul Sartre, *The Age of Reason,* trans. Eric Sutton [New York: Alfred A. Knopf, 1948], p. 146).

on Existentialism, which they branded as idealistic and decadent. They asserted that it smacked of Fascism. They called him a nihilist.[12] When Roger Garaudy labeled Sartre a graveyard digger, the latter retorted by saying that he had better be that—an honest occupation, after all—than serve as a lackey in the Communist Party. Garaudy takes the Existentialists to task for their reliance on metaphysical speculation, their retreat into absolute subjectivity, their isolation from the social conflicts of their age. "Sartre and his kind never felt themselves part of the masses, one with men and their history. So to him freedom is not creative participation in the dialectics of necessity."[13] Sartre's concept of freedom is irrational, without content, for it postulates a world of contingency whose future cannot be predicted.

> In Sartre, freedom, which is an absolute choice, has nothing to do with reason; history, drowned in subjectivity and the perpetual waiting for a justification that never comes, has nothing to do with science. This should suffice to expose the basically obscurant character of existentialism.[14]

Existentialism, Garaudy charges, contains no points of agreement with Marxism. In fact, it contradicts Marxism. "From its doctrine of free will to its idealist theory of knowledge, from its negation of scientific history to its indifference toward science, existentialism castrates man."[15] Garaudy sums up his indictment by characterizing Sartre's philosophy of freedom as confused, anarchic, impotent. "Nothing in his philosophy opens the road to action. That is why this philosophy is profoundly reactionary."[16]

Unruffled by these nasty aspersions, Sartre continued to move in the direction of the revolutionary Left. Together with other Existentialists he organized the Rassemblement Démocratique Révolutionaire (R.D.R.), which would cooper-

---

12. "Whatever may be said in criticism of Sartre's ethics, it does not seem fair to call him a nihilist even by implication" (Norman N. Greene, *Jean-Paul Sartre: The Existentialist Ethic* [Ann Arbor, Mich.: The University of Michigan Press, 1960], p. 161). There is no reason why the term "nihilism," rightly construed in context, should be used as an invidious, personally damaging epithet.
13. Roger Garaudy, *Literature of the Graveyard,* trans. Joseph M. Bernstein (New York: International Publishers, 1948), p. 9.
14. *Ibid.,* p. 11.
15. *Ibid.,* p. 13.
16. *Ibid.,* p. 15.

ate with the militant working class while asserting its right to criticize Stalinist Communism when the occasion for such criticism should arise. It appealed directly to the French proletariat and announced that it would remain democratic in spirit. In 1950, when Sartre was convinced of the existence of Soviet labor camps, he did not remain prudently silent. When the Korean War started, he sided with the Soviets, who were devoted to the cause of peace. More and more he allied himself with the Communists and reserved his most opprobrious epithets for those who were opposed to Communism. "An anti-Communist," he wrote, "is a rat."[17] Or: "An anti-Communist is a dog; that is what I will always hold."[18]

The articles he published in his newspaper dealing with the May 28th Demonstration and the June 4th Strike (they have been brought together in *The Communists and Peace*) are a dreary disappointment. The events themselves, the violent controversies that broke out, the personalities involved in the debate, the factional quarrels—all these, eroded by time, have lost their significance and savor. What we get is a series of talmudic disputations, political infighting. Sartre vigorously defends the leadership of the Communist Party, the policy of the Soviet Union, and the character of the proletariat. At one point he writes:

> When the worker is reduced to his worn-out body, to the gloomy daily awareness of his exhaustion, death seems to him all the more absurd the more his life loses meaning; death inspires in him a horror all the stronger the more tired he is of living: the bosses have nothing to fear—neither revolt nor a man power shortage—when the worker has no other reason to live than the fear of dying. . . . Common sense, a cool calculation of the chances—everything tells him to let go, to give up the struggle against enemies who have weapons, troops, money, machines, and science.[19]

But the workers have not given up; they will achieve organizational unity and under the auspices of the Party carry out their messianic mission.[20] For the worker, Sartre proclaims,

17. Burnier, *Choice of Action*, p. 74.
18. Joseph H. McMahon, *Human Beings: The World of Jean-Paul Sartre* (Chicago and London: The University of Chicago Press, 1971), p. 7.
19. Jean-Paul Sartre, *The Communists and Peace*, trans. Martha H. Fletcher (New York: George Braziller, 1968), p. 82.
20. "A fortiori it is scarcely possible at the present day to take seriously the claims made for the practical relevance, in a country like France, of Marxism-

"the Party is his freedom. Today, a worker in France can express himself and fulfill himself only in a class action directed by the C.P. . . ."[21]

As editor of *Les Temps Modernes,* Sartre informed his readers that Marxism was the only valid philosophy of our time. Since Marxism has been led astray by the epigones, he rejects their call for revision and resists their attempt to rehabilitate the pre-Marxist synthesis. "His desire is rather a project to restore to Marxism its original vital impulse."[22] During the fifties he arrived at the conclusion that Existentialism has been superseded, though until then it had refused to surrender to Marxism. Sartre was now convinced "both that historical materialism provides the only valid interpretation of history and at *the same time* that existentialism remains the only concrete approach to reality."[23] Sartre agrees with Engels that men are the makers of history but adds that they shape it within a particular environment that conditions their response. Man is not only a product of the socioeconomic forces acting upon him but is also an agent who affects the tempo of social change and determines the direction of the historical process.

Sartre is a Marxist, but is he to be regarded as a Communist? Is Existentialism not to be looked upon as but a footnote in the science of Marxist hermeneutics? In his essay "Marxism and Existentialism," Sartre accords primacy to Marxism, but he does not rescind the major importance he formerly attributed to human freedom nor does he revoke his views on the contingency of freedom. In *Being and Nothingness,* he had said: "Being is without reason, without cause, and without necessity; the very definition of being releases to us its original contingency."[24] But it is meaningful to question the origin of the for-itself: the question of "Why" that it raises. "Everything happens as if the world, man, and

Leninism. There are signs that this fact is beginning to be perceived even by Communists, who on these grounds may well come to revise the traditional view of the proletariat as the class destined to make an end of capitalism." George Lichtheim, *Marxism in Modern France* (New York and London: Columbia University Press, 1966), p. viii.

21. Sartre, *The Communists and Peace,* p. 131.
22. R. D. Laing and D. G. Cooper, *Reason & Violence: A Decade of Sartre's Philosophy 1950-1960* (New York: Pantheon Books, 1971), pp. 25-26.
23. *Ibid.,* p. 37.
24. Jean-Paul Sartre, *Being and Nothingness,* trans. Hazel E. Barnes (New York: Philosophical Library, 1956), p. 619.

man-in-the-world succeeded in realizing only a missing God."[25] In taking up the ethical implications of his ontology, Sartre asserts that there are no categorical imperatives. "Man makes himself man in order to be God. . . ."[26] Existential psychoanalysis refuses to recognize the existence of values apart from the creation of these values by human subjectivity.

Sartre has tried to cope with the difficult task of reconciling these inconsistent and incompatible positions. If Existentialism espouses a philosophy of universal determinism, it commits intellectual suicide. Sartre tried hard to find some plausible and rationally persuasive way of combining his existentialist outlook with his new ethic of revolutionary commitment, but the results were deplorable. Raymond Aron cogently asks: "What is this 'common ground' of Marxism and existentialism? I would define it as *the calling into question of both the destiny of the individual and the historical destiny of mankind.*"[27] Sartre failed to create a fully convincing version of Marxianized Existentialism.[28] "With no other criterion than the truth of the party, with no other certitude than the rejection of the present, the militant, whether Marxist or existentialist, is in fact a nihilist."[29] Aron demonstrates that "it is fundamentally impossible to call oneself an existentialist and a Marxist at the same time. . . ."[30] He shows why "these two philosophies are incompatible in their intentions, their origins, and their ultimate ends."[31] Hence an Existentialist, if he

25. *Ibid.,* p. 623.
26. *Ibid.,* p. 626.
27. Raymond Aron, *Marxism and the Existentialists* (New York and London: Harper & Row, 1969), p. 12.
28. A number of critics have rushed to the defense of Sartre. Frederic Jameson rebuts Sartre's detractors by contending that the acceptance of Marxism as a philosophy "does not seem to preclude the adherence to some other kind of philosophy; that one can be both a Marxist and an existentialist, phenomenologist, Hegelian, realist, empiricist, or whatever" (Jameson, *Marxism and Form,* p. 207). The *Critique of Dialectical Reason* is not "a radical break with the position of *Being and Nothingness*" (ibid., p. 208). In *Sartre: The Radical Conversion,* James F. Sheridan sets out to refut the charges made by a number of critics in England and the United States that there is a fundamental contradiction between Existentialism and Marxism. "Sartre became convinced that capitalism was a social and political order which *systematically* kept the greater part of mankind in a near sub-human status and thus was wholly inconsistent with the ideology of freedom it professed. Until it was overthrown, *men* would not be fully free, and thus *man* would not be fully his freedom" (James F. Sheridan, *Sartre: The Radical Conversion* [Athens, Ohio: Ohio University Press, 1969], p. 17).
29. Aron, *Marxism and the Existentialists,* p. 15.
30. *Ibid.,* p. 28.
31. *Ibid.,* p. 28.

believes in the truth of his philosophy, cannot become a convert to Marxism.

Sartre the Existentialist had vehemently denied that human decisions are dictated by the inexorable logic of events, the immanent dialectic of history. Man is not at the mercy of his material environment. And he had advised writers not to align themselves with the Communist Party. "How can the politics of Stalinist Communism, Sartre asks, be compatible with the honest practice of the literary craft? . . . If the work of art cannot accommodate itself to bourgeois didactic standards, neither can it make its peace with Communist utilitarianism."[32] Though he has of late conveniently ignored or forgotten these antinomies, Sartre fashioned for himself a Marxist system that, though subtly Existentialized in some ways, represented a repudiation of his Existentialist philosophy. By 1960 there is no mistaking the depth and strength of his adherence to Marxism.

> Existentialism, he now conceded, was only an ideology, a parasitic system existing in the margin of knowledge, whereas Marxism was a philosophy, the most advanced and comprehensive of which the present generation was capable.[33]

Whatever "deviations" are to be found in his interpretation of Marxism, his loyalty to the Revolution is not to be questioned. Sartre means what he says when he writes: "I consider Marxism the one philosophy which we cannot go beyond. . . .[34]

The invasion of Hungary by the Red Army and the brutal suppression of the uprising in that land aroused the wrath of Sartre. The Soviet Union was guilty of firing upon the Hungarian proletariat. Sartre cited evidence to prove his point that the Hungarian workers who took up arms had no intention of effecting a compromise with capitalism. Sartre thus demonstrated his independence of judgment: the Party leaders in France and the Soviet Union had no power over him; he could not be silenced. He analyzed the harm committed by the Stalinist dictatorship, the implications of the

---

32. Charles I. Glicksberg, "Existentialism *versus* Marxism," *The Nineteenth Century and After* 147 (May 1950): 335-41.
33. David Caute, *Communism and the French Intellecutals 1914-1960* (New York: The Macmillan Company, 1964), p. 257.
34. Jean-Paul Sartre, *Search for a Method*, trans. Hazel E. Barnes (New York: Alfred A. Knopf, 1963), p. xxiv.

monolithic emphasis on establishing Socialism in one country, and the flagrant contradictions that emerge in Stalin's officially endorsed—and stringently enforced—version of Marxism.[35] As a political realist, however, Sartre proclaimed his belief that, in a backward country like Russia, Stalinism was necessary as a salutary disciplining force.

His occasional outbursts of disaffection did not weaken his revolutionary zeal. In 1971 he published his book on Flaubert (which he defended as a thoroughly political work), but he had actually given up the practice of literature and devoted himself wholly to the Communist cause. He is the committed writer *par excellence,* the patron saint of left-wing groups. He turned down the Nobel prize and announced his complete support of the student rebellion in 1968. The function of the intellectual, he explained, has been drastically changed. His special task is to write through the masses, for the masses, and with the masses. He must turn over to them his body of technical knowledge. His privileged status, Sartre announces, is ended. The intellectual is guilty of bad faith if he remains self-absorbed, concerned only with his own problems. He must acknowledge the fact that it is the toiling masses who made it possible for him to become an intellectual. Therefore, Sartre reasons, since he owes his acquisition of learning to the workers, he "must be with them and in them. . . ."[36]

Sartre has acted as the committed revolutionary while re-

35. "On the one hand, the propaganda and the Polyanna novels of 'socialist realism' appeal to a quite nauseating optimism: in a socialist country everything is good, there is no conflict except between the forces of the past and those which are building the future; the latter must necessarily triumph. The failures, suffering, death, all are caught up and saved by the movement of history. It even seems opportune for a while to produce novels without conflicts. In any case, the positive hero knows nothing about internal difficulties and contradictions; for his part, he contributes, without flinching and without mistakes, to the construction of socialism, his model is the young Stakhanovite; a soldier, he knows nothing of fear. These industrial and military idylls appeal to Marxism: they depict for us the happiness of a classless society. On the other hand, the exercise of dictatorship and the internal contradictions of bureaucracy necessarily engender an unavowed pessimism: since one governs by force, men must be evil; these heroes of labor, these so devoted high functionaries, these Party militants so upright, so pure, a mere puff can blow out their most blazing virtues: there they are counterrevolutionaries, spies, agents of capitalism; habits of integrity, of honesty, thirty years of faithfulness to the C.P., nothing can protect them against temptation. And if they deviate from the line, one soon discivers that they were guilty from birth" (Sartre, *The Ghost of Stalin,* p. 79).

36. *The New York Times Magazine,* October 17, 1971, p. 38.

maining in all respects a French intellectual.[37] Germaine Brée reports that though the French people still respect him, he is no longer as influential a figure as he was in the past. His authority had waned. He has had no appreciable effect on the course of politics. "Sartre, in other words, has become an exemplary though controversial figure rather than an actually effective one. He is now a figure of the past. . . ."[38]

37. "If man has freedom of choice, by what existentialist right does Sartre insist that Marxism is the only 'valid' choice? Sartre has never convincingly answered this question" (John Ardagh, *The New French Revolution* [New York and Evanston: Harper & Row, 1969], p. 357). Adam Schaff, the Polish philosopher, also underlines the unreconciled contradiction between Sartre the Existentialist and Sartre the Marxist. Schaff rejects the subjectivist foundations of Existentialism. Whatever choices the individual makes, he "always does so socially, in the sense of the social· conditioning of his personality" (Adam Schaff, *A Philosophy of Man* [New York: Monthly Review Press, 1963], p. 29). Schaff therefore concludes that the marriage of Existentialism and Marxism cannot possibly be consummated. Gradually "the force and logic of Sartre's own arguments lead him to forsake exactly those Existentialist traits that he wished to incorporate into Marxism: the subjectivity of the individual with the resulting humanism, and the individual's creative freedom in social, political, and historical events" (Walter Odajnyk, *Marxism and Existentialism* [Garden City, N. Y.: Doubleday & Company, 1965], p. xxii). *Critique of Dialectical Reason* marks an extreme modification of his Existentialist views so as to bring them closer to the Marxist position. "In fact, on the basis of the *Critique de la Raison Dialectique*, it is necessary to conclude that Sartre is now a Marxist and no longer an Existentialist" (*ibid.*, p. xxii). Sartre "has buried Existentialism in a Marxism of his own making. . ." (*ibid.*, p. 170).
38. Germaine Brée, *Camus and Sartre: Crisis and Commitment* (New York: Dell Publishing Co., 1972), p. 3.

15

Albert Camus: Art versus Politics

But here, for the first time, literature betrayed him [Sartre]: the literary act is neither a political act nor a demonstration of virtue.[1]

Camus never pretended to be transforming the world or the human condition by writing novels; that is why he continued to write them.[2]

Perhaps the central problem of political philosophy today is the validation of moral norms. It is extremely difficult to envisage the emergence in our time of a universally accepted "solution" to this great quandary, which is endemic to a culture characterized by value pluralism and dominated by the scientific ethos.[3]

1. *From Absurdity to Commitment*

Many critics seem to feel that it is necessary for them to choose between the two men, Sartre and Camus, in their

1. *The New York Times Book Review,* August 13, 1972, pp. 6, 22. Review by Albert Memmi of Germaine Brée's book *Camus and Sartre.* The review is translated by Paul Auster.
2. *Ibid.,* p. 22.
3. Fred H. Willhoite, Jr., *Beyond Nihilism: Albert Camus's Contribution to Political Thought* (Baton Rouge, La.: Louisiana State University Press, 1968), p. 186.

quarrel over the issue of Communism and the crucial question of political "commitment." One must be right and the
other wrong. The two writers were temperamentally different.[4] One was the theorist, the philosopher, the professional
revolutionary, the existentialist leader converted to Marxist
praxis, the believer in the use of violence. As a militant Marxist, Sartre became an enthusiastic, though at times, critical,
friend of the Soviet Union. The decision he made to devote
his energy to the creation of a "committed" literature did not
turn out as he had planned. His productivity as a novelist
came to an abrupt halt.

Camus was not impressed by Sartre's crusade for commitment. Nor was he impressed by Sartre's public role as *the*
committed writer of his age, the dedicated friend of the proletariat the world over. Camus refused to function as the
voice of the Communist Party, faithfully echoing its decrees
and justifying its foreign policy at every juncture. He was
primarily a novelist, a playwright, a man of letters, not a
trained ideologist. As a journalist, however, he was embroiled
in various controversies of his day. The traumatic historical
events that he witnessed or in which he participated left their
mark upon him: the deadly menace of Fascism, the Second
World War, the Occupation, the part he played in the French
Resistance, the war in Algeria, the problem of colonialism,
the Stalinist dictatorship, and the threat posed by an organized system of Communism that was secretive, cunning,
and unscrupulous. Camus responded, of course, to the challenge of these events. "But he was not a propagandist, nor a
crusader, and he propounded no theory or system to which
he sought to convert the world."[5]

The kind of politics a writer approves of and practices depends, as I pointed out in the case of Céline, in large measure on his conception of the character of man. Camus had
rejected the promise of immortality that Christianity held out

4. Germaine Brée, in *Camus and Sartre*, is fair-minded in defining the nature of
the conflict between the two men. She demonstrates that Sartre's theory of
committed literature, his belief that the writer must become involved in the
revolutionary struggle, is out of touch with the realities of our time. "Without
in any sense presuming to pass judgment on the men and on their work, it is
Camus's position that has seemed to me, though not the easiest, the most
fruitful for the artist." Germaine Brée, *Camus and Sartre: Crisis and Commitment*
(New York: Dell Publishing Co., 1972), p. x.
5. *Ibid.*, p. 124.

to the faithful. He could not believe in the reality of a life after death. His early writing celebrated the sensuous pleasures the good earth affords. The absurd man realizes that death is the end; since he will not be given a second chance, he must endeavor to enjoy each moment of life as it passes; it may be his last. Camus discovered that in this final crisis, as man encounters the dark angel of death, reason is of no avail. Regardless of all that a man accomplishes during his earthbound pilgrimage, death sooner or later overtakes him. Man is forced by necessity to protest against this outrageously unjust fate. If Camus sided with the metaphysical rebel, it was because the latter condemned God for imposing this unjust sentence of death on mankind. "The rebel fights death," says Willhoite, "not necessarily because he is afraid to die, but because it seems to deprive life of meaning; likewise he protests against suffering for which he sees no justification."[6] Though he never completely abandoned the nihilism of his early manhood, Camus did not fall into a state of absolute despair. He never gave up his quest for meaning. "For him the search for meaning is what the question of being, of ultimate truth and human dignity, is for Sartre."[7]

The absurd was ubiquitous, an unavoidable consequence of the human condition, yet Camus refused to accept the logical implications of the absurd; he questioned the extent of its power over mankind and finally revolted against it. Even if life proves to be ultimately meaningless, man still has a vitally important task to carry out in the realm of history, which is ruled by the fiat of the human will. In his preliminary reflections on the ideas that were eventually incorporated in *The Rebel,* Camus writes: "Torn between the world that does not suffice and God who is lacking, the absurd mind passionately chooses the world."[8] From the start Camus was resolved to revolt against the absurdity of existence. He vowed he would not become resigned to this intolerable fate. "With all my silence, I shall protest to the very end. There is no reason to say: 'It has to be.' It is my revolt which is right. . . ."[9] There

6. Willhoite, *Beyond Nihilism,* p. 108.
7. Leo Pollman, *Sartre and Camus,* trans. Helen and Gregor Sebba (New York: Frederick Ungar Publishing Co., 1970), p. 116.
8. Albert Camus, *Notebooks 1942-1951,* trans. Justin O'Brien (New York: Alfred A. Knopf, 1965), pp. 45-56.
9. Albert Camus, *Notebooks 1935-1942,* trans. Philip Thody (New York: Alfred A. Knopf, 1963), p. 54.

is, therefore, little justification for neatly classifying Camus's career as falling into two distinct and separate stages: first comes the myth of the absurd, which is then followed by the period of revolt. The two concepts, that of the absurd and that of revolt, cannot be studied in isolation; they are in conflict throughout the body of Camus's plays and novels. *The Plague,* like *The State of Siege,* gives expression to Camus's revolt against the hegemony of the Absurd, but they also reveal the baleful presence and power of the absurd. Similarly, *The Stranger* discloses "the revolt" of Meursault, and *Caligula* foreshadows in a way the later motif of human solidarity.[10]

If the physical universe, the world of Nature, is utterly indifferent to the needs and hopes of man, then the latter has the option of saying No to conditions as they exist and becoming a rebel. In this way he salvages his pride and asserts his dignity as a human being. Camus's heroes rebel against the oppression of the absurd. They are the leaders of "revolt"—a revolt that is relative, not absolute.

> At all times the rebel must be aware of a *limit,* beyond which he must not pass, on pain of redeeming transgression with his own life. And yet the absurd presents a terrifying paradox. It is in itself a total experience: life is never the same again.[11]

Camus's steadfast perception of the absurd did not prevent him from shouldering his responsibilities as a writer, but what did these responsibilities consist of? He would not be drawn into the trap of aligning himself with a political party of the Left and lending it unconditional support. He would not, like Sartre, subordinate his vocation as a writer to the practical necessities of politics. If the writer gives himself wholeheartedly to a cause or joins a political movement, he runs the danger of getting his hands soiled—a theme that Sartre handled with ironic insight in his play *Dirty Hands.* Politics, the ruthless struggle for power, often corrupts the idealism that motivated the writer to set forth on his political mission. Such a perversion of his aim need not have taken place if he had realized at the outset that his imaginative work will not of itself start a revolution. The current talk of "commitment" is semantically vague and misleading, a

10. See E. Freeman, *The Theatre of Albert Camus* (London: Methuen & Co., 1971).
11. *Ibid.,* p. 157.

mélange of ill-assorted and confused sentiments. Of course the writer wishes to be committed, but to what? That is the question.

In his study of the subtle and far-reaching ways in which Camus was influenced by the concept of commitment, Emmett Parker says: "Camus believed that the artist is obliged by his very art to bear witness to man's basic right to freedom and justice in the face of the historical aberrations of his time."[12] Camus's career demonstrates the temptations that beset the writer who commits himself politically. At the age of twenty-one, when he was still a student at the university, he became involved in politics. He joined the Communist party, but his membership was of short duration. He was repelled by the Party's adoption of a policy that combined opportunism with expediency. In 1939 he lost whatever enthusiasm he had once felt for the Soviet Union. His early disenchantment with the power politics of the Communist Party explains in large part his reluctance—as a writer who cherished his freedom as an artist, his inalienable right to freedom of expression—to tie himself closely to some political organization. "The problem of just how deeply the intellectual's commitment should involve him in political affairs occupied a place in Camus's thought for some time after his break with the Communists. . . ."[13] In his pursuit of the ideal of justice, the writer must shut his ear to the ideological songs the sirens sing. Camus struggled hard to preserve his artistic integrity and to purge his mind of all cant.

> Neither the artist whose supreme dedication is to his art—which to Camus meant dedication to the truth above all else—nor the intellectual who cultivates his doubts and prefers to "keep his eyes open" is likely to adapt very easily to the restrictions imposed by political party discipline.[14]

Though the artist in these parlous times must take a stand, this does not mean that he must swear allegiance to some political system and act strictly in accordance with its dictates. Which, Camus asked himself, should come first: art or politics? Camus became convinced that "the artist could better

12. Emmett Parker, *Albert Camus: The Artist in the Arena* (Madison, Wis.: The University of Wisconsin Press, 1964), p. xi.
13. *Ibid.*, p. 11.
14. *Ibid.*

serve the revolutionary cause by submitting to the discipline of his art instead of to political party discipline."[15] Less arrogant than Sartre in the presentation of his views, he contended that the writer is not a privileged being whose political pronouncements deserve special consideration. Camus, who looked upon himself as primarily an artist, became not a crusading anti-Communist like Arthur Koestler, but a principled non-Communist.[16]

Throughout his life Camus consistently affirmed that the writer must bear the burden of responsibility to society. Camus drew the line at the injunction preached by Marxist critics that the writer must take part in the political struggle waged by the Left. The intellectual, the artist, has no particular competence in the field of politics. As a rule, he knows too little at firsthand about the socioeconomic conflicts of his age: neocolonialism, strikes for higher wages, imperialistic wars, monopolistic control, but he must not, out of a sense of humility, keep silent, for then he allows the *status quo* to remain unchallenged. He must not forfeit his right to utter his cry of protest when things are in the saddle and injustice rides mankind. "The writer who allows himself to be fascinated by the political Gorgon," Camus warned, "is doubtless making a mistake. But it is also a mistake to pass over the social problems of our time in silence."[17] Despite his limited knowledge and his realization that his words will not abolish the evil or the injustice he is denouncing, the writer must speak up.

There is no inconsistency between Camus's participation in the Resistance movement and the philosophy of the absurd expressed in *The Stranger, Caligula, The Misunderstanding,* and *The Myth of Sisyphus.* Because he would not accept the leadership of the Communist Party nor agree that the end justified the means, his political enemies labeled him an absurdist.

15. *Ibid.,* p. 12.
16. Brée's study points up the differences between these two writers "that made them unmixable and in many ways antithetical. . . . When Camus was directly involved, he usually became more actively involved than Sartre who has accepted no specific concrete responsibilites in the vertical sphere. His support of the Spanish Republicans and his friendship with the Spanish exiles lasted as long as his life; during the war he was far more deeply engaged in specific underground activities than Sartre who, on the whole, stayed on the sidelines." Germaine Brée, *Camus and Sartre,* p. 82.
17. Albert Camus, *Lyrical and Critical Essays,* ed. Philip Thody, trans. Conroy Kennedy (New York: Alfred A. Knopf, 1969), p. 353.

They make no mention of the fact that Camus, the alleged incorrigible absurdist, joined the Communist Party toward the end of 1934, which assigned him the task of carrying on propaganda work among the Moslem people, and that he left the Party in 1935 (though some believe that he retained his membership card through 1937). They do not refer to his position as an editorial writer for *Alger-Républicain,* which dealt with Algerian political problems. Once he achieved recognition as a novelist, the French reading public paid no attention to these politically motivated calumnies and listened to his utterances as if he were an oracle even on matters outside the realm of literature. Roger Quilliot is one of the few French critics who sets the record straight in relation to Camus's involvement in politics.

> The fact that he [Camus] came to literature by way of a novel set in poverty, or that his first theatrical work should have paid vehement homage to the dead strikers of Oviedo in a text in which the class struggle erupts with virulence, could be only a literary accident or the result of a crisis of political puberty. However, among the writers who have counted during the past fifty years, Camus is one of the rare ones—along with Aragon or Eluard—to have played an active role for several years in a political party, and more precisely, the Communist Party.[18]

Because he was neither a fanatic nor a camp follower, he was regarded with intense disfavor by critics on the Left. He exposed the limitations of the proposed Communist method for insuring the success of the proletarian revolution. He showed that both Communism and Fascism issued from the same philosophical source. The course of action followed by the devotees of German National Socialism bore out the thesis Camus had argued: that the death of God and the collapse of the moral sense led the Nazi leaders to believe that they could rely for the success of their plan to conquer the world on military power alone. The Nazis and the Communists assumed that there were no universal moral standards, that the fate of history is determined by the triumph of superior force. As Camus pointed out in *The Rebel,* they were firmly convinced that the end justified the means. Communism and Fascism thus represented an unprecedented outburst of nihilistic passion. Hitler practiced

18. Roger Quilliot, *The Sea and Prisons: A Commentary on the Life and Thought of Albert Camus,* trans. Emmett Parker (University, Ala.: The University of Alabama Press, 1970), p. 117.

genocide in a "mad" organized effort to wipe out the Jewish people. Stalin resorted to terrorism in order to get rid of his "enemies" and to achieve the collectivization of the land; he killed those "kulaks" who opposed his plan and deported millions of muzhiks.

It took considerable courage for a French writer to attack Stalin and the Soviet Union after the war was over. It was more prudent to avoid a clash, to remain discreetly silent. Camus would not compromise his principles and defended the cause of constitutional democracy. As a result he was the target of scurrilous attacks by the left-wing press; he was damned as a renegade, a reactionary, an agent of Imperialism.[19] He sought to find a solution to the problem of determining

> the nature, status, and place of moral judgments in politics. He believed that the collective tragedies of the twentieth century occurred in large measure because of ideologies which, rather than surpassing nihilism, embraced it in what proved to be a death-grip—in the form of allegiance to nothing but brute force or to a distant future condition of historical perfection.[20]

Camus condemned the atrocities committed by both sides in the Algerian war and warned that the use of terrorism would not be conducive to a peaceful settlement of the conflict. Some critics rebuked Camus for his "betrayal" of the Algerian cause. Conor Cruise O'Brien considers Camus's action "a fall." As he says:

> One may feel—as the present writer does—that Sartre and Jeanson were right, and that Camus's voice added to theirs instead of turning against them, would have rallied opinion more decisively and earlier against imperialist wars, not only in Algeria but also in Indochina—Vietnam and elsewhere. One may experience horror at the sight of the moral capital of *La Peste* being drawn on in support of the values of the Cold War and colonial war.[21]

19. "In an important series of articles entitled 'Ni Victimes ni Bourreau,' published in *Combat* in November 1946, Camus attacked Marxism in general and the Soviet Union in particular because of the disquieting information coming out about the Stalinist dictatorship. These articles appeared to justify charges that Camus had forsaken his early left-wing intransigence, and a Marxist intellectual, Emmanuel d'Astier de la Vigerie, virtually accused Camus of being a crypto-Capitalist and 'fils de Bourgeois' all along." Freeman, *The Theatre of Albert Camus*, p. 91.
20. Willhoite, *Beyond Nihilism*, p. 186.
21. Conor Cruise O'Brien, "Camus, Algeria, and 'The Fall,'" *The New York Review of Books*, October 9, 1969, p. 12.

2. *The Moral Stance of the Rebel*

Camus would not accept a doctrine, be it Christianity or Marxism, on faith. He had to work out his own principles, his own code of ethics. As a rebel he opposed those forces which denied his humanity and affirmed those values which formed the basis of a viable humanism. Camus declared that when God died, the rebel was born. In this age of metaphysical revolt, the crucial problem godless man faces is to formulate a morality that requires no support from the supernatural. By committing an act of rebellion, the individual overcomes his alienation; he is no longer alone. "I rebel—therefore we exist."[22] The metaphysical rebel wants to remake the world by putting an end to the reign of injustice.

> Metaphysical rebellion is a claim . . . against the suffering of life and death and a protest against the human condition both for its incompleteness, thanks to death, and its wastefulness, thanks to evil. (p. 24)

Once the rebel has abandoned his faith in God, he is saddled with the responsibility of himself creating the order of justice. Man has become God. There is no one above him to whom he must account for his actions.

But can man devise a system of morality that will shape his conduct without seeking validation from God? Man establishes the principle of law, which determines the precise guilt of the offender and the kind and degree of punishment to be meted out. History then becomes the ground of human aspiration and effort. The rebel acts on the assumption that man can find fulfillment in the world of time. The revolutionary is different in character, aim, ideology, and method of attack. The latter justifies his ruthless will to power by virtue of his plan to impose world unity by force. He believes in the use of violence and is prepared to commit crimes in behalf of his supreme revolutionary purpose. The will of the masses is not to be balked by appeals to constitutional grounds of legitimacy or moral law. The workers are sovereign, they become God. Out of this secularized faith in the proletariat as the redeemer of corrupt and oppressive society emerges the

---

22. Albert Camus, *The Rebel*, trans, Anthony Bower (New York: Alfred A. Knopf, 1961), p. 22.

same type of tyrannical rule that Communism vowed to overthrow. The Revolution, once it is successful, uses terrorism against those who criticize or resist its decrees. Stalin seizes dictatorial power and the Soviet Union becomes a totalitarian State. The ideology handed down by the Party, which Stalin controls, is to be followed by the faithful without question, without even the faintest hint of mental reservation. Rebellion that is not held back by moral restraint becomes irresponsible and its history is a record of appalling crimes. The revolutionary movement of the twentieth century fought under the banner of pragmatic amorality. The triumph of the Revolution overrides all considerations of morality. What matters is the achievement of the ultimate goal. All actions are arbitrary. "The sky is empty, the earth delivered into the hands of power without principles" (p. 148).

Camus, far from being dazzled by the grandiose promises of Marxism, critically examines its major weaknesses. A curious mixture of utopian optimism and quasi-scientific objectivity, it confidently prophesies the inevitable smash-up of capitalism, the defeat and extinction of the bourgeoisie, and the triumphant emergence of the dictatorship of the proletariat, which will in the future be succeeded by the ultimate achievement of Communism—the classless state. The path that history actually follows does not conform to the Marxist forecast of the future; there are mistakes, setbacks, betrayals, defeats, ideological blunders, counterrevolutionary opposition, but the end result, despite these frustrating delays, is never in doubt. The dictatorship of the proletariat is somehow wickedly transformed into the despotic dictatorship of one man, but that is only a minor, temporary deflection from the appointed goal of Communism.

Marxism represents a pseudo-religious eschatology that attracts true believers throughout the world, despite its false prophecies and its failure to make good on its promises to the proletariat. Though it is hostile to religion and religious institutions, it functions like a tightly knit religious organization whose members must profess the orthodox creed and obey its scriptural commandments. It consists of its sacred dogmas and its ruling myth, its martyrs and its patron saints. A religion stripped of transcendence, Communism readily masters the manipulative techniques of politics. The proletariat are entrusted with the historic mission of liberating

mankind from the fate of alienation. The golden age they
will usher in "justifies everything" (p. 208): the suffering, the
bloodshed, the assassinations, the crimes. "The demand for
justice ends in injustice if it is not primarily based on an ethical justification of justice; without this, crime itself one day
becomes a duty" (p. 209).

The millennium has not come. As the desired end—the
classless paradise—is indefinitely postponed, many devout believers become disillusioned. Those who visited the Soviet
Union discovered, like Gide, that the realities they had observed ran counter to the radiant image of the ideal commonwealth that Communist spokesmen pictured it to be.
These recalcitrant facts were dialectically interpreted and they
ceased to be facts: they became bourgeois slanders, Trotskyist
lies, the vile propaganda of reactionary circles. The leaders of
the Communist Party perfected the art of casuistry, systematic distortion of the truth, the deliberate falsification of the
historical record. The Soviet Union instituted a modified version of State capitalism. The Russian proletariat are still
asked to make sacrifices for some collective shibboleth. In
an economy geared solely to production, the people were denied their birthright of freedom. "Revolution . . . is nothing
but slavery" (p. 219).

Camus's critique of Marxism reveals by what unscrupulous,
Machiavellian methods the leaders of the Communist Party in
the Soviet Union sought to increase their power. The Party
was the supreme authority in determining the nature of
truth. It could revise the text of history by changing the
character of the past. Its ambition went beyond this limited
aim: it believed it could change human nature by a process of
conditioning. Diehard rationalists, the Communist leaders
ruled out the element of the irrational; they rejected the
Freudian concept of the unconscious. Men are bundles of
conditioned reflexes and they can be taught to practice the
virtue of obedience to authority. The revolutionary, once he
is invested with power, becomes the accuser, the merciless
judge, the executioner, all in one. He knows that men are
expendable. History accepts no alibis. He who is not for the
Revolution is against it. The individual who does not hold
"the correct" Marxist outlook is potentially guilty of treason.
The Grand Inquisitor rules unchallenged in the Fatherland
of the Proletariat.

Such an exposé in *The Rebel,* Camus knew full well, would earn him the implacable hatred of the Communist Party in France. It caused the rupture of his friendship with Sartre. He never regretted the step he had taken. He was not convinced by the Sartrean logic, which held that rebellion must culminate in revolution. He believed that the rebel turns against the revolutionary. "Every revolutionary ends by becoming either an oppressor or a heretic" (p. 249). He turns into a destructive nihilist. Camus does not bid man to give up this world in moral despair. Man must create and abide by the value that enables him to judge the vicissitudes of history, and he can find this supreme value in the ethic that underlies rebellion. This ethic categorically denies that man is but an object, a pawn to be moved about at will in the ruthless chess game of power. To protect ourselves against this source of nihilistic infection, we must recognize a nature common to all men and establish a limit beyond which it is dangerous to go.

Is the rebel to remain silent while "legalized" murders are committed with impunity? Camus advocates a humanistic philosophy that sets limits to human ambition. The rebel knows he is not omniscient. Unlike the revolutionary, he does not act in terms of absolute principles and thereby attempt to legitimize whatever evils are committed in his time. The rebel, on the other hand, confines himself to the sphere of the relative and strives only for what is possible. Rebellion, acting within a framework of limited aims, does not resort to terrorism to achieve its ends. It dedicates itself to the never-ending struggle against evil, and in doing so it is careful not to violate the libertarian tradition. "Man can master, in himself, everything that can be rectified. And after he has done so, children will still die unjustly even in a perfect society" (p. 303). Since it is a movement that affirms life, rebellion has no use for the revolutionary abstractions that do violence to the true nature of man. It refuses to sacrifice the needs of the present on the altars of an unknown or problematical future. The adventure of revolutionary romanticism comes to an end when man realizes at last that he is not God.

By the time Camus was awarded the Nobel Prize in 1957, many Europeans regarded him as the conscience of the race of man, who voiced the need for justice and compassion in an age given over to terrorism, concentration camps, death factories, and genocide. He spoke out with lucid yet impassioned conviction on the major issues that confronted his age. Whatever the theme he dealt with as a journalist—the war in Algiers, neocolonialism, capital punishment, Fascism, Communism, responsibility—his work was instinct with a profound awareness of the necessity for preserving a number of basic human values. Committed to the defense of these values, Camus endeavored to combat the political nihilism that argued that might was the final arbiter of right and that nothing mattered in the last analysis except the victory gained by superior force of arms. Camus never yielded to absolute despair nor lost his faith in man. The world was absurd, but not the destiny man chooses for himself or the ideals he struggles to establish on earth.

Once Camus made known his humanist position, his reaction after 1945 to the political crises and conflicts of his time was strikingly consistent. He did not bother to conciliate the antagonistic voices on the Left. He was his own man. When Gabriel Marcel protested against the fact that *The State of Siege* is situated in Spain, Camus replied that the play is an attack on totalitarianism wherever it happens to flourish. "No one in good faith can fail to see that my play defends the individual, the flesh in its noblest aspects—in short, human love—against the abstractions and terrors of the totalitarian state, whether Russian, German, or Spanish."[23] The bureaucratic State, absolutist in its exercise of power and repressive in function—that is the monstrous evil which must be abolished.

In seeking to make reason prevail in Algeria, Camus condemned the enormities committed on both sides. If terroristic methods are used and the innocent are made to suffer, then nihilism triumphs. There is no justification for crime, no matter who commits it. He was opposed to the war and labored hard to avert the tragedy that was about to befall Algeria. Like Sartre, he attacked the counterrevolutionary regime installed in Hungary with the aid of Soviet troops and tanks. The Hungarian intellectuals, Camus charged, were intimidated, imprisoned, and executed because they had dared to protest against the intolerable conditions in their land. What happened in Hungary, he declared, underscored the bankruptcy of the forces of the Left. Though he continued

23. Albert Camus, *Resistance, Rebellion and Death,* trans. Justin O'Brien (New York: Alfred A. Knopf, 1960), p. 78.

to defend the cause of freedom, he urged the artist not to succumb to the spirit of hatred for life and of contempt for the human race. The writer cannot afford to cut himself off from society, but he must not become subservient to the wielders of political power.

B. IN ENGLAND

16

Poetry and Radicalism in England

1. *The Marxist Evangel*

art posed problems for Marx and his successors when they attempted to incorporate it within their overall view of social and historical phenomena.[1]

During the thirties the fight against Fascism lent a note of special urgency to the contribution of embattled Marxist literary critics. They told the poet not only what subjects he should write about but also how he should treat this material and what conclusions he should draw. The fight against capitalism, the evil source of social and economic inequality, the struggle of the proletariat to make Communism prevail throughout the world, though at present it was necessary to protect the Soviet Union against its enemies—these were to be given primary stress. These Marxist critics were ideological missionaries who knew the liberating truth of the class con-

1. Henri Arvon, *Marxist Esthetics,* trans. Helen R. Lane (Ithaca, N.Y. and London: Cornell University Press, 1973), p. 3.

flict. Marx had proclaimed it, Lenin had expounded it, and Stalin was implementing and perfecting it. These critics preached an aesthetic of commitment that was viable and completely valid and they brooked no half-hearted ideological allegiance, despite the fact that Marx and Engels and their disciples were unable to solve the difficult problems that their study of literature and art raised. Writers who were lacking in doctrinal purity and passion were reminded of Lenin's anathemas against politically uncommitted literature:

> Let us rid ourselves of men of letters without a party!... The cause of literature must become a part of the general cause of the proletariat.[2]

Nothing that departs from the Marxist-Leninist synthesis can possess any real merit.[3]

Not that the Communist spokesmen encountered no opposition during the turbulent thirties. In England at this time there were Party members and fellow travelers who were opposed to the use of revolutionary violence. Many were pacifists. When the question of art and its reason for being arose, particularly its relation to the world of politics, dissension made itself felt among the left-wing literati. Moreover, Stalin's hostility toward intellectuals led them to reexamine the exact nature of their loyalty to the Party. In Great Britain they resisted the demand that they obey Party directives, without demurrers of any kind. Their membership in the Party declined sharply in numbers; in 1926 there were over ten thousand who had joined the Party, but by 1930 they had dwindled to a little more than a thousand. The Communists in Great Britain were inclined to support moderate rather

2. *Ibid.,* p. 15. Lenin's article, "Organization and Party Literature," to which the quotation refers, dealt with Party polemics and propaganda, not with imaginative literature. The article was intended to provide guidelines for the writer of publications issued by the Communist Party.

3. John Strachey points out that writers like Stephen Spender and W. H. Auden "have been very severely taken to task for their lack of insight into the social and political theory of the working class movement. And no doubt they are by no means perfect masters of Leninism and Marxism. But it would be a mistake, I think, to suppose that on that account they are bad poets. It would indeed be a blunder if we tried to pretend that a man was a bad poet because he was a bad Marxist, and a good poet because he was a good Marxist" (John Strachey, "Fascism and Culture," *International Literature,* no. 4 [September 1934], p. 108).

than radical proposals. It was the outbreak of the Spanish Civil War that inspired them to take sides.[4]

Though the writers in England were on the whole more resistant to Marxist propaganda than their counterparts in the United States and France, one English critic achieved wide recognition as the author of *Illusion and Reality* (1937), a brilliant if not altogether successful effort to judge all literature, but particularly poetry, in the light of historical materialism. Christopher Caudwell (pseud. of Christopher St. John Sprigg) was a versatile, highly gifted, and productive writer.[5] What Caudwell adds that is new in the practice of Marxist criticism is an outgrowth of his ambitious attempt to use scientific knowledge drawn from physics, psychology, and anthropology and combine it with the basic Marxist conceptions to form a synthesis that could illuminate the nature of literature. *Illusion and Reality* is an amazing book; it not only lays the foundation for a new system of aesthetics, which is a fusion of Marxism, Freudianism (drastically revised), the philosophy of science, anthropology, and symbolic logic; it also tries to furnish a comprehensive interpretation of the universe and of human nature.

"The Future of Poetry," the concluding chapter of *Illusion and Reality*, reveals the limitations of Caudwell's method of criticism. Bourgeois culture, he announces, is on its last legs;

4. "Spain was the first and last crusade of the British left-wing intellectual. Never again was such enthusiasm mobilized, nor did there exist such a firm conviction in the rightness of a cause" (Neal Wood, *Communism and British Intellectuals* [New York: Columbia University Press, 1959], p. 57).
5. After leaving school, Caudwell obtained a job on the *Yorkshire Post*. He soon set out for London, where he edited the journal *British Malaya*. Together with his brother, he started an aeronautical publishing firm. Enterprising, prodigiously gifted in many ways, he invented a mechanical part that could be used in the automobile. As richly diversified in his interests and activities as the Renaissance man, he achieved more before he reached the age of thirty than most people accomplish in a lifetime, if they accomplish anything at all. His unflagging productivity in such varied fields as literature, science, physics, and literary criticism that applied Marxist categories, gave proof that here was a rare spirit. In the course of his short life he composed eight detective works of fiction, one novel, and a goodly number of poems and short stories. His technical capability found an outlet in the writing of five books on aviation. He will be remembered chiefly for his three major contributions to Marxist literary criticism: *Illusion and Reality, Studies in a Dying Culture,* and *Further Studies in a Dying Culture.* He joined the Communist Party in 1935 and left for Spain less than a year later when civil war broke out in that land. "He did not mix with other Party intellectuals or engage in Party intellectual work, preferring the company of 'proletarian' communists, and sharing with them the menial chores and routine activities of Party life." *Ibid.,* p. 89.

it has reached its final crisis, the terminal stage of its fatal illness, and the new society is about to emerge from the womb of time. The economically exploited proletariat can achieve freedom only by abolishing the bourgeoisie. The proletariat is not only the most long-suffering class in capitalist society; it is also the class destined to assume the responsibility of leadership and play a creative role in the birth of the new social order. Caudwell assures us that without an understanding of the deepening revolutionary crisis and the historic mission of the proletariat in building the collective society of the future, it is impossible to gain adequate insight into the nature of modern art. For proletarian art, Caudwell declares,

> expresses the movement of the proletarian class itself, and this movement is to annihilate its existence as a class by becoming coincident with society as a whole.[6]

In the course of developing this Marxist thesis, Caudwell contrasts bourgeois freedom with proletarian freedom. He reaffirms his conviction that art, too, is a social product. One fails to comprehend how this cluster of Marxist abstractions[7] gives one special insight into the secret of modern art. For these abstract statements, about art as a productive problem, about proletarian consciousness and bourgeois consciousness, about proletarian freedom as contrasted with bourgeois freedom, are difficult to apply to the concrete work of art.[8]

In England it took the intellectuals some time before they recovered from their early infatuation with Marxist doctrine. As W. H. Auden said in his *New Year Letter:*

6. Christopher Caudwell, *Illusion and Reality* (New York: International Publishers, 1947), p. 280.
7. In his study of Caudwell's aesthetics, David N. Margolies asks the big question: "What is a Marxist aesthetic?" His reply is as follows: "There is no accepted or established definition of a Marxist aesthetic and perhaps it is the absence of such a definition that has allowed careless writers so to confuse Marxist criticism that they classify as Marxists all sorts of critics, from those who base themselves to some degree on Marxism to those whose work bears no relation to Marxism at all. This tends to make the term 'Marxist criticism,' unless it is defined, rather meaningless" (David N. Margolies, *The Function of Literature: A Study of Christopher Caudwell's Aesthetic* [New York: International Publishers, 1969], p. 9).
8. Attempts have been made to restore and enhance the reputation of such critics as Georg Lukács and Herbert Marcuse, the prophet of the New Left. See *Marxism and Form*, by Frederic Jameson, which examines the Marxist method employed by such European critics as Adorno, Walter Benjamin, Ernst Bloch, Lukács, and Sartre.

> We hoped; we waited for the day
> The State would wither clean away,
> Expecting the Millennium
> That theory promised us would come.
> It didn't.[9]

In thus cutting themselves off from Communism, the English writers were not betraying "the cause"; they were not, to quote Auden once more, repenting of their last infraction by seeking "atonement in reaction." It was against the absolute imperatives of Communist ideology that they revolted. Their ill-starred adventure in the politics of utopian engineering taught them that there is no single road that leads to salvation. They desired as much as ever to contribute to the building of a rational, humane, and just society, but they were not convinced that this could best be achieved by a revolutionary seizure of power. Their observation of conspiratorial methods in action made them realize the priceless value of democratic institutions, and they rallied to the defense of their imperiled heritage of freedom. If they showed so much anxious concern for the autonomy of art and the freedom of the artist from external constraints, it was not because they were the unwitting dupes of an "ideology" that exalted their status as belonging to a privileged group or because they were covertly protecting their "class" interests, but because they honestly believed that art is a fundamental need of man.

2. C. Day Lewis

> we felt "from each according to his need" or "freedom is the knowledge of necessity" to be concepts as inspiring as Christ's sayings in the Sermon on the Mount; we believed that a second world war was on its way.[10]

Together with his like-minded friends, Lewis was at the time fully convinced that the capitalist system was doomed, that they were called upon to eliminate such calamitous evils as Fascism and mass unemployment, that only Communism could bring about the nationalization of the means of pro-

9. W. H. Auden, *The Double Man*, in *Collected Longer Poems* (New York: Random House, 1969), p. 102. *New Year Letter* was published in *The Double Man* in New York in 1941.

10. C. Day Lewis, *The Buried Life* (London: Chatto & Windus, 1960), p. 208.

duction. As he looked back upon the past from the vantage point of 1960, when the younger generation took pride in their calculated nihilism, professing to believe in nothing,[11] the thirties seemed to shine forth as a decade when men believed in good social and political causes. He considered it extremely fortunate that youth then believed they could do something about the social and political ills of their age.

The portrait of himself that Day Lewis draws in his candid autobiography reveals a sensitive, humane, and engaging personality. Because of the extreme leftist views he voiced in the thirties, he became involved in many a scrape. When he published *The Magnetic Mountain,* which was daringly revolutionary in content, the trustees of the school where he was employed as a teacher did not utter a single note of outrage or disapproval. The author accounts for this forbearance by saying that the few guardians who read it assumed, "after the English manner, that since it was poetry it could have no bearing on real life."[12] Day Lewis had become a member of the Party, but he was an unorthodox Communist; he was too scrupulous in his regard for moral values. His troubled conscience had compelled him to join the Party, even though he knew this step would mean the loss of his job on the College staff. It was "a real plunge, even in the Thirties, with a wife and two children and no private income, to give up a salaried job for the life of a free-lance writer" (p. 206).

In accepting the Communist doctrine, Lewis was acting in accordance with his beliefs. Like Auden and Rex Warner, he had given up the Christian faith, and he now craved a cause to which he could devote himself wholeheartedly. Marxism offered a solution for the problems of the world. Besides, he then longed to throw off "the intolerable burden of selfhood" (p. 209) and become an anonymous unit in a crowd. He was aware at the time that his devotion to Communism was mixed with a religious element. He responded to the romantic vision his mind conjured up (images derived from Russian

11. Jimmy Porter, the protagonist in *Look Back in Anger,* describes with lyrical nostalgia that quickly turns into bitter, accusatory rage, the special appeal the decade of the thirties has for his generation. "I suppose people of our generation aren't able to die for good causes any longer. We had all that done for us in the thirties and forties. . . . There aren't any good, brave causes left" (John Osborne, *Look Back in Anger* [New York: Bantam Books, 1950], pp. 104-5).

12. Lewis, *The Buried Life,* p. 204.

films) of heroic workers driving a tractor toward the dawn of a new day. He hated the Enemy, the Capitalist, and he despised the middle class, which was responsible for shoring up "the System." He had composed "revolutionary" poetry before he became a Party member. In retrospect, he was convinced that it was not his reading of Marxist texts that brought him to Communism but his "heritage of romantic humanism, a bent of mind quite incompatible, as I would discover, with the materialism and rigidity of Communist doctrines" (p. 211). Nevertheless, he felt that he had done the right thing. Though his new political faith was shaken by recurrent seizures of doubt, this experience during the thirties at least filled him with the elixir of hope.

In his skeptical moments he could not ignore the major faults of Communist practice: its pursuit of ends without worrying about the immoral means used, its Machiavellian shifts of policy, its reliance on the propaganda of the lie. Though his political activity was dictated by his conscience, his conscience also protested vehemently against some aspects of this activity, "and finally put an end to it. . ." (p. 209). He could not as a poet reconcile himself to the political role he was expected to play. His political activities consumed more time and energy than he could afford. Whereas his conversion took place quitely, without fireworks, his "revulsion—not from Communism but from the self which political activity had fostered—was almost apocalyptic" (p. 222). His political duties now seemed to him pointless; he wanted to write poetry.

Though Day Lewis dreamt of the classless society that the future would bring to birth, he was no Marxist minuteman of the Revolution. In *A Hope for Poetry* (1934) and in *Revolution in Writing* (1935), he analyzes the nature of the problem confronting the modern poet and the kind of social responsibility he must bear. Though he tries to keep faith with the Marxist outlook, he is opposed to the use of propaganda in poetry. He had gone beyond the mood of bitter or sophisticated disillusionment that characterized many English poets who spoke for "the lost generation." He, too, had known doubt and despair but he rose above them and sang with fine gusto of the beauty of the natural world and the joy of life, rediscovering, as it were, the glory of sunlight, the reviving pulse and renewed creative power of Nature, the procession of the seasons, the dynamic rhythm of life in the cities, and the essential worth of man. Gone is the morbid whine of the introverted, intellectualized self. Here is God's plenty: music and gladness and blithe acceptance. He transcended the sterile logic of introversion by creative acts of affirmation, by the surrender of his personal will to the infinitely varied influences of the universe.

His recoil from the excesses of romantic individualism led him to embrace the Marxist philosophy of collectivism. *The Magnetic Mountain* describes how the lover becomes rebel, how the mind of the poet is aroused by the necessity for revolutionary action. The magnetic mountain represents the classless society, which is the ultimate goal of Communism. Capitalism is abolished; the benighted past is left behind. Lewis projects the vision of a brighter and happier world for mankind. He bids the workers to cower no longer in the darkness. When the zero hour is signaled, they will be the leaders, the "wielders of power and welders of a new world."[13]

What Lewis is pleading for is not the creation of a Socialist paradise but the building of a world that stresses not possessions but social justice. Lewis's contribution to the then growing corpus of "revolutionary" poetry consisted not only of *The Magnetic Mountain* but also of *Noah and the Waters*. The latter work, originally designed for a choral ballet, is in reality a Marxist morality play, like Mayakovsky's *Mystery-Bouffe*. A conflict is depicted as going on in Noah between the old life of capitalistic exploitation and the new life of the Flood. A similar struggle, though it takes place in the mind of the poet, is described in "The Conflict." For a time, Lewis declares, poetry gave him the wings to soar above the dust and frenzied cries of the battlefield; it could ease his personal sorrows; but the unhappy consciousness of living between two worlds, without belonging to either, forced upon him the realization that poetry is not enough to save a man. Man can win the inestimable prize of freedom only through his knowledge of social reality and by his acceptance of necessity. He must be prepared to fight for his beliefs, regardless of the seemingly insuperable odds arrayed against him.

The "spirit of the times" demanded that the writer "com-

13. C. Day Lewis, *Collected Poems* (London; Jonathan Cape, 1954), p. 116.

mit" himself unequivocally as a partisan in the class struggle. "Certainly, writers of my own generation are interested in politics to an extent unequalled among English writers since the French Revolution."[14] The isolated individual dooms himself to passivity and impotence; he cannot launch a revolution. Lewis predicted that as the political struggle became more intense, the writer would be forced to choose between Communism and Fascism—a theme that Communist propaganda stridently emphasized. If the alliance between literature and left-wing politics should turn out badly, the writer can still turn to psychology for guidance. Freud's discovery of the unconscious "altered all the values of the human equation" (p. 68). Lewis went so far as to say that Freudianism offered man "a revolutionary idea of the nature of his own soul" (p. 69). It might give rise to a new religion of love.

As a poet who stemmed from the middle class, Lewis wondered uneasily how he could leap over the barrier that separated him from the working class. It would be useless for him to go "slumming" or to wear the garb and adopt the speech of that class. He must establish a living contact with the workers, and such a contact meant that they must work together and live together, "sharing the same economic conditions and the same language" (p. 76). Lewis asserts that it is "the life instinct" that drives the writer to participate in the revolutionary movement, for Communism offers "the widest scope to love. . ." (p. 79).

Day Lewis draws up a scathing indictment of the leaders who corrupted Western civilization. In *Noah and the Waters* he warns that the posture of neutrality cannot be maintained in the face of the worsening crisis. In "The Conflict" he prophesies that those who keep apart from the class struggle are doomed, since it is impossible to sustain life in no man's land. Unlike some of his Marxist critics, Day Lewis saw no reason why the poet, once he has been converted to Communism, should abandon poetry, if it is a natural function, and take up the task of revolutionary agitation as a full-time job. Why should his political conversion blind him to the true nature of poetry? Day Lewis stresses the need for technical excellence. A poem, he contends, "may have been written by a reactionary bourgeois, and yet be a very good poem and of

14. C. Day Lewis, *A Time to Dance* (New York: Random House, 1936), p. 66.

value to the revolutionary; *The Waste Land* is such a one" (p. 89). Day Lewis took the trouble to recapitulate these commonplaces of literary criticism in order to strengthen the driving force of his thesis that the poet should be accorded unrestricted freedom of choice in selecting his subject matter. Why should the "proletarian" poet be required to confine himself to the single, all-absorbing theme of the Revolution? Nor should the revolutionary strain in modern poetry be construed to mean the inclusion of edifying propaganda. If the revolutionary poet is true to himself, he will not rely on such trite symbols as hammer and sickle.

It is evident that Day Lewis was no orthodox Marxist. Whenever the character of poetry was brought into question, Lewis demonstrated that he had no patience with those Communist critics who urged the poet to be up and doing, with a heart for any fate that insured the ultimate triumph of the Revolution. Day Lewis clung to his conviction that poetry, as poetry, was historically of value to the Revolution. Why, then, should the poet surrender his proper calling and engage in political activism on the Left front? "A good poem enters deep into the stronghold of our emotions: if it is written by a good revolutionary, it is bound to have a revolutionary effect on our emotions, and therefore to be essentially—though not formally—propaganda" (p. 89).

3. *Auden's Career: From Freud to Marx to Kierkegaard*

Of the three English poets we are examining in this chapter, Auden is the most daring and accomplished experimentalist. He is full of cerebral tricks, sallies of wit, verbal surprises, stylistic pyrotechnics, and high animal spirits. His poetry, charged with intense creative energy, diagnoses the illness of his age and prescribes the medicine that he hopes and believes will cure it. Like Day Lewis, he dreamed for a time of the Golden Age to come, the egalitarian society about to leap into being from the womb of time. But it was the urgent quality of his search for meaning in a world suffering from economic dislocation and threatened by another catastrophic global war that made his poetry during the early thirties seem so alive. His political affirmations at the time sprang from his realistic, if then still limited, knowledge of the world at large. What he gleaned from the teaching of Karl Marx was supplemented and counterbalanced by his study of Freud. He was at no time a fanatical, fire-breathing Marxist, the strident preacher of a revolutionary ideology. In fact, he was not a Marxist in the orthodox sense. He was more interested "in psychotherapy than in social mechanics: the former precedes and, in large measure, contains the answer to the latter."[15] And his conception of "love" was not consonant with the Marxist canon. Though he was definitely attracted during the thirties by the role of militant Communist, "he was as often seen as the poet-as-physician, diagnostician and healer of a sick society. . . ."[16]

Auden's social diagnosis is set forth in "The Dance of Death," which attempts to portray the death of a class. Death the dancer—the main character—symbolizes modern capitalism. Though many of his followers believe that Death loves them, he is in reality exploiting them for his own profit. At last the People become aware of their collective strength and their historic destiny. While the People are frantically debating which path to follow—to forge ahead or cling to the past—there is a thunderous crash, and the dancer falls to the ground in a fit. Nothing can revive him, however, and Death, or capitalism, dies, but not before he has drawn up a will, which is a rollicking, rhymed version of dialectical materialism and its effect on history. At the end, Karl Marx, accompanied by two young economists, appears and announces that the instruments of production have overcome the victim. "He is liquidated."[17] In the production of "The Dance of Death" by the Group Theater, the actors tried to involve the audience in the action.[18]

15. Richard Hoggart, *Auden* (New Haven, Conn.: Yale University Press, 1951), pp. 116-17.

16. Katherine Bail Hoskins, *Today the Struggle* (Austin, Tex., and London: University of Texas Press, 1969), p. 193.

17. W. H. Auden and Christopher Isherwood, *The Dance of Death* (London: Faber and Faber, 1933), p. 38.

18. Auden's plays of this period were influenced by Bertolt Brecht's work. Brecht effectively introduced songs into his social dramas and employed light verse for purposes of cutting satire. That is how Brecht created a genuine feeling of rapport with his audience. "During his stay in Berlin in 1928-29 Auden seems to have been greatly impressed by this achievement. . ." (Monroe K. Spears, *The Poetry of W. H. Auden* [New York: Oxford University Press, 1963], p. 90). For a more detailed critical analysis of the alleged influence of Brecht's poetry and his experimental plays, particularly *Mahagonny* and *Die Dreigroschenoper*, see Frederick Buell, *W. H. Auden As a Social Poet* (Ithaca, N.Y. and London:

Auden interpreted the class war in terms that were human and concrete, combining the eschatological vision of Marx with the psychological insights he derived from Freud, Jung, and Groddeck. Before the revolution could succeed, Auden pointed out, the heart of the worker must be transformed. He must root himself in the primordial earth, renew his life-giving contact with Nature, preserve his integrity, and learn the secret of being alone. The demise of the old, fractious, possessive self must give way to a new love that will mark the coming of the individual soul to maturity.

Letters from Iceland (1937), by Auden and MacNeice, describes the journey of the two poets through the magnificent northern landscape of Iceland. The trip enabled Auden to view his own land in perspective and to pass judgment on its failings. He is suspicious of the concerted effort being made to achieve technological efficiency in social living. As a boy he enjoyed most of all studying books about machines. He then planned to become a mining engineer. He relates how he came to choose the poet's vocation. T. S. Eliot showed him the way.

The Ascent of F 6 (1936), by Auden and Isherwood, is a poetic drama that pictures England as still driven by imperialistic ambitions. Selfishness is the prime mover in the tainted world of politics; greed, the desire to acquire wealth and fame and power, corrupts the leaders of the State. The ascent of F 6 provides the framework of the plot. The mountain must be climbed if the natives are to be subdued and the empire kept intact. M. F. Ransom, a scholar and dreamer who realizes full well the vanity of worldly power, is chosen as the sacrificial victim. At first he rejects this assignment but his mother persuades him to undertake this expedition and find the Demon that legend says occupies the topmost peak. The fabric of the story is held together by an inwoven thread

Cornell University Press, 1973), pp. 88-97 and 101-2. To what extent was Brecht of importance in shaping the career of Auden as poet and playwright? There was no direct Brechtian influence on Auden, though the two writers had much in common; "they both sought solutions to the problem of political engagement through literature. . ." (Buell, *W. H. Auden As a Social Poet*, p. 90). Both writers at this time wove political motifs into the warp and woof of their plays. Auden, like Brecht, was interested in avant-garde experiments that were satirical and polemical in content. Though the two writers had much in common, they differ sharply in their political views and in the character of their commitment. Auden was no Marxist soothsayer, no true believer.

of symbolism and allegory. "Nothing is revealed but what we have hidden from ourselves,"[19] says the Abbot, who knows that men desire evil and must therefore be kept within bounds. In the end, the rulers are destroyed. "For you can only rule men by appealing to their fear and their lust; government requires the exercise of the human will: and the human will is from the Demon."[20] The other alternative, the Abbot declares, is complete abnegation of the will. When Ransom is left alone, he cries out to be saved from the destructive power of his will. After the death of his companion, Ransom too craves death. And the Figure he beholds at the summit, after its draperies fall away, is that of his mother when she was young.

On the Frontier (1938), by Auden and Isherwood, is a spirited tract for the times, a blow struck in the fight against Fascism. A chorus of workers chant couplets, each of which portrays the miserable kind of life they lead and voices their determination to find a way out. Valerian, the head of the Westland Steel Trust, is the power behind the ranting demagogic dictator who protects the interests of the moneyed class that supports him. He is cultured but cynical, devoid of any faith except his belief in the invincibility of power that is backed by wealth. For the masses he feels only contempt. They were put on earth to serve as beasts of burden. They dream of utopias that will give them a taste of paradise, they protest against what they call injustice, but they inevitably turn to a master for guidance. This capitalist is convinced that Nature despises the underdog. Valerian plans to establish absolute control over the State. The workers keep up their hope. They continue to fight for a better world and if they die in the struggle they know their place will be taken by others.

We learn of the state of hostility that exists between Westland and Ostnia. Inflamed by propaganda, the people in both these countries are fiercely patriotic, convinced that the other side is bent on war. But the young are not deceived by the flood of vicious oratory that pours forth from the loudspeakers. They know, like Eric who goes to prison because he

19. W. H. Auden and Christopher Isherwood. *Two Great Plays: The Dog Beneath the Skin* and *The Ascent of F 6* (New York: Vintage Books, 1962), p. 153.
20. *Ibid.*, p. 154.

believes it is wrong to kill, that they have been born into a world of hate and fear, a world in which the common people cannot satisfy their basic needs. The voice of the chorus is then heard, suggesting that once the people are united in fraternal solidarity they will strip the ruling class of its monopoly of wealth and power. Finally, the soldiers revolt and Valerian is killed. While in prison, Eric learned that the struggle he had waged was his own struggle. He could not stand apart from this war of the classes.

At this stage of his career Auden believed that the Economic Man was slated for extinction. Unlike the orthodox Marxist, he felt that the guilt for the exploitative crime of the past is present in all of us. The insulated, self-sufficient ego must be slain. The hubristic mania, the inordinate will to power, is bound to culminate in a tragic but redemptive fall. What can still save us is the experience of love. The political struggle must be preceded by a disciplined process of self-purification.

In *Journey to a War,* by Auden and Isherwood, there is a minimum of political commentary. Auden witnessed the suffering of the Chinese, a supremely civilized people, the victims of Japanese aggression. Auden was then hammering home his belief that this war was but the local manifestation of a struggle in which all men are involved, the intellectual and the man of action, the lover and the scientist, the poet and the hungry peasant. He reviews the movements of civilization, the alternating cycles of faith and doubt, and observes that while the intelligence has made great strides forward, the heart of modern man is stunted. It was the Industrial Revolution that generated the deadly hatred of the class war.

The year in which *Journey to a War* was published —1939—marked the end of Auden's attachment to Marxism. The poem "September 1, 1939" reflects the profound change that has taken place in his political orientation. It consists of mordant reflections on the state of the world as he sits in one of the dives on Fifty-Second Street in New York City. He detects the offensive smell of death spreading over the face of the earth. He has cast off the alluring abstractions spelled out by the Marxist evangel. He need invoke no dialectic to know that evil inevitably begets evil. The neurotic compulsion that drives the human race to acts of wholesale murder, that compels them to engage in a demented carnival of mass slaughter, is caused by the romantic error that inspires men and women to seek what is impossible of fulfillment. This self-engrossed, narcissistic quest for love must be abandoned.

Once Auden gave up his adherence to Marxist doctrine, his poetry took a new direction. After his arrival in the United States, he came under the influence of Kierkegaard and Niebuhr, an influence that weaned him away from the arena of radical politics. Now he came to grips with the moral and religious problems of his age. His conversion was by no means a sudden one. He now looked upon man as a fallen creature, tainted with a disposition to do evil, a victim of original sin. Absolute values exist, he maintained, even though they cannot be proved. Religiously committed, Auden, like Niebuhr, held that man today falls into sin because he refuses to acknowledge his limitations as a finite being. Governed by overweening pride and presumption, modern man thinks he can usurp the throne of God. Auden, who has lost his faith in the philosophy of the Enlightenment, now rejects the naive optimism of the liberal who assumes that man is naturally good. He accepts the principle of redemptive love, which lies at the heart of the world religions. If the Marxist dream of the classless society no longer appeals to him, it is because he now perceives that mankind as it wanders blindly from birth to death will never achieve a condition of perfect happiness on earth.

The new Auden is more concerned with the cumulative and enduring force of tradition, the conflicts of the religious consciousness, and the dimension of eternity, than with the ephemeral challenge of politics. Times change, governments are overthrown, famine stalks the land, epidemics familiarize the masses with the grotesque horror of death, world wars are fought, revolutions break out, but the face of eternity remains untroubled. In "The Sea and the Mirror, A Commentary on Shakespeare's *The Tempest*," Auden pictures humanity waltzing merrily across the tightrope of time, ignoring the imminence of death, blind to the danger of falling down into the gulf that yawns beneath them. Auden is powerless to dispel the mystery that surrounds us on all sides. Prospero frees Ariel and gazes into the future, where death waits for him. Prospero is the intellectual who seeks to acquire supernatural power. Ariel represents man's real self. In "Caliban to the Audience," Auden describes the demoralized condition of modern man, who regards Science, Religion, and Art as "fictions" that have no bearing on life. Industrial civilization is the curse from which twentieth-century man needs to be delivered, since it hides from him his true state of being.

After the Fall, man is benighted, spiritually lost, not knowing where to turn or what fate to choose. He cannot distinguish between reality and appearance. In his desperate quest for ultimate meaning, man has reached the farthest frontier of consciousness. Beyond it he cannot go. *The Age of Anxiety* (1947) added further confirmation of the fact that Auden had left far behind him the Marxist vision of the Proletarian Heaven on Earth.

In preparing the collected edition of his poetry, Auden revised his past work in the light of his religious conversion. After his commitment to Christianity, Auden accepted the doctrine "that the good life in its fullness can never be approximated on earth save with the aid of supernatural grace, and never wholly realized save in Eternity in the City of God."[21] In keeping with this faith, Auden revised a number of key passages. Whereas the original version depicted man exulting in the power of his will to build the structure of human justice, the lines were subsequently altered so that in the new context justice is no longer human but superhuman. It is exalted as divine, as is indicated by the personification of Justice.[22]

That, in general, is the method Auden pursued: by means of slight verbal changes, lines that were formerly secular in meaning now give off religious overtones. For example, Joseph Warren Beach shows how Auden took a satirical passage from "The Dog Beneath the Skin," a parody of ecclesiastical eloquence, and presented it as "a profound and edifying exposition of religious truth."[23] What had originally been intended as political propaganda is transformed into religious preachment. Marxist symbols are invested with Christian connotations. Agape replaces the trinity of Freud, Marx,

21. Joseph Warren Beach, *The Making of the Auden Canon* (Minneapolis, Minn.: The University of Minnesota Press, 1957), p. 7.
22. *Ibid.,* pp. 7-8.
23. *Ibid.,* p. 11.

and Engels. In the past Auden had assumed that man
created God in his own image,[24] but now he deals with such
themes as original sin, the Incarnation, the Absolute, and the
Eternal. He has ceased to be the rebel against the Establishment represented by the Church and the State. Whatever
degree of commitment he once felt for the cause of political
radicalism had by this time fallen to zero. He is aware that
the world today, as it has been in the past, is infested with
hideous evils and full of suffering, but he considers it a fatal
illusion, born of the romantic exaggeration of the vocation of
the artist to believe that by creating works of art he can
eradicate the source of evil or reduce the misery of mankind.
"Where social evils are concerned, the only effective weapons
are two: political action and straight reportage of the facts.
Art is impotent."[25]

4. Stephen Spender: The Repudiation of Communism

Spender possesses a pure lyrical gift. He eschews the or-
namental, the oratorical, and the didactic. His lines communicate their burden of meaning with a bare but poignant
simplicity. Only through the medium of concrete and sensuous images can he present his social and political views. He
avoids the abstract and the doctrinaire. Like Auden, he seeks
to transcend the isolated, encapsulated ego. His aim is "to
advance from friends to the composite self,"[26] though he is
not at his best in poems of this description. His finest poems
call to mind the impassioned beat of Shelley's lyrics; they are
imbued with the same intensity of feeling and they voice the

24. Monroe K. Spears defends Auden on the ground that the religious vision
transcends the earlier outlook. As for the criticism Joseph Warren Beach, in
The Making of the Auden Canon, directs at Auden's method of altering the earlier poems and giving them a religious rather than Marxist cast, Spears points
to the fact that Beach, a secular humanist and a liberal in his political orientation, is fundamentally unsympathetic to Auden's religious convictions and
therefore fundamentally biased in his assessment of Auden's poetry during
the last two decades (Spears, *The Poetry of W. H. Auden,* p. 202). For a cogent
and perceptive analysis of the reasons why Auden between 1936 and 1941 became a religious poet, a Christian existentialist, see François Duchene, *The Case
of the Helmeted Airman: A Study of W. H. Auden's Poetry* (Totowa, N.J.: Rowman
and Littlefield, 1974), pp. 93-119 *et passim.*
25. W. H. Auden, "The Real World," *The New Republic,* December 6, 1967, p. 26.
26. Stephen Spender, *Collected Poems* (New York: Random House, 1955), p. 10.

same tender and compassionate cry at the spectacle of insensate cruelty or unmerited suffering.

He had not foreseen, he confesses, how the will grows exhausted, paralyzed into immobility, how the brightness of the early vision of the ideal gradually fades in the common light of day. But he is not mourning his own loss of innocence. He captures the passive, apathetic mood generated by the years of economic depression. He describes men without work wandering aimlessly through the streets or idling forlornly on the corner. He writes with imaginative empathy about these human derelicts, helplessly draining away the empty hours of life. It is the human predicament that haunts the mind of the poet. He sounds no strident appeal to the unemployed to take up their quarrel with the capitalist foe or to raise high the red banner of revolution. His compassion includes within its sweep all sorts and conditions of men—the poor, the prisoners massive like blocks of stone in their cells, the ugly, bedraggled prostitute. The fact that men must live in squalor, without a definite aim or purposeful goal, he finds unutterably depressing.

In *Vienna* (1935), a narrative poem that develops an ambitious and complex theme—the corruption of bourgeois society as evidenced by the recent murder of five Viennese Socialists—Spender is too rhetorical in his indignation to be fully convincing. He is more at home in the short lyric, even when he takes up themes of social protest. In one memorable poem he wonders how it happened that money and work could conceal the obvious and enduring love of man for man. In this poem he strikes a confident note of affirmation, of faith in the future. And this faith requires no Marxist exegesis. It embodies the heart of Spender's political message. He is calling upon youth to rebuild the structure of society before it collapses and buries them beneath its ruins. Let all our senses be touched and transfigured by love. We must surrender our dream of paradise, abandon our reliance on the past, and strengthen the sinews of our will to achieve the desired social goal.

> No spirit seek here rest. But this: No man
> Shall hunger: Man shall spend equally.
> Our goal which we compel: Man shall be man.[27]

27. *Ibid.,* pp. 49-50.

In *Trial of a Judge* (1938), Spender undertakes the difficult task of indicting the Nazi regime. The play represents his farewell to liberalism. The idealists must forsake their attitude of detachment and support the workers in their fight against Fascism. The crimes the Nazis committed are too horrible to be portrayed with uncompromising realism. In five acts Spender analyzes the reactions of a judge and his anguish at seeing justice about to be perverted at the behest of the corrupt and accommodating powers of the State. He had sentenced to death five terrorists for an act of murder. Pressure is exerted on the Judge to release the murderers, and he grants the reprieve.[28]

We can trace the steady growth of Spender's political insight. In the second and third parts of *The Still Centre* (1939), he included those poems which were inspired by his political concerns. Though born of an immediate experience or activity, they embody attitudes that extend beyond the moment and the occasion. The third part is of particular interest in that it deals with the Spanish Civil War. Spender tells us that the reason why he failed to strike a more heroic note at the time was "that a poet can only write about what is true to his own experience, not about what he would like to be true of his experience."[29] He resisted the strong pressure then brought to bear on poets to write about what lay beyond the limited range of individual experience. He composed poems of a more personal nature.

His tenderness and his pity are expressed in "An Elementary Class Room in a Slum." What, he asks, can Shakespeare and the map of other lands mean to these children of the poor with their stunted bodies, trapped as they are in a fog-shrouded slum? The more concrete the experience—a battle, an air raid—the more vividly realized as a rule is the poem. In "Two Armies," written while he was in Spain, he describes in poignant imagery the two armies, enemies during the day, asleep in the silence of the night as if they were united by a common suffering.

For Spender, like other liberal-minded intellectuals in

28. "The liberal judge, having briefly compromised with the forces of fascism and then reversed himself, is ostensibly being tried for treason to the Fascist state; but he is really on trial in his own mind for his initial willingness to acquiesce in injustice for the sake of preserving order and avoiding violence." Hoskins, *Today the Struggle*, p. 161.
29. Stephen Spender, *The Still Centre* (London: Faber and Faber, 1941), p. 10.

Europe and the United States, Spain symbolized the climax of their struggle against Fascism. Here was history in the making. The civil war in Spain led a number of writers to join one of the foreign brigades that fought on the Loyalist side.[30] The savage battles that took place between the workers, untrained in the use of arms, and Franco's Moors, the resistance of the people pitted against the Insurgent armies and the planes provided by Hitler that swooped out of the sky and rained bombs on unprotected Loyalist divisions, the rank injustice of the policy of nonintervention pursued by France and England—all this fanned their indignation to a white heat. The record of these tragic years is preserved in *Poems for Spain,* edited by Stephen Spender and John Lehmann.[31] In "Arms in Spain," Rex Warner fiercely denounces those who sent munitions to the Insurgent forces. In the poem "Spain," Auden affirmed the need to participate in this crucial struggle against the powers of reaction that effectually prevent the implementation of the humanistic ideal. As Spender points out, to many who were involved in this war action itself became a kind of living poetry that gave proof of their total commitment. They felt, like Auden, that the fate of civilization was being determined on the blood-soaked battlefields of Spain. They associated Republican Spain with all that is progressive and life-sustaining: freedom, democracy, the survival of culture. In "Full Moon at Tierz," John Cornford voiced his conviction that the men in the International Brigade are fighting for the future. Written before the poet engaged in the storming of Huesca, this poem contains a number of charged lines that gave utterance to this young man's faith in the Party as he stands alone before the test of his nerves in the ordeal of battle. He prays that he will prove equal to the occasion, that he will be as hard as the metal of his gun. Then he weakens the sheer lyrical thrust of the poem by tacking on a coda that consists of versified Party slogans:

> Our fight's not won till the workers of all the world
> Stand by our guard on Huesca's plain,

---

30. In 1955 Auden wrote: "Nobody I know who went to Spain during the Civil War who was not a dyed-in-the-wool stalinist came back with his illusions intact." Quoted in Spears, *The Poetry of W. H. Auden,* p. 86.
31. Published in London in 1939 by the Hogarth Press.

Swear that our dead fought not in vain,
Raise the red flag triumphantly
For Communism and for liberty.[32]

5. *Spender and the Problem of Commitment*

As we have seen, the threat of Fascism during the thirties induced a number of writers to heed the urgent prompting of their conscience and support the Communist cause. Spender witnessed the rising tension in Germany, the deadly conflict for power between the Nazis, unconscionable in their methods of beating down all opposition to their aims, and the Communists. Berlin suffered from poverty, unemployment, and inflation. The Jews were under attack by Hitler's Storm Troopers. The intellectuals were on the defensive. Those whom Isherwood and Spender knew personally in Germany belonged to the Left. Though Spender sympathized with the Communists, he could not accept the drastic solution they proposed. He hated war and believed in social justice, but he "could not accept the proposition that to resist evil we must renounce freedom, and accept dictatorship and methods of revolutionary violence."[33] Where did he stand? Did he believe in Socialism? Though he felt guilty because of his role as a mere spectator, he could not subscribe to the political philosophy of Communism. He would not give in to the demand of the Marxists that he discard his "liberal concepts of freedom and truth. The Marxist challenge . . . that the opponents of Communism were concerned only with *their* freedom, *their* truth, and that all ideas were rationalizations of their interests, made me think out for myself the position of the freedom of the individual."[34] He insisted that it was pos-

---

32. John Cornford, though a member of the Communist Party, joined the P.O.U.M. He gave his unqualified allegiance to the Party. In the militia of the P.O.U.M. he met men who had left the Party because of their conviction that the Kremlin, and Stalin in particular, had betrayed the Revolution, but the bitter disillusionment of these ex-Communists only strengthened Cornford's loyalty to the Party. The Party and the International, he declared, "had become flesh and blood to me. Even when I can put forward no rational argument, I feel that to cut adrift from the Party is the beginning of political suicide." Peter Stansky and William Abrahams, *Journey to the Frontier* (Boston and Toronto: Little, Brown and Company, 1966), p. 341. See Hoskins, *Today the Struggle*, pp. 228-20.

33. Stephen Spender, *World Within World* (London: Hamish Hamilton, 1951), p. 133.

34. *Ibid.*, p. 135.

sible to transcend the pressure of class interest and bear witness to truths that served no vested privileges.

He was in Vienna when he heard the startling news of the
Spanish Civil War. Harry Pollitt, the secretary of the British
Communist Party, asked him if he would support the Loyalist
cause by joining the Party, despite the doubts he harbored
about the Moscow Trials. Spender had been active for a time
in the United Front movement. At meetings held with other
writers he discussed the question "whether there was a necessary connection between politics and literature."[35] Everyone,
it seemed to him, was now becoming involved in politics.
"The sense of political doom, pending in unemployment,
Fascism, and the overwhelming threat of war, was by now so
universal that even to ignore these things was in itself a political attitude."[36] Politics spoke with the decisive accents of fate,
but he did not condemn those writers who held different
views. Even when he was in close accord with the Marxist
outlook on many vital issues of the day, he persisted in his
heretical belief that the liberation of man could not be ef-
fected solely on an economic and ideological basis; a spiritual
transformation would have to take place as well.[37]

The critical writing Spender published during this period
reveals his struggle to define and abide by the values in
which he believed. In *The Destructive Element* (1935), he
examines the work of one writer, Henry James, in depth and
seeks through him to establish a criterion of value. He sees
the contemporary writers engulfed by the destructive element, that is, "by the experience of an all-pervading Present,
which is a world without belief."[38] Uprooted from the main
tradition of their culture, their link of continuity with the
past broken, they suffer from an excess of consciousness;
their egotism is immense, but not counterbalanced by any
humane or moral discipline; they seem to have no sustaining
faith or purpose in life. In an age of sharply fluctuating val-

---

35. *Ibid.*, p. 249.
36. *Ibid.*
37. In this connection Francis Scarfe writes: "The poet cannot afford to present
   more than . . . the essence. the idealism of a political creed. And it becomes
   obvious that, bound to universal and not to local truths, there is little hope for
   the poet outside a general humanitarian outlook." Francis Scarfe, *Auden and
   After* (London: Routledge, 1942), p. 44.
38. Stephen Spender, *The Destructive Element* (London: Jonathan Cape, 1935), p.
   14.

ues, social conflicts, political unrest, widespread economic distress, and psychic maladjustments, the role of the poet is often regarded with suspicion. Why is he fiddling with verses while Rome burns? Hence the inner compulsion that drove some poets to emphasize the social value of their contribution. From now on, Spender declared, poetry must be rooted in life and not serve as an outlet for private dreams.

Spender then set out to defend the legitimacy of the political subject in literature. He opposed the aesthetic bias that argued that the work of the imaginative writer should be nonpolitical in character. What he meant by "political," however, was not what the Marxists meant when they employed the term. He asserted that the greatest art is moral in spirit and substance even if it advances no moral or political doctrine. He maintained that the writer must not yield to the weakness of suspending his own judgment in order to underline the importance of some political thesis. He must avoid the danger of becoming the slavish echo of a political creed. Even more to the point is the warning he sounded against the writer who "knows" the nature of man and the direction in which history will move in the future, for "as an artist"[39] he possesses no such knowledge. In short, poetry is essentially communication or revelation, not indoctrination.

What subject, then, shall the modern writer choose? Intuitively Spender realized that without organic beliefs of some kind, beliefs passionately held and yet valid beyond the personal needs of the moment, a writer is doomed to sterility. What a writer uses for his material is intimately bound up with what he believes. The trouble with some of the writers he discusses—D. H. Lawrence, T. S. Eliot,[40] and Wyndham Lewis—is that the beliefs that made them moral writers bore no correspondence to the world around them. The political movements of the age possess a moral significance far greater than that which inheres in the life of the individual. If the world is to be saved from destruction, we must break out of our locked-in ego.

Spender, like Day Lewis, was drawn to Communism because it presented a satisfying picture of a just world toward

---

39. *Ibid.,* p. 20.
40. Spender remarks that to T. S. Eliot "it seemed impossible to accept any belief that is not a religious belief: one either rejects all belief . . . or else one accepts a religious belief in salvation and damnation." *Ibid.,* pp. 146-47.

which men of good will could strive. It inspired the writer to embody in his work the coming of that far-off event—the dawn of the classless society. "The writer who grasps anything of Marxist theory feels that he is moving in a world of reality, and in a purposive world, not merely in a world of obstructive and oppressive *things*."[41] The precise practical method by means of which the ideal state will be established is not of paramount importance to the artist. It is not his concern at all. He knows that the economic system is not sacrosanct and immutable. It was made by man. If man changes, so must the system. That is all the writer needs to know.

Spender would not endorse the dictum that the proletarian artist must be a dialectical materialist. It is not sound critical practice to castigate writers because of their bourgeois origin or because their work, though it gives an honest and moving portrayal of life, is not sufficiently revolutionary. Writers should be permitted to write what they genuinely feel and believe. "Unless artists insist on their right to criticize, to be human, and even 'humanitarian,' Communism will become a frozen era, another ice age."[42] Communism operates, Spender complained, on too arbitrary and sectarian a basis. It is wrong for the writer to cram himself full of the Marxist world outlook, its philosophical premises, its economic interpretation of history, and its dialectical abstractions. The future may well belong to Communism, but the artist, if he is to keep faith with his creative mission, will have to travel a road infinitely more difficult thatn the one mapped out for him by Marxist theoreticians. The Marxist outlook, Spender concludes, is not "adequate to produce considerable art; it is adequate only to use art to serve its own purposes. The real objection to the Communist ideology in writing is that it is not self-critical."[43] The value of literature is not determined by the degree to which it meets the requirements of ideological conformity.

Forward from Liberalism records the various stages of the spiritual and intellectual journey he had to take before he was ready to accept the Communist creed. A sort of psychoanalytic confession of the complex process that bade him to join the militant Left, the book reveals the emotional

41. *Ibid.*, p. 228.
42. *Ibid.*, p. 235.
43. *Ibid.*, p. 254.

elements that affected his political conversion. A large part of its contents consists of a paraphrase or restatement of the basic Marxist principles, but he goes further than that: he furnishes an illuminating analysis of the relation of politics to art and of art to politics. Perhaps the most memorable section of the book, because it is the most personal in content, is the one called the "Inner Journey," in which Spender discloses the doubts that assailed him and then shows how he overcame them.

Unlike the liberals of the past, he realized that political issues are decided finally not by acts of Parliament but "by the industrial interests which control the liberal democratic state."[44] Spender formulated no narrow materialistic conception of politics. Politics offers the means whereby democracy is made truly effective, but democracy, if it is to become effective in the life of a nation, must be enlarged to include economic and cultural as well as political democracy. It is impossible for the writer to remain neutral, disinterested, uncommitted. If he cuts himself off from the struggle of his time to build a classless, egalitarian society, he is driven to interpret the world from a romantic viewpoint. The realities of industrialism, neocolonialism, and economic exploitation do not impinge on his creative mind, which has arbitrarily excluded them as alien to his field of vision, but the result is that his creativity is rendered anemic and he feels himself to be utterly ineffectual and impotent, a writer without an audience and without anything vital to say to his generation. This version of romanticism as inescapably neurotic—neurotic because it is regressive in its retreat to an Arcadian past or to a pure primitiveness—manifests itself in opposition to the predominant power of machinery, the tyranny of the technological complex. The romantic cult of beauty proves itself to be bankrupt "when brought up against the naked realities of the capitalist world."[45] Romanticism failed because it was sentimental in its attitude toward the world and because its protests against the advance of industrialism were entirely unrealistic. "Machinery, all the instruments of production, instead of being against us, are on our side, if they are used, not for the exploitation of a majority by a smaller minority,

44. Stephen Spender, *Forward from Liberalism* (London: Victor Gollancz, 1937), p. 17.
45. *Ibid.*, p. 30.

but for the benefit of the whole society."[46] There is no need to destroy machinery; it is the profit motive that must be abolished.

In *Forward from Liberalism,* Spender rejects the policy of reformism. What the Popular Front must aim at is the establishment of a world state that is classless in structure. Though in sympathy with pacifism and at heart opposed to violence, he admits that exceptional situations might arise in which he hopes he would possess the courage to act violently. He now believes violence to be justified. "It seems to me that, although there are important principles of human conduct, these are never absolute."[47] He must either fight for freedom or submit to tyranny. There is no middle ground. One is compelled to take sides.[48] The Austrian Socialists were right in defending themselves against the attacks of the Heimwehr in 1934.

In the section called "The Inner Journey," Spender explains that he is trying "to do a portrait of the mind of a person whose sympathies are idealist and liberal in the present moment of history. In my opinion the mind of that person should be directed towards communism."[49] The liberal's insistence on exercising his freedom of thought creates a difficult problem. His presumptive right to criticize, to voice his doubts, arouses the hostility of those political realists who are at the head of the Party.[50] It is the proletariat who will lay the foundations of the classless society and shape the history of the future. The artist will contribute to the spiritual and imaginative enrichment of the new Socialist civilization. This book, Spender announces, "is an act of my will, it is an assertion in behalf of two things I very much care for, justice and poetry. If you like, I believe that the revolution must be an example of poetic justice."[51] Spender sums up his position by saying that he is a Communist because he is a liberal who believes in objective truth and supports the cause of political justice. He feels certain "that in the modern world

46. *Ibid.,* p. 36.
47. *Ibid.,* p. 252.
48. "A moment comes when those who are not with the classless society are against it." *Ibid.,* p. 71.
49. *Ibid.,* p. 169.
50. This provides further proof of the attitude of suspicion and distrust the Party leaders manifested toward intellectuals.
51. Spender, *Forward from Liberalism,* p. 196.

communism—the classless, internationalist society—is the final goal of liberalism."[52]

Later, looking back upon this period in his life, Spender perceived that he was naive in expecting the revolution to set an example of poetic justice. He realized that he had not stated his case convincingly. He had engaged in "historical analysis and political equivocation"[53] for which he was unfitted. He felt that he would have presented a stronger case if he had simply tried to stress the moral issue, illustrating it with material drawn from his own experience. The dogmatic preachment of Communism defeats its own ends. That is so because Marxism, while it emphasized the economic factor, betrayed no inclination to allow the philosopher and the artist to search for the truth without being bound by an antecedent set of conclusions. The primary stress Communism placed on the philosophy of materialism, its arbitrary adherence to the myth of the proletariat as saviors of mankind, the obsessive insistence of the Party that all other causes must yield precedence to the revolution—all this created "a mental prison of Socialist ideas. . . ."[54]

Spender could not get himself to believe in the messianic role of the proletariat or in the doctrine of historical inevitability. Nor was he prepared to use immoral and unscrupulous means to reach the ultimate revolutionary goal. And he refused to sacrifice his freedom of thought. "I could not believe that it was politically reactionary to believe in God or to hold views about nature or humanity which were not 'scientific' in the Marxist sense. . . ."[55] In the final analysis, when it came to a showdown, he saw no reason why he should surrender his judgment to the Party leaders.[56]

52. *Ibid.,* p. 203.
53. Spender, *World Within World,* p. 201.
54. Spender, "Writers in the World of Necessity," in *Modern British Writing,* ed. Denys Val Baker (New York: The Vanguard Press, 1947), p. 146.
55. *The God That Failed,* ed. Richard Crossman (New York: Bantam Books, 1951), p. 243.
56. *Ibid.,* p. 274.

17

Arthur Koestler and the Revolution Betrayed[1]

The emotional need that drove many intellectuals to embrace Communism was largely religious in character, though in public they explained their motives as part of a world-historical movement.[2] Later, after casting off this pseudo-religious absolutism, the ex-Communists tried to atone for their past excesses by telling the truth about their former relation to Communism. Of the essays published in *The God That Failed*, Arthur Koestler's confession is the most poignantly revealing, the most impassioned in its repudiation of the ideology he had once sworn by, the most unsparingly documented. By the time he decided to leave the Party, he

1. Arthur Koestler was born in Hungary. He lived for a time in a kibbutz in Palestine. Later he became the editor of a leading newspaper in Berlin. He finally decided to settle in England amid a people who admire personal qualities, not ideologies. Since he is an English citizen and writes his books in English, he has been included in this chapter among the English writers.
2. Frederic Jameson retorts that this type of invidious accusation cuts both ways. Anti-Communists make much of the fact—to them it is a "fact"—that Marxism is at bottom a religion, but it is branded "a shamefaced religion, a religion which does not wish to know its name. Yet it has always seemed to me a peculiar reproach. . ." (Frederic Jameson, *Marxism and Form* [Princeton, N. J.: Princeton University Press, 1971], p. 171). By identifying Marxism as basically religious in content and in its appeal, the anti-Communists in effect reduce the religions of the world to secular ideologies.

knew to what an alarming extent faith, in politics as in religion, springs from irrational sources. He became converted to Marxism because he lived, as he then believed, in a disintegrating capitalist society longing for the bread and wine of faith. The son of middle-class Hungarian parents, he became an influential European journalist. In 1931 he decided to become a member of the Communist Party. In the literature of Marxism he found the answer to all his tormenting doubts, the key that would unlock the enigmas of history, the dialectic that could resolve the wasteful conflicts of society. He learned to regard the Party as infallible at all times. It was his experience in a Spanish prison that compelled him to face the bitter, disenchanting truth about his espousal of the Communist cause. While waiting to be executed by Franco's guards, he was taught the lesson that induced him to forsake his revolutionary romanticism. He saw now that "the end justifies the means only within very narrow limits; that ethics is not a function of social utility. . . ."[3]

During the forties and fifties Koestler searched his conscience to discover the reasons that impelled him to join the Communist camp. His craving for the absolute of faith was so strong that he was ready for "the leap."

> In the nineteen-thirties conversion to the Communist faith was not a fashion or craze—it was a sincere and spontaneous expression of an optimism born of despair.[4]

Courageously, in novels and essays, he portrayed the personality of the Communist who finally perceives that the Soviet Union is not the Earthly Paradise. Koestler turned to the depth psychology of Freud to unravel the tangled skein of unconscious motives that lead "the true believer" to choose the fate of martyrdom. In *Arrival and Departure,* he shows what happens to a revolutionary who, as the result of an inner conflict between the call of love and his desire to offer himself as a sacrifice for the Revolution, develops a "beautiful" neurosis. Why did Peter Slavek accept and act on the ethical beliefs preached by Communism? As hidden

3. *The God That Failed,* ed. Richard Crossman (New York: Bantam Books, 1951), p. 68.
4. Arthur Koestler, *Arrow in the Blue* (New York: The Macmillan Company, 1952), p. 274.

memories come to light, he begins to realize that these beliefs and ideals were only pretexts. When he is under psychoanalytic treatment, his dream-sequences indicate that his revolutionary ardor had been stimulated and fed, not by an objective assessment of the historical situation but by an infantile sense of guilt caused by intense sibling rivalry. His fanatical dedication to the revolutionary movement had been an unconscious means of atoning for his guilt complex. It did not matter whether he was a hero of the proletariat or a martyr upholding the Catholic faith. When he realizes what has been the matter with him all along, his craving for the fate of martyrdom, he resolutely turns his back on the past.

Koestler gradually became convinced that the Revolution had been betrayed. The left-wing intellectuals were themselves responsible for this shameful betrayal. *Dialogue with Death* narrates Koestler's experiences while serving as a newspaper correspondent in the Spanish Civil War. He was lucky to escape with his life. The account he gives of his reactions while listening to the bursts of rifle fire that announced that another batch of Republican soldiers had been put to death, reveals the traumatic nature of the ordeal through which he then passed.

Disillusioned, uprooted, bitter as he reviews the events of his past, the ex-Communist continues to feel vaguely guilty even as he goes through the elaborate ritual of atonement. He must start a new life. He has lost his former dogmatic confidence that the Revolution will automatically transform human nature. The revolutionary writer who has thrown off the ideological spell that held him so long in mental bondage must find a new, dynamic purpose in life. It is this painful experience of awakening from the messianic delusions of the past that Koestler analyzes in his anti-Communist fiction.

The Gladiators illustrates Koestler's obsessive theme: the ambiguous morality of politics, the pitfalls that lie in the path of those who struggle to establish perfect justice on earth. *The Gladiators* develops the paradox, which also informs Sartre's play *The Devil and the Good Lord:* that the will to do good often entails the use of evil means and hence brings about evil consequences. Spartacus sees that the revolution for which so much blood had been shed was doomed. He is trapped, forced to fight, and his slave legions are slaughtered by the Roman troops. But this disastrous defeat was foreshadowed by a series of events long before the actual massacre took place. The slaves were overcome because they had lost their revolutionary fervor. *The Gladiators* ends on a pessimistic note: freedom is not easy to achieve; men, the mediators of the revolutionary dialectic, are essentially imperfect. As Koestler points out:

> The century of abortive revolutions was completed, the Party of justice had lost out, its strength was spent and exhausted. Now nothing could impede the greed for power, nothing barred the way to despotism, no barrier to protect the People was left. He whose grasp is the most brutal can rise to untold heights: dictator, emperor, god.[5]

The terrible dilemma of the Communist who loses his revolutionary faith is brilliantly depicted in *Darkness at Noon*, which explores the devious psychology of the dedicated Communist, the complex set of motives that originally prompted him to join the Party Militant, and the reasons why he finally decided to leave it. How far, Koestler asks, is the revolutionary saint prepared to go in his fanatical devotion to the utopian future? Is he willing to employ "evil" means in order to achieve desirable ends? Is he sufficiently disciplined, like the masked Comrades in Brecht's *The Measures Taken*, to end the lives of others if the millennium can thus be more quickly reached? And yet circumstances often arise when the most humane of men feel justified in killing those who are the enemies of the ideal. The utopian revolutionary is not held back by moral considerations. In *Darkness at Noon*, Ivanov the Communist is not troubled by finicky scruples about the sanctity of life. Those who oppose the Revolution are simply put out of the way. But Rubashov, who is made of different clay, wonders why hosts of innocent victims must be slain on the altars of the Revolution. Rubashov ponders this moral problem as he broods about his past: did not the needs of the collectivity justify all such actions?

Koestler's original intention in writing *Darkness at Noon* was to portray how a few prisoners react when they are sentenced to death in a totalitarian country. Each one discovers that he is "objectively" guilty, though he had not committed the par-

---

5. Arthur Koestler, *The Gladiators* (New York: The Macmillan Company, 1939), p. 391.

ticular crime for which he was given the death penalty.[6] In their intense preoccupation with the means, these men had lost sight of the ultimate goal. Koestler's protagonist, Rubashov, has a first name, Salmanovich (Solomonson), which identifies him as a Jew, though Koestler states that he was not aware of it at the time.[7] The novel demonstrates, among other things, that there is nothing to choose between the two totalitarian regimes: the Right and the Left. Koestler's unconscious provided him with a rich harvest of memories that revealed the unmitigated tyranny of Stalinist rule. His unconscious dictated the flow and shape of the plot. Painful incidents out of the blurred past, names, faces, gestures, snatches of conversation broke through the barriers of repression he had erected and fell into a preordained pattern. The novel seemed to write itself. He had no need to worry about the way in which the central conflict would be resolved:

> I knew, for instance, that in the end Rubashov would break down and confess to his imaginary crimes; but I had only a vague and general notion of the reasons which would induce him to do so. These reasons emerged step by step during the interrogations of Rubashov by the two investigating magistrates, Ivanov and Gletkin. The questions and answers in the dialogue were determined by the mental climate of the closed system; they were not invented but deduced by the quasi-mathematical proceedings of the unconscious from that rigid logical framework which held both the accused and the accuser, the victim and the executioner in its grip.[8]

Rubashov was a composite symbol of the old-guard Bolsheviks who had given their whole life to the revolutionary movement, only to witness its later betrayal by Stalin. When they are brought to trial, they act out obscene, groveling, hysterical confessions of guilt. Koestler believes that these incredible confessions were the direct result of the G.P.U.'s method of grilling its victims, breaking down their will, their power of resistance, by dire threats, intimidation, and torture. But what

6. One critic calls *Darkness at Noon* "one of the masterworks of political ethics in the twentieth century." George Kateb, *Utopia and Its Enemies* (New York: The Free Press of Glencoe, 1963), p. 37.
7. Arthur Koestler, *Invisible Writing* (New York: The Macmillan Company, 1954), p. 394.
8. *Ibid.*, p. 395.

convinces Rubashov at last of his "objective" guilt is a long
process of dialectical reasoning that justifies his acceptance of
the death sentence as an act of sacrifice for the Cause. Even
if the revolutionary had acted in good faith, this did not absolve him of blame. Subjective intentions were beside the
point. If one is "objectively" in the wrong, he must suffer the
consequences.

A born dialectician, the professional revolutionary controls
his feelings so that in every situation that arises he will act
rationally, in accordance with his beliefs. But how can a
Communist in the service of a political Party that does not
hesitate to use immoral means against its enemies—how does
such a man settle accounts with his irreparably damaged conscience? He knows the shattering truth now: the Revolution
has been betrayed, but at this juncture he must perforce obey
orders and keep silent. Victims of a nightmarish but irrefrag-
able system of logic, the former leaders of the Revolution
were arrested, imprisoned, tortured, forced to "confess" their
crimes. If the Party is always right, then why should they
complain when they themselves are caught in the net?[9] Be-

9. When the purges took place and the trials were held that "proved" the guilt
of many old revered revolutionary figures, there were loyal Communists
throughout the world who believed in the truth of these "confessions." Koestler's "explanation of the astounding confessions issuing from the former Bolshevik leaders at the Moscow trials had perhaps the widest currency. Yet it is
a hypothesis as mistaken in terms of historical probability as it is on the level
of artistic discrimination. For Koestler, the old Bolsheviks caved in because
they had signed their personalities away. . ." (W. D. Redfern, *Paul Nizan:
Committed Literature in a Conspiratorial World* [Princeton, N. J.: Princeton University Press, 1972], p. 97). According to Caute, however, Koestler's theory, as
it appears in *Darkness at Noon,* was not too limited in scope and arbitrary in its
interpretation. Gletkin tells Rubashov that because Russia is a backward country it needs scapegoats. It does not matter what means are used to keep her
going and enable her to survive until the next triumphant revolutionary upsurge. Gletkin, the inflexible Stalinist interrogator, admits that the accused did
not accept this approach; "some were susceptible to torture while others were
promised their heads, or those of their relatives" (David Caute, *Communism
and the French Intellectuals* [New York: The Macmillan Company, 1964], p.
132). In his recent study of Bukharin, Stephen F. Cohen charges that Koestler
in *Darkness at Noon* was guilty of spreading a misconception by portraying
Rubashov as having agreed to sign the confession in order to repudiate his
opposition to Stalin and thus help to strengthen the Party. This version of the
protagonist as a "repentant Bolshevik and morally bankrupt intellectual prevailed for two generations. In fact, however, as some understood at the time
and others eventually came to see, Bukharin did not really confess to the
criminal charges at all" (Stephen F. Cohen, *Bukharin and the Bolshevik Revolution: A Political Biography, 1889-1938* [New York: Alfred A. Knopf, 1973], p.
372).

lieving as they do in the verdict that history pronounces, they have no legitimate grounds for making a fuss when the Party decides that their days of usefulness are over.

Koestler's interpretation in *Darkness at Noon* of what must have happened to the accused revolutionaries that led them to harp on their guilt, was severely criticized. He endorses Gletkin's theory that the human organism can stand just so much "psychic" torture, and when that point is reached the man gives in. In fact, there is no need to utilize the standard types of physical torture. The accused are deprived of sleep, they are questioned relentlessly under a powerful glaring light day after day, until they lose all consciousness of time and can no longer distinguish between truth and falsehood, reality and imagination. Their mind seems to float on a sea of hallucination; the voice of the interrogator sounds unreal; their memory begins to play them false. They reach a state of exhaustion when they cease to care what happens. What does anything matter: honor, decency, surrender, death? They are at the mercy of one overwhelming desire: to sleep.

Rubashov represents the type of revolutionary who is driven by a stern and stubborn sense of duty. In all things he must conform to the professional ideal that had guided his life in the past. Despite the pain that racks him, despite his readiness to sign the incriminating document his captors have prepared for him, he haggles over minor details. Alone in his cell, he argues endlessly with himself as he reviews his career. His interminable monologue, his introspections, reveal the austere discipline he had imposed on himself as a Communist. Now he is able to commune with that "grammatical fiction," the "I," which he had long ago consigned to oblivion. He sets down his confused thoughts in a diary, which the prosecutor uses against him.

Through his eyes we behold the corruption of the regime, the spirit of ideological conformity that is made to prevail, the despotic control of the masses. Rubashov, as a revolutionary, had paid no heed to "bourgeois" distinctions between good and evil. Truth, he had argued, is identical with utility. The Party, in pursuing its ends, has had to sacrifice many men. Now it is his turn to be the scapegoat. Inwardly he is convinced that the fate of the individual is of no significance; the forward march of Communism must not be halted even if the victories it wins cost the lives of millions. Had not

Rubashov acted, and without compunction, on the premise that the Party could do no wrong?

> The Party is the embodiment of the revolutionary idea in history. History knows no scruples and no hesitation. Inert and unerring, she flows towards her goal. At every bend in her course she leaves the mud which she carries and the corpses of the drowned.[10]

In the solitude of his cell it is these theories that rise up to haunt him. He sees that his past was a horrible lie. How could he have believed that the Party incarnated the will of history? He perceives that the Soviet Union no longer represents the ideals of the Revolution. It has become a dictatorship, a bureaucracy.

But if this is what Rubashov thinks, then he is indeed guilty of counterrevolutionary opposition. The Party in power affirms its belief in truth as an expression of expediency. Whatever is conducive to "success," whatever helps to kindle the fire of faith in the masses, even though myths, painted in black and white, are specially invented for their consumption—all this is to be approved by the loyal members of the Party. Had not Rubashov acted on the assumption that the end justified the means? Rubashov, by thus probing the depths of his conscience, not only destroys his usefulness to the Party but also proves a traitor to the revolutionary cause. Ivanov argues: "The principle that the end justifies the means is and remains the only rule of political ethics. . . ."[11] It is this Machiavellian system of ethics that Rubashov is beginning to reject. Are human beings to be treated as if they were chemical elements in a test tube? If social utility is to be regarded as the sole criterion of moral value, then Rubashov realizes that he must yield to the demands of the Party, for only in that way can he be useful. Since the old revolutionaries have outlived their usefulness, they must make their exit from the stage of history. As Rubashov waits to be executed, he wonders whether it is not possible to run amok in pure reason and even to commit atrocious crimes in its name. Perhaps, he brooded, minutes before he was put to death, there lay the chief source of the evil: the elimination

10. Arthur Koestler, *Darkness at Noon*, trans. Daphne Hardy (New York: The New American Library, 1948), p. 36.
11. *Ibid.*, p. 113.

of the ethical standard. Perhaps in the future, his mind speculated, a new movement would spring up. "Perhaps the members of the new party will wear monks' cowls, and preach that only purity of means can justify the ends."[12]

Scum of the Earth, like *Dialogue with Death,* is a record of Koestler's adventures in prison and concentration camps and of his flight from France. Though the author's introspection, his fears and despair, lend the story dramatic intensity and verisimilitude, the events he describes are symbolical of the tragedy not of one anti-Fascist fighter but of hundreds of thousands on the continent of Europe who fled before the advance of the Nazi Juggernaut. These refugees now found themselves trapped in France, the classic land of liberty. How some men degenerate under misery and privation while others, through all the vicissitudes that flesh is made to bear, retain their essential sanity—all this is movingly told in a book that is both more objective and more truly inspired than Feuchtwanger's *The Devil in France.* It also furnishes an excellent psychological analysis of the collapse of France: the lack of morale, the insidious work of the fifth column, the petrifying fear of revolution, the indifference and confusion of the masses. The people hated Hitler, but only because he threatened to upset the *status quo.* The common man had acquired a feeling of contempt for lofty ideals. The Munich act of appeasement had destroyed any creed worth fighting for.

What was even worse, the hopes of the Left had been smashed ruthlessly by the dictatorship. After serving as a loyal Communist for seven years, Koestler left the Party in disgust. He had learned a mortifying but salutary lesson.

> We had realized that Stalinism had soiled and compromised the Socialist Utopia just as the Medieval Church had soiled and compromised Christianity; that Trotsky, although more appealing as a person, was in his methods not better than his opponents; that the central evil of Bolshevism was its unconditional adaptation of the tenet that the End justifies the Means; that a well-meaning dictatorship of the Torquemada-Robespierre-Stalin ascendancy was even more disastrous in its effect than a naked tyranny of the Neronian type; that all the parties of the Left had outlived their time, and that one day a new movement was to emerge from the deluge.[13]

12. *Ibid.,* p. 185.
13. Arthur Koestler, *The Scum of the Earth* (New York: The Macmillan Company, 1948), p. 17.

The dream of the ideal once incarnate in Soviet Russia was dead, and for those intellectuals who had once believed in it, the failure of their dream produced an unparalleled darkness and depression of spirit. They no longer had any faith in the historic destiny of the proletariat. Though they fought in the war, they fought without conviction or hope.

Some of the essays in *The Yogi and the Commissar*, which provoked a violent literary controversy, were written in the heat and stress of the war and bear the mark of special pleading, yet the outlook is eminently sound and reaches out beyond the restricted perspective of the temporal. In the midst of the war Koestler stressed the neglected truth that Fascism is a state of mind and that it cannot, therefore, be defeated by force of arms alone. Indicative of the new direction his mind was taking as he explored the nature of the human personality, is his insistence that the myth of the rational man must be exploded. Like Erich Fromm in *Escape from Freedom,* he shows how hard the human being, suffering from a split personality, is driven by the demon of the irrational. This split personality is due to the conflict between the thalamus, the storehouse of feeling and emotion, and the cortex, the organ of logical thought.

Koestler goes on to say that politics, especially in its more fanatical outbursts, has committed irreparable blunders by ignoring this aspect of the human personality, for it conceived of the psyche as a perfectly working mechanism of thought, a rational instrument of control. There it went sadly astray; the Goddess of Reason could not maintain her throne. The belief in the inevitable triumph of reason reached a horrendous climax in the eruption of subliminal passions in Germany. Nor were the activities of the Communists, at the other end of the spectrum, calculated to save men from the feeling that their primary spiritual needs and aspirations were being frustrated. Communism provided no firm anchorage for the emotions. The frustrations finally broke through all barriers in what Koestler calls "the Return of the Repressed." When the intervention of the cortex failed, the thalamus took its revenge.

In *The Age of Longing,* the penitential ex-Communists sound shrill warnings of the catastrophe that is about to befall the world, the imperialistic aggression that the Soviet power is preparing to unleash. Bitter, disillusioned, hopeless, without a country or a cause, all these men possess, now that their utopia lies crushed, is their vision of humanity redeemed in the distant future. The Dark Age is about to engulf Europe, which is stricken with the death wish. Julien, the most complex character in the novel, speaks of his gang of émigrés as the dispossessed—"the dispossessed of faith; the physically or spiritually homeless. A burning fanatic is dangerous; a burnt-out fanatic is abject."[14] These dispossessed and spiritually homeless people know that the old world is dying, but they have no conception of the new world that is to replace it.

Apart from his attacks on Communism and the Soviet dictatorship, Koestler made a valuable contribution in exposing the doctrinaire fraudulence of Marxist aesthetics, which wished to exploit literature and art for the sake of hastening the proletarian revolution. In a speech delivered at the International Congress of the P.E.N. Club, Koestler described the temptations the novelist must fight against. He may decide to withdraw from the world and shut himself within his own room, where he can pursue beauty undisturbed, thus becoming a virtual Yogi of the arts. The other temptation is to open wide the window of his room and portray, if not participate in, the dynamic swirl of events going on outside. The third temptation, "the hole-in-the-curtain method," represents a compromise: the novelist leaves his window partly open and gets a limited perspective, a peephole view of the world.

According to Koestler, the perfect novel calls for a window that is open to all the winds and vistas of the world. Though the novelist should have an all-encompassing knowledge of the forces that shape his world, he must be more than a "realist." Though he must portray life against the setting constituted by the dominant tendencies of his age, these background factors—war, science, politics, labor conflicts, Communism—must be assimilated and given life in terms of the experiences the characters undergo. The novelist is not a reporter. In creative fiction, whatever is told must be imaginatively reenacted, convincingly *lived*. For that reason the writer must keep the windows of his room wide open and must take the long view.

14. Arthur Koestler, *The Age of Longing* (New York: The Macmillan Company, 1951), p. 28.

The function of the intelligentsia is to be critical, noncon-formist, a creative and therefore "revolutionary" source of protest. It is the duty of the writer to contrast the life man actually leads with the kind of life he might lead. This vision of the ideal places the artist in perpetual opposition to the society of his time, and the hostility of society deepens the process of neurotic alienation. Because of their alienation, the literati suffer from an exacerbated guilt-complex, an occupa-tional neurosis. The case of Koestler versus the Communists is virtually closed. Though Koestler is still productive, he has stopped writing about politics. His diatribes of the forties and fifties are dated, but he was influential at the time in helping a number of writers free themselves from a closed-in system of political absolutism that repressed their creative activity. He taught them that there is more between heaven and earth and in the heart of man than is included in the philosophy of Marxism.[15]

15. See Appendix.

18

George Orwell and
the Morality of Politics

So long as a political ideology frees and stimulates the creative imagination it will be a brilliant matrix for the production of literature and art. But unfortunately it is the fate of most political ideologies to be narrow, to misrepresent and oversimplify the complexities of the world, to insist on the rightness of a single way, to fanatically constrict those operations of the imagination on which art feeds. And when this is the case (with either Marxist dogma or any other narrow ideology), then what demands for its health the infinite freedom of fantasy is forced into the rigid framework of an intellectual creed which nullifies its power. This is why there is so seldom a fruitful symbiosis between political insistence and creativity in the arts.[1]

No one any longer believes in the *simpliste* notion of workers charged with an easily recognisable identity, causing them to be distinct as though all manual workers had black faces, and all who were not manual workers white faces. No one believes any longer in the myth of all these black-faced people rising in revolt, killing all the white-faced people and there being henceforth a black-faced world.[2]

1. Albert William Levi, *Humanism and Politics* (Bloomington and London: Indiana University Press, 1969), pp. 303-4.
2. Wyndham Lewis, *The Writer and the Absolute* (London: Methuen & Co., 1952), p. 193.

He was a socialist, who popularized a severe and damaging criticism of the idea of socialism and of its adherents.[3]

1. *The Literary Contribution of George Orwell*[4]

The imaginative writer may not be the legislator, acknowledged or not, of mankind, but he has been on many occasions the outspoken accusing conscience of his age.[5] He not only records all that he sees, feels, and experiences but also attempts to interpret the meaning of the human adventure, the conflicts and crises of his time, and to impose a pattern of significance on the welter of events. Like many of his illustrious predecessors, he often exercises a quasi-prophetic function. George Orwell, novelist, journalist, literary critic, professed Socialist, predicted during the thirties the smash-up that was bound to come, the outbreak of the Second World War. He saw it all with preternatural clarity of vision, but he knew that his warning of the impending catastrophe would not be heeded. He went ahead with his self-appointed role of social critic, diagnosing the sickness of modern technological society, exposing the ubiquitous and irrepressible power of the acquisitive impulse, and revealing the various ways in which the cash nexus corrupts and degrades the soul of man. His early novels delineated with naturalistic objectivity the sordidness of middle-class life in England: the unrelieved boredom, the frustrations, the vulgarity, the smoldering resentment, the competitive mania.

The key to Orwell's character is to be found in *Down and Out in Paris and London* (1933). Though it is called a novel, it is actually a sober, factual account of Orwell's initiation into the life of the lower depths. In this story the narrator is the persona of Orwell himself, who is recounting a series of painful firsthand experiences. It is extreme poverty, hopeless and debasing, that he pictures for us, the soul-crushing poverty of

3. Raymond Williams, *Culture and Society* (New York: Harper & Row, 1958), p. 286.
4. Some parts of this first section are based on the following article: Charles I. Glicksberg, "The Literary Contribution of George Orwell," *Arizona Quarterly* 10 (Autumn 1954): 234-45.
5. Offhand one recalls the courageous example set by such writers as Voltaire, Zola, Camus, Dickens, Carlyle, Shelley, Gide, André Breton, Solzhenitsyn, and Sartre.

the slums. In such an ugly and cruel environment, where the struggle for survival is pitiless and unremitting, it is terribly difficult to preserve one's self-respect. The only redeeming feature of poverty, Orwell discovers, is that it destroys all reasons for worrying about the future. The victim feels a sense of relief, almost of pleasure, in being at last down and out.[6]

The second half of the book describes the kind of life Orwell led as a tramp in London, a pariah, homeless, despised, the object of countless insults and humiliations. He documents the economic situation that then existed in England: the tatterdemalion bands of outcasts, filthy, infested with sores and lice, but not at all dangerous, for they were underfed and physically degenerate, without spunk or spirit. After a few months of hunger and hardships, these creatures that once were men lose their nerve. The experience of being an outcast bred in Orwell a hatred of all class distinctions. It taught him that, contrary to the belief held by the educated classes, there is no gulf separating the poor from the rich. He saw that beggars are thoroughly human, not to be condemned out of hand as despicable parasites.[7] What these derelicts and misfits craved was work even more than money. Orwell ends his tale with a spirited analysis of why tramps exist by the tens of thousands. He assails the notion, born of class prejudice, that they are all desperate characters, monsters of iniquity. Though he has painted a harrowing picture of the hell in which these poverty-stricken wretches live, he insists that he has explored only the fringes of this infernal region, which is located in the heart of London.

In *Burmese Days* (1934) Orwell comes to grips with the problem of imperialism. A bitter, savagely realistic book, it is neither cynical nor despairing in tone. It is a lament over the fact that the decent folk, the good, kindly, humane people, either fail in life or come to a bad end, while the cunning and the selfish, the mean, the aggressive, and the callous,

6. Peter Stansky and William Abrahams offer a psychological explanation of Orwell's compulsive decision to enter the lower depths. He had served in Burma as an agent of imperialism; "he must be punished (and who better able to punish him than himself?) for having been one of the oppressors." Peter Stansky and William Abrahams, *The Unknown Orwell* (New York: Alfred A. Knopf, 1972), p. 236.
7. It is these flashes of compassionate insight that make this book of comparable value to Jack London's *The People of the Abyss*.

somehow reach their goal. A shocking satire of the iniquitous white man's rule in Upper Burma, this novel shows how the caste system operates. What a glaring contrast we behold between the avowed ideal of carrying the white man's burden, bringing the benefits of civilization to "the heathen," and the stark actuality that Orwell depicts—the disease, the grinding poverty of the natives, the unconscionable exploitation of labor, and, above all, the degradation of the colonized, the contempt that the rulers, buoyed up by the myth of racial superiority, feel for these coolies.[8] The men who accept these official posts in the jungle of Burma[9] are a corrupt lot, lazy, bored, alcoholic, unspeakably cruel. The only code they live by is that of solidarity with their own kind; those of the lesser breed without the law are rigorously excluded from associating with the lordly whites.[10]

The novel develops two related themes: the first dwells circumstantially on the abominations of the caste system, the current of hatred that flows between the two races, the brutality of the whites toward the natives. Connected with this motif is Orwell's contention that this kind of life infects the soul of the whites, saps their moral energy, and turns them into beasts. Orwell detested these colonical officials, their false airs, their righteous rhetoric, their cowardice, their silly pretense of superiority, their knuckling under to wealth or a title. The natives know that so long as the English remain in power, they are doomed to endure a state of servitude.[11]

8. Albert Memmi, a Jew born in Tunis, wrote *The Colonizer and the Colonized*, a trenchant essay that spells out the dialectic that governs the relationship between the colonizer and the colonized. It is of necessity a relation that is rooted in hatred. The colonizer endeavors to banish his own guilt as an exploiter by looking down upon the natives as the children of Caliban, inferior by birth, backward, fit only for a servile condition. Memmi attacks the structure of colonialism, its *raison d'être*. "For me, oppression is the greatest calamity of humanity. It diverts and pollutes the best energies of man—of oppressed and oppressor alike. For if colonization destroys the colonized, it also rots the colonizer." Albert Memmi, *The Colonizer and the Colonized*, trans. Howard Greenfield (New York: The Orion Press, 1965), p. xvii.

9. Born in Bengal of an Anglo-Indian family, Orwell served with the Indian Imperial police from 1922 to 1927.

10. E. M. Forster describes a similar alignment of forces in *A Passage to India* during the trial of Aziz.

11. With inexorable logic Albert Memmi analyzes the reasons, psychological, social, political, and economic, why the colonizer is bound to fail in his desperate effort to subjugate the natives whom he exploits. Sartre, in his introduction to *The Colonizer and the Colonized*, remarks: "Colonization denies human rights to human beings whom it has subdued by violence, and keeps them by

How can they fight against a small but well-armed army of occupation? Though the English came to this jungle town of Kayauktada with the intention of letting the Burmese enjoy the fruits of civilization, the most flourishing institution in this country is the prison. Corruption is rampant. The members of the European Club, all pure white, are determined, regardless of the wishes of the Government at home, to blackball any candidate who is colored. They play bridge, they gossip, they curse the weather and the ignorant natives, and they regularly drink themselves into a state of sodden insensibility. The most intemperate foe of "the blacks" is Ellis, local manager of a company, though the others, with the exception of Flory, are almost as bad. Ellis refuses to allow Dr. Veraswami, to whom he refers as "a dear little nigger-boy," to be admitted into the Club. He will have none of this new-fangled liberal idea of fraternizing with pot-bellied "niggers" smelling of garlic, even though there are clubs in India that have let down the bars. Ellis will not compromise. He wants to be backed by the others in a case like this, "when it's a question of keeping those black, stinking swine out of the only place where we can enjoy ourselves."[12] Let Flory, if he so wishes, be friendly with Dr. Veraswami, but it is carrying matters too far to demand that this undesirable person become a member on the same footing with all the others in the club. Orwell comments that there was nothing hypocritical in this vitriolic attack; Ellis is completely sincere in his racism.

> Ellis really did hate Orientals—hated them with bitter, restless loathing as of something evil or unclean. Living and working . . . in perpetual contact with the Burmese, he had never grown used to the sight of a black face. Any hint of a friendly feeling towards an Oriental seemed to him a horrible perversity.[13]

Here was an intelligent man and a capable worker for his firm, but Orwell classifies him as a type of Englishman, an incorrigible monomaniac in his race prejudice, who should never have been sent to the East. Unfortunately, his type was not uncommon among English colonials.

force in a state of misery and ignorance that Marx would rightly call a sub-human condition." Memmi, *The Colonizer and the Colonized*, p. xxiv.

12. George Orwell, *Burmese Days* (New York and London: Harcourt, Brace and Company, 1950), p. 23.
13. *Ibid.*, p. 24.

The racial prejudice that Ellis and the others (with the exception of Flory) take for granted is implicit in Ellis's definition of the role of the white man in Burma. The white man's function is to rule, to govern "a set of damn black swine who've been slaves since the beginning of history, and instead of ruling them in the only way they understand, we go and treat them as equals."[14] Ellis carries his racism so far as to feel incensed when the native Christians, even the Eurasians, are permitted to worship in the Christian church. It is an abominable mistake for these missionaries to preach the dangerous doctrine of equality. Mrs. Lackersteen, the one white woman in the post, believes firmly in keeping the natives in their place, instead of spoiling them by introducing democratic reforms. India was definitely going to the dogs; the good old days of undisputed domination by the whites are over. Mr. Macgregor, who is in charge of things, dislikes the use of the ugly word "nigger," which is not officially countenanced in India. He is not a bad sort, as officials go; he has no prejudice against Orientals so long as they are kept within proper bounds; he does not like to see them wantonly insulted. But Ellis refuses to accept Macgregor's politic distinction that the Burmese are Mongolians. For him a black skin, whatever its racial origin, is taboo. No natives (except as humble servants) are to be permitted to pollute the precincts of the Club. The trouble with the English and the Empire, Ellis asseverates, is that they have treated the natives too softly. There must be no doubt as to the nature of the relationship established: master versus slave.

Flory, the persona of the author, is the only one who is revolted by all this nasty talk of race prejudice by men who look upon themselves as the agents of justice and the torch-bearers of civilization to the lowly heathen. It is because of his sympathy for the underdog and his appreciation of Burmese art that Flory is regarded by the others as a Bolshevik. All these colonizers hark back nostalgically to the good old days when no native dared to be insolent, when the Government took a firm stand, and when natives were, for the slightest offense, immediately ordered to be flogged. For a new spirit sweeps the land; the natives are sullen, resentful, mutinous, filled with nationalist hopes and aspirations. Flory

14. *Ibid.*, p. 25.

finally discerns the truth about the English colonizers and their vaunted Empire. "The Indian Empire is a despotism—benevolent, no doubt, but still a despotism with theft as its final object."[15] The Army established its rule and created a world in which there is no freedom, not even of thought. Frustrated, powerless to revolt, Flory drowns his misery in drink while listening to these reactionaries boast of the methods they will use in dealing with the nationalists. Flory reflects: "The time comes when you burn with hatred of your own countrymen, when you long for a native rising to drown their Empire in blood."[16]

All of Orwell's novels deal in one way or another with the social problem: the curse of poverty, the concentration of wealth in the hands of the few, the insensate competitive struggle in business, the impossibility in this age of gigantic corporations and technological control of "coming up for air." A fearless critic of our money-mad civilization, Orwell shows that it worships the one true God: Mammon. There is no avenue of escape for those who cannot fit into the present scheme of things. Capitalism destroys the spirit of man by denying him the opportunity of leading a decent life. The manic obsession with money, the exhausting effort required to survive economically, the fear that haunts the little man of losing his job—this is mordantly presented in *Keep the Aspidistra Flying* (1936).[17]

In *Keep the Aspidistra Flying*, Orwell gave vent to his hatred of the anonymous and impersonal economic forces that turned a man into a thing, a robot. Brought up in genteel poverty, Gordon Comstock seeks to make his mark in the world, and as a result develops a paranoiac antipathy for its shabby business ethics, its class snobbery, its idolatry of wealth. He is a writer who cannot produce what the publishers will print or the public read.[18] Unknown, desperately poor, he has the courage to despise the world in which practically everything—culture, literary recognition, fame—depends on the acquisition of money. He protests against

15. *Ibid.*, p. 68.
16. *Ibid.*, p. 69.
17. The aspidistra is the symbol of middle-class respectability.
18. Orwell, like George Gissing, never became a popular novelist; he evinced no desire to gain that coveted but dubious distinction. An accidental conjunction of historical events brought *Animal Farm* and *Nineteen Eighty-Four* to the attention of a wide public.

these false values by giving up his position in a publicity agency and accepting a dead-end job selling books. His "protest" is futile and self-defeating. He is still unable to write. Poverty now grinds him down into the dust. He does not have enough money to buy food, clothing, and tobacco, and this deprivation undermines his morale. He becomes convinced that this oppressive sense of economic insecurity is responsible for his creative impotence. He fights off the temptation to rejoin the wage-earning multitude, chained to a job and fearful of being fired and rendered destitute.

Orwell drives home his belief that the British Empire with its pyramidal class structure and its faith in the cash nexus is doomed. In fact, he believes that Western civilization as a whole is sick at heart and secretly wishes to die. It will perish not with a whimper but a bang. The protagonist hears the noise of "the whole western world going up in a roar of high explosives."[19] Poor Gordon, in the meantime, continues to suffer from a crushing sense of failure. He is waging a hopeless struggle against overwhelming odds. Early in life he had realized that modern commerce is a huge swindle, that "money-worship has been elevated into a religion. Perhaps it is the only really felt religion that is left to us. Money is what God used to be."[20] It is the only measure of good and evil in the world. Gordon knows that it is this terrible protracted battle to maintain an appearance of respectable poverty that prostitutes the soul of man. He rejects the goal of "success" in life. He is not willing to pay the price. He would rather go under.

In the end, however, he must give in. Experience has taught him that to embrace poverty is no solution. Lack of money damages both the mind and soul, disintegrates the precious feeling of selfhood, and saps the strength of the body. Without money it is impossible to keep hope alive. Nothing comes out right for the man without money; he is rejected, made to feel contemptible. Like Céline, Orwell portrays the spiritually debasing effects of poverty. No one can live sanely, uncorrupted, in a materialistic society. "To abjure money is to abjure life."[21]

19. George Orwell, *Keep the Aspidistra Flying* (New York: Harcourt, Brace and Company, 1956), p. 21.
20. *Ibid.*, p. 43.
21. *Ibid.*, p. 237.

Coming Up for Air (1939) is structurally not effectively integrated, though it fits in logically with the emerging pattern
of Orwell's creative development and his political commitment at the time. Orwell's purpose in this novel is clear: to
demonstrate that the hard-working members of the lower
middle class are slowly becoming aware of the kind of world
they live in; to show that they are trying desperately to come
up for air, only it is too late for them to break free. The end
is imminent.

We are introduced to George Bowling, a fat insurance
agent who lives in a middle-class suburb; a wage slave married to a fretful, nagging wife, he is responsible for supporting her and the two children she has borne. She worries constantly that the family will wind up in the poorhouse. George
Bowling is the protagonist who tells the story, which is a
piercing lament for an idyllic past that cannot be reclaimed: a
past lived in the countryside where youngsters could wander
in the fields, go fishing, play truant from school, rob birds'
nests, and live a carefree life. But a new age of large-scale
business corporations and thriving industrialism has arrived.
His father is gradually driven into poverty by his loss of
trade, and after a number of years the old town is swallowed
up. In the meantime, George has fought in the war; he has
held various jobs and finally—a lucky break for him—
becomes an insurance agent. The past is irretrievably gone.
There is no possibility of going back in time. When he returns to his boyhood town in order to recapture the sense of
the past by going fishing and attempting to catch the large
perch he had once seen in this hidden pool, everything is
hideously altered. Industrialism has triumphed. The factories
are turning out munitions, the bombers zoom steadily over-
head, the next war is about to begin.

Orwell makes the reader feel the dreary, stultifying routine
of the lower-middle-class household: the crowding, the
meanness, the insecurity, the unrelieved boredom. The
houses on Ellsmere Road stand like prison cells, all in a row.
Each white-collar worker shivers with dread that the boss will
fire him, while the wife upbraids him at home and the children suck his life's blood. Each one in this community aspires
to a state of respectability, dreams of owning his own home,
while he is perpetually pursued by nightmarish visions of
economic disaster. "Everyone that isn't scared stiff of losing

his job is scared stiff of war, or Fascism, or Communism."[22]
The people are apprehensive about what will happen when
the enemy bombers launch their attack.

George Bowling cannot sweat the fear out of his system; he
knows what the future holds in store for him and his kind.
The modern world is streamlined, mechanized, heartless. Nature has been wiped off the map. What a contrast this presents to the England Bowling had known in his childhood:
the peaceful rural landscape, the fish in the pool, and the
people who had never heard of Hitler or machine guns or
concentration camps and were not afraid of losing their jobs!
In those days they were sustained by the reassuring knowledge that after their death the order of things would remain
substantially the same. They did not need to believe in personal immortality, and they were not afraid to die. "It's easy
enough to die if the things you care about are going to survive" (p. 126). The war changed all that in a flash. The old
order went up in flames and smoke. It proved to Bowling
that society was not everlasting. There was nothing to believe
in any longer, and people were perfectly willing to sell themselves for the sake of a job. Since there were not enough jobs
to go around, they engaged in cutthroat competition, each
one out for himself.

In a number of striking passages, *Coming Up for Air* anticipates *Nineteen Eighty-Four*. When Bowling hears the roar of
murderous rage directed at Hitler, he is frightened by the vision he beholds of what will inevitably follow. The world of
the future will resound with the hoarse cries of tribal hatred;
it will be a world ruled by slogans.

> The coloured shirts, the barbed wire, the rubber truncheons.
> The secret cells where the electric light burns night and day, and
> the detectives watching you while you sleep (p. 176).

This protagonist conjures up a dreadful picture of frenzied
crowds, a million strong, cheering their Leader under the
impression that they worship this man when they really hate
his guts. The novel provides a rough sketch of the totalitarian world that Orwell later described more bitterly and with
greater understanding in *Nineteen Eighty-Four*. The young

22. George Orwell, *Coming Up for Air* (New York: Harcourt, Brace and Company,
1950), p. 18.

succumb to the same propagandistic appeals that his generation had been fed in the First World War. There is, Bowling
realizes, no further possibility of coming up for air. Even the
air the populace breathes is polluted. "Coming up for air!
But there isn't any air. The dustbin that we're in reaches up
to the stratosphere" (p. 257). And all this is fated, not to be
turned aside. And through his persona, Orwell reiterates the
message of doom that the future holds in store for man: the
bursting bombs, the rubber truncheons, the colored shirts
marching in unison, the shouted slogans, while "the
machine-guns [are] squirting out of bedroom windows" (p.
267). He knows in his bones that Fascist tyranny is coming.

> I only know that if there's anything you care a curse about, bet-
> ter say good-bye to it now, because everything you've ever known
> is going down, down, down into the muck (p. 269).

2. *George Orwell: The Conscience of the Left*[23]

A born nonconformist, Orwell never compromised on fundamental issues. He belonged to no school of thought and
was the promoter of no particular political *ism*. He was no
sectarian, no dogmatist. Even the Socialism he professed was
latitudinarian in character. Tough-minded, independent in
his outlook, he was not to be bribed, bamboozled, or intimidated. Before passing judgment he subjected every idea,
whatever its officially approved status, to a thoroughgoing
critical examination. He is not only "sincere" (sincerity is, after all, a subjective category and the road to hell is often
paved with "sincere" intentions) but also honest and truthful.
It is this spirit of truthfulness that led him to denounce
British imperialism in *Burmese Days* and to write *The Road to
Wigan Pier* for the Left Book Club; it was his spiritual and
intellectual probity that induced him to enlist in the Spanish
Civil War and to attack the Stalinists for their betrayal of the
revolutionary cause. Later he heeded the inner call to write
Animal Farm, a scathing satire of Communism, and his anti-

---

23. Oxley says that "most often he [Orwell] has been seen as 'the conscience of the
Left'—as a man who spent much of his life pointing out to radical socialists
that in their fight against West European Fascism they ran the danger of making themselves blind to that other form of totalitarianism known as Stalinism"
(B. T. Oxley, *George Orwell* [New York: Arco Publishing Company, 1969], p.
18).

utopian novel, *Nineteen Eighty-Four*. It is not without good reason that he was called "the conscience of the Left."

The Road to Wigan Pier (1937) serves a double purpose: it is a defense and at the same time an astringent critique of Socialism. Orwell provides unforgettable descriptions of the industrial towns of England: the mines, the smoke and grime, the smells, the dirt. He gives a vivid account of a coal mine he visited. What an infernal world this is, this nether region where men must dig for coal! The sight of the miners at work arouses deep-seated feelings of guilt in Orwell, for all intellectuals owe their material comfort to these toiling men underground. Orwell is not indulging in humanitarian sympathy or spouting Socialist sentiments. He knows what he is talking about. He had lived among these workers, studied their income, estimated the skimpy budget on which they had to make ends meet, seen the unemployment figures, and watched the unhappy plight of the idle and the use they made of their enforced leisure time. If they did not engage in cultural or creative pursuits, it was because they enjoyed neither privacy nor peace of mind; they were deprived of hope and had nothing to look forward to. Orwell, on first getting to know the unemployed, was amazed to discover that many of them felt ashamed because they were without jobs. They had been misled by the cant of the newspapers and the moral values of the lower middle class to which they felt they belonged. They have no idea of what has happened to them. Their prevalent attitude is that the individual is himself to blame if he is thrown out of work. Orwell cries out against this unjust and outrageous state of affairs. Why must industrialism give rise to so much ugliness and squalor and cause so much human waste and suffering?

Orwell traces the origin of his own attitude toward the matter of class consciousness. He dwells on his own past, his birth into the lower-upper-middle class. He analyzes the bias that many feel about the members of the lower class. He was taught, for example, that they smell, and no logical argument can prevail against a conditioned reflex of physical repulsion. That is how snobbery based on class distinctions is inbred. Orwell is convinced that every middle-class person secretly harbors some type of class prejudice, which can be easily aroused. Even if such a person becomes a Socialist or a Communist, his tastes in this respect scarcely change.

Orwell was educated at an English public school. At the age of seventeen or eighteen he was both a snob and a revolutionary. "I was against all authority."[24] He considered himself a Socialist at the time, though he knew nothing of the working class. However much he might be moved by their economic woes, he did not like to associate with them. After his period of service in the Indian Imperial Police in Burma, he came to hate imperialism. Upon his return to England, he resigned from the police force. He would have no part of "that evil despotism" (p. 179). He suffered from painful reminiscences of the past. He remembered the faces of the men whom he had bullied, the servants he had struck. He felt weighed down by an enormous burden of guilt, which he had to expiate. He had reduced his sense of justice to a simple formula: the oppressed were always right and the oppressor always wrong. It was, he later conceded, a mistaken theory, but he saw that it was the natural result of his having played the part of the oppressor. "I wanted to submerge myself, to get right down among the oppressed, to be one of them and on their side against the tyrants" (p. 180). He developed an extreme hatred of oppression in all its forms. Failure—that seemed to him at that time the only virtue he could admire.

Orwell here confesses the sense of guilt that lacerated his conscience and prompted him to sink to the lowest stratum of the working class, the unfortunate victims of economic injustice, the unemployed, the utterly destitute. The motives that drove him to take such a drastic step were highly complex. He was at that time not particularly drawn to Socialism. He wanted to share the worst conditions the working class had to endure, to confront the real meaning of poverty, to experience the hardships of joblessness and the hopeless struggle waged by those laid off from work against the iron laws of economics, to feel the psychological consequences, traumatic in their impact, of being deprived of a regular weekly wage. Such a lucid explanation seems to smack too much of a subsequent process of rationalization. The masochistic spirit of self-sacrifice that impelled him to embrace a life of utter failure was neither logical nor consciously arrived at. Quasi-religious motives of expiation were uncon-

24. George Orwell, *The Road to Wigan Pier* (New York: Harcourt, Brace and Company, 1958), p. 172.

sciously at work, even though Orwell called himself an atheist. He wanted to merge with the down and out, the tramps, the beggars, the outcasts, and even the criminals. "What I profoundly wanted, at that time, was to find some way of getting out of the respectable world altogether" (p. 181). He would uproot himself, get rid of everything he owned. He would change his name and start life anew, stone broke. He would join these people and "see what their lives were like and feel myself temporarily part of their world" (p. 182). When he touched bottom then perhaps the weight of his accumulated guilt would fall away from him. He put on a disguise and by fraternizing with tramps managed to learn the ropes. At first he was held back by his unconscious fear of the working class; he expected they would attack him for his quixotic folly and presumption; they would discover his real motives, accuse him of spying upon them, and throw him out. He went on the road, lived in flop-houses, and found that the life he was leading made him happy.

> Here I was, among "the lowest of the low," at the bedrock of the Western world! . . . And down there is the squalid mud and, as a matter of fact, horribly boring sub-world of the tramp (pp. 182-83).

The experience was liberating; it was an adventure that brought him a feeling of release.

No such feeling of release took possession of him when he was gathering his material for *The Road to Wigan Pier*. The world of industrialism was terribly depressing. He regarded as deplorable the way in which "the idea of Socialism is bound up, more or less inextricably, with the idea of machine-production" (p. 220). The utopian ideal that the Socialists hold up with such enthusiastic fanfare is one that is completely mechanized. His impulse to protest against a world dominated by machinery was checked by the sober realization that such a world is here to stay. But he continued to fight against the tendency to worship mechanical progress as "an end in itself, almost as a kind of religion" (p. 221). He saw that society in the future would be subject to the control of technological totalitarianism. All work in the future would be done by machinery, and the demand for productive efficiency would transform the character and function of the proletariat. Orwell warns Socialists "that the machine itself may be the enemy" (p. 235).

An independent Socialist, Orwell in *The Road to Wigan Pier* attacked those Socialist dogmas he considered false and harmful. He was never a believer in the mystique of the Revolution. At no time did he become a fellow traveler, and he was not in the least impressed by the Communist eschatology. It is characteristic of the man that, when he went to fight in the Spanish Civil War, he became a member of the POUM. *Homage to Catalonia* is one of the best accounts of what actually took place in one sector of the far-flung front. Orwell is not bothered by considerations of loyalty to the Party. With unflinching honesty he pictures the political situation that existed in Spain and specifies the reasons that caused the initial revolutionary élan to die out. Because of the repressive policy followed by the Comintern, which obeyed the dictates of Stalin, the early revolutionary promises were not kept. What astonished Orwell the most was the fact that the Communist Party, with the full support of the Soviet Union, was opposed to the revolution in Spain. "It was the Communist thesis that revolution at this stage would be fatal and that what was to be aimed at in Spain was not workers' control, but bourgeois democracy."[25] The Russians drove a hard bargain: they supplied weapons only on the express condition that the revolution would be aborted. Orwell concluded that Communism in this historic instance was anti-revolutionary in character.

Orwell had come to Catalonia with the intention of reporting events for English newspapers. When he arrived in Barcelona he was immediately struck by the charged atmosphere of the city; a revolution was in the making: the workers had seized a number of buildings, revolutionary symbols were scrawled on every available wall; the interiors of churches had been stripped of their sacred objects and many church edifices had been demolished. Shops had been "collectivized." The working man wearing proletarian clothes was treated with respect; the people of wealth and substance, the bourgeoisie, were not be seen. Here was something worth fighting for. This marked the first stage in the development of the workers' State; it had eliminated all bourgeois and counterrevolutionary elements. It breathed a spirit of vital hopefulness. "Above all," Orwell wrote, "there was a belief in the revolution and the future, a feeling of suddenly having

25. George Orwell, *Homage to Catalonia* (New York: Harcourt, Brace and Company, 1952), p. 51.

emerged into an era of equality and freedom. Human beings were trying to behave as human beings and not as cogs in the capitalist machine."[26]

Under the inspiriting influence of the emotions called forth by his observations, Orwell enlisted and was soon involved in the thick of the fighting. As luck would have it, he was put into the POUM division. At that time, however, he was not particularly interested in the political situation. His object in joining the militia was, as he put it, to fight against Fascism and, positively, to fight for the triumph of decency. The quirk of fate that had landed him in the POUM militia soon made him aware that what was happening in Spain was not merely a civil war; it was the beginning of a revolution. He never regretted his service on the front lines, the dangers he faced. On the field of battle he had broken away from the clutches of corrupt capitalist society. "I had dropped more or less by chance into the only community of any size in Western Europe where political consciousness and disbelief in capitalism were more normal than their opposites."[27] Here at last he could live on a plane of perfect equality. "One had been in a community where hope was more normal than apathy or cynicism, where the word 'comrade' stood for comradeship and not . . . for humbug!"[28] But the dream of equality soon ended. Orwell was wounded, and the enmity of the Communists forced him to go into hiding and flee for his life to England.

By 1946 Orwell had become convinced that the Fascism of the Left was essentially the same as the Fascism of the Right. In his devastating satiric fable, *Animal Farm* (1946), he makes this appalling truth known. We see how the system works at close range, the strategy Communism in power uses to get rid of the opposition. The masses (the sheep) are encouraged to bleat and baa in chorus, thus drowning out all querulous reactionary complaints. In the beginning, on the Manor Farm, old Major, the prize boar, preaches a doctrine of liberation to his congregation in the barn: the dogs, the pigs, the hens, the cows, the cart-horses, the goat, the donkey, the cat. Old Major tells them of the cruel injustices of which they have been the victims. The land was being exploited to en-

26. *Ibid.*, p. 6.
27. *Ibid.*, pp. 103-4.
28. *Ibid.*, p. 104.

rich the owner, Mr. Jones, whereas under the order decreed by nature all the animals could easily live in comfort: that is, if the fruit of their labor were not stolen from them by greedy and unscrupulous human beings. Just as the capitalist is the deadly enemy of the proletariat, so is man the implacable foe of animal democracy. All they have to do, the old Major assures them in his harangue, is to put man out of the way, and they will cease to feel the ravages of hunger. All forms of exploitation will be abolished. Man is a vicious parasite who keeps a major share of the harvest for himself and allots his animal slaves only enough wages to keep them from starving. He urges them to revolt against the tyranny of man. Major ends his fiery speech by declaring that all men are enemies and all animals comrades. He bids them beware of the despot they are about to overthrow, for everything man touches is infected with evil. He has taught them the revolutionary hymn "Beasts of England," and they all sing it with a will.

The Revolution succeeds. When old Major (Lenin) dies, the struggle for leadership is waged by two young boars: Snowball (Trotsky) and Napoleon (Stalin). Though the former is the author of original ideas and is endowed with a talent for delivering eloquent and impassioned speeches, the latter is more cunning and unconscionable and triumphs over his rival. Snowball is driven out and the animals on the farm are reduced to a state of fearful submission. The pigs meet in secret, presided over by Napoleon, and their decisions are approved by the general assembly. There are no debates because there is no opposition. Napoleon is always right, even when he contradicts himself. If anything goes wrong, it is caused by the fiendish machinations of Snowball. Those who criticize or protest against any measure are "liquidated." A number of prominent pigs publicly confess that they had been in league with Snowball and conspired against Animal Farm. They, too, are "liquidated," their throats torn out. Terrorized by this slaughter of the innocent, the animals finally perceive that this repressive regime is not what they had bargained for when they threw off the yoke of the human race, but it is suicidal to think of rebellion. No one dares to speak up; the police dogs are everywhere. The old revolutionary song is now banned.

The utopian aspirations that the revolutionaries fought for

have been forgotten. The bureaucrats are in control and they grow more prosperous and powerful each year. The common animals, however, are permitted no luxuries. According to Napoleon, happiness comes from self-sacrifice. Though most of the animals still go hungry and lead a wretched existence, they are consoled by the thought that in their realm all animals are equal. Then they behold the astonishing sight of the ruling pigs, Napoleon in front, proudly walking erect on two legs. Now the sheep shout in chorus the latest slogans; that two legs are better than four and that while all animals are equal some animals are more equal than others. Napoleon now seeks to prove to his "friends," recently his enemies, that they have nothing to fear from him. He harbors no revolutionary designs. He has no intention of stirring up rebellion among the animals on the neighboring farms.[29]

Nineteen Eighty-Four, the novel that brought him fame, is too heavily charged with the passions and prejudices aroused by political controversies to be read with aesthetic detachment. Even if we regard it as purely a work of fiction, a futuristic fantasy, the implications are nonetheless inescapable: this seeming fantasy is uncomfortably close to the truth of reality. Here is a prophetic but authentic picture of what

29. Despite his growing reputation as a writer, Orwell encountered serious difficulties in getting the manuscript of *Animal Farm* accepted for publication. His past record as a volunteer in Spain, his service in the P.O.U.M. organization, his unsparing attacks on the Communists for persecuting the Spanish anarchists and for betraying the revolutionary cause, made him a *persona non grata* during wartime. He had composed *Animal Farm* in 1943 and 1944, when Russia was England's ally. His opposition to Stalinism was well known. It was therefore not surprising that Gollancz rejected *Animal Farm.* Though Jonathan Cape recognized its literary merits, it also decided to reject the book on political grounds. The firm of Faber and Faber also declined it, and again for political reasons. Frederic Warburg brought it out. Orwell's introduction to this volume was not printed. In an essay called "The Freedom of the Press" (which was identified as Orwell's by Bernard Crich), Orwell assailed the form of literary censorship that was practiced in wartime England. It was voluntary, and therefore dangerous, since it established orthodoxy of opinion as the prescribed norm, and the dominant orthodoxy right now called for unqualified praise for all things Russian. The British intelligentsia dutifully echo the beliefs disseminated by Russian propagandists. Liberal writers exalt the figure of Stalin and declare themselves to be on the side of the Soviet Union. In this essay, the banned introduction to *Animal Farm,* Orwell contends that no opinion, however unpopular, should be silenced. Reaffirming his faith in freedom of thought and expression, Orwell says: "For quite a decade past I have believed that the existing Russian regime is a mainly evil thing, and I claim the right to say so, in spite of the fact that we are allies with the U.S.S.R. in a war which I want to see won" (George Orwell, "The Freedom of the Press," *The New York Times Magazine,* October 8, 1972, p. 76).

man can (and in some countries has already) become: he is regimented, intellectually cowed, rendered spiritually submissive, arrested and imprisoned without a trial, tortured until he confesses his crimes, efficiently "purged." Writers have stopped composing rhapsodic forecasts of utopian fulfillment in the future. Having lost faith in himself and his potentialities, man has ceased to believe in the future. He lives in a technocratic age in which individuality is dismissed as a bourgeois concept, anachronistic and decadent. The mass man, anonymous and properly conditioned in thought and controlled in behavior, "inherits the earth." The living truth, the "correct" ideas, are dictated from above. History is "corrected," and thereby "falsified," to suit the needs of the State. The citizen is watched even in the privacy of his "home," and he is punished if he deviates from the required norm of conformity. The punishment, carried out in secrecy, is swift and drastic. The culprit disappears from the haunts of the living.

History can be tampered with because objective truth is outlawed. The State decides what is to be believed, what is to be accepted as truth and what is to be cast aside as falsehood. Since it controls all the media of communication, it is invested with the power to decide what the people shall love and hate, affirm and deny, swear allegiance to and repudiate. Members of the Party must participate in periodic hate rituals—a kind of revivalistic session in which the collective emotion of frenzied hatred is generated—and woe befalls those members who fail to register the full quota of concentrated hatred.

Each one wears the uniform of the Party. The Police Patrol hovers in the air, ready to swoop down upon the guilty person. Everyone is under the constant surveillance of the Thought Police. This is London in 1984, under the new regime, with its established Ministry of Truth and its inverted creed that war is peace, that freedom is slavery, and that ignorance is strength. In this poisoned atmosphere of organized hate sessions (a villain named Emmanuel Goldstein is dubbed the Enemy of the People), it is dangerous to trust others; one must be extremely careful not to betray his inner thoughts even by a glance. In this police State, children spy upon and betray their parents. Gone is the human capacity to experience tragedy, the ability to feel either joy or sorrow. This is an age of continuous wars, though the populace never knows what the war is about or against whom it is being fought. They are, however, given the official assurance that the enemy is the incarnation of absolute evil. In this nightmarish world the victims resort to the use of "doublethink."

> To know and not to know, to be conscious of complete truthfulness while telling carefully constructed lies, to hold simultaneously two opinions which cancelled out, knowing them to be contradictory and believing in both of them, to use logic against logic, to repudiate morality while laying claim to it, to believe that democracy was impossible and that the Party was the guardian of democracy . . . that was the ultimate subtlety: consciously to induce unconsciousness, and then, once again, to become unconscious of the act of hypnosis you had just performed. Even the word "doublethink" involved the use of doublethink.[30]

Nineteen Eighty-Four surpasses even *Darkness at Noon* in its delineation of the horrors of the totalitarian state. The Party member is "a credulous and ignorant fanatic whose prevailing moods are fear, hatred, adulation, and orgiastic triumph. In other words, it is necessary that he should have the mentality appropriate to a state of war."[31] As long as a state of war exists, the multitude can easily be aroused to a pitch of hysteria. The last section describes in detail how those guilty of a though crime are broken in spirit until they are willing not only to say what is expected of them but also to believe in the literal truth of their own confession. The excruciating pain they suffer under these scientifically administered tortures is so extreme that they cannot hold out any longer; they are ready to confess to any crime of which they may be accused—espionage, sabotage, treason. It is the Party intellectuals who conduct these clinical experiments in the administration of pain until the culprit's power of resistance is completely destroyed. He is badgered night and day; questions are hurled at him without respite; his mind weakened by total lack of sleep and rest, he becomes involved in a series of contradictions until he tearfully agrees to sign the document that has been drawn up for him. In the end he must submit to the will of his torturers. To resist is a sure sign of madness. The Party, which is immortal, determines the character of objective truth. If the Party decrees that two plus two is

30. George Orwell, *Nineteen Eighty-Four* (New York: The New American Library, 1950), pp. 29-30.
31. *Ibid.*, p. 146.

five, then that is the correct answer. The Party is absolute power incarnate, and its aim is to create a world of fear, terror, and treachery. "The old civilizations," the torturer explains, "claimed that they were founded on love and justice. In our world there will be no emotions except fear, rage, triumph, and self-abasement."[32]

All this is concretely embodied in the action of the novel and the inner struggle of the leading characters. Though *Nineteen Eighty-Four* is an autonomous world of fiction, its compelling power derives in large part from the fact that what we are reading is a documented history of what is to come. It is a challenging statement of Orwell's social philosophy, a warning of the political disaster that will befall England in the near future if its people do not rise up in wrath and put an end to the totalitarian threat.

Orwell's life was instinct with paradox. He has been called "perhaps the most paradoxical English writer of his time."[33] He possessed a strong sense of social responsibility but repeatedly attacked the way in which authority was exercised. He fought against absolutism in politics. If he opted for Socialism, he was not unaware of the dangers that collectivism posed. He sought in his writing for the press to work out a strategy of reconciliation betwen responsibility and revolt, authority and freedom. He is one of the few English writers of the thirties and forties who kept their integrity intact. For him Socialism meant "brotherhood, fair play and honest dealing,"[34] ideas of decency that he had drawn from writers like Dickens. An influential journalist and literary critic as well as novelist, he endeavored to tell the unadulterated truth in an age of political corruption and propagandistic lies, and his moral strength supported him through this ordeal.

Of the literary men of the Left who were productive during the hectic thirties, few emerged with their character unsmirched, their integrity uncompromised. In England, the writers were hurled out of their comfortable middle-class existence by the catastrophic events of the time: the terrible

32. *Ibid.*, p. 203.
33. Richard J. Voorhees, Jr., *The Paradox of George Orwell.* Purdue University Studies. Humanities Series (1961), p. 15.
34. George Woodcock, *The Crystal Spirit: A Study of George Orwell* (New York: Minverva Press, 1966), p. 28.

threat to freedom posed by the rising tide of Fascism; the economic depression and the widespread suffering it caused; the rabble-rousing oratory of Hitler that accompanied his policy of rearmament and territorial annexation; the bumbling diplomatic efforts of England's craven leaders to appease this "fanatic" and thus keep the peace; the horrendous reports of the atrocities committed by the Nazis—the burning of the books, the rounding up of Jews and their shipment to concentration camps, the crematoria that worked night and day to put an end to the Jewish race; the defeat of the Loyalist forces in the Spanish Civil War and the growing suspicion that the Soviet Union had betrayed the Revolution in Spain; the outbreak of the Second World War and the signing of the Hitler-Stalin pact.

In the meantime, members of the Communist Party in England and a host of fellow travelers were put to the test. Ugly rumors were circulated during the thirties that the Soviet Union was conducting a wholesale reign of terror. Men and women, the reports from the underground charged, were arrested and thrown into prison and then, if they were lucky, sent to a forced labor camp. The unlucky ones mysteriously disappeared. Auden, in *The Age of Anxiety,* declared that "the Night of the Knock" had arrived. The leading Bolsheviks of the October Revolution were accused of a variety of heinous crimes—spying for a foreign power, sabotage, and treason. At the notorious Moscow Trials they abjectly confessed their crimes against the State, beating their breast in penitential self-hatred. The roll call of those who were executed after being found guilty should have been enough to create doubt in the most loyal devotee of the Party, but they did not flinch. Bukharin, Radek, Lunacharsky, Zinoviev, Kamenev: they were charged with the crime of organizing a terrorist organization under Trotsky's command. Brought to trial in August 1936, all—except one—confessed their guilt and were put to death. In March 1938, Bukharin, Rykov, Krestinsky, and sixteen other "traitors" were brought to trial. Yagoda, the former head of the OGPU and the one who masterminded the earlier trials, was among the victims chosen to die. The comrades in England insisted that these men were enemies of the Soviet Union and deserved the punishment meted out to them. Stalin, the leader of the Soviet Union, was not condemning these wretched creatures to death without sufficient cause. It was unthinkable that the heads of the Communist Party in Russia would connive at fabricating a monstrous lie. Hence the comrades in England, France, and the United States attacked anyone who portrayed these events in a bad light.

Then Khrushchev, addressing the Twentieth Congress of the Communist Party in the Soviet Union in 1956, revealed to an astounded world the truth about the Moscow Trials: these prisoners had been reduced to a state of abject compliance; their will to resist was broken by means of physical torture; they had further been threatened with the death of their families if they did not carry out orders. They were beaten or shocked by electricity till they were reduced to a state of unconsciousness. Finally, their faculty of judgment was destroyed; they could not longer distinguish between truth and error. After undergoing this relentless pressure, the prisoner lost his sense of self and agreed to sign any confession his torturer placed before him.

Orwell emerged from this crisis of conscience with his honor unimpaired. He was one of the few not deceived by the strident propaganda promulgated by the Left. He was repelled by the abstractions that Marxism preached. He did not deny that men had to be fed; that came first in the order of time, but this alone did not reach to the heart of the problem that mankind faced. Orwell did not subscribe to the orthodox Marxist version of the class war nor did he accept the mystique that attached itself to the proletariat.[35] The workers

35. Communist propaganda was itself to blame for encouraging this tendency to picture the proletariat as the standard-bearers of the Revolution, the saviors of society. Actually it is the Communist Party that leads the proletariat and decides what it should do. The assumption that there is an "identity of interests between the communist parties and the proletariat" is not supported by historical fact (Franz Borkenau, *The Communist International* [London: Faber and Faber, 1938], p. 374). "This leading role of the proletariat in the upheavals of our time has proved to be the Utopian element of Marxism" (*ibid.,* p. 421). Originally a term of contempt designating a social class of inferior status, *proletariat* was given an exalted signification by Marxism. Objectively considered, a proletarian is a wage earner whose source of income is exclusively derived from his labor power in a competitive labor market. A wage earner by birth, he remains one for life. He owns no property; his freedom to bargain is no more than a legal fiction. His freedom to turn down a job is literally the freedom to starve, since he has no other source of income. How did he happen to emerge as, in the modern sense, belonging to a self-conscious social class? First, capitalism tended to commercialize human labor, to hire it at the lowest price as if it were a commodity whose value could be measured in terms of money. The worker thus ceased to possess the traits

he met in England did not regard themselves as belonging to the proletariat; most of them adhered to a middle-class outlook.[36]

3. *The Morality of Politics*

Orwell distinguished himself as a political critic by his uncompromising intellectual honesty. His originality lay in his courage to take an independent position where others became fierce partisans or straddled the controversial issues of the day. Scorning all semantic dodges and rhetorical obfuscation, he ferreted out the truth, regardless of whose ox he gored. The essays he included in *Dickens, Dali and Others* (1946) reveal the persistence of his interest in the moral problem. He delighted in the exuberant vitality and creative power of a novelist like Dickens. He shows that Dickens stood politically nowhere left of center. He is no "proletarian" writer, an active revolutionary or champion of reform. Dickens had no intention of changing the world by instituting legisla-

that identified him as a human being. He became a thing, a cipher, a tool, a "hand." His existence was insecure, since he was subject to the capricious fluctuations of the market. Alienated from the object he produced, he derived no joy from his work. He was but a cog in the industrial machine. The cash nexus reduced him to a condition of permanent inferiority. Bound together by their mutual grievances, their economic dependence, their stigma of inferiority, the workers finally achieved a sense of class solidarity. Through their unions they were able to rise above their degraded status. Their defense mechanism took the form of a proud apocalyptic assertiveness. The old pejorative meaning of "poor," "wretched," "low" attached to the name of the proletariat is transformed into an honorific badge. "The case of 'proletarian' may perhaps be significant as a specific case of defense mechanism in operation. A resentful, unconscious overemphasis on one's own worth and dignity is called forth by the painful and agitating experience of being undervalued by one's fellows" (Goetz A. Briefs, *The Proletariat* [New York and London: McGraw-Hill Book Company, 1937], p. 46). Because he was despised as vulgar and degraded, the proletarian nursed a burning sense of injustice. He consoled himself with the thought that from him issued the power that built civilization and sustained the life of culture. Finally, rejecting the religion of the earthly masters who had cruelly deceived him in order to exploit him more effectually, he substituted "class" for God. Alone he was helpless; united with his fellow workers he was invincible, destined to rule the earth. An embarrassing example of the lavishly eulogistic mood that was generated by the "proletarian" theme is C. Day Lewis's poem, "The Road These Times Must Take," in which he asks why, when we see a Communist, do we feel small? This poem was published in the *Partisan Review* 1 (November-December 1934): 37.

36. See Ruth Ann Lief, *Homage to Oceania* (Columbus, Ohio: Ohio State University Press, 1969).

tive remedies and abolishing economic evils. His criticism of society was exclusively moral, and Orwell praises this attitude as being more constructive than the Marxist solution. It is not only the economic structure, Orwell argues, but also the nature of man that must be transformed. There is no sense, Orwell contended, in changing institutions if the heart of man is not likewise transformed. Though Dickens is not a revolutionary writer *"in the accepted sense,"* Orwell points out that "it is not at all certain that a merely moral criticism of society may not be just as 'revolutionary'—and revolution, after all, means turning things upside down—as the politico-economic criticism which is fashionable at this moment."[37]

In his illuminating interpretation of Dickens, Orwell refutes the romantic conception of progress. We live now in an age of realistic political awareness. We have learned, to our cost, that there is always a tyrant ready to take over. Orwell sums up the matter incisively when he declares that two viewpoints are tenable:

> The one, how can you improve human nature until you have changed the system? The other, what is the use of changing the system before you have improved human nature? They appeal to different individuals, and they probably show a tendency to alternate in point of time. The moralist and the revolutionary are constantly undermining one another.[38]

For Orwell, the central—and tormenting—problem of our time is that of preventing power from being abused. Though he does not resolve the conflict between the moralist and the revolutionary, his sympathies are unquestionably with Dickens, who believed that individual regeneration must precede any kind of social reconstruction.

If Orwell rejects the Marxist canons of criticism, he is equally unsparing in exposing the wishful thinking of liberals like H. G. Wells and Bernard Shaw, with their utopian faith in the uses of reason, sanity, and science. Such an obsession he classifies as psychopathological because it blithely disregards the forces that are actually shaping the course of history. The liberals have, like the Communists, been cherishing a pipe dream of perfection, believing fervently as they did in

37. George Orwell, *Dickens, Dali, and Others* (New York: Harcourt, Brace and Company, 1946), pp. 22-23.
38. *Ibid.*, p. 23.

the abstract ideal of rational enlightenment, mechanical progress, internationalism, the golden age to be realized in some paradisiacal future. The people of the world, however, are ruled by other sentiments: patriotism, nationalism, xenophobia, and feelings of superiority to foreigners, atavistic emotions. Orwell therefore concludes that the ardent apostles of twentieth-century rationalism, the zealous upholders of the cause of world federation bound together by ties of brotherhood, blundered badly. Their cardinal mistake lay in attaching themselves to abstractions, theories, principles, bloodless ideas, in failing to perceive that the dynamic energy that drives the world springs predominantly from emotional and irrational sources. Like Koestler, Orwell became aware of the destructive forces of evil at work in the world.

The hard-hitting essays included in *Dickens, Dali and Others* are written with genuine conviction. No Party fanatic, no inflamed partisan, no narrow-minded propagandist, Orwell tries to practice the difficult virtue of freedom of conscience and untrammeled independence of thought. It is not surprising that he has been viciously slandered by Communist writers as a reactionary, a hireling of the capitalist press.[39] Unaffected by such scurrilous attacks, Orwell practices the complex art of literary criticism with distinction. He is discriminating, fair-minded, objective in his insights. He treats every subject he takes up from a number of different and mutually enriching perspectives. For example, the essay on "Boys' Weeklies" develops into a profound study of the psychology of taste, the nature of aesthetics, and, surprisingly enough, the use of propaganda. Orwell's range of cultural interests is wide. In reading his criticism, we are privileged not only to sample the rich and varied contents of his mind but also to comprehend some of the major obsessions of his age.

One of the most virulent obsessions, of course, is political, and Orwell tackles the political theme with the courage that is almost invariably the mark of the born dissenter. Though he maintains that every novelist, whether he admits it or not, propounds a "message" and therefore contributes to "tenden-

39. Howard Fast, who later renounced his allegiance to Communism, paid Orwell these amiable compliments: "Orwell himself . . . is one of the crassest and most inept political propagandists who ever put pen to paper, and every one of his childish and wicked little opium dreams bears clearly the label: 'Made in Wall Street' " (Howard Fast, *Literature and Reality* [New York: International Publishers, 1950], p. 98).

tious" literature, he qualifies the force of this statement by pointing out that while all art is propaganda, it does not follow that all propaganda is art. *Shooting an Elephant* (1950), a posthumous collection of essays, contains some excellent criticism. The title essay, written in 1936, describes Orwell's experience when he was a sub-division officer in Lower Burma and had to shoot an elephant. The interest of this essay lies primarily in its analysis of the politics of imperialism, the hostility and hatred that the British colonizers aroused in the natives, and in its conclusion that imperialism is an evil thing. In "Politics vs. Literature: an Examination of 'Gulliver's Travels,'" Orwell discusses the character of the totalitarian state, how it regiments public opinion by the unscrupulous use of psychic and moral agencies, and dwells at some length on the intolerable features of Swift's projected utopia. He cannot agree with Swift that life is foul and vile; in spite of everything, and Orwell suffered severely from both poverty and sickness, life was for him immensely worth living. Then in a passage that luminously reveals the man as well as the writer, Orwell sums up his critical position:

> It is often argued, at least by people who admit the importance of subject-matter, that a book cannot be "good" if it expresses a palpably false view of life. We are told that in our age, for instance, any book that has genuine literary merit will also be more or less "progressive" in tendency. . . . The views that a writer holds must be compatible with sanity, in the medical sense, and with the power of continuous thought; beyond that what we ask of him is talent, which is probably another name for conviction.[40]

Orwell died at an early age, before he could fulfill all his potentialities as a writer. His distinctive genius lay not in the field of the novel but in the art of social satire. He was in some ways a twentieth-century Swift but, fortunately, without the latter's misanthropy. Despite the outrageous abuse of political power in his time and the sinister spread of totalitarianism, Orwell continued to believe in the idea of freedom and equality:

> All through the Christian ages, and especially since the French Revolution, the Western world has been haunted by the idea of

40. George Orwell, *Shooting an Elephant* (New York: Harcourt, Brace and Company, 1950), pp. 175-176.

316 THE LITERATURE OF COMMITMENT

freedom and equality; it is only an *idea,* but it has penetrated to all ranks of society.[41]

Orwell really belongs to the tradition built up by the great English liberals of the nineteenth century, who stressed so eloquently the need to defend freedom of speech, freedom of inquiry, freedom of thought, and freedom of conscience. In "Why I Write," first published in 1946, Orwell specifies the different motives, apart from the need to earn a living, that prompt men to become writers. First in order of importance comes the impulse born of egoism: the desire to be in the limelight. Then Orwell lists what he calls aesthetic enthusiasm: the "desire to share an experience which one feels is valuable and ought not to be missed."[42] Next he cites the historical impulse, the desire "to see things as they are. . . ."[43] The fourth motive is political in nature. Orwell defines "political" in a broad sense: "Desire to push the world in a certain direction, to alter other people's idea of the kind of society they should strive after."[44] Here, too, he underlines his personal belief that "no book is genuinely free from political bias. The opinion that art should have nothing to do with politics is itself a political attitude."[45] Yet in "Inside the Whale," which appeared first in 1940, Orwell warns of the dangers the writer runs if he becomes politically committed.

> On the whole, the literary history of the 'thirties seems to justify the opinion that a writer does well to keep out of politics. For any writer who accepts or partially accepts the discipline of a political party is sooner or later faced with the alternative: toe the line, or shut up. It is, of course, possible to toe the line and go on writing—after a fashion. Any Marxist can demonstrate with the greatest ease that "bourgeois" liberty of thought is an illusion. But when he has finished the demonstration there remains the psychological *fact* that without this "bourgeois" liberty the creative powers wither away.[46]

41. *Ibid.,* p. 74.
42. George Orwell, *An Age Like This, 1920-1940,* in *The Collected Essays, Journalism and Letters of George Orwell,* ed. Sonia Orwell and Ian Angus (New York: Harcourt, Brace & World, 1968), 1: 3.
43. *Ibid.,* 1: 4.
44. *Ibid.*
45. *Ibid.*
46. George Orwell, "Inside the Whale," *New Directions in Prose and Poetry* (Norfolk, Conn.: New Directions, 1940), p. 235. In a stenographic record of a speech delivered by Lunacharsky, the latter asserted that he had no use for the idea advanced by writers and artists that they must have freedom in order to be

Though Orwell seems to be inconsistent at this point, there is no real contradiction in his outlook, not if we bear in mind the distinctions he makes in his use of the ambiguous term "commitment." As I have shown, he has been a politically committed writer from the start, but he never accepted the discipline of a political party. Unlike Koestler and Camus, he never joined and was never tempted to join the Communist Party.

The same kind of semantic distinction must be brought to bear on Orwell's text when he discusses the proper and illegitimate function of propaganda. In a talk on "The Proletarian Writer,"[47] Orwell reaffirms his belief "that every artist is a propagandist. I don't mean a political propagandist. If he has any honesty or talent at all he cannot be that. Most political propaganda is a matter of telling lies, not only about the facts but about your own feelings. But every artist is a propagandist in the sense that he is trying, directly or indirectly, to impose a vision of life that seems to him desirable."[48] Though some critics might question this *ad hoc* definition of propaganda, it is in line with his general trend of thought. He understood the difference that separated art from propaganda. In a broadcast he gave in 1941 on "The Frontiers of Art and Propaganda," he remarks that the literature of the past decade has been "swamped by propaganda."[49] Since the thirties, society has been troubled by a mounting sense of insecurity. In such a world of conflict and crisis, the writer cannot afford an attitude of Olympian detachment. He is forced to choose between two warring camps: Fascism and Socialism. "Literature had to become political, because anything else would have entailed mental dishonesty."[50] But

able to create. Lunacharsky proceeds to demolish this stupid bourgeois prejudice. "We cannot but hurl repressions against those authors and artists who use their great weapon of art, science or philosophy against us. Freedom of the press in the bourgeois sense is an erroneous and false thing, an internally contradictory thing" (A. Lunacharsky, "The Role of the Proletarian State in the Development of Proletarian Culture," *International Literature* no. 4 [September 1934], p. 115). In his critical essays and journalistic contributions he labored hard to expose the fallacy that resides in such a one-sided and intolerant conception of freedom.
47. Delivered over the BBC and printed in *The Listener* in December 1940.
48. George Orwell, *My Country Right or Left, 1940-1943*, in *The Collected Essays, Journalism and Essays of George Orwell*, ed. Sonia Orwell and Ian Angus (New York: Harcourt, Brace & World, 1968), 2: 41.
49. *Ibid.*, 2: 123.
50. *Ibid.*, 2: 126.

what are the consequences of this decision on the writer's part to become politically committed? Not until 1939 did a number of "committed" writers discover "that you cannot really sacrifice your intellectual integrity for the sake of a political creed—or at least you cannot do so and remain a writer."[51] Again and again, Orwell reiterates his conviction that "there is no such thing as genuinely non-political literature. . . ."[52] In "Politics and the English Language," he repeated his contention that "in our age there is no such thing as 'keeping out of politics.' "[53] Certainly Orwell did not keep out of politics. He was careful to distinguish clearly betwen his bounden duty as a writer and his political obligations as a citizen. Orwell has been downgraded by some critics because his political outlook is confused, but he made no pretense at being a political scientist who had worked out a comprehensive system of political values.[54] He was primarily a writer, a literary critic, a social satirist. As the conscience of the Left, his views on the issue of commitment deserve to be remembered.

> When a writer engages in politics he should do so as a citizen, as a human being, but not *as a writer*. I do not think that he has the right, merely on the score of his sensibilities, to shirk the ordinary dirty work of politics. Just as much as anyone else, he should be prepared to deliver lectures in draughty halls, to chalk pavements, to canvass voters, to distribute leaflets, even to fight in civil wars if it seems necessary. But whatever else he does in the service of his party, he should never write for it. He should make it clear that his writing is a thing apart.[55]

51. *Ibid.*
52. George Orwell, *Such, Such Were the Joys* (New York: Harcourt, Brace and Company, 1953), p. 71. The essay "Writers and Leviathan" was first published in *Polemic* in January 1946.
53. *Ibid.,* 4: 137.
54. For an attack on Orwell as deficient in the field of political "science," see D. A. N. Jones, "Arguments Against Orwell," in *The World of George Orwell,* ed. Miriam Gross (New York: Simon and Schuster, 1971), pp. 154-63.
55. Orwell, *Such, Such Were the Joys,* pp. 70-71.

19

Bertolt Brecht: The Prophet of Commitment

At one point in his book *Brecht and Ionesco,* the author informs us that a work of literary art cannot be explicated as the sum and substance of a particular doctrine. To do so is to ignore its special and distinctive embodiment as art, "the uniqueness of its form."[1] Despite this tribute paid to the intrinsic virtue of form fused organically with content, the author regards the act of political commitment as constituting a "significant" factor in conditioning those attitudes and insights which shape the artist's vision of the world. Wulbern is aware of the difficulties that stand in the way of arriving at an objective assessment of Brecht's commitment to Communism and the precise effect of this commitment on his work as a playwright. Wulbern is convinced that this act of political commitment plays a crucial part in determining the way in which the artist gives full expression to his creative vision. He treats Brecht with unfailing sympathy and unstinted admiration. Had he taken the trouble to show exactly how this significant factor functions in the context of Brecht's plays, he would have made a valuable contribution to Brechtian schol-

1. Julian H. Wulbern, *Brecht and Ionesco: Commitment in Context* (Urbana, Ill., and London: University of Illinois Press, 1971), p. 10.

319

arship. Unfortunately he does not tackle this complex aesthetic problem. He offers no corroborative proof.[2]

Wulbern points to the complexity of Brecht, the man and dramatist, whose utterances were in contradiction to what he preached at other times. It is no easy matter to analyze his work in relation to his political radicalism. Not all of Brecht's manuscripts (which are kept in the Brecht-Archiv in East Berlin) bearing on his politics have been published. As for critical studies of Brecht, these are too often polemical in tone. In the West, the dominant judgment is that Brecht, a die-hard, evangelical Communist, produced propaganda rather than art. Wulbern assures us that he will attempt to present a more objective and "integrated" interpretation. There is no inherent conflict, he argues, between a writer's commitment to Marxism and his dedication to art. Then he adds this qualifying and ambiguous proviso: "provided that the artist is talented, honest, and cunning enough to couch his perception of the truth in terms which have some appeal to the regime."[3]

Emotionally, Brecht was from the start of his literary career inclined to take the side of the underdog, the poor, and the oppressed. In fact, if he refrained from putting his philosophy of political commitment into practice, it was because of his cynicism, which he defined as "his lack of capacity for enthusiasm, and his inability to think 'politically.' "[4] He frankly confessed his ideological deficiencies, his defect of character: he could not resolve his problem by means of adopting some positive doctrine of political engagement. But it is this cynicism, this aversion to unrestrained outbursts of enthusiasm, that led him to accept the Marxist system. With mounting fascination he had taken up the study of the writings of Marx, who became his mentor, the very voice of his conscience. Brecht declares that when he read Marx's *Das Kapital* he was able to understand his plays. "Naturally I didn't discover that I had written a whole pile of Marxist plays without knowing it, but this Marx was the only audience for my plays that I had ever seen. . . ."[5] Here was a unified body of rational thought that prescribed an effective remedy for the economic ills of the world.

2. *Ibid.*, p. 11.
3. *Ibid.*, p. 27.
4. *Ibid.*, p. 32.
5. *Ibid.*, pp. 33-34.

Certainly the most gifted and influential exponent of the literature of political commitment in our time is Bertolt Brecht. No modern writer dwells more intently on the close connection that exists between politics and art, ideology and literature. The miseries that afflict twentieth-century man, the conflicts that corrupt his basically "good" nature, the economic privations he is made to suffer, the evils that oppress him, these are the result of bad social management. Man can gain control of his social destiny. Brecht seeks to eliminate as far as possible the element of make-believe, the technique of illusion, and portray the world as it "really" is. The critical version of social reality that Brecht presents on stage[6] is basically congruent with the aesthetic propounded by Chernyshevski, Pisarev, and Dobrolyubov. Whereas the dramatist can exhibit the damage inflicted by alienation, this alienation can be overcome only when Communism is established.

Since Communism was based on scientific principles, Brecht wished to create dramas that would embody the scientific outlook. That was how he hoped to change the world. He envisaged a radical, experimental theater that would play a constructive role in furthering the revolutionary cause. His didactic plays preached, as in *The Measures Taken,* that the individual member must subordinate his fractious will to the will of the Party. Brecht was, however, too talented a dramatist to conform mechanically to the precepts promulgated by Party leaders or follow the prescriptive formulas of Socialist realism. Fully convinced that the theater could be legitimately—and fruitfully—used for propagandistic purposes, he labored hard to educate his audience with his morality plays, parables, *Lehrstücke*, all of which were meant to furnish an authentic picture of social reality. For Brecht, the Marxist playwright, economics is the determinant of fate.[7]

In his youth he had passed through a period of bitter

6. "Reality, always understood as social reality, and art belong together most intimately; art is a critical reproduction of reality." Hans Egon Holthusen, "Brecht's Dramatic Theory," in Peter Demetz, ed., *Brecht* (Englewood Cliffs, N. J.: Prentice-Hall, 1962), p. 109.

7. "All the larger issues of human existence he [Brecht] subordinated to one purpose only—class warfare. His plays lack any true conflict; they are, in a deeper sense, undramatic since their issue is a foregone conclusion" (H. F. Garten, *Modern German Drama* [London: Methuen & Co., 1959], p. 243. Garten, in his distaste for ideologically slanted plays, overstates his case.

nihilism. In plays like *Baal* and *Drums in the Night,* he portrayed man as a carnivorous beast who engages in a mad struggle for power in a cruel and meaningless world. After his conversion to Communism, Brecht sought to analyze the social forces that corrupt man and transform society into a jungle. His faith in Communism enabled him to transcend the negative passion of nihilism. Henceforth he devoted his creative energy to promoting the cause of Communism. To carry out this mission most effectually he devised a new dramaturgy that would do justice to his Marxist vision of society redeemed.

The bourgeois dramatist uses the theater as a house of illusion. In order to strengthen the illusion presented on the stage, he utilizes the art of psychic distance. The Expressionists, for example, attempted to act directly on the mind of the spectator and thus change his notion of "reality"; on the other hand, they exploited the resources of the creative imagination in order to appeal to the subjectivity of the people in the audience. Brecht for his part deliberately experimented with a type of play that would do away with this objectionable and distracting element of illusion. Influenced by Piscator, he created dramas that would involve the spectators in the action taking place on the stage. His work would tear down the artificial barriers that preserve aesthetic distance and transform the aesthetic experience in the theater into a meaningful encounter with social reality. The aim of the "epic theater" is to analyze and illuminate the conditions that bring about poverty, economic exploitation, and war. Hence Brecht used a number of ingenious devices that would remove or greatly reduce "the illusion" that the "staged" production tends to generate. For example, the actors, by directly addressing the audience, make it clear that they are only actors. Or by the use of a narrator or commentator, Brecht hoped to break down the process of empathy. In keeping with his self-appointed mission as a committed playwright of the Left, Brecht campaigned vigorously in behalf of a workers' theater that would reject the noxious notion of art as enchantment and endeavor to convince the audience that man can become the master of his environment.[8]

8. Oscar Büdel, "Contemporary Theater and Aesthetic Distance," in Demetz, ed., *Brecht,* pp. 59-85. Büdel says: "The playwright himself assumes his audience will no longer accept theater as theater, that it is too aware of the theater as being a 'swindle,' not real (and here, not only the play, but also the playing of

Epic theater was an experiment designed by Piscator in the twenties to make the drama an instrument of political enlightenment. Epic theater is synonymous with proletarian or revolutionary theater. It was intended from the day of its inception to be a theater of social revolt, a political theater. The purpose of the epic theater, Piscator declared, "is to learn how to think rather than to feel. . . ."[9] It was a theater that wrestled with the crucial problems of the age instead of providing narcotic entertainment, escapist fantasies, or titillating sex extravaganzas. The epic or proletarian theater hoped to leave behind the effete and artificial world of "art" by producing plays that would exert a positive political influence on contemporary affairs. Revolutionary in aim and content, this type of theater would stage plays that emphasized the theme of the class war. Indeed, Piscator was from the start a firm believer in literature as a form of "direct action."[10]

Piscator's experiments transformed the theater into a forum, a legislative assembly, with the audience assigned the task of deliberating on the major issues of the time.[11] "It was the stage's ambition to supply images, statistics, slogans which would enable its parliament, the audience, to reach political decisions."[12] In Piscator's theater "aesthetic consider-

the actor is involved). Therefore, the playwright too wishes to make known his awareness of the unrealness of the theater by analytically dissecting it, by playing with it, or making fun of it; and it is quite indicative that in a great many such plays this aesthetic problem occupies a central position: theater within the theater. . . . Perhaps there is an effort on the part of the playwright to affirm the truth of art to life again by making fun of art as art" (*ibid.*, pp. 84-85).

9. Maria Ley-Piscator, *The Piscator Experiment: The Political Theatre* (New York: James H. Heinemann, 1967), p. 13.
10. Ernst Schumacher, "Piscator's Political Theater," in Demetz, ed., *Brecht*, p. 88.
11. David Caute is outspoken in his judgment of Piscator's revolutionary commitment, his attempt to use the theater as an educational and didactic vehicle, and the nature of his influence on Brecht. "Piscator was both a communist and a revolutionary Marxist who believed that the only hope for the world was a proletarian revolution followed by a dictatorship on the Soviet model. Brecht adopted this point of view with a part of his mind, even if his heart proved recalcitrant, and this attitude carried him out of the fellow-travelling orbit. While he shared with the vast majority of fellow-travellers a distrust or contempt for socialist realism on the Soviet model, the agitprop plays he produced in the early thirties were Marxist, didactic and 'revolutionary' in a style not associated with the literary work of fellow-travellers. Possibly the 'Schweik' or 'Galileo' element in his nature kept him out of the Party, but the critical factor was the unacceptability to Moscow of an aesthetic style and philosophy he refused to abandon." David Caute, *The Fellow-Travellers: A Postscript to the Enlightenment* (New York: The Macmillan Company, 1973), p. 49.
12. *Brecht on Theatre*, trans. and ed. John Willett (New York: Hill and Wang, 1964), p. 131.

ations were entirely subject to political."[13] Documentary
material was eagerly utilized since it helped to produce a
more realistic effect.[14] Piscator sought to create a theater that
would apply the basic ideas of Marxism, and Brecht later followed his example. The modern world has drastically
changed man into a creature who belongs to a given class.
Hence the subjective suffering or the personal problems of
the individual are no longer suitable subjects for the playwright. It is the fate of the masses that he must depict. He
must uncover the cause of economic exploitation and oppression and thus lead the audience to rebel against a society that
allows such things to go on.

> The principles of epic theater are rigorously applied in plays
> that Brecht describes as "exemplary." The action is reduced to
> the dimensions of a short "fable," the purpose of which is to il-
> lustrate a political lesson. Theater becomes entirely functional; its
> one purpose is to arouse the consciousness and the revolutionary
> will of the masses.[15]

Bertolt Brecht valued the pioneering work of Piscator and
tried to apply some of Piscator's techniques to his own productions at the Volksbühne. He had collaborated with Piscator in constructing a number of technical devices on the
stage. Piscator, whom Brecht calls "without doubt one of the
most important theatre men of all times,"[16] introduced various technical innovations that vastly increased the capacity of
the theater to deal with modern controversial themes. Particularly important was his use of the film as an organic part
of the setting. The film and film projections could be
employed effectively as an adjunct method of narrating
events and providing essential statistics.

Brecht pleaded the cause of Communism in plays that
stressed the inevitability and universality of the class war.
Henceforth he believed in the revolutionary function of the
theater "as a means of teaching and transforming his society."[17] He would expose the ideological swindle by means of

13. *Ibid.*
14. See the chapter on "The German Revolutionary Theater," in Henri Arvon, *Marxist Esthetics*, trans. Helen R. Lane (Ithaca, N. Y., and London: Cornell University Press, 1973), pp. 71-82.
15. *Ibid.*, p. 80.
16. *Brecht on Theatre*, p. 77.
17. John Willett, *The Theatre of Bertolt Brecht* (London: Methuen & Co., 1959), p. 75.

which the ruling class preyed with a good conscience upon the poor, the ignorant, and the weak; his plays would gradually make men understand the principle of causality and demonstrate that the methods that worked so well in science could be applied with equally good results to the urgent task of social reconstruction. Believing as he did that Marxism was scientifically valid in its approach, he wanted the working class to learn how to think critically, to question all things, to challenge the most sacred truths with methodological skepticism, and thus discover the secret of how to bring the iniquitous rule of capitalism to an end. They must not accept the teachings of those leaders, be they priests or savants, who preach that all is right with the world and that human nature cannot be changed. As a committed "proletarian" playwright, Brecht produced plays that were doctrinaire. In keeping with his pedagogic purpose, he often simplified the issues in conflict, as in *The Good Woman of Setzuan.* The "moral" theme is driven home as if with a sledgehammer. All morality is conditioned by the economic factor. Man must first satisfy his hunger; only after this need has been satisfied does he face the moral problem. Hence his characters, as in *The Caucasian Chalk Circle,* are drawn as stock types, personifications of virtue or vice,

Though Brecht interprets the plight of modern man from a Marxist point of view, he does not indulge in overt Communist propaganda. He reveals how life under capitalism results inevitably in shady moral compromises, in the loss of personal integrity, and finally in the bitterness of disillusionment. To survive in this ruthless competitive world, one must be cunning. *Mother Courage* paints a hideous picture of the evil destructive forces at work in society. Brecht informs us that in this play he meant to show that in wartime it is not the little people who are in charge of big business. And under the cover of war, business goes on as usual. Hence, those who keep faith with their human virtues find themselves betrayed and undone. Last of all, Brecht stressed the message in the play that "no sacrifice is too great for the struggle against war."[18] Though the ordeals that Mother Courage has to endure awaken our compassion, Brecht had no intention of presenting her as a tragic or heroic figure. He wanted to

18. *Brecht on Theatre,* p. 220.

underline the fact that this huckster had learned nothing from her experience.

The Threepenny Opera (1929) employs the form of the opera to focus on the evil contradictions and cancerous growth of capitalist society. A spirited parody based on John Gay's *The Beggar's Opera,* a mix of acerbic satire and cynical laughter, it points an accusing finger at the venality of the middle class, its sordid business schemes, its ethic of cutthroat competition. The organization of thieves is shown to resemble closely that of the sanctimonious, middle-class operators. In a light-hearted manner and without reference to the proletariat as the class destined to abolish the evil of exploitation, Brecht develops his thesis that it is the economic system that makes men behave unconscionably. It is capitalist society, at war with itself, that insidiously corrupts human relationships. In a world geared solely to insure profit, humanity is defrauded and debased.

Later, while in flight from his native land, which was ruled by Hitler and his Nazi supporters, Brecht composed his *Threepenny Novel,*

> which is, to some extent, a glossary to accompany the opera. There he makes an effort to turn his subjective uneasiness into an effective criticism, or I should say, usable criticism. He situates his characters in a more precise context: the imperialistic era whose essence and decline were announced at the same time by the Boer War. Above all, he creates a new character, the soldier Fewkoombey, thus individualizing the proletariat which, up until that time, he had left in the shadows of anonymity. In the opera we were witnessing the conflicts of the great, forgetting their victims. The novel reminds us that the social stakes of the drama are to be found elsewhere: in the exploitation of the masses by a few people.[19]

Brecht eliminates the element of suspense. He does not hesitate to use the auctorial privilege of omniscience so that he can inform the reader what is going to happen. The plot of the novel moves at a slower pace, the tone is more sardonic, the attack on capitalism more severe and sustained. Fewkoombey, the soldier who had been wounded in the leg by a bullet in the Boer War so that the lower half of the leg had to be amputated, is held up as the victim of society. Here is

19. Walter Weidell, *The Art of Bertolt Brecht,* trans. Daniel Russell (New York: New York University Press, 1963), p. 30.

George Fewkoombey, an honest and honorable man, reduced as a cripple to beggary, and he is prevented from practicing this lowly profession. He must be subsidized and protected by Peachum, who specializes in the profitable science of squeezing alms out of passersby. George learns to his astonishment that this "new profession was just as well organized as any other, perhaps even better. . . ."[20] Brecht rubs in the caustic social satire. Destitute and helpless, this ex-soldier finds that there is nothing he can do to earn his keep. His wound calls forth no pity. His condition constitutes a telling argument against war, but wars are necessary if the fruits of empire are to be retained.

Brecht exhibits the crookedness of business, the methods used to fleece the government. The law of the jungle still prevails, the law that makes possible the survival of the fittest. Each man looks out for himself and the devil take the hindmost. MacHeath, who uses various aliases, believes in the principle of competition, the ethical correctness of ambition, which drives a man to get ahead of his rival, undersell him by fair means or foul, put him out of business. Wars represent an excellent investment, since they raise the morale of a nation and promote the life of trade. Polly Peachum hoodwinks the man her father wishes her to marry. She learns how MacHeath operates his shops, and at a profit. MacHeath, once called the "Knife," has committed murder in pursuing his "professional" career as the head of a gang that disposed of its booty by a bold and original scheme. Now MacHeath seeks to expand his "business" ventures, and that requires money. He is following in the footsteps of that eminent family the Rothschilds. MacHeath knows what he is doing; the profit motive governs the behavior of all men. "Free" competition is the bedrock of civilization. The masses can easily be duped and exploited.

These realistic insights into human nature fitted in with Brecht's political commitment. He would adapt the theater to political ends and prove that society, far from being at the mercy of fate, can be rationally managed. By his strategic use of the alienation effect, he hoped that his plays would demonstrate that the scientific method endows man with the Promethean power to change the world, to create a society

20. Bertolt Brecht, *Threepenny Novel,* trans. Desmond I. Vesey; verse trans. Christopher Isherwood (New York: Grove Press, 1956), p. 11

that functions harmoniously and is fully productive. The themes Brecht selects for dramatic embodiment uncover the source of man-made evil: hunger, economic misery, greed, imperialism, war. Capitalism draws up and enforces its own binding rules. One must play the game. If the player foolishly clings to virtue, he will be devoured alive. If man is the architect of his own misfortunes, it is because he has allowed the "I" and not the "We" to prevail.

Brecht's epic theater is based on an aesthetic that is closely related to the propagandistic function of the drama. His technique of alienation is designed to act upon the audience so that they will join the ranks of the revolutionary fighters. This technique comprises a whole repertory of devices. As Peter Demetz remarks:

> Epic acting, inscriptions projected upon the stage, a particular use of songs, music, choreography and scenic design, which counteracts the fable, commenting on rather than supporting it—all of these elements "alienate," as Brecht says, certain events of the play from the realm of the ordinary, natural and expected.[21]

The epic theater dispenses with psychological dissection, the analysis of introspective states, the vagaries of subjectivity. Relying wholly on "behavioristic" criteria of human nature, Brecht announced that "the individual" died long ago. In the complex modern world, the human being becomes what he is as the result of all the social pressures brought to bear upon him. The epic form, Brecht declares, is the only one that presents these pressures and processes in action and thus make it possible for the drama to furnish "a comprehensive picture of the world."[22] Brecht welcomed the fruitful interaction of film and drama. Holding up a mirror to social reality, Brecht dealt with the typical. His object is to demonstrate that there is no continuity of the ego. Man is an atom whirled about in the constantly changing flux of social relations. "We have to show things as they are."[23] The epic drama projects events as seen from a given social and historical perspective that brings out the political implications of an action or event.

From 1933 to 1947, during the period of exile in Scandinavia and the United States, Brecht learned the art of

21. Demetz, ed., *Brecht*, p. 3.
22. *Brecht on Theatre*, p. 46.
23. *Ibid.*, p. 15.

stagecraft from the ground up; together with Piscator he produced plays that experimented with new techniques.[24] The traditional drama, Brecht became convinced, had outlived its usefulness. A modern audience, he felt, can learn nothing from such playwrights as Ibsen and Strindberg, since they are the defenders of an individualism that is obsolete. The new theater must invent a dramatic art that will affect the behavior of people. Brecht explains his method of procedure as a dramatist. He seizes on those traits of behavior which prove most helpful to the human race in its struggle for survival, and then shows these traits on the stage and underlines them. In effect, he writes parables: if one behaves in this manner then the following will occur, but if one acts differently then the opposite results will take place. "This isn't the same thing as committed art. At most pedagogics."[25] What strikes one immediately in this terse description of his method is its cold-blooded reasoning, its manipulative ratiocination; the play is transformed into an edifying lesson, a pedagogic exercise, a didactic demonstration that emphasizes that man is helpless if he acts alone; he must join forces with the proletariat and thus acquire collective strength. In carrying out this program Brecht was forced "to deal with political matters. . . . I don't mean that all playwriting ought to be political propaganda. . . ."[26]

In "Theatre for Pleasure or Theatre for Instruction," Brecht confronted a problem that has bedeviled both critics and dramatists through the ages: is art to provide pleasure or edification, delight or instruction? As a committed Marxist playwright, Brecht never hesitated as to which side he espoused. The only difficulty he faced was to show that there was no earthly reason why a theater that aims primarily to "instruct" the audience cannot also furnish a premium of aesthetic pleasure. Brecht's epic theater consisted chiefly of *"Zeitstücke"* or *"Lehrstücke"*; that is to say, it was harnessed to a didactic revolutionary purpose.

Brecht argued that new technical developments—the mechanization of the stage, the spotlight, the projection of

24. For an account of Piscator's work with films in conjunction with the production of plays at the People's Theater *(Volksbühne)* in Berlin, see Leif Furhammar and Folke Isaksson, *Politics and Film,* trans. Kersti French (New York and Washington: Praeger Publishers, 1971), p. 36.
25. *Brecht on Theatre*, p. 67.
26. *Ibid.*, p. 68.

films on a screen, the use of music—vastly enriched the resources of the playwright and lent greater freedom and flex-
ibility to his treatment of material so that he could now portray his characters as actively immersed in the complex life of
society. The environment could be delineated as a vital, pervasive force that determines the fate of the characters on
stage. The background could serve to account for the events
enacted on the stage. By means of huge screens, the audience
can behold other events, occurring at the same time, that
have a determinate effect upon the action. The film, too, can
project statistics and documentary material that negate or
confirm what the characters report. In addition, the actors
must not identify themselves wholly with their assigned role.
By remaining detached from the character whose name they
bear, they are "clearly inviting criticism of him."[27]

Alienation is utilized to counteract the effect of empathy
and awaken the spectator to a critical understanding of what
is taking place on the stage. Alienation removes the crust of
habit and the veil of familiarity that conceal the truth of what
is actually happening in the world, so that what is commonly
regarded as "natural" proves, when viewed from this "alienat-
ing" perspective, to be "unnatural." Whereas the spectator
who consumes the traditional fare of the theater is led to believe that social conditions are part of an eternal, unalterable
scheme, that suffering is the inescapable fate of mankind, the
epic drama leads the audience to pass through a profoundly
different and heartening experience. The alienated observer
in the Brechtian theater says to himself that such abominable
conditions must not be allowed to exist. He perceives that
man-made suffering can be ended. He ceases to be a passive
"voyeur."

All this is in line with Brecht's interest in producing plays
that were instructive. He knew what themes were best suited
for representation on the stage, such subjects as war and social conflicts, the market for oil, the structure of the family,
"religion, wheat, the meat market. . . ."[28] The choruses could
be used to inform the spectator about the relevant facts he
had no knowledge of. Films, statistics, the actions of world
leaders and the reasons that were supposed to govern their
actions—all this trained the spectator to become critical of

27. *Brecht on Theatre*, p. 71.
28. *Ibid.*

events in his social environment. The new theater thus calls forth the philosophical and observant mind, but it is intended only for those philosophers who wish not only to explain the world "but also to change it."[29] As this formulation with its paraphrase of a famous proposition stated by Marx in the *Eleven Theses on Feuerbach* indicates, the philosophy expounded on the stage of the epic theater would be Marxist in content. To the reiterated charge that such a proposal converted the theater into a classroom, Brecht replied that the common distinction drawn between learning and enjoyment is a factitious one. It is perfectly possible, he maintained, to make learning in the theater a truly enjoyable process.

But if the theater is to be made a predominantly edifying institution, then the epic dramatist must decide what role knowledge is to play in his work. Brecht summarily disposes of the objection that art and knowledge, literature and science, serve two different and incompatible ends. Though he concedes that art and science operate on two separate and disparate levels, he insists that scientific understanding is essential to the playwright. In his own case he found that he could not write his plays without levying tribute upon one or two sciences. Intuition or observation is not enough; if the dramatist is to do justice to his theme these must be supplemented by the tested facts of sociology and economics. And such knowledge, integrated within the body of the play, can be imaginatively transmuted into poetry.[30]

Much of this has to be taken on faith. Brecht tells us what he sets out fo do and the ingredients he pours into his scientific and dialectical prescription for epic drama, but he does not reveal the secret of his creative method. His dramaturgy constitutes a mighty challenge to the traditional conception of

29. *Ibid.*, p. 72.
30. In "Literature and Signification," Barthes praises Brecht for his originality in transforming the status and function of the theater. He considers Brecht to be a brilliant and daring innovator who "understood that the theatrical phenomenon might be treated in cognitive and not purely emotive terms; he was able to conceive the theatre intellectually, abolishing the (stale but still tenacious) mythic distinction between creation and reflection, nature and system the spontaneous and the rational, the 'heart' and the 'head'; his theater is neither pathetic nor cerebral; it is a justified theater. Next he decided that the dramatic forms had a political responsibility. . ." (Roland Barthes, *Critical Essays*, trans. Richard Howard [Evanston, Ill.: Northwestern University Press, 1972], p. 262). That is why Brecht used placards, music, song, and costumes. The ideological theater he created "takes sides with regard to nature, labor, racism, fascism, history, war, alienation. . ." (*ibid.*, p. 263).

the drama. It is possible, of course, to admire the moral indignation that informs his work, the passion for social justice
that motivates his technical innovations, without accepting his
politically slanted theories as valid. Good intentions, even
when they are backed by a pious recital of Marxist principles,
do not always make for good art. Like such gifted Marxist
critics as Lucien Goldmann and Georg Lukács, Brecht regards "correct" ideology or *Weltanschauung* as the supreme
criterion of worth in the drama. Such an aesthetic outlook
fits in with Brecht's desire to turn the theater into a forum
for the critical discussion of ideas, a propagandistic medium
that will justify the need for revolutionarly action. In calling
for the development of such a doctrinaire art, Brecht envisages a new type of drama that will address itself to the crucial
themes of the modern age, and these themes are, as we have
already noted, focused on the proliferation of huge industrial
corporations, the class conflict, the battle against poverty, disease, and war.

Brecht is the founding father of this type of drama, Marxist in content, in which the protagonist is no longer delineated as the victim of an inexorable fate. Man can direct
the course of his social destiny. Brecht hopes that the epic
theater can provide "the ideological superstructure" that will
radically change the collective life of this age. If this means
that the theater must be didactic in its treatment, so be it;
there is no reason, Brecht repeats, why didactic plays cannot
be entertaining. The theater does not cease to be theater because it is didactic. If it provides good theater, it is bound to
be entertaining as well.[31] The reading of Marx's *Das Kapital*
enabled him to comprehend what he was driving at in his
plays. Not that he had unconsciously composed a whole series
of Marxist plays, but he looked upon the heroic figure of
Marx as "the only spectator for my plays I'd ever come
across."[32]

Brecht's avowed purpose in writing and producing epic
drama was to influence the social behavior of the spectator.
But a theater that is geared to shape the social behavior of
the people in the audience is a theater based on Pavlovian
premises. It assumes that the emotions of the audience can

31. *Brecht on Theatre*, p. 80.
32. *Ibid.*, pp. 23-24.

be experimentally controlled. The epic theater, which is meant to be popular, instructive, and utilitarian, must do more than analyze and explain; it must generate the power to stir the masses to action. Political in its orientation, it takes for granted that art can be legitimately used as a potent weapon in the class war. Brecht, in short, despite his disclaimers, is writing propaganda in behalf of the play that carries a revolutionary message.[33] Here again, he wanted to take the Marxist thesis that it is not enough to interpret the world; one must change it, and apply it to the theater.[34]

Brecht was too talented an artist to accept the bogus doctrine of Socialist realism promulgated by Zhdanov. The playwright who includes factory hands and peasants in his work does not thereby give birth to an authentic "proletarian" masterpiece. It is essential to educate the masses but there is no justification for feeding them a steady diet of trash. A truly Socialist art, Brecht warned, cannot ignore the question of quality, which "is politically decisive."[35] Brecht, however, approved of the goal that Socialist realism set for itself. Socialist realism, he declares, demands that the writer realistically portray the collective life of man by artistic means. It incorporates its material within a Socialist framework. "In the case of Socialist Realism a part of the pleasure which all art must provoke is pleasure at the possibility of society's mastering man's fate."[36] But when it was a question of art versus doctrinal orthodoxy,[37] Brecht courageously rejected the belief that art could be produced by ideological fiat. Nor would he agree that the administrative bureaucracy of the Party were competent judges of artistic excellence. Though Mayakovsky thought otherwise, he denied that the production of poems lay within the jurisdiction of the Party. After all, the Commissar cannot organize the

---

33. Barthes, in "The Tasks of Brechtian Criticism," dismisses as superficial the type of criticism that condemns Brecht's plays because they are Communist in content. Barthes denies that Brecht's theater is thesis-ridden or vitiated by propaganda. Brecht employs Marxism as a method of interpreting the world (Barthes, *Critical Essays*, pp. 71-76).
34. *Brecht on Theatre*, p. 248.
35. *Ibid.*, p. 267.
36. *Ibid.*, p. 269.
37. In "Brecht in 1969," Martin Esslin shows that though Brecht was a Marxist, his judgments were frequently not in line with Marxist orthodoxy as prescribed by the Party in East Berlin (Martin Esslin, *Reflections: Essays on Modern Theatre* [Garden City, N. Y.: Doubleday & Company, 1969], pp. 61-73).

production of poems "as on a poultry farm."[38] Art must not be subject to the arbitrary decrees of some government committee. *"It is only boots that can be made to measure."*[39]

Until the production of *The Measures Taken*, Brecht had not introduced the theme of Communism in any of his plays. In this play, written in 1930, Brecht defended the necessary murders that the Communist Party required at times of its disciplined members.[40] He demonstrated the impossibility of practicing virtue and manifesting compassion in a selfish, hate-corroded, competitive world. At the same time, the play exalts the ideal of working for the ultimate good of the race: the death of capitalism and the birth of the classless society. When he composed *The Measures Taken*, Brecht tackled the difficult problem of how to justify the resort to violence. However noble his motives may have been, the one who endangers the success of a Party mission must be killed: this is the stern morality the Revolution enjoins upon its followers. Communism must triumph—that is the sole touchstone of ethics, the only moral issue to be considered. In *The Measures Taken*, the sacrificial victim himself approves of the decision. He dies but the Communist Party lives on.

In this controversial play Brecht wanted to demonstrate, in the character of the young comrade who yields to an impulse of compassion, why it is necessary to submit to Party discipline. The comrades, all five of them, swear to consider only what serves the good of the Party; they are to subordinate their private selves and become anonymous workers for the revolutionary cause. But the young comrade, because of his humanitarian impulsiveness, endangers their mission and the five must flee if they are not to be slain by the Kuomitang. They cannot dispose of the young comrade, who had removed his mask and thus revealed his identity; he must be made to disappear. He admits his guilt and accepts death at their hands; he is shot and his body thrown into a quicklime pit. The action all took place in the past and is being reenacted by the four agitators, who wish to be absolved of blame. They are judged to be not guilty. The end sought justified the means.

38. *Brecht on Theatre*, p. 269.
39. *Ibid.*, p. 270.
40. Auden, in "Spain 1937," had written the lines:
    Today the inevitable increase in the chance of death;
    The concrete acceptance of guilt in the fact of murder;

This is unquestionably Brecht's most deeply committed play, but it failed to call forth the desired response. He was severely criticized by Communist critics for creating a harmful image of the Party. Critics in the West interpreted the play as an attempt to resolve the tragic conflict between the promptings of conscience and the compulsion of duty to an abstract and inhuman political ideal. Wulbern attempts to explain why, after this contretemps, Brecht ceased to write didactic plays of this type. He had learned his lesson. In 1930 Brecht believed there was an unavoidable conflict between the aspirations of the individual and the demands the Party imposed on him. This conflict forms the heart of this play, *The Measures Taken.* He had displayed poor judgment in thus giving vent to his feelings and the Party duly censured him for his ideological error. Hence "he found ways of circumventing and placating the dictates of socialist realism and still expressing what he felt to be the truth. . . ."[41]

Brecht did not disguise his political beliefs.[42] For a period of thirty years he was fairly orthodox in his Communist views. His critical reflections on the drama, his innovations in the theater, his technique of alienation, are in accord with his commitment as a Marxist. He hoped that his creative contributions would help to change the world in keeping with the plan drawn by Marx, Engels, and Lenin. This doctrinaire bias sometimes led him to simplify the life of man and to indulge in black-and-white contrasts: capitalism and Communism, the repressive past and the redemptive future. He invoked the theory of the class war to account for all the contradictions of society. The abstractions of dialectical materialism frequently take over and distort the working of his imagination. "So Marxism often degenerates into a means of stylizing the actual course of events, facing the reader with gross over-simplifications, and leading to awkward intellectual shuffles whenever what was White . . . has abruptly to be reclassified as Black."[43]

Hostile critics have magnified these contradictions in his

41. Wulbern, *Brecht and Ionesco,* p. 117.
42. Brecht appeared before the House Committee on Un-American Activities and flatly denied that he had been or was now a member of the Communist Party. There is reason to doubt the truth of this statement, but Brecht was then fleeing from the Nazi armies and was seeking asylum in the United States. See "From the Testimony of Bertolt Brecht," in Demetz, ed., *Brecht,* pp. 30-42.
43. Willett, *The Theatre of Bertolt Brecht,* p. 197.

career, the various masks he donned, his praise of Stalin.[44] Brecht failed in his objective of turning the epic theater into a classroom, just as his quixotic experiment of converting the *Communist Manifesto* into hexameters was a dismal failure.[45] Brecht was, of course, under pressure to conform to the ideological dictates of the Party. He relied on the resources of irony as a protection against the temptations that beset him because of his political commitment. Hence his protagonists were not so "positive" as Communist critics would have liked them to be.[46] His plays, his poetry, his career, his faith in Marxism, his conversion to Communism, and his work in the theater—all this reveals the drawbacks and dangers of political commitment.

44. In her essay on Brecht, Hannah Arendt mentions his ode to Stalin "and his praise of Stalin's crimes, written and published while he was in East Berlin. . . ." (Hannah Arendt, *Men in Dark Times* [New York: Harcourt, Brace & World, 1968], p. 210). She points out that the poem praising Stalin was omitted from Brecht's *Collected Works*. Brecht revealed no awareness of the crimes committed by Stalin in the thirties; the Moscow Trials elicited no reaction from him; he remained a member of the Party; he kept silent about what happened during the Spanish Civil War.

45. Willy Haas reports that Brecht continued experimenting with the *Communist Manifesto* for at least a quarter of a century. Fragments of this abortive effort have been preserved. Peter Huchel published them in *Sinn und Form*, the journal of the Academy of Arts in East Germany. Here are the famous first lines of the *Communist Manifesto* transposed into hexameters:

Wars are destroying the world and a specter is stalking
    the rubble,
not emerged from the wars, it has long been observed
    during peacetime,
threat to the powerful men but a friend to the poor in the
    cities,
visiting the indigent kitchens, deploring their half-empty
    dishes,
waiting then for the fatigue at the gates of the mines and
    the shipyards,
calling on people in prison and walking in, lacking a per-
    mit,
seen at the desk of the clerks, even heard in the halls of
    the college,
driving at times giant tanks and flying the death-bringing
    bombers,
speaking in various languages, silent in many.
Popular guest in the slums and the ghetto, and fear to the
    palace,
now it has come here to stay, and its name is communism.

Willy Haas, *Bert Brecht*, trans. Max Knight and Joseph Fabry (New York: Frederick Ungar Publishing Co., 1970), p. 31.

46. "Just as he mocks the sentimentality, humanitarianism, and idealism of the liberal West, so is he curiously reluctant to celebrate the 'brighter side' of Communism, to create a 'positive hero,' or even to follow his own declared intention to depict man 'as he might become.' " Robert Brustein, *The Theatre of Revolt* (Boston and Toronto: Little, Brown and Company, 1964), p. 258.

Part V
COMMITMENT AND REVOLUTION
IN THE SOVIET UNION

20

Mayakovsky: The Suicide of a Committed Poet

Mayakovsky's creative work and his meteoric career cannot be summed up by means of some honorific or pejorative label. Here was a writer who dedicated himself completely, both his talent and his life, to the Revolution.[1] This meant that he had to drive himself hard in order to produce the kind of doctrinaire, didactic writing the Communist Party demanded. He attended political meetings, visited factories where he was enthusiastically applauded when he read his poems, and diligently wrote the kind of propaganda needed, drawing the design and devising the title for thousands of posters. He was extremely proud of these creations, even

---

1. Those who have no knowledge of the Russian langauge are not in a position to judge the merits of Mayakovsky's poetry in the original tongue. A translation can suggest but faintly the achievement of this highly gifted poet. The recent study by Edward J. Brown, *Mayakovsky: A Poet in the Revolution*, furnishes an excellent critique of Mayakovsky's art, his prosodic patterns, his rhyme schemes, his use of neologisms and puns, his ventures in symbolism, and his reliance on the poetic tradition of his land, despite his truculent Futurist heresies and his proclaimed readiness to scrap the cultural heritage of the past. Brown stresses that Mayakovsky's poems themselves should be the object of close critical study. "His imagery, syntax, and vocabulary exist independently of his life and can be studied without reference to it" (Edward J. Brown, *Mayakovsky: A Poet in the Revolution* [Princeton, N. J.: Princeton University Press, 1973], p. 3).

339

though, as he said in 1926, he was rapidly becoming a newspaper man, turning out edifying and morale-uplifting feuilletons and slogans, but he was equally proud of his role as journalist.

Though he was willing to make the sacrifice and play the role of a journalist composing impassioned propaganda in behalf of the new revolutionary order, he could not altogether suppress the insurgent creative vision and lyrical élan that were an intrinsic part of his being. He could curb neither his irrepressible spirit of irony, even when it was directed against himself, nor his tough-minded craving for independence. After the death of Lenin, the Party bureaucrats endeavored to strengthen their position of power by creating and maintaining a stifling atmosphere of ideological conformity. Despite his genuine desire to be of service to the revolutionary cause, Mayakovsky refused to become their mouthpiece and thus earned their enmity.

He kept faith with the Muse of political activism. He made a determined effort to subdue his rebellious ego. He had to play two disparate and conflicting parts: poet and agitator, lyricist and propagandist, lord of creation and sloganeer.[2] He had hailed with delight the vision of a Proletarian Paradise built on the ruins of the old capitalist system, for then the revolutionary would surely come into his own. In the meantime, the Revolution had to be fought for, and when it had established itself in the land it had to be defended against its enemies. In the early years of hardship, danger, and struggle, the poet responded quickly to the call of the Party. He disciplined himself to produce "useful" work for the Soviet Union: topical, hortatory verses; posters; propaganda. In all this he exemplified the inspiring image of "the committed" poet. He supported the Russian people and the cause they believed in; for the time being he silenced his creative self in order that he might as a poet serve his country in a capacity similar to that of a worker in the factory or a soldier in the ranks. He experimented boldly with the new forms: agitprop

2. Mayakovsky's poetry reflects the stormy vicissitudes of his life: the aesthetic views he espoused, the hostile critics with whom he feuded, the women he loved, the political faith he held. "Mayakovsky demands of the critic that he be aware as much as possible of everything that existed in the bright foreground of the poet's own life: artists, poets, critics, revolutionaries, Roman Jakobson and David Burliuk, Lily Brik and other intriguing women, the 'quiet Jew' Pavel Ilych Lavut and the People's Commissar Lunacharsky, as well as the iconic political figures Lenin and Stalin" (ibid., p. 5).

verses meant to be recited, poems instinct with social significance—scathing, mocking, polemical, denunciatory. But his basically anarchic temperament suffered severely while it subjected itself to this regimen.

In his youth Mayakovsky had begun writing as an arch-individualist, a rebel against stifling conventions. Then, as an aggressive Futurist, he voiced his contempt for the regnant dogmas of romantic poetry. He rejected the absurd anachronistic role of pastoralist; he was the lusty, brawling singer of modern industrialism, and his vocabulary, in keeping with the character of his theme, was earthy, iconoclastic, dynamic. When the October Revolution broke out, he supported it loyally in every way possible for him as a poet.

He earned the title of poet laureate of the Revolution. He wandered through the length and breadth of Russia, declaiming his poems in factories and on battleships; he delivered morale-building speeches suited to the time and the occasion. While he was thus faithfully carrying out his day-to-day assignments, the lyrical urge, so long held in check, was stirring in his blood. Despite this inner conflict, he continued to defend the Revolution. He strove to become the collective voice of Communism, and assumed that this would draw him closer to the working class. Alas, the plan did not work out as he had hoped. His contribution as a poet was later harshly criticized on personal as well as ideological grounds. The Bolshevik leaders did not take kindly to his work. Lunacharsky, though he encouraged the poet, regarded him as an adolescent who repeatedly proclaims that he is a genius.[3] Lenin, after reading "150 Million," declared that it is "hooligan communism."[4] Mayakovsky's career was viewed with suspicion, if not scorn, as a form of ego-exhibitionism. His writings failed to conform to the dictates of the Party pundits. He never questioned the humanistic aims of the Revolution; he took them for granted; what he could not countenance was the crude method the Party leaders used in measuring the purity of the ideological content of poetry. What he inveighed against was the philistinism of the bureaucratic cadre; it was blinkered men of this description who were guilty of betraying the Revolution.

His active participation in the Revolution made it possible

3. Wiktor Woroszylski, *The Life of Mayakovsky*, trans. Boleslaw Taborski (New York: The Orion Press, 1970), p. 250.
4. *Ibid.*, p. 275.

342   THE LITERATURE OF COMMITMENT

for him to transcend the feeling that overcame him from
time to time that he was alone, cut off from his fellow men.
The Revolution gave him "new strength and peace of
mind."[5] He gladly performed the tasks that were required of
him. He was eager to wield his pen as if it were a bayonet.
This was no time for love or lyricism. In his poem "Vladimir
Ilyich Lenin," written in 1924,[6] which is dedicated to the
Russian Communist Party, Mayakovsky exalts the Party as the
one thing that will never betray him. In "Homewards!"
(1925) he asserts that he embraced Communism because
without it, for him, "there is no love."[7] That is why he longs
ardently to become an integral part of the Soviet productive
system and wants to deploy the pen so that it will equal the
power of the gun. In "At the Top of My Voice" (1930) he
describes how, despite his disenchantment with propagandist
poetry, he crushed under foot the throat of his own songs.[8]
In this anti-poem he renounces the vocation of poet. The
lyricist lapsed into silence while his alter ego, the rambunc-
tious propagandist, took command.

Unlike such exiles as Bunin, Andreyev, Zamiatin, Ivanov,
Artzybashev, Kuprin, and others, Mayakovsky was never
tempted to leave his native land. When Yesenin lost faith in
the new regime and committed suicide in 1925, Mayakovsky
was shocked. He could not condone such an abject failure of
nerve. The thought that this new revolutionary world belonged to him filled him with boundless elation. A picturesque Bohemian defying the philistines, this tall, handsome
Futurist wore lemon-colored blouses[9] and chanted "praises of
the poet Vladimorovich Mayakovsky."[10] Though he was in

5. Viktor Shlovsky, *Mayakovsky and His Circle,* ed. and trans. Lily Feiler (New York: Dodd, Mead & Company, 1972), p. 97.
6. Professor Brown says that Mayakovsky "succeeded in consecrating a great poem ['Vladimir Ilich Lenin'] to a political cause. It is anything but a pro-paganda pot-boiler" *(Mayakovsky,* p. 20).
7. *Mayakovsky and His Poetry,* ed. and trans. Herbert Marshall (New York: Hill and Wang, 1965), p. 342.
8. *Ibid.,* p. 404.
9. Ezra Pound, when he first came to London at the beginning of his career, wore, according to Ford Madox Ford, "trousers made of green billiard cloth, a pink coat, a blue shirt, a tie hand-painted by a Japanese friend, an immense sombrero, a flaming beard cut to a point, and a single blue ear-ring." Quoted in Charles Norman, *Ezra Pound* (New York: The Macmillan Company, 1960), p. 53.
10. Jürgen Rühle, *Literature and Revolution* (New York and London: Frederick A. Praeger, 1969), p. 14.

the thick of the political conflicts and controversies of his age, he did not join the Communist Party. In his autobiographical sketch "I Myself" (1928), he reveals why he held back. The grim reality of life in the Soviet Union shattered his artistic dreams as well as his political aspirations.

What went wrong? Why did this darling of the gods, this poet laureate of Communism, finally take his own life? The suicide note he wrote discloses nothing that has a direct bearing on his underlying motive. Yet the evidence, however oblique or circumstantial, is there just the same: cumulative, overwhelming, utterly damning. His decision to pour his creative energy into propaganda work, the time he spent in coining slogans and designing posters, the poems he wrote as the hour and the occasion demanded, this self-imposed labor proved in the end to be a thankless task, a crushing burden. He became a target for attacks launched by journalists, Party officials, literary critics, and rival poets. They found fault chiefly with the ideological content of his work. He was not, they complained loudly, reflecting the views of the workers or satisfying their fundamental needs. His detractors disliked the type of man he was as well as his poetry. They were repelled by his eccentricities, his blatant campaign of self-advertisement. His poems were condemned as mannered, idiosyncratic, incomprehensible.

Though there is no demonstrable proof that Mayakovsky's suicide was caused principally by the conflict that raged within him between his anomalous role as poet laureate of the Revolution and his desire to express himself fully as a lyric poet, the essential facts of his life[11] seem to confirm this

11. These facts are scrupulously presented in a documented biography by Woroszylski. The compiler of this monumental work gathered his material from a variety of sources (reminiscences, interviews, newspaper records, book reviews, theatrical criticism, reports issued by the Communist Party, Mayakovsky's own autobiographical recollections, the testimony of his friends, his sisters, and the women he loved). Woroszylski describes the method he used in painting this composite portrait of the poet. "I want to look at Vladimar Mayakovsky from the outside, excluding conjecture, hypotheses, and my own emotions. Only records of various kinds will be allowed to speak" (Woroszylski, *The Life of Mayakovsky*, p. v). It was the philistinism of his land, Mayakovsky felt, that had oppressed and crushed his spirit. If he was fed up with the kind of agitprop that he had produced in such abundance, he had no one to blame but himself. He was aware that a poet must not be forced, "but he can force himself" (*Mayakovsky and His Poetry*, p. 34). In the last year of his life, Mayakovsky was depressed by his isolation as a poet; he wanted to establish contact with the masses and become a member of some literary organization

supposition. Among the negative forces that drove him to his death—his "failure" as a lover, his increasing sense of isolation, the jeering, derisive attitude of the audiences to whom he read his poems, the cruel criticism to which his exhibition, "Twenty Years' Work," was subjected—must be included the unrelenting persecution of Party leaders.[12]

Mayakovsky had early in life pledged his loyalty to the Revolution. At the age of thirteen he had engaged in conspiratorial work. He distributed illegal publications. He had been shadowed by Russian secret agents and arrested three times. The Governor of the prison where Mayakovsky was confined reported that this youth incited the inmates to acts of disobedience. Even in his teens Mayakovsky was faced with the difficult problem of deciding how much of his time and energy he should devote to the Revolution. How could he afford to neglect his ambition to become an artist, though at the time (he was then sixteen years old) he did not know which career, painting or poetry, he would pursue. He was convinced that he must allow nothing to stand in the way of

that represented the proletariat. But his efforts in this direction proved self-defeating. His friends were incensed by his decision to join RAPP (the Revolutionary Association of Proletarian Writers). Why had he surrendered to "the enemy"? His surrender to RAPP "was probably the one event that made his suicide inevitable" (Brown, *Mayakovsky*, p. 367).

12. Mayakovsky, who is the paragon of revolutionary commitment, was not actually hounded to his death by the Party bureaucrats. His politicized aesthetic, his agitational and propagandistic poems, his idealized declaration of faith in the Party in "Vladimir Ilyich Lenin," all this was born of his will to dedicate his art to the Revolution. "The pressures on him to do this were complex and varied, but they came largely from inside himself. The image we sometimes have of a genuine poet required by a state bureaucracy to give up his real self in favor of agitation and propaganda is totally false. . . ." (Brown, *Mayakovsky*, pp. 7-8.) It cannot be denied, however, that the Party functionaries frustrated the poet. Their aesthetic blindness, their philistine taste, their demand for ideological conformity in the arts, their persistent harassment of Mayakovsky, their rooted dislike of this flamboyant Bohemian, this Futurist who displayed his ego in public, their attempt to prevent the production of his plays and the publication of his work—all this deepened his sense of alienation and contributed to his decision to end his life. Jerzy Peterkiewicz maintains that it requires no singular gift of analysis to fathom the political motives behind Mayakovsky's suicide. ". . .A serious analyst of politics could offer a straightforward explanation of Mayakovsky's suicide. When he shot himself in 1930, less than thirteen years after the Bolshevik revolution, the officials of Soviet literature with their customary hypocrisy first frowned on this individualistic departure from the earthly paradise, then put the propagandist on a higher monument, restored his tough images and covered his final despair" (Jerzy Peterkiewicz, *The Other Side of Silence* [London: Oxford University Press, 1970], p. 26).

his creative fulfillment. David Burliuk recalls that Mayakovsky, whom he first met in September 1911, was a tall young man, unkempt, but with a handsome face that made him look like an Apache. A colorful and dynamic personality, Mayakovsky was an impressive reader of his own poetry in public. His lyrics captured the frenetic rhythm of the streets and the exciting night life of Moscow.

Mayakovsky enthusiastically endorsed the spectacular aesthetic program of Futurism. Marinetti's iconoclastic manifestos had been translated and published in Russia in 1914. Marinetti extolled the life of danger, the vertiginous release of energy, the intoxication of travel at high speed. He praised the hardy virtues nourished by war. Groups sprang up in Russia to support the cause of Futurism. Mayakovsky was particularly impressed by Marinetti's contemptuous rejection of the fossilized past. The manifesto "Slap to the Public's Taste," which Mayakovsky, together with the other Russian Futurists, signed, rejoiced in the challenging image it presented and voiced its opposition to academicism and the worship of Pushkin. In and out of season, the Futurists sounded their barbaric yawp that the dead past must be buried and forgotten, the sooner the better. The yellow tunic he wore as a Futurist poet was a symbol of defiance; this was how he expressed his disdain for the literary Establishment, the members of which upheld tradition as a pious cult. He was irritated by the smug and affluent middle class, which had no understanding or appreciation of art. Rejected by a society that knelt in adoration before the Golden Calf, the modern artist, like his nineteenth-century predecessors in France, displayed his utter detestation of middle-class values. Alfred Jarry, who in *Ubu Roi* had reviled his audience with a barrage of scatological insults, demonstrated his eccentricity by leading a tortoise on a leash. But there was no trace of the Dadaist in Mayakovsky. There was nothing nihilistic or decadent in his attitude toward the world or toward man. By means of the poems he published and recited, as well as by his intractable behavior, he was creating the legend that pictured him as an ebullient, self-confident poet. Brashly he announced that he knew, or pretended that he knew, his own intrinsic and incomparable worth as a poet. As a Futurist he regarded himself as a daring innovator, the native genius who would bring to life the beauty of the new, ultramodern

art. Some of the poems he wrote during this period were designed to shock the conventional reader, to provoke the ire
of the public. When he recited the poem "You Have It!," he
deliberately baited his audience by accusing them of wanting
to trample on the fragile hearts of poets. He shouted at them
that they constituted a mob in whose collective face he will
spit with joy.[13] Such a rash, intemperate statement of his feelings was not calculated to win the Russian people over to his
side.

His flamboyant self-assurance and unflagging productivity
accounted for his early successes, but as he grew older he
found that the Soviet critics did not care for his poetry.
When his work was vilified, he was filled with bitterness and
resentment. Gone or largely curbed was the spontaneous élan
with which as a young man he had recited his lyrics before
wildly enthusiastic audiences in all parts of Russia. He had
eagerly tendered his services to the Soviet Union when it had
to fight against its internal enemies and defeat the armed
forces sent by the imperialistic powers in a plot designed to
smash the Revolution, but after a time he began to feel unhappy in the role he was expected to play.[14] He could not
approve of a regime that valued ideological conformity more
highly than original works of art.

His enemies never forgot and never forgave his heretical
devotion to Futurism. He had toured the provinces and
sought to gain supporters for the Futurist movement. In
1913 he wrote *Vladimir Mayakovsky*, which was planned for
production under his direction. It was staged as a Futuristic
performance. Some who saw this "play" thought it was not
only a failure but a fiasco. In 1913 and 1914 he was stigmatized as an ego-futurist. He was charged with "the crime"
of espousing an unrestrained individualism. Mayakovsky

13. Pasternak was not fooled by these histrionic outbursts: the Futurist swagger,
the braggadocio, the boorish attacks on the audience. Mayakovsky, he
realized, was still a young man, and that accounted in the main for his affecta-
tions, his brash poses. Pasternak detected the sensitivity, the shyness, and the
gloom, which Mayakovsky's eccentric and offensive behavior tried to cover up.

14. Helen Muchnic declares that Mayakovsky struggled hard to subdue his restive
private self and to control his personal feelings, so that he could give himself
wholly to the Revolution. "Mayakovsky's whole life was a self-willed, defiant
submission to what he conceived to be his public role." Helen Muchnic, "Literature in the NEP Period," in *Literature and Revolution in Soviet Russia, 1917-
1962*, ed. Max Hayward and Leopold Labedz (London: Oxford University
Press, 1963), p. 39.

struck back at his hostile critics. "I am neither cubo- nor ego-. I am a prophet of mankind of the future!"[15] The critics were not the only ones to jeer at him. Many Russian poets were antagonized by the preposterous theories the Futurists propounded, and they rated the poetry produced by the Russian Futurists as outrageously bad. Mayakovsky turned furiously on his detractors, making fun of the insipid verses the conservative poets wrote.

Despite, or perhaps because of, the controversies he provoked, Mayakovsky was fast becoming a legendary figure in 1914. In that year Maxim Gorky published a favorable article on Futurism. He predicted that the Futurists would grow and mature and in time create truly valuable work. Of Mayakovsky he said that here is a young man who is idiosyncratic and undisciplined in his behavior, but no one could deny the originality of his talent.

The First World War went on and the Russian armies, poorly equipped with weapons and badly trained, suffered disastrous losses. The Russian soldiers in the trenches threw down their guns and refused to fight. When the Czarist regime was overthrown, Mayakovsky greeted this event, which marked the triumph of the October Revolution, with rapture. At a meeting held in 1917 in support of leftist trends in Russian art, Mayakovsky said that he had come to this meeting in behalf of the artists "who have raised the flag of revolution—art is in danger."[16] In this time of social upheaval, the artist must temporarily step aside and acknowledge that politics comes first. When someone in the audience objected to the ideas Mayakovsky had advanced, the poet replied as follows: "Long live the political life of Russia and long live art free from politics!"[17] These words reverberate with prophetic overtones.

The subject of proletarian literature and art was vigorously debated at this time. Some critics maintained that the definition of proletarian culture should be based on the Party membership of the artist. Mayakovsky dissented, for Party affiliation is no guarantee of talent. These discussions on art and politics, in which he participated freely, voicing his convictions with forthright sincerity, foreshadow the stormy con-

15. Woroszylski, *The Life of Mayakovsky*, p. 85.
16. *Ibid.*, p. 175.
17. *Ibid.*, p. 177.

troversies in which he would become involved in the future—a repressive future when he would be forced to censor his own work and silence his innermost beliefs. He had greeted the new revolutionary dispensation with heartfelt ecstasy. He was never faced with the problem whether to accept or reject the new order. "It was my revolution."[18]

Now that the Revolution had established itself, the urgent question arose: What was the proper function of the writer in a Socialist state? What direction should the emergent "proletarian" art take? How much freedom should the artist be granted? Mayakovsky's Futurist recommendations were turned down. He was regarded as too much of an extremist. He was prepared to jettison the art of the past and concentrate all energy on creating the distinctively new proletarian art. In *Mystery-Bouffe,* he gave vent to the utopian dreams his imagination had nourished. In this play he renounces the clamorous Futurist ego. Discarding the persona of the Russian Hamlet, he dons the mask of the revolutionary evangelist. He wrote plays for the Russian theater, which he then believed must be reconstructed from the ground up.

Artists working in and for the Russian theater were at first given *carte blanche.* There was no interference with their productions, no ideological demands were made, there was no censorship, and no attempt to impose Party control. Hence the early twenties gave expression to a rich variety of plays. In vigorous opposition to the traditionalists, a group of innovators were convinced that the new experimental theater would reveal the miracles wrought by the Machine Age and derive enormous benefits from the achievements of technology. Meyerhold, who sided with the innovators, opened the theater to the first Soviet play, *Mystery-Bouffe,* which was produced on November 7, 1918, in celebration of the first anniversary of the Revolution. Meyerhold knew that Mayakovsky would be one of the leading contributors to the Soviet theater. In 1918 Mayakovsky sent a letter to the Central Committee describing the contents of *Mystery-Bouffe.* The first act, he said, would show how the whole world is flooded by the rising tide of revolution. Only the proletarians survive this cataclysmic change. The second act introduces the motif of secular salvation. Walking on the waves as if on dry land,

18. *Ibid.,* p. 186.

toward the ark, is not Christ—who has had some experience in such practice—but the simplest of men. "Standing on top of workbenches and furnaces, he delivers a great sermon on the mount, the promise of a future paradise on earth. . . ."[19] He represents the collective will of the workers. The last act affirms the beauty of the earth and the sheer wonder of existence, now that the Revolution is a *fait accompli.* Mayakovsky, who acted in the production, took the part of the speaker: "Simply a Man."

This revolutionary fable is replete with resounding slogans and the clichés of the class war. "Meyerhold treated this allegory with all the rigid schematization of the propaganda poster."[20] It reminds one of the old morality plays, even though it is explicitly atheistic in outlook. The worker who beholds the light of freedom replaces, as in *Everyman,* the sinner who repents as he hears the dread death summons, and the energizing myth of the seizure of power by the proletariat supplants the beatific Christian vision of redemption in Heaven. Mayakovsky prophesies that the victorious proletariat will build the Commune, and in fifty years they will launch their aerial fortresses to conquer distant lands. This first version of *Mystery-Bouffe* was violently criticized and afer three scheduled performances it was withdrawn.

In 1921 Meyerhold produced *Mystery-Bouffe* in a new version the author had written. The plot tells how the Unclean, the rejected and oppressed working class, become revolutionary fighters. The villains in the play are the merchants, the speculators, the conniving politicians, leaders like Clemenceau and Lloyd George. At the end, the Unclean overcome all opposition. Driven to act by the politics of their hungry stomach, they throw off their chains and wake up from their long slumber of ignorance and apathy. Refusing to be gulled by the so-called democratic promises of the reactionary forces, they take matters into their own hands and unleash the October Revolution.

The Christ who appears before these legions of the Unclean belongs to no class or race or nation. He symbolizes the Man of the Future. In his Sermon on the Mount he confides to his listeners the liberating truth that there is no Heaven;

19. *Ibid.,* p. 234.
20. *Meyerhold on Theatre,* trans. and ed. Edward Braun (New York: Hill and Wang, 1969), p. 161.

they have been hoodwinked by a theological fiction. The only real Heaven is the one built by human hands on earth. Then this modern Christ—the Christ of Communism—holds up before the entranced multitude the miracle wrought by technology.[21]

The workers then force their way through the regions of Hell and overpower the Devil. What tortures can Beelzebub inflict that they have not already suffered at the hands of capitalism? In Paradise, Jehovah brandishes his thunderbolts in vain. The workers storm the ramparts of heaven and take away his weapons. Then Mayakovsky paints what is meant to be an enticing picture of the terrestrial paradise: factories operating at full speed and at full capacity, the rapid growth of cities, locomotives streaking across the golden landscape, steamboats on the rivers and oceans, the horn of plenty made available to all. This technological utopia is located, of course, in Russia. Mayakovsky rapturously describes the plenitude of goods the populace now enjoy and the state of happiness they attain: skyscrapers towering above the horizon, steel bridges, the earth transformed into a fruitful garden. Electric tractors, electric thrashers, electric baking machines: these inventions bear witness that the millennium has arrived. Shop windows display a profusion of the best consumer merchandise. All this has been achieved under the aegis of the Sickle and Hammer. The moral is painstakingly spelled out for all to read: the machines now belong to their true owners—the workers. The Locomotive Engineer proudly chants his song of triumph: all these miracles have been wrought by the proletariat. The curtain rings down as a chorus of the Unclean jubilantly sing their victory chorale. They have at last thrown off the chain of slavery and gained the summit of freedom.

Mayakovsky was by this time confident that he knew the right answer to the question of what the new revolutionary culture should consist of. Art should not be kept in lifeless museums, but become an integral part of the life of the streets: it should be displayed in street cars and in factories. His poem "Orders for the Army" proclaimed the need to raze museum walls and utterly destroy the worthless heritage

21. On his visit to the United States in 1925, Mayakovsky wrote "My Discovery of America," which articulates his growing awareness of the drawbacks and dangers of uncontrolled technological expansion.

of the past. The classics, he announced in stentorian tones, were no longer to enjoy a privileged status.[22]

The revolutionary vanguard affirmed the necessity for liquidating the past, and the Futurists applauded such a move. Unfortunately, the degree of public favor they enjoyed was fast diminishing. In 1918 Lunacharsky published an article, "A Spoon of Antidote," in which he welcomed Mayakovsky's shift from the romantic stance to the "revolutionary-collectivist routine"[23] Despite Lunacharsky's measured praise, the tide of public opinion turned against the Futurists. They were dismissed as arrant egotists who were not worthy of making a contribution to the body of proletarian literature in the making: literature that expressed the authentic spirit of the Revolution. These loud-mouthed boasters and arrogant interlopers should be taught a salutary lesson.

Mayakovsky was certainly not backward in making known his allegiance to the Revolution and his feeling of solidarity with the Russian masses. His poem "One Hundred Fifty Million," he asserted, was a genuine expression of the Russian folk. But his reiterated vow of commitment to Communism did not insure his work against the official voice of censure. His plays, exercises in propaganda but not the kind the Party hierarchy approved, were held up for publication. The Communist Party put an end to this irritating movement known as Futurism. Mayakovsky was gradually pushed out of his position of leadership. His production of propagandistic verse, his public speeches, his efforts not to run counter to the ideological pronouncements of the Party, resulted, alas, in an adulteration of his poetic substance. He was beset on both sides: by Communist politicians who demanded unconditional obedience to the Revolution (as they interpreted it) and his poetic conscience, which struggled to maintain high artistic standards. Lenin asked Lunacharsky bluntly if he was not ashamed of giving his approval to the publication of "One Hundred Fifty Million." "This is absurd, stupid, mon-

22. In a letter Alexander Blok wrote to Mayakovsky (December 17-30, 1918) but never mailed, the older poet said that he hated museums as much as Mayakovsky, but he wished to point out that "destruction is as old as construction, and just as 'traditional.'" Woroszylski, *The Life of Mayakovsky*, p. 248.
23. *Ibid.*, p. 250.

strously stupid, and pretentious."[24] In 1922 Osip Mandelstam recognized that Mayakovsky possessed a close knowledge of the complexity of world poetry, but in his efforts to produce poetry for the Russian masses he excluded from it all that was obscure and allusive, hammering home the naked message. Such propaganda poems, cut off from their cultural roots, ceased to be poetry. Mayakovsky has written some excellent cultural poems. Mandelstam finds it a pity that he should have impoverished himself in this manner.

The noose was being more tightly drawn, but slowly, by degrees, around Mayakovsky's neck. During the period of the NEP, ideologists were in the saddle. Bureaucrats, philistines of the kind that Mayakovsky despised, were invested with the power to determine the value of works of art. Russia was steering a new course. Avant-garde figures were treated with suspicion and open dislike. Mayakovsky reached a point in his development when he questioned "the usefulness" of his creative work. He would repudiate his role as a poet, and he composed poems that called for the death of poetry. He read his ode on Lenin before a large literary audience. At the end, he was heckled by people who asked a number of irrelevant but hostile questions: Was he a member of the Communist Party? Why had he not joined? The campaign of persecution was under way. In November 1925, Alexander Voronsky called Mayakovsky "an extreme individualist and an eccentric."[25] Voronsky singles out for invidious comment the pervasiveness of the "I" in Mayakovsky's poetic effusions. He was sincere in his devotion to the Revolution, but it was held against him that he failed to grasp its true meaning. Mayakovsky was not one to suffer calumny in silence. In "The Message to Proletarian Poets" he spoke out boldly against the slogan-mongers and the bureaucrats.

Mayakovsky was deeply moved by Ysenin's suicide, though he publicly criticized the poet for choosing the easy way out, for losing heart in the face of the mighty challenge posed by Communism. Mayakovsky declared that he intended to take upon himself the task of dissipating the aura of glamor surrounding Ysenin's end. In place of "the easy beauty of death,"[26] he would chant hymns in praise of life and the steady

24. *Ibid.*, p. 274.
25. *Ibid.*, p. 356.
26. *Ibid.*, p. 396.

march of the future toward the goal of Communism. This was no flourish of ideological trumpets on Mayakovsky's part. He was not simply uttering his Everlasting Yea and casting a vote of confidence in Communism. He meant what he said. Communism must remove all obstacles that stand in the way of freeing mankind from the evil clutches of the past and thus enable it to take rightful possession of its heritage. Suicide is no solution but a defeat for the human spirit.

Mayakovsky continued the practice of touring the cities in many parts of Russia, but these recitals were not an unalloyed success. Increasingly he was baited by the audience. His enemies had discovered his Achilles' heel, and they concentrated their fire on this vulnerable spot. Since Mayakovsky regarded himself as a proletarian poet, why does he use the incriminating "I" so excessively? Why does he stress "I" so obsessively and to a sickening degree? The literary critics reproached him for indulging in obscurity. That is why the workers were unable to understand his poetry. In May 1927 Vyacheslav Polonsky repeated the charge that Mayakovsky displayed traits of insufferable egotism. Posing as a blustering nihilist, Mayakovsky tried to attract attention to himself by whatever means best suited his purpose. More damaging to his reputation was the indictment that as a revolutionary poet he failed to capture the spirit of Russia and its people. His cardinal sin was that he had not celebrated the heroic achievements of Socialist construction.

The attacks on Mayakovsky increased in number and in virulence. He was "officially" out of favor. *The Bathhouse* was poorly received. The play was considered to provide unintelligible and indigestible fare for the masses. *The Bathhouse,* produced in 1930 by Meyerhold, is an outspoken satire of the Soviet bureaucracy. We are introduced to an inventor who is working furiously to finish his time machine. He approaches the Chief of the Federal Bureau of Coordination, Pobedonosikov, for financial help. But the Inventor gets lost in a labyrinth of red tape. The Chief represents the typical bureaucrat, puffed up with self-importance, taking no interest in his job. He spends his time coining slogans, quarreling with his wife, and making plans for his vacation. The inventor follows this official home in the hope of gaining a hearing. The machine suddenly becomes active. We learn of the Future Age of Communism. In the year 2030, all problems have been solved. The Phosphorescent Woman reveals the prodigious achievements of the Soviet Union. The feckless bureaucrats have been fired. Pobedonosikov wonders whether the play is not saying that people of his stripe are of no use to Communism.

Mayakovsky was sharply rebuked for this caustic satire. It was a slap in the face of the regime and its leader—Stalin. "It was hinted that he was a reactionary, a Trotskyist, or worse. Stalin, who had been keeping a watchful eye on Mayakovsky, encouraged the attacks."[27] Mayakovsky was finding out that it is by no means an easy matter to serve as the revolutionary spokesman of his people. The audiences to whom he read his poetry were becoming more antagonistic. The acrimonious critical articles that appeared in the press reflected the attitude of the Party leaders. In their eyes he was unreliable, since he dwelt on the negative features of life in the Soviet Union.[28]

Mayakovsky wrote The Bedbug, a trenchant satire of the bureaucrats and the untrained Party office-holders, those who boast of their proletarian origin and their bona fide membership in the Party. Prisypkin is a nonentity who nevertheless wields some influence because he belongs to the Party. Unfortunately, he is the host on whom a bedbug is feeding. In this fantasy, Mayakovsky predicts the victory of Communism in 1970, when Prisypkin is thawed out of his frozen state. But what does this futuristic utopia consist of? Mayakovsky projects a disheartening vision of the degradation of the Marxist dogma: the new order is puritanical in attitude, mechanical in its operation. Sex is tabooed as a bourgeois fetish; neither alcohol nor tobacco can be purchased by the man who drinks or smokes; love is ruled out as a romantic illusion derived from a deluded and discreditable past. When Prisypkin gets his bearings, he ignores these restrictive laws. He drinks heavily. Through the medium of sa-

27. James M. Symons, *Meyerhold's Theatre of the Grotesque: The Post-Revolutionary Productions, 1920-1932* (Coral Gables, Fla.: University of Miami Press, 1971), pp. 15-16.
28. Patricia Blake says: "During the two years before his suicide he came closest to an awareness of the nature of the society he had once acclaimed. He saw the conflict between the ideals and the reality of communism, between the individual and the community, between the artist and the bureaucrat." Vladimar Mayakovsky, *The Bedbug and Selected Poetry*, trans. Max Hayward and George Reavy and ed. Patricia Blake (New York: Meridian Books, 1960), p. 37.

tire, Mayakovsky reveals his painful disenchantment with conditions as they exist in the Soviet Union.

This comic extravaganza portrays the negative and annoying features of life in Russia: the flourishing black market, the snobbery that prevails, the ridiculous airs of superiority put on by those who are Party members or who hold office. Prisypkin, a buffoon, insists that he must have a Red wedding, a class-conscious ceremony that will do justice to his exalted social position. The clowning, the comic ingredients, and the cutting dialogue highlight the disconcerting fact that this proletarian paradise is rife with discontent. The Revolution is losing its momentum. The nation suffers from food shortages and an insufficiency of housing accommodations. What is more, the land is plagued with lice. Prisypkin is a materialist: he has a definite liking for bourgeois comforts. That is what he fought for, after all; these are precisely the rewards he expected to receive. "And who knows? Maybe just by looking after my own comfort I can raise the standards of the whole working class!"[29] A fire breaks out and Prisypkin, by a happy combination of circumstances, is saved and preserved in alcohol.

Fifty years later, the Institute for Human Resurrection brings him back to life by scientific means. He beholds a new world in which wars no longer occur. Some "decadent" words like "suicide" and the ideas that are connected with them, have fallen out of use; they are obsolete and their archaic meaning is recorded in the dictionary. Other obsolete terms are "business," "surrealism," and so on. Mayakovsky is poking fun at the Soviet regime and the grandiose utopian schemes it has hatched. Life is geared to one purpose only: the building of dams, bridges, tractors, and railroads. The propagation of children is encouraged so as to provide the manpower that will achieve this technological ideal.

Restored to life, Prisypkin feels out of place in this strange environment, but he sees a bedbug and experiences a sense of kinship with it. The present generation observe the extraordinary antics and regressive behavior of Prisypkin, who guzzles beer and smokes cigarettes. When the Professor tells him that society wishes to rehabilitate him and raise him to

29. Vladimir Mayakovsky, *The Complete Plays of Vladimir Mayakovsky*, trans. Guy Daniels (New York: Washington Square Press, 1968), p. 157.

the human level, Prisypkin, turned rebellious in his despair, cries out: "To hell with society, and to hell with you, too!"[30] He voices the secret thought of those in the audience when he complains: "What *is* all this? What did we fight for? Why did we spill our blood if I, a leader in our new society, can't enjoy myself doing the new dance steps. . . ."[31] The closing scene shows Prisypkin in a cage, sitting on a bed with his guitar; the bedbug is in a glass cage. When he sees the audience watching him, he shouts at them: "Citizens! My people! . . . Why am I alone in this cage?"[32]

Mayakovsky was resentful of the way he was being treated: the political attacks on his work, the friends who turned against him, the inimical tone of the press when his name was mentioned. In "At the Top of My Voice" (1930) he sought to justify his work as a poet and the active part he had played in the revolutionary struggle. Not at all penitent or apologetic, he confesses that he is fed up with turning out agitprop poems. For a number of years he had suppressed his song. Defiantly he predicts that his poetry will live and be read by the generations to come, despite the infamous conspiracy that was organized to silence him. He has not changed his colors. He is still a staunch Communist, the uncompromising foe of those who would defraud the workers of the fruits of their victory.

Despite this proud affirmation of faith in his calling, his position as a writer was rapidly becoming untenable. He felt both angry and dejected. His decision to join RAPP, the Russian Association of Proletarian Writers, left him more isolated than ever. On March 23, 1930, the year in which he took his life, he delivered a speech on the occasion that celebrated his twenty years of creative work. He assured his audience that he could easily have turned out poems that would win public approbation: popular but ephemeral productions that like gaudy butterflies would not outlive the day of their birth. One part of his speech constituted a brief but moving *apologia pro vita sua*. Throughout his career his chief occupation was to denounce what he considered wrong, to fight against those tendencies which he believed were harmful to the Russian people. He pointed out that "at every given point

30. *Ibid.,* p. 185.
31. *Ibid.,* p. 186.
32. *Ibid.,* p. 195.

one had to defend revolutionary literary views, fight for them and fight against the fossilization which does occur in our thirteen-year-old republic. . . ."[33] He referred to the abuse that had been heaped on his head. This exhibition of the life and work of Mayakovsky was designed to refute the slanderous campaign directed against him. He wanted to prove that he was, in fact, a writer-revolutionary, one who "takes a very active part in the everyday life and building of socialism."[34] Less than a month later he fired a bullet through his heart.

Mayakovsky had played the game of Russian roulette on a number of occasions in the past. On April 14, 1930, he decided to play the game in dead earnest. Why did he take his own life at the age of thirty-six, when he was at the height of his powers? Why, without warning, did he suddenly decide to end his life?[35] His suicide was, in effect, a repudiation of his role of revolutionary commitment. The conflict in him between the spontaneous poet and the propagandist, the lyricist and the self-conscious ideologist, wore him down. His self-inflicted death was a portent of the disaster that would befall many writers during the thirties under the totalitarian rule of Stalin. The individual, stripped of significance, was trapped in a world that seemed to be governed by irrational and inexplicable forces. The human personality was conditioned to repel the intrusion of mystery. The tragic dimension had no place in Communist society.[36] Few writers of talent could survive in such a climate of terror and repression. The truly

---

33. Woroszylski, *The Life of Mayakovsky*, p. 510.
34. *Mayakovsky and His Poetry*, p. 401.
35. In chapter 14, "The Heart Yearns for a Bullet," Brown takes up the challenging theme of the poet's suicide. Brown, *Mayakovsky*, pp. 352-68.
36. In her essay on the concept of tragedy in Russian and Soviet literature, Helen Muchnic writes: "Every wise question must have its sufficient answer, and any question that cannot be answered is a foolish one and should not be asked. There is no such thing as mystery, there is only obscurantism. . . . The Soviet man is a function of his society; his value is determined by the degree of his usefulness to it; he stands or falls by his adequacy as an instrument; his values are given him; his emotions, the very meaning of his life, are judged in relation to the society he serves. No Soviet hero can be tragic; he is bound to win out, because the world is with him" (Helen Muchnic, "Concept of Tragedy in Russian and Soviet Literature," in *Literature and Revolution in Soviet Russia, 1917-62*, ed. Max Hayward and Leopold Labedz [London: Oxford University Press, 1963], pp. 264-65). See the valuable book by Raymond A. Bauer, *The New Man in Soviet Psychology* (Cambridge, Mass.: Harvard University Press, 1952).

gifted Russian artist, if he escaped the fate of liquidation during the thirties, found life difficult—and boring.[37] The dogma of Socialist realism, rigidly enforced, prevented the growth of an autochthonous literature. The determined effort to harness the creative energy of Soviet artists for political ends failed miserably.[38]

37. "Communist utopia turned into Stalinist reality: the dreamed-of paradise turned out to be a new class and terror regime worse than the Czarist one. The tendencies in the art of the Revolution—its love of truth, its indictment of all evil, and its passionate desire for change and betterment—now turned against Communism itself" (Rühle, *Literature and Revolution*, p. 135).
38. "Art and politics have their own laws. They can move, stimulate, and inspire one another. . . . But the attempt to make them agree must bring on a collision. . . ." (*ibid.*, p. 140).

21
Commitment, Coercion, and Conformity

1. *The Politics of Political Conformity*

Many writers, including those who work in the capacity of responsible editors or occupy important posts in the Writers' Union, think that politics is the business of the government and the
Central Committee. As for writers, it is not their business to occupy themselves with politics. A work if written well, artistically,
beautifully—give it a start, regardless of the fact that it has rotten
passages that disorient our youth and poison them. We demand
that our comrades, both those who give leadership in the literary
field and those who write, be guided by that without which the
Soviet order cannot live, *i.e.,* by politics, so that our youth may be
brought up not in a devil-may-care spirit, but in a vigorous and
revolutionary spirit.[1]

Literary creation cannot change the world. That is the business
of politics. And woe to mankind if the politicians fail to join in
this alteration of consciousness.[2]

---

1. Andrei A. Zhdanov, *Literature, Philosophy, and Music* (New York: International
   Publishers, 1950), p. 31.
2. Wilhelm Emrich, *The Literary Revolution and Modern Society and Other Essays,*
   trans. Alexander and Elizabeth Henderson (New York: Frederick Ungar Publishing Co., 1971), p. 78.

Zhdanov's emphasis on the political content and propagandistic function of literature was used by the Party leaders to
justify their authoritarian control over the arts in the Soviet
Union. During his long reign, Stalin did not make the mistake of underestimating the importance of the arts in the life
of the Russian people. Like Lenin, he was determined to get
rid of every organ of opinion in the land that did not dutifully follow the policy prescribed by the Communist Party.
He left nothing to chance. When RAPP was dissolved, a new
organization, the Union of Soviet Writers, was formed. This
organization consisted largely of time-serving yes-men, writers who could be trusted to carry out the will of their master.
The All-Union Congress of Writers, which met in Moscow in
1934, declared that Socialist realism was henceforth to be accepted by the faithful as the official aesthetic outlook, the
approved method to be used in the production of Soviet literature. Art, this Congress maintained, must be realistic in
content, socialist in politics, affirmative in tone. The Commissar who supervised the literature and the arts was consistently
hostile to formalistic art, and this negative attitude persisted
even after the death of Stalin. The denunciation and persecution of those who were guilty of the sin of formalism rested on the assumption that such art pays excessive attention
to matters of form and style at the expense of the socialist
orientation of the work.

> Actually, what the Soviets saw and still see in so-called formalistic
> art is the expression of a doomed society, namely, the decadent
> bourgeoisie. They object not to alienation from content as such
> but to alienation from one particular, narrowly prescribed
> content—namely, illustrating their own social dogma.[3]

Negative criticism, eccentricity, experimental caprice, subjectivity the preoccupation with art for art's sake, the sterile
esoteric cult of aestheticism, the anarchy of the uncurbed
Bohemian imagination, the solipsistic fantasies of the romantic dreamer—all this is the unmistakable mark of decadence
and is therefore sternly forbidden.[4]

When the New Economic Policy (NEP) was in effect, those

3. Hellmut Lehmann-Haupt, *Art Under a Dictatorship* (New York: Oxford University Press, 1954), p. 231.
4. See chap. 5, n41, for the remark by Georg Lukács on the decadence of contemporary bourgeois literature.

old Bolsheviks who held important posts in the government did not want the State apparatus to establish control over the arts. When the NEP came to an end, Stalin transformed the Communist Party into a powerful organization, which he controlled, that would endeavor to politicize all the realms of art. From that time on, art in the Soviet Union would be judged by its ideological fidelity to the Communist cause, and in practice this meant loyalty to the Stalinist dictatorship.

Those writers in the Soviet Union who sought to capture the fugitive shapes and shadows that body forth the life of the imagination, found it extremely difficult to survive during the years when the Stalinist regime enforced its demand that their conception of reality and their portrayal of human nature *must* in all essential respects be in accord with Marxism-Leninism as interpreted by the leaders of the Party. Under Stalin's tutelage, Socialist realism was meant to strengthen and extend Party control over all literary productions. Here we behold a bureaucratic attempt to make literature serve a pedagogic and didactic purpose. The novelist was expected to create a picture of the collective life of the land that would exalt the service rendered by the positive hero, the Stakhanovite who lives devoutly for the Revolution and reverently echoes the ideological creed of the day. Russian writers were unable to apply these prescriptive principles to their work in fiction, for these *ex cathedra* standards were extremely vague, so that the writer had nothing to guide him. Yet he knew—it had happened to other writers—that his novel, when finally brought before the public, would be dissected with unsparing harshness if it failed to satisfy the criteria of ideological fidelity the Party critics had set up. But the implacable negative judgments of these zealous guardians of the cultural heritage to which proletarian genius would soon give birth had, as the French critic Henri Arvon points out, no justification "other than the political needs of the moment."[5] Those strong-willed writers who could not be bribed or intimiated were reduced to silence. Suspected of treason or disloyalty, those literary men who did not agree with the then mandatory Party line were banished from the Soviet Union or imprisoned and shipped later to a concentration camp. Babel died in confinement in 1941. Boris Pilnyak

5. Henri Arvon, *Marxist Esthetics,* trans. Helen R. Lane (Ithaca, N. Y., and London: Cornell University Press, 1973), p. 83.

was branded an enemy of the people. Meyerhold was probably put to death in a Moscow prison in 1940. The estimate is that from 1936 to 1939 four to five million people, many intellectuals among them, were the victims of various cruel forms of repression.[6] About four to five hundred thousand of this number were shot to death.

Some day the fully documented history of the sadistic Stalinist persecution of writers will appear. *The Gulag Archipelago* does not exclude the dire fate meted out to writers and artists and intellectuals in general from Solzhenitsyn's comprehensive coverage, but he does not confine himself to the literati. The story of how Olesha incurred the displeasure of the powers that be offers an instructive example of the way writers who were ideologically suspect were punished for their literary infractions. Olesha's novel *Envy*, published in 1927, was at that time well received. It was not long, however, before the hapless author found himself in deep trouble. He was charged with the serious "crime" of formalism. It seems that the "positive heroes" he had created in *Envy* did not appeal to the public nor to those officials who could impose censorship. Many readers unaccountably identified themselves with "the superfluous man" in the novel, the protagonist who is supposed to embody the worst traits of the petty bourgeois. He exudes the poison of envy, resentment, spite; he indulges in futile reveries that disclose his longing

6. See Roy A. Medvedev, *Let History Judge*, trans. Colleen Taylor, ed. David Joravsky and Georges Haupt (New York: Alfred A. Knopf, 1971), p. 239. In *Uncensored Russia*, the editor Peter Reddaway presents material taken from the underground journal *A Chronicle of Current Events*. The book gives a documented account of the repressive measures taken against those citizens who criticized conditions in the Soviet Union. These dissenters are arrested, their apartment ransacked for incriminating material (books, manuscripts, letters, photographs), which is seized; they are tried, invariably found guilty, and sentenced to serve time in prison. Some are judged to be insane and sent to a psychiatric hospital, which is actually a prison. Stalin's spies, informers, and secret police instituted a reign of terror unparalleled in the history of the world. The editor remarks: "By the years 1937–38, when the population of the concentration camps rocketed to 9–10 millions, these graves for the living had, ironically, become the last notable refuge of free expression. A rich literature of songs developed in them, often with strong political overtones. . ." (*Uncensored Russia: Protest and Dissent in the Soviet Union*, ed. and trans. Peter Reddaway [New York and Toronto: American Heritage Press, 1972], p. 18). When Stalin died in 1953, there was some relaxation of the censorship laws; most of the ten to fifteen million inmates of concentration camps were released. But a liberal regime was not established. In 1966 the practice of *samizdat* was resumed. See the chapter "The Camps and Prisons," in *ibid.*, pp. 203-26.

for the return of the good old days. Olesha, it was charged, had not handled his theme properly; his treatment failed to do justice to the stirring realities and epic achievements of Soviet life.

A writer caught between two worlds, Olesha harks back nostalgically to the traditional society of the nineteenth century, the golden period of childhood. He is unable to make the required adjustment to the dynamic world of the present: the tempo of industrialization, the emergence of the new Soviet man, the code of behavior enforced by the Revolution. He is unable to write about the subjects the Party recommended as suitable. Unlike those Soviet writers who were assigned to live with the workers on the site where a dam or a factory was being constructed and who could compose novels based on their observations, he could not produce such fiction on command. He lacked the versatility of Ehrenburg. He was not endowed with the facile talent to invent characters who would personify the heroic worker in Russia. He hoped—but it was in vain—that he would be allowed to discover his own characteristic themes: the idyllic dreams the young cherish, the kind of love they yearn for.

Envy reveals the depth of Olesha's hankering for the lapsed and discredited values of the past: the life of feeling as opposed to the rationalism that is rampant today. The "positive heroes" in *Envy* are Andrei Babichev, the "genius" presiding over the food industry, and Volodia Makarov, Babichev's protégé, a student of engineering, whose chief aim in life is to control his emotions and to function efficiently like a well-oiled machine. These two characters are meant to demonstrate the folly and waste of the revolt led by the "malcontents" and the "maladjusted" of the new social order. Ivan Babichev, Andrei's brother, challenges the myth that glorifies the machine. Kavalerov, the other "superfluous man," suffers from a tendency to daydream. He suffers from the disease of Oblomovism.[7] Volodia, the destined leader of the future, is contemptuous of those useless creatures who cling pathetically to the dead past. In delineating the character of Kavalerov, Olesha shows that those people who possess a lively imagination encounter only suspicion, scorn, and the

---

7. *Envy* was influenced by the novel *Oblomov*, by Ivan Goncharov, which was published in 1857.

laughter born of incomprehension. Superfluous men like Ivan Babichev and Kavalerov cannot survive in the U.S.S.R.

Kavalerov, for example, has a fixed habit of personifying things in his environment that he feels are hostile. He projects his feelings onto the objects around him: the furniture and his blanket, which malevolently frustrate his intentions. He watches the movements of Andrei Babichev, the type of man who is not thus "persecuted" by things. He studies him intently: his well-tailored suit, his eating habits, his pince-nez. Andrei possesses inexhaustible energy and initiative and is full of original ideas. He is endowed with charisma. Has he not been singled out for praise by a Commissar? Compared with him, Kavalerov is an utter nonentity.

Andrei, in supreme control of the food industry, is the innovator of a huge communal kitchen that relieves housewives of the burdensome task of preparing their own meals. He saves them hours of needless labor. Olesha pictures this positive hero in action: briskly issuing orders to his staff of workers, conducting business deals, signing contracts. He is the extrovert, the doer, whereas Kavalerov is the passive bystander, not fitted for any occupation, his innards as well as his mind eaten through with the acids of envy. He vows that he will prove to the world that he is as good as Babichev, though when he is in his presence he is rendered speechless and cannot make the proper retort.

Andrei, moved by pity, had picked up Kavalerov where he lay, dead drunk, outside the door of a bar. He had been thrown out when he furiously insulted a group in the bar who had dared to laugh at him. He is astounded by the tream of foul abuse that issues from his lips. He feels as if ₂ were locked inside an absurd dream, but the humiliation which he was subjected is no dream. When he wakes up, is lying on a sofa in Andrei's apartment. Andrei tells him ιt Volodia, an excellent soccer player, whom he loves as if ˙ere his own son. He praises this lad of eighteen as an ɒlary representative of the younger generation. He con- ς "a completely new human being."[8] If Volodia returns, ˙ov will have to leave. Kavalerov is hurt by this disclo- t he will soon be replaced by this paragon of virtue. ιegrace brother, Ivan Babichev, appears on the scene

lesha, *Envy and Other Works*, trans. Andrew R. MacAndrew (Garden Ci-
˙.: Doubleday & Company, 1967), p. 15.

and announces that he has invented a machine called Ophelia. He threatens Andrei, but the latter orders him to be off or he will have him arrested. Andrei characterizes Ivan as "a lazy bum, a harmful, contagious man."[9]

Kavalerov realizes that he is making no favorable impression on Andrei, who pays no heed to his words. Born at the beginning of the century, he is critical of present conditions in Russia. Whereas Europe offers an open market for talent, in Russia the individual is deprived of the opportunity to achieve success. Insurmountable barriers are placed in the path of the gifted man. Kavalerov confesses what is ailing him. He desires to exhibit his colorful and commanding personality. He would like to taste the intoxicating fruit of glory. In Communist society the individual is ignored. He counts only as an atom in the collectivity. He demands "a great deal of attention."[10] The personality in this benighted land counts for naught. The creative ego perishes in a desert of indifference and neglect. The various roads to fame are permanently closed. Poor Kavalerov dreams of suddenly doing something absurd so that the people who worship efficiency and value the utilitarian and realistic attitude will be startled, and then he will say: "that's your way and this is mine."[11] Or he will kill himself, without reason, "to show that everyone is free to do what he pleases with himself."[12]

The contrast between the two men—Kavalerov, the hapless dreamer, bitter in his resentment of the new men in Soviet life, and Andrei, the brilliant, enterprising manager, forms, together with the contrast between Andrei and his ne'er-do-well brother, the heart of the conflict. Kavalerov broods on the irremediable failure his life has been; at twenty-seven he has accomplished nothing. He is not famous, his dreams of grandeur will never be realized. Nor will love come his way. He will have to settle for the erotic favors of the widow, greasy from her job as cook for a cooperative. Having succeeded in nothing he must come at last to this degrading pass of sharing the bed and the sexual possession of this fat, unappetizing widow of forty-five.

9. *Ibid.,* p. 16.
10. *Ibid.,* p. 17.
11. *Ibid.,* p. 18.
12. Such strictures, born of anarchistic tendencies, offended the Commissar mentality. Like Dostoevski in *Notes from Underground,* Olesha was affirming the power of the irrational.

Andrei is a veritable dynamo, bursting with energy, full of plans for the marketing of meat products. He is helping to build the new world of Communism. Kavalerov refuses to be impressed by such feats of business efficiency. Andrei is unlike the heroes whom history honored in the past. Kavalerov is well aware that he has no record to boast of. Granted, he is not a productive worker, but why must he therefore be reduced to a blank, a minus quantity? Andrei had used Kavalerov to read the proofs of copy dealing with the production of salami. Does Andrei, the high and mighty Salami Chief, regard him as belonging to the lumpenproletariat, fit only for menial work? He will show this upstart what's what. Furious because he has been ignored, treated like an inferior, he begins to suspect that Andrei wishes to marry Valia, that he is persecuting his brother because Ivan is intellectually superior. Bursting, like Dostoevski's underground man, with repressed rage and *ressentiment*, he intends to frustrate the plans of this vile schemer. He will join forces with Ivan and thus gratify his thirst for revenge. He remarks that he is fighting "for tenderness, for pathos, for individuality."[13]

Inwardly he knows he is headed for a bad fall. His plot will be foiled. He meets Volodia Makarov, the young man who represents the future. In his haste to leave Andrei's apartment he retrieves what he thinks is the insulting letter he had written Andrei but it turns out that he had snatched a letter by Volodia that expresses his idolatry of the machine. Volodia acknowledges that he is a human machine or is, as he hopes, fast becoming one. Tht is what he aspires to be. He takes extraordinary pride in the efficiency of the machines in the workshop where he is employed.[14] He intends to marry Valia.

Kavalerov's envy is so intense that it leads him to believe in his paranoiac fantasies. He is humiliated repeatedly; his encounters with "the enemy" result in his abject defeat, and each experience in abjection adds fuel to his sick craving for revenge. He is pathetic in his abortive efforts to prove to the world that he is no clown. Ivan, another misfit, hates his brother. He insists that the machine he has invented will destroy Andrei. He will not allow Volodia to marry his daughter Valia. Later he stops his brother's car and creates a public

13. Olesha, *Envy and Other Works*, p. 44.
14. *Ibid.*, p. 49.

scene. He is arrested and kept in jail for ten days. He is threatened with deportation if he again violates the law. He is the foe of the established regime because he believes that many precious human feelings "are scheduled for liquidation."[15] He specifies that such feelings as pity and pride, tenderness and love, will be eliminated. Socialism will replace these feelings with a new set of responses that will compose the soul of man.[16] The true, steadfast Communist will have outgrown the sentiment of pity. Suicide will be forbidden. The distinctively human passions have been outlawed. The new Soviet man has no use for these anachronistic and anomalous feelings and tramples them under his feet. The old generation is dying. Kavalerov, who has become "the lover" of the fat widow, feels keenly the degraded condition to which he has fallen. He looks upon his past life as morally irresponsible; "he had overestimated his own importance. . . ."[17] But this contrite confession by the superfluous man was not enough, alas, to save Olesha from the inquisition of hostile revolutionary critics. He had erred grievously, it appears, by making the reader sympathize with such ne'er-do-well, negative, anti-social characters.

Other works of fiction by Olesha confirm the impression that he felt alienated and unwanted in a Socialist country that feverishly worshiped the Moloch of the machine and demanded that the writer restrict his subjectivity to a minimum and adopt the method of Socialist realism. He could not become a part of this mechanical collectivized rhythm. He dwelt in the invisible land of the imagination, where perception did not follow the normal pattern.[18] The writer who dwelt in this land of sensitivity and imagination did not concern himself with science or politics or the abstractions of dialectical materialism.

Olesha realized that his creative vision was limited in scope. Compared to the prodigious achievements of the Soviet Union—the October Revolution, the triumph of Communism, the discoveries of science, and the wonders wrought by technology—his literary contributions were of little worth.

15. *Ibid.*, p. 71.
16. *Ibid.*, pp. 71-72.
17. *Ibid.*, p. 120.
18. For Olesha the invisible land was "the land of sensitivity and imagination" (*ibid.*, p. 149). This "definition" appears in the story "The Cherry Stone."

Hence his reiterated cries of sheer frustration. When the newspapers proudly report the heroic accomplishments of Russian workers building power stations, railroads, new towns, he is overcome with envy. Why is he so backward, so ineffectual, so barren as a writer? Incapable of deriving his germinal material or inspiration from the outer world, he feels that he is a useless being. Introspective and self-tormented by temperament, Olesha resembled the protagonist of Thomas Mann's story, *Tonio Kröger;*[19] he was convinced that the writer's vocation brought only misery and misfortune upon him, since neither money nor fame could possibly compensate him for the occupational fate that deprived him of the simple but genuine joys of life. His creative work forced him to peer constantly into the depths of the self, and this "absorption . . . always leads in the end to the thought of death and the fear of death. . . ."[20] The hackneyed advice the unsuccessful writer in the Soviet Union is invariably given, that he should merge with the masses, proved of no help, and Olesha was tired of hearing such clichés.

He would very much like to be different: to abandon introspection and to look back with nostalgia upon the vanished past, to voice the ideals and aspirations of his people, to participate in the collective effort of creating the new Soviet man. Unfortunately, he was not equipped for such a task. In a speech he delivered at the First Congress of Soviet Writers, he admitted that Kavalerov saw the world through the eyes of the author. At first he was deeply hurt when the critics berated him for introducing a character that was vulgar, repulsive, essentially reactionary in his outlook. He wanted to feel that he was utterly wrong and that the verdict pronounced by the Communist literary critics was absolutely right.[21] Later, however, he became convinced that he must not tamely accept the verdict of the critics but fight hard to preserve the integrity of his personal vision, the freshness and purity of his perceptions. He knew he was not capable of handling "public" themes in keeping with the prescriptive criteria set forth in Socialist realism. His confession at the time sums up

19. For an analysis of *Tonio Kröger,* see Charles I. Glicksberg, *Modern Literary Perspectivism* (Dallas, Tex.: Southern Methodist University Press, 1970), pp. 45-46.
20. Olesha, *Envy and Other Works,* pp. 175-76.
21. *Ibid.,* p. 215.

not only Olesha's dilemma but also that of those writers in the Soviet Union whose political commitment did not satisfy the ideological gods. He had to humble himself, to suffer the humiliation of comparing himself to a worker or to a member of the Party. Such a comparison reduced him to a mere nothing. "How can one do that and go on writing?" To those pioneers who blazed a path through the wilderness, collectivized the land, and assured victory on all fronts, he addresses a number of questions that he considers of fundamental importance. "Who are you?" he asks. What longings take possession of you? "Do you ever dream? . . . How do you love? How do you feel about the world? . . . Do you know what tenderness is?"[22]

In the end, of course, Olesha had to give in. He had to acknowledge that he was guilty of "formalism." He had to disavow his ideological heresies. He was a great admirer of Shostakovich, the Russian composer, but then *Pravda* proclaimed its *ex cathedra* judgment that his opera was not music but cacophany. Was the writer of the article in *Pravda* wrong? But the *Pravda* article concerned itself with fundamental principles. "It is the opinion of the Communist Party; either I am wrong or the Party is wrong."[23] The latter possibility, however, is ruled out: the Party cannot be wrong. The Party correctly emphasizes the interdependence of social life and the need to labor tirelessly for the good of the people. At this point Olesha capitulates:

> If I am not in agreement with this line, in any particular context, the whole complex framework of the life about which I think and write falls to pieces for me personally. If I do not agree with the articles in *Pravda* about art then I must cease to care for a great deal in this life which seems to me fascinating.[24]

He proceeds with his penitential recital:

> If I do not agree with the Party in a single point, the whole picture of life must be dimmed for me, because all parts, all details of this picture are bound together and arise one out of the other, therefore, there must not be a single false line anywhere.[25]

22. *Ibid.*, p. 218.
23. Olesha, "About Formalism," *International Literature*, no. 6 (June 1936), p. 87.
24. *Ibid.*
25. *Ibid.*, p. 88.

That is why he readily admits "that in this matter, the matter of art, the Party is as always right."[26] Here is the petty issue to which this brouhaha finally reduced itself: the demand of the Party that the erring artist do penance by publicly admitting that in matters pertaining to art the Party is *always* right.[27]

2. *The Literary Pogrom in Action*

The directives promulgated in the Soviet Union in the name of Socialist realism were so general in meaning that they could be interpreted in a variety of ways. Karl Radek, for example, asserts that Socialist realism must follow this method: "Select all phenomena which show how the system of capitalism is being smashed, how socialism is growing, not embellishing socialism but showing that it is growing in battle, in hard toil, in sweat."[28] Fedor Gladkov, author of *Cement,* declares: "One undoubtedly should write 'what and as is' but one cannot stop at that. From the point of view of Marxian dialectics art is faced with the problem of not only portraying what is but also what should be, that is, art must present reality in motion, advancing and developing. This is party art. . . ."[29] It was this bold attempt, by means of the categorical commands that Socialist realism enjoined the writer to obey, to politicize the arts, to create that noxious oxymoron party art, and to make doctrinal conformity the touchstone of liter-

26. *Ibid.*
27. One of the themes that engaged the attention of Russian novelists dealt with the conflict between the individual and Communist society. Russian Communism demanded that the individual seek not personal but collective fulfillment. Instead of giving in to his variable moods and indulging in daydreams, he should behave according to the precepts of Marxist morality and obey the law of reason. "But man continues to defend his right to irrational impulses, impetuous love, disarming tenderness, unaccountable passions. He has vagaries of mind and heart, he dreams of freedom, he rebels against the shackles of dogma, duty, social usefulness, and political conformity. This conflict assumes tragic form because of the necessity of adaptation to new conditions created by the Revolution. The lonely fate of the individual becomes a fate of suffering and failure." Marc Slonim, *Soviet Russian Literature* (New York: Oxford University Press, 1964), p. 119.
28. Karl Radek, "Contemporary World Literature and the Tasks of Proletarian Art," in *Problems of Soviet Literature* (New York: International Publishers, 1935), p. 181.
29. Fedor Gladkov, "My Work on 'Cement', *International Literature,* no. 1 (April 1934), p. 142.

ary merit—it was this attempt that drove many writers into the refuge of silence. Those who refused to play the game were cruelly punished.

In her documented memoir about her husband, the gifted poet Osip Mandelstam, Nadezhda Mandelstam reveals the ghastly truth of the enormities committed in Russia during the years of Stalin's dictatorship. Rumors were heard in the West about these atrocities: purges, assassinations, liquidations, concentration camps, but these rumors were furiously denied by the Communist press and labeled as canards spread by the hirelings of capitalism. The melodramatic scenes enacted at the Moscow Trials were not faked. After the death of Stalin, the Party leaders denounced the cult of personality and Khrushchev divulged that the ugly rumors about Stalin's monstrous crimes were based on fact. And the widow of the persecuted poet tells the horrifying story of the reign of terror Stalin had unleashed. A woman of indomitable courage, she shared the exile of her husband. After his mysterious death, she fought to stay alive in order to safeguard his secretly hidden manuscripts and to prevent his memory from perishing in the minds of the new generation. A gifted woman in her own right, she did not succumb to the weakness of self-pity or hurl hysterical recriminations at the evil man directly responsible for her misery. She did translations (she knew French, German, and English) with her husband, but attached no importance to this work. After Osip died, she supported herself by teaching English in the provinces. Later she was appointed chairman of the Department of the English Language at a teachers' training college.

The Russia she describes is a land infested with informers: friends spy on their friends; neighbors send in reports— anonymously, of course—of the traitorous activities of their neighbors. Everyone is under suspicion. Nadezhda Mandelstam tells us of the night when the secret police visited their apartment and searched the premises thoroughly for incriminating evidence. The search and the arrest were supposedly carried out under the provisions of the law. The poet's manuscripts were carefully examined throughout the night. Nadezhda at that time did not know why her husband was arrested, and there was no point in making inquiries. To those who naively ask why such things happen, the poet Akhmatova replies: "What do you mean, *what for?* It's time you understood that people are arrested for nothing."[30] Everyone in the Soviet Union is potentially capable of betraying his country and therefore actually guilty. The friends of Mandelstam begged Gorky for help, but there was nothing he could do. In 1934, arrest followed by exile did not mean that the victim was doomed to disappear forever from the ranks of the living; the arrested person later returned from exile and was permitted to reside in Moscow. Hence the Mandelstams were not unduly alarmed, but they could not undo Osip's "treasonable" mischief in writing a poem bitterly satirizing Stalin. In one version he calls Stalin "the murderer and peasant-slayer" (p. 13). Such a flagrant case of lese majesty could not be forgiven, not by the vindictive and paranoiac Stalin.

The terrible ordeal the Mandelstams had to endure—the constant spying to which they were subjected, the arrest, the imprisonment, the exile—is told with marked restraint. The author keeps her anger and indignation under control; there are no fierce outbursts of hatred. Determined to bring the past back to life, she has not forgotten a single important detail of her journey through hell. With matter-of-fact realism she relates how she saved a number of her husband's manuscripts by hiding them or by distributing them among a number of friends who she felt could be trusted. Unfortunately most of the manuscripts were lost at the time of his sudden arrest. In her distress over her husband's plight, she appealed to Bukharin for help, but she did not tell him about the poem satirizing Stalin. In this instance, she was forced to lie. When he heard about the lines that lampooned Stalin, he washed his hands of the case.

Mandelstam had originally been sentenced to serve in a forced labor camp, but this was changed and he was exiled to the town of Cherdyn. The remarkable thing about these arbitrary punishments was that many people believed they were just. People were afraid to talk openly. It was dangerous to voice heterodox opinions. No one felt safe. "Nobody trusted anyone else. It sometimes seemed as though the whole country was suffering from persecution mania, and we still haven't recovered from it" (p. 34). Employees reported their suspicions of their fellow workers or their supervisors; students betrayed their teachers. On all sides there were infor-

---

30. Nadezhda Mandelstam, *Hope Against Hope*, trans. Max Hayward (New York: Atheneum, 1970), p. 11.

mers, recruited by the security service, who could not be identified. The Mandelstams were under constant surveillance; every move they made was watched by security agents. "We lived among people who vanished into exile, labor camps or the other world, and also among those who sent them there" (p. 37).

Yet the spark of human decency, kindness, and compassion was not altogether extinguished. Despite the ubiquitous spying, the systematic indoctrination, the harsh punishment meted out to those who disobeyed the regulations, there were some courageous souls who on occasion violated the rules. The reign of terror forced people to conceal their humane feelings, but Nadezhda Mandelstam is convinced that these feelings "are ineradicable and cannot be destroyed by any amount of indoctrination" (p. 39). Despite all the cruel suffering that fell to her lot, she continued to believe that the good in man was indestructible. During these years when terrorism knew no bounds and the vulnerable body was brutally beaten by the secret police, it was better, Nadezhda asserts, to scream than to keep silent as a way of affirming one's human dignity. "If nothing else is left, one must scream. Silence is the real crime against humanity." (p. 43). When she and her husband were sent into exile, they knew that Osip was to be "preserved."

The author of this memoir does not state her views on Communism or engage in ideological debates. She avoids political abstractions. She confines herself to the task of scrupulously recording the series of horrifying events through which she lived; she states the bare facts and allows these to speak for her. The bare recital of these facts constitutes a more damning indictment of the Stalinist regime than all the maledictions she might have hurled at the man who was responsible for these infamies. She describes the interrogation to which her husband is subjected; he readily admits that he wrote the satire. After 1937, prisoners did not as a rule emerge alive from these "interrogations," though Nadezhda did not then know for certain that this was so. Osip was deprived of sleep and questioned every night without letup. The prison where these tortures were inflicted was the Lubianka; the object was to break the spirit of the victim, destroy his will to resist, drive him over the border into insantiy.

Osip Mandelstam was a man of courage. Utterly devoted to

his work as a poet, he felt he had something important to say and refused to be browbeaten into silence. He expected to be killed by Stalin's agents, but he was resolved to speak out. He had witnessed the inhuman consequences resulting from the enforced collectivization of the land, he had seen the peasants who were starving to death, and he knew that this was all the handiwork of Stalin, whom he called a "murderer and peasant-slayer" (p. 158). Pasternak, however, blamed Mandelstam for his foolhardiness in writing a poem of this kind. He said: "How could he write like that when he's a *Jew?*" (p. 161).

The Marxian dialectic had confidently relied on the power of reason, but here in the Soviet Union the logic of the Revolution had culminated in the triumph of the irrational and the irrepressible upsurge of evil. How could one possibly gloss over this epidemic of "terror"? How account for its occurrence? Those writers who prudently made their peace with Stalin were impelled by the need not to be deprived of their creative calling. Some believed that this repressive regime would stay in power. Others kept their faith in Communism by arguing casuistically that the reported atrocities inevitably accompanied the birth-pangs of a new world.[31]

31. As this was written, *The New York Times* reported: "Two decades after his death on March 5, 1953, Stalin enjoys great latent prestige among the Soviet people and a much more favorable reputation than Nikita S. Khrushchev, the man who dared denounce him for his political purges" (*The New York Times,* March 5, 1973). Roy A. Medvedev adamantly opposed the trend that would rehabilitate the image of Stalin. He would put a stop to it by documenting the truth about Stalin's crimes. During the early thirties, the Communist Party was exalted as a religious body. It did not err and it was privy to everything that happened. "For the sake of the Party and the state a Communist had to do anything; the Revolution justified any cruelty" (Roy A. Medvedev, *Let History Judge,* trans. Colleen Taylor, ed. David Joravsky and Georges Haupt [New York: Alfred A. Knopf, 1971], p. 146). The Party did not stand in Stalin's way as he systematically got rid of those he regarded as belonging to the opposition. It was Stalin who ordered the killing of Kirov. Zinoviev and Kamenev were tried and found guilty. An unusual feature noted in the trials of Zinoviev, Kamenev, and other defendants in August 1936 is that they all confessed their part in the killing of Kirov and in planning to kill Stalin and other Soviet leaders. These men were shot and other Trotskyite "enemies" were rounded up. Radek, arrested in 1936, accused Bukharin of belonging to a secret terrorist organization. Bukharin denied the charges brought against him, but he was arrested just the same in 1937. The trial of these "enemies" of the Revolution was held in 1938. Medvedev concludes that "all these trials were completely fraudulent. They were a monstrous theatrical presentation that had to be rehearsed many times before it could be shown to spectators" (*ibid.,* p. 179).

Nadezhda describes the dazzling illusions that led the early Bolsheviks to persist in their conspiratorial course of action, even though it involved them in lies, duplicity, political murder. After the dawn of the twentieth century, a concerted attempt was made to create the ideal society, the scientific Utopia, which would guarantee happiness to all. Though this vision of the perfect social order had its roots in the humanism and democracy of the preceding century, this attachment to humanism and democracy raised barriers to the fulfillment of the dream of social justice. This age was therefore vilified as weak-willed, addicted to rhetoric and the strategy of compromise, "and people now looked for salvation in a rigid order and authoritarian discipline."[32] Stalin was installed as the Supreme Pontiff, the Leader whose commands had to be obeyed. He was the master magician who hypnotized the masses into carrying out his will. He instituted a reign of terror that transformed everyone in Russia into a victim. "Everybody is a victim—not only those who die, but also all the killers, ideologists, accomplices and sycophants who close their eyes or wash their hands. . . ."[33] Incredible as it may seem, vast numbers of "suspects" were tracked down who were at heart loyal Communists. They committed no act of treason and harbored no subversive thoughts.[34]

3. *The Age of Fear*

The commitment to Communism that Russian writers professed was not enough to prove their political trustworthiness. They had to go the whole hog: practice the art of Socialist realism, eschew the heresy of formalism, and sup-

---

32. Mandelstam, *Hope Against Hope*, pp. 254-55.
33. *Ibid.*, p. 297.
34. Eugenia Semyonovna Ginzburg, author of *Journey into the Whirlwind* (New York: Harcourt, Brace & World, 1969), was a teacher in the local university. She was married to a man who was an official in the Communist Party. Despite her unblemished record, she spent eighteen years in prison, labor camps, and Siberia. A devoted supporter of the Communist Party, she followed the Party line, though, privately, she saw no reason for idolizing Stalin, but she was careful not to voice her misgivings about Stalin. Nevertheless, she was brought under suspicion and pronounced guilty of failing to attack a professor whom she knew and expose his Trotskyist ideas. Her frantic denials could not save her. Her unmerited punishment did not lead her to repudiate her faith in the Communist Party.

port the leadership of the Party. When Stalin died, the Party did not relax its control over the printed word. Both Andrei Sinyavsky (Abram Tertz) and Yuli Daniel (Nikolai Arzhak) loved their country and its people, but they also loved the truth and were thus opposed, as storytellers, to what in Russia was known as "the cult of personality": the worship of Stalin. They were charged with the crime of smuggling their manuscripts out of the country and publishing their defamatory and slanderous works abroad. The minutes of the trial show us how the rulers of the state, which was totalitarian in structure, brazenly posed as the guardians of proletarian freedom. Sinyavsky had been an ardent Komsomolet, a member of the Communist Youth League. A number of traumatic experiences led him to lose his faith in Communism and he became a non-Marxist. He was a Jew. When his father was arrested in 1951, he caught his first glimpse of the arbitrary way in which the claims of justice were disregarded in the Soviet Union. The doctor trials in 1952 revealed the insidious spread of anti-Semitism among the Russian people.[35]

Sinyavsky had written a brilliant polemic, *On Socialist Realism,* which sharply criticized the literary dogmas the Stalinist hierarchy had originally promulgated. How absurd it was to issue specific instructions as to how fiction should be written! Sinyavsky pointed that the enforced method of Socialist realism resulted in a number of internal contradictions. He compounded his guilt, in the eyes of his accusers, by affirming his faith in the truth of reality that is brought forth by fantastic art. His contention at the trial that he was not a political writer fell on deaf ears, and he was sent to a concentration camp in Siberia. He refused to confess his "crimes." He steadfastly defended his course of action: all he had done was to champion the cause of freedom for the imaginative writer.

This notorious trial was held in February 1966. It was a foregone conclusion that the two writers would be convicted. The surprising feature of this case was that they did plead guilty as charged but maintained they had done no wrong. In effect, they put the Soviet Union on trial by demonstrating that it brooked no dissent. Yuli Daniel had protested against the barbarous purges that took place when Stalin wielded ab-

35. See Andrei Sinyavsky, *For Freedom of Imagination,* trans. Laszlo Tikos and Murray Peppard (New York and Chicago: Holt, Rinehart and Winston, 1971).

solute power. He had dared to shed light on the horrible past: the assassinations, the mass imprisonment of "heretics" and "enemies of the State," the liquidation of four to five hundred thousand victims. In *Moscow Speaking,* he had taken as his theme the belief that under no circumstances must men forfeit their humanity. They should follow the imperative dictates of their consciences. Daniel firmly argued in court "that there should be no prohibited subjects in the life of society."[36] Sinyavsky, equally outspoken and unyielding, did not deny that he had attacked the Stalinist dictatorship, but in his final plea he sought to distinguish literature proper from the bastard genre known as propaganda. His writings, he said, were neither pro-Soviet nor anti-Soviet propaganda but simply un-Soviet in content.

The Russian Supreme Court sentenced both contumacious writers to hard labor in a concentration camp—Sinyavsky, the major offender, for seven years, Daniel for five. Thirteen years after the death of Stalin the writer who deviated from the Party line was guilty of committing a crime against the State. A number of writers applauded the verdict. Mikhail Sholokhov violently attacked those critics, in and outside of Russia, who considered the punishment as unjust. These two writers were traitors.[37]

The persecution of these writers by the post-Stalinist regime aroused wider interest abroad in their work. As Mihajlov points out, the work of Sinyavsky marked a refreshing departure from the dead level of mediocrity represented by the products of Socialist realism. Sinyavsky is not bound by political norms. He pays no attention to Party directives. With the courage born of his imaginative insight he challenges the dogmas fathered by scientism and its positivistic assertions about the nature of reality. Why assume that the visible world is the sole basis of reality and that man must of necessity adjust to it? As Mihajlov says: "His vision of our horror-laden time is not social but metaphysical."[38] Fiction instinct with such an anomalous vision was not published in the Soviet Un-

---

36. *On Trial: The Soviet State versus "Abram Tertz" and "Nikolai Arzhak,"* trans. and ed. Max Hayward (New York: Harper & Row, 1966), p. 81.
37. Sholokhov declared indignantly: "I feel ashamed, not for those who slandered our homeland and flung mud at everything most sacred to us. They are amoral. I am ashamed for those who tried and are trying to defend them. . . ." *The New York Times,* April 2, 1966.
38. Mihajlo Mihajlov, *Russian Themes,* trans. Marija Mihajlov (New York: Farrar, Straus and Giroux, 1968), p. 4.

ion. Communist writers are not supposed to be concerned about questions relating to the ultimate meaning of life. Such questions relating to the ultimate meaning of life. Such questions are non-sense, the *Wletschmerz* characteristic of bourgeois capitalism, the tainted heritage of a decadent past. Man, collective man, is the architect of destiny, the creator of history. Communist life in the future will be intelligently planned and efficiently organized. In his millenarian fantasy, Trotsky declared that the morbid fear of death will eventually be overcome so that the new man will no longer cling to "stupid and humiliating fantasies about life after death."[39] The emancipated man

> will make it his purpose to master his own feelings, to raise his instincts to the heights of consciousness, to make them transparent . . . and thereby to raise himself to a new plane, to create a higher social biological type, or, if you please, a superman.[40]

Russian writers were not inspired by such apocalyptic visions. They are not tempted by such eschatological speculations but devote themselves dutifully to the task of dealing with the urgent problems of their age: the attempt to increase production quotas, the mystique of the machine and the worker's relation to it, the use of speed-up methods, the building of dynamos and tractors. Made-to-order fiction of this description was faithfully documented but woefully lacking in psychological complexity. Novelists did the best they could with such assignments.[41] They were afraid to disobey.

39. Leon Trotsky, *Literature and Revolution* (New York: Russell & Russell, 1957), p. 255.
40. *Ibid.*, pp. 255-56.
41. "Marx blamed capitalism for men's alienation from their human potential, but the industrial process is the same in any social system, no matter what kind of rhetoric is used to explain its goals. I am not here claiming that the industrial process is intrinsically antiaesthetic, or that the relationship of a man to his industrial labor is a *priori* a demeaning one. But the Soviet effort to demonstrate the contrary in hundreds of novels is surely unconvincing. The novel with a machine at its center confers moral worth on the men who tend it, according to the success with which they make it work. Men become appendages of the machine. . . . But relationships that bear the aesthetic impress of the machine cannot fail to demonstrate its tonelessness, its unvarying geometry, its statistical uniformity" (Rufus Mathewson, "The Novel in Russia and the West," in Max Hayward and Edward L. Crowley, eds., *Soviet Literature in the Sixties* [New York and London: Frederick A. Praeger, 1964], p. 8). What all this technological planning left out was the element of mystery, the *x* that represents the unknowable in the human equation.

One novelist, Alexander Afinogenov, wrote a remarkable play called *Fear*. The hero of the play, Professor Borodin, who had investigated what basically motivates the behavior of people in Russia, comes to the conclusion that in eighty percent of the cases the dominant emotion was fear.

> We live in an age of great fear. Fear compels talented intellectuals to repudiate their mothers, to lie about their social origins, to worm themselves into high positions. Fear dogs a man's footsteps. . . . We are all rabbits. How, then, can anyone work creatively?[42]

In his diatribe *On Socialist Realism,* Sinyavsky denied that the writer's picture of reality must conform to the principles of dialectical materialism. He ridiculed the philistine notion that literature must be affirmative, optimistic; that it must praise the correct leadership of the Communist Party and predict the inevitable triumph of Communism the world over; that it must create characters who, instead of being governed by their emotions, are "objectively" conditioned and suffer from no "spiritual" conflicts or contradictions. The dedicated writer reveals the forward march of history toward the end goal that Communism is destined to reach. This is the earthly paradise to be realized, this "the Purpose which Fate destined for mankind."[43]

Once writers like Sinyavsky, Daniel, and, later, Solzhenitsyn courageously set an example, the submerged forces of the opposition began to rise to the surface.[44] In 1966 a group of writers took the unheard-of step of warning the Russian leaders that the conviction of Sinyavsky and Daniel on the ground that they had slandered the Soviet Union created a dangerous precedent. The petition, signed by sixty-three

42. Quoted in Vera Alexandrova, *A History of Soviet Literature,* trans. Mirra Ginsburg (New York: Doubleday & Company, 1963), p. 42. In "I Am Afraid," Zamyatin discusses the strange silence that has overtaken Russian writers. He knows what is troubling them, what keeps them silent. "It is that literature can exist only where it is created, not by diligent and trustworthy officials, but by madmen, hermits, dreamers, rebels and skeptics." Yevgeny Zamyatin, *A Soviet Heretic,* ed. and trans. Mirra Ginsburg (Chicago and London: The University of Chicago Press, 1970), p. 57. "I Am Afraid" first appeared in 1921.
43. Abram Tertz, *On Socialist Realism,* trans. George Dennis (New York: Pantheon Books, 1960), pp. 30-31.
44. See the following works: Peter Reddaway, *Uncensored Russia* (New York: American Heritage Press, 1972); *In Quest of Justice,* Abraham Brumberg (New York: Praeger Publishers, 1972); and Abraham Rothberg, *The Heirs of Stalin: Dissidence and the Soveit Regime* (Ithaca, N. Y.: Cornell University Press, 1972).

writers, was addressed to the 23rd Congress of the Soviet Communist Party. The text of this petition[45] did not agree with the judgment of the court that the writing of Sinyavsky and Daniel was anti-Soviet. Liberal thought found expression in an underground monthly newsletter called *Political Diary,* which was circulated among a small group of Soviet intellectuals. *Political Diary* supported Solzhenitsyn's right to be published in the Soviet Union. The poet Yevtushenko, looking back upon the appalling crimes that Stalin had committed, asserts that the dictator's worst crime was the corruption of the human spirit.

45. *The New York Times,* November 19, 1966.

22

The Moral Protest of Solzhenitsyn

The central problem of socialist realism is to come to terms critically with the Stalin era. ... If socialist realism—which in consequence of the Stalinist period became at times a term of abuse, even in the socialist countries—desires to regain the level it had reached in the nineteen-twenties, then it must rediscover the way to depict contemporary man as he actually is.[1]

1. The Stormy Petrel of Russian Letters

Solzhenitsyn is the stormy petrel of Russian letters, the novelist who insists, no matter what the cost or the consequences, on divulging politically embarrassing truths. He will not submit to the restraints imposed by "the higher authorities" nor will he be swayed by their official condemnation, their campaign of vilification in the press, their harass-

1. Georg Lukács, *Solzhenitsyn,* trans. William David Graf (Cambridge, Mass.: The MIT Press, 1971), p. 10. The veteran Marxist critic from Hungary endeavors to rehabilitate the term "Socialist realism" by infusing it with a new liberalized content. He feels that it is safe to speak out and correct past errors of omission, now that the world knows of the atrocities committed during the Stalinist reign. The record shows that no one living inside Russia during that period of time was left unmarked by this traumatic experience.

ment, their decision to drum him out of the Writers' Union on various trumped-up charges. He was not to be intimidated. That is why he was considered to be dangerous and was punished severely for his refractoriness.

In the United States, the censored writers, the rebels, and the muckrakers are accorded the welcome light of publicity; their cases are covered in the newspapers; they are hailed by the avant garde as the defenders of freedom of expression. Hence they achieve a certain measure of notoriety (the artistic merit of their work is not in question at this point). Writers like Joyce, Dreiser, D. H. Lawrence, Henry Miller, James Jones, William S. Burroughs, Ken Kesey, and Allen Ginsberg became widely known because of their willingness to violate the moral conventions of their age.

But in a closed society, as in the type of totalitarian dictatorship Stalin had established in the Soviet Union, the dissenting writer was effectually silenced. Indeed, he was lucky if that was the worst fate that befell him. He could have been imprisoned or sent to a concentration camp or "liquidated." When Stalin died, hope arose that during the thaw the censorship would be lifted. But labor camps for the ideologically sinful still exist in the Soviet Union. Some protesters are diagnosed as psychotic and are consigned to mental institutions. Solzhenitsyn had been arrested on the ground that he had spread anti-Soviet propaganda among his friends. Though he was a Communist in his political beliefs, he was opposed to the Stalin cult and did not appreciate the distinctive merit of Soviet writing.

After he was released from a labor camp, he wrote *One Day in the Life of Ivan Denisovich,* which was highly praised on all sides. But Solzhenitsyn was too outspoken not to be brought under attack. His efforts to get *Cancer Ward* published were futile. He wrote a letter to the Fourth Soviet Writers' Congress, in which he denounced the censorship and the harm it did to native literature. He said that it was wrong to compel the writer to revise his manuscript at the behest of some Party bureaucrat. Imaginative literature cannot be judged by the time-conditioned standards of what is politically permissible. Literary values change in response to changes in the political climate. Dostoevski, Mayakovsky, and Bunin were once looked upon with disfavor. "Literature cannot develop in between the categories of 'permitted' and 'not permitted,' 'about this you may write' and 'about this you may not.' Literature that is not the breath of contemporary society, that dares not transmit the pains and fears of that society, that does not warn in time against threatening moral and social dangers—such literature does not deserve the name of literature. . . ."[2]

At a session of the Secretariat of the Union of Soviet Writers, Solzhenitsyn revealed the kind of persecution to which a dissident writer was subjected in Russia. His categorical denials that he had sinned ideologically produced no results. The Secretariat wanted him to make a public statement that would berate the enemies of the Soviet Union in the West for the propagandistic use they made of his work published abroad. In his own defense Solzhenitsyn countered the charges brought against him. Why should *Cancer Ward* be called anti-humanitarian when what it tries to show is that "life conquers death"?[3] Why should he conceal the truth or distort it? The writer's function is not to take sides in a political controversy. The task of the writer

> is to select more universal and eternal questions, [such as] the secrets of the human heart and conscience, the confrontation between life and death, the triumph over spiritual sorrow, the laws in the history of mankind that were born in the depths of time immemorial and that will cease to exist only when the sun ceases to shine.[4]

When *The First Circle,* which Solzhenitsyn could not get published in the Soviet Union, appeared in England and the United States where, like *Cancer Ward,* it sold very well, pressure was brought to bear on him so that he would be forced to leave the Soviet Union. In a speech addressed to collective farmers, Sholokhov, the novelist who could be depended on to support the powers that be, referred caustically to those literary pests who are eager to do the bidding of the moguls of capitalism in the West and, by using secret channels, get their work published abroad. He declared that writers in the Soviet Union wish to get rid of them.[5] Solzhenitsyn would not leave the country nor acknowledge that he was politically

---

2. *Solzhenitsyn: A Documentary Record,* ed. Leopold Labedz (New York and London: Harper & Row, 1971), p. 84.
3. *Ibid.,* p. 121.
4. *Ibid.*
5. *The New York Times,* November 28, 1969.

at fault. When he was awarded the Nobel Prize for Literature, he could not obtain a visa. The attacks on him in the Russian press did not let up. In an interview published in *The New York Times*,[6] he spoke of his painful and protracted struggle to keep on writing in the face of persecution, public abuse, and ostracism. He was denied access to Government archives for his research, his mail was examined, he was watched by the security police. What gave this man, the most gifted novelist of his land, the courage and the fortitude to stand alone?

Born on December 11, 1918, he formed early in life the ambition to become a writer. He studied mathematics at Rostov University and was proficient in his work, though he felt no inclination to spend his entire life specializing in this field. It was his proficiency in this subject that led to his being transferred from a concentration camp to a sharashka, where he stayed for four years. Later, when he was sent into exile, he was permitted to teach mathematics and physics. This position made it possible for him to resume his writing. He had graduated from Rostov University in 1941, just before Russia was invaded. At first he was assigned to drive horse-drawn vehicles; his health was poor. Later, because of his schooling in mathematics, he was sent to an artillery school, from which he graduated in November 1942 and was then given command of an artillery position-finding company. He served in this capacity on the front line until he was arrested in 1945 in East Prussia. In his correspondence with a school friend he had been incautious enough to refer to Stalin disrespectfully, though they used a pseudonym for the Soviet leader. The authorities found further damning evidence in his manuscript stories and personal reflections. This man was not to be trusted. He was sentenced in July 1945, without being present, to eight years in a detention camp.

He was an inmate of several correction work camps. Then, as a mathematician, he was transferred to the scientific institute of the MVD-MGB and there spent some years. In 1950 he was sent to the newly established Special Camps for political prisoners. In such a camp, in the town of Ekibastuzin, Kazakhstan (described in *One Day in the Life of Ivan Denisovich*), he worked at various occupations. While there he was operated on for a tumor but the condition that brought

6. *Ibid.*, April 3, 1972.

on the tumor was not cured. Only later did he learn what was wrong with him.[7] After serving the full length of his sentence he was not set free but was required to spend the rest of his life in exile in southern Kazakhistan. He was not the only one on whom such dire penalties were imposed. Such drastic punishments were at the time frequently handed out to political offenders.

In March 1953, after Stalin died, Solzhenitsyn was permitted to go out without an escort. His cancer, in the meantime, was growing worse; at the end of 1953, unable to eat or sleep, he felt that he was about to die.[8] He arrived at the cancer clinic in Tashkent (as described in *Cancer Ward*) and was cured of his carcinoma during 1954. While teaching, he secretly resumed his prose writing. He did not dare ask his close acquaintances to read his manuscripts, but he could not indefinitely preserve his secret. He wanted his work to be judged by professionally trained critics. Then, in 1961, he offered *One Day in the Life of Ivan Denisovich* for publication; it was a move fraught with danger, but this time he was lucky.

2. His Literary Contribution

To be awarded the Nobel Prize for Literature in 1970—that was a wonderful vindication for a writer whose work could not be published in his own land. The Swedish Academy singled out his three novels—*One Day in the Life of Ivan Denisovich, Cancer Ward,* and *The First Circle*—for high praise; it spoke of "the ethical force with which he has pursued the indispensable traditions of Russian literature."[9] The award granted to this proscribed writer underlined the fact that he stood head and shoulders above the ruck of approved Russian novelists who followed the precepts of Socialist realism. In an age ·of servile conformity, he disregarded the aesthetic compulsives of the Commissar in charge of letters and arts,[10] and emulated the example set by such illustrious

7. "Solzhenitsyn's Life," by Aleksander I. Solzhenitsyn, in *ibid.*, July 4, 1971.
8. *Ibid.*
9. *Ibid.*, October 9, 1970.
10. Andrei A. Zhdanov took it for granted that Soviet literature, since it exemplified the standards of Socialist realism, was infinitely superior to the bourgeois literature of the West. Earnestly he proclaimed the aesthetic gospel of Communism. "While selecting the best feelings and qualities of the Soviet man and revealing his tomorrow, we must at the same time show our people what they must not be, we must at the same time show our people what they

predecessors as Dostoevski, Turgenev, and Tolstoy. He is, of course, no Tolstoy, but he resembles him in his resolute dedication to the truth, his outspokenness, his moral courage. Like Tolstoy, he is a moralist who has been forced by the exigencies of history to take up the political theme.

Perhaps Solzhenitsyn's work might not have received worldwide attention and acclaim had the Russian cadre of leaders not committed the stupid blunder of suppressing his writings so that they had to be smuggled out of Russia and published abroad. The concerted effort to silence him failed. Much of what he wrote was based on his own experiences as a prisoner in a research institute, an inmate of a concentration camp, a patient in a cancer research hospital. His aim in writing *One Day in the Life of Ivan Denisovich* was to shatter the hypocritical pretense, the lie officially endorsed by the press, that all was well in the Fatherland of the Proletariat. Solzhenitsyn realistically portrayed life there as a vast concentration camp, a jail, a madhouse. He made the Russian people realize the they were locked, as in a prison, within an oppressive and iniquitous system, which condemned them as guilty without the formality of a trial and punished them cruelly for crimes they did not commit. They led fearful, harried lives, at the mercy of a mindless dictator who could carry out his paranoid homicidal fantasies with impunity. Like a vengeful God of old, he was omnipotent and ubiquitous, but there was this fundamental difference: Stalin was unconscionable. And the people were powerless to defend themselves against his tyranny.

They were thrust into concentration camps or prison or shipped off to Siberia for infractions of the law they were supposed to have committed in their minds. Though most men succumbed to the corruption of evil, there were always a few, Solzhenitsyn revealed, who refused to quench their spark of humanity. These were not satisfied merely to stay alive: they fought against the forces in their environment that would destroy them spiritually. Those particularly who lost everything they prized in the world could not be intimidated; they had nothing more to lose.

must not be, we must castigate the remnants of yesterday, remnants that hinder the Soviet people in their forward march. Soviet writers must help the people, the state, and party to educate our youth to be cheerful and confident of their own strength." Andrei A. Zhdanov, *Literature, Philosophy, and Music* (New York: International Publishers, 1950), p. 43.

One Day in the Life of Ivan Denisovich is supported by a wealth of concrete documentary details. The narrator, Ivan Denisovich Shukhov, is identified by a number—Prisoner 854. The penal colony in which he is imprisoned contains representatives of all strata of Soviet society, from the highest to the lowest—former administrative officials, generals, gypsies, soldiers, peasants, workers. The inmates have been rounded up and sentenced under Article 58 of the Criminal Code, which could condemn a man to prison or exile for a period of ten or twenty-five years. Solzhenitsyn depicts the conflict in these victims between their self-interest and their social idealism. "Over all of Russian society there looms the specter of the penal colony, of the informer, the torturer and interrogator, the camp guard."[11] Possessed of a rigorous moral imagination that will not compromise with the truth, Solzhenitsyn contends that men are personally responsible for their behavior. It is their duty to fight against evil and injustice, no matter what the cost.[12]

One Day in the Life of Ivan Denisovich belongs in the category of "Now-it-can-be-told" fiction. Solzhenitsyn shows that these crimes against the Russian people were the "natural" result of totalitarianism. His novel is a modern political version of Kafka's *The Trial*. The sentences imposed on these men—ten years, twenty-five years—were utterly without legal justification. Those installed in the seats of power disregarded the restraints of the law or interpreted the law to suit themselves.

11. Abraham Rothberg, *Alexander Solzhenitsyn: The Major Novels* (Ithaca and London: Cornell University Press, 1971), p. 16.
12. Unlike Sinyavsky, Solzhenitsyn does not repudiate the philosophy of Marxism (he does later on) but he is essentially a moral rather than a political writer. Though Marx was a materialist and confronted things as they are, his moral presuppositions are evident in his condemnation of the iniquities of capitalism. "His life and work seem to proclaim a unity of theory and practice, of science and advocacy, that characterizes the ethical *Weltanschauung* rather than the positive value-free science. Even his own disciples seem uncertain whether Marx revolutionised the foundations of ethics or showed that it could have no foundation" (Eugene Kamenka, *The Ethical Foundations of Marxism* [New York: Frederick A. Praeger, 1962], p. 1. Is Marxism as the *praxis* of science divorced from all moral values? Or is its revolutionary humanism profoundly ethical in content? Solzhenitsyn raises the crucial problem of how the individual is to react when the Communist Party orders him to do things that he feels are wrong. Is the Communist morally justified in defying Party commandments? Perhaps his defiance is motivated by inner weakness, by subjective factors. If he trusts his own moral convictions, he is presuming to set himself up as judge. Adam Schaff, a Polish Marxist, admits that "the final decision can only be made by the individual concerned" (Adam Schaff, *A Philosophy of Man* [New York: Monthly Review Press, 1963], p. 78).

The prisoners found that the wisest policy to follow was not to trust the future but to go on living from day to day, hour to hour, so as to eliminate all painful thoughts and safeguard themselves against the shock of disappointment. Ivan Denisovich had been charged with treason; he had been captured by the Germans and confined within a prisoner-of-war cage, but he managed to escape. His story is not believed; he must have collaborated with the Germans.[13] One Russian soldier, a machine gunner, is imprisoned because it is discovered that his father was a kulak.

The First Circle continues the indictment. Though the State-controlled press fulminated furiously against this novel, it is not a spiteful polemic, a deliberate attempt to discredit the Communist regime. If it calls attention to the abominations perpetrated by Stalin and his secret police who were recruited from all walks of life, it does so on moral grounds. The goal of Marxist humanism, the dream of founding a workers' state in which each would contribute according to his ability and receive support according to his needs, the utopian vision of a classless, egalitarian society—all this is implicitly affirmed and never repudiated. Those who are accused of seditious activity, disloyalty to the State or the Party, spying for "the enemy" (who is invisible but present everywhere), are the ones who cling to the Marxist ideal. In the name of security, people are bribed or blackmailed into spying for the regime. These informers, never identified, do their nefarious work in the home, in school, in factories, in the labor camps, and in the "sharashka" where the action in this novel takes place. This sharashka, located on the outskirts of Moscow, is called the Mavrino Institute. It houses 281 zeks, who are intellectuals trained in physics, mathematics, engineering, and linguistics. They have been brought to this Institute to work on a secret electronics project. If they prove restive or intractable, they will be relegated to a lower circle of hell—to a concentration camp in the Arctic region or Siberia. The novel recounts the events of four days, from December 24 through December 27, 1949. A new purge is

13. In his short story, "An Incident at Krechetivka Station," Solzhenitsyn touches upon the scandalous treatment accorded "returnees" during the war—"troops who had been surrounded, had capitulated to the Germans, and after being retaken by Soviet forces were being shipped off to detention camp" (Alexander Solzhenitsyn, *Stories and Prose Poems*, trans. Michael Glenny [New York: Farrar, Straus and Giroux, 1971], p. 179).

about to get under way, which will reach its climax in the Doctor's Plot in 1953.

The novel paints a revolting portrait of Stalin: his egregious vanity; the cult of personality that catered to his boundless egotism; his unmitigated cruelty to those who opposed his will; his mistrust of those who were close to him and did his bidding; his vengefulness; his obsessive fear of assassination; his chronic insomnia. Solzhenitsyn does not spare the man; he ridicules his pretensions to knowledge in the field of linguistics, his atrocious style, the inescapable limitations of his mind.

The opening scene pictures the humane impulse of a well-known young diplomat; he wishes to warn the doctor who had taken such good care of his mother against turning over any medical knowledge to the foreigners he meets abroad. A trap has been set for the doctor. State Counselor Second Rank Innokenty Volodin hesitates to make the call; he is aware that it is dangerous to use the telephone. Impulsively disregarding the danger of being caught, he tries to warn the doctor. The rest of the plot describes the intensive efforts of the Mavrino Institute to decode sound patterns so that the identity of the man who made the call can be determined.

The zeks who are assigned to the Mavrino Institute have been selected from a number of concentratons camps, where the inmates are forced to endure hardships that defy description. Compared to the place they came from, the Institute seems to offer a foretaste of heaven. Lev Rubin, the philologist, assures the newcomers that they are still inhabitants of hell, though they have been elevated to the first circle. Rubin, a Jew as well as a Communist, had served during World War II as a major in the "Section for Disintegration of Enemy Armed Forces"; his task was to induce Germans in the POW camps to work for the Russian cause behind the enemy lines. In his efforts to convert these German prisoners, he began to feel affection, even pity for them, and this led to his arrest.

The chief protagonist is Gleb Nerzhin, a man of courage and stubborn conviction. A mathematician, thirty-five years old, he is assigned to work with Rubin on the telephonic communications project. He had first sensed that something was grievously wrong in the Soviet Union when as a youngster he was revolted by the chorus of flattery reserved for Stalin and by the ghastly spectacle of the old Bolsheviks confessing their guilt in court. He regards Stalin as the evil dragon who devours all those who in his pathological judgment are or might prove to be dangerous. He has reduced the Russian people to a state of ignoble submissiveness. Many are infected with the lust for power, their demented ambition held in check by no moral principle. In this corrupt society, the mediocrities, the cunning, the sycophants, the unscrupulous, forge ahead. The police enlist a secret army of informers. At the Mavrino Institute the free employees are officers who have been trained for the job of surveillance. After graduating from the school that prepared them for this work, they were told that the zeks in the Mavrino Institute were dangerous criminals who had plotted against the Russian people.[14]

The characters in *The First Circle* are individualized; they are human, made of flesh and blood, idiosyncratic. They speak out at times on matters that concern them deeply. Nerzhin discusses the meaning of life, the secret of happiness. The years he has spent in prison developed in him the habit of reasoning things out for himself. The skepticism he had adopted saved him from the vice of dogmatism. Whereas Rubin, the dialectician, stoutly supported the penal system the Soviet Union devised under the benevolent rule of Stalin, Nerzhin is not fooled by the propaganda machine the State uses; he has rid himself of loyalties that have not undergone a critical examination. After reading the works of Lenin, he cannot stomach Stalin's pedestrian, nondescript prose. Lev Rubin asserts that the Soviet Union is making the right political moves. He virtually absolves Stalin of wrongdoing. After all, had Stalin not succeeded in industrializing the nation, collectivizing the land, and defeating the Nazi armies?

Most of the zeks are not deceived in their estimate of Stalin. Some of them are spiritually incorruptible. But those who are placed in positions of power are hypocrites and liars, men without a conscience. These favored men are granted privileges according to their rank. The offices they occupy are filled with portraits of Stalin, the Great Generalissimo,

14. "Solzhenitsyn sympathizes with those who are crushed or warped by the regime, approves of those—like Sologdin—who outwit the regime, but those he admires and loves are those who resist the regime on principle, who deny it their cooperation, who are willing to risk torture, the camps, even death for principle or their own integrity." Rothberg, *Alexander Solzhenitsyn*, p. 91.

the Most Brilliant Strategist of All Times and Peoples.[15] He is the Plowman, the Leader of all Progressive Humanity, the Best Friend of Counterintelligence Operatives.[16]

In three chapters (18, 19, and 20) Solzhenitsyn analyzes the character of Stalin, whose figure has given rise to an incredible cult of hero worship. We see him in his fortified retreat, the man whose pronouncements are echoed throughout the land, whose name is given to cities, schools, farms, battleships, factories. This little man with a double chin who is unable to sleep at night has been transformed into a legend, a myth, a veritable God. He is the infallible Leader. He is the subject of a biography that has sold millions of copies. He is afraid of doctors, medications, and injections. He wishes to live till ninety at least and be remembered forever by a grateful posterity. But there are dastardly enemies who must be disposed of, the traitor Tito for one.

Stalin has succeeded in his aim of silencing all opposition; he has revised the works of Lenin, altered the historical record, blotting out the names of those who had disagreed with him on the goals of Socialism. Now there was this upstart Tito. Stalin had taken care of all his opponents by exiling whole populations to Siberia, by locking them within a prison cell, or by having them killed. Yet he still felt insecure. Solzhenitsyn cannot forgive this despot and his monstrous fantasies of destroying at one blow his enemies the world over. Stalin's vast construction projects were glorified by the press as heroic achievements, though they had been built by slave labor.

Solzhenitsyn hates Stalin for demoralizing the character of the Russian people and for transforming Russia into a land teeming with informers. Ruska, in *The First Circle*, is repelled by the sight of people seeking and obtaining privileges. He was later urged to volunteer his services as a paid informer. Solzhenitsyn adds:

> Ruska and his whole generation had been taught to believe that "pity" was a shameful feeling, that "goodness" was to be laughed at, that "conscience" was priestly jargon. At the same time they were taught that informing was a patriotic duty, was

15. Alexsandr I. Solzhenitsyn, *The First Circle*, trans. Thomas P. Whitney (New York and Evanston: Harper & Row, 1971), p. 70.
16. *Ibid.*, p. 71.

the best thing one could do to help the person one denounced, and would improve the health of society.[17]

Outside the sharashka, informers are recruited. Veterans returning from the front are shocked by their observation of privileges granted according to rank. And literature, under Stalin's paternal supervision, is in a bad state. The books that are published are uniformly dull, for the Russian writers must subscribe to the tenets of Socialist realism. The writers who manage to survive do so by prudently avoiding tabooed subjects. Literary as well as political circles encourage the spread of anti-Semitism, though it is not called that. And Stalin is foremost in his persecution of Jews. Throughout the novel Solzhenitsyn uncovers the festering realities of life in Stalinist Russia. One zek remarks:

> Do you remember how, long ago, we read that the Ford assembly line is the most inhuman aspect of capitalist exploitation? But fifteen years have passed and now we acclaim the same assembly line, renamed the "flow line," as the best and newest form of production.[18]

In *Cancer Ward* Solzhenitsyn portrays life in a hospital where cancer patients are given specialized treatment. Even as they face the prospect of imminent death, some of them betray the fact that they suffer from a moral as well as physical source of infection. Like *One Day in the Life of Ivan Denisovich* and *The First Circle*, *Cancer Ward* is based on the author's own experiences and observations. Solzhenitsyn, like Oleg Kostoglotov, the principal character in *Cancer Ward,* had been confined in a concentration camp. While there he was operated on for the removal of cancer. Later, when he was exiled to Kazak, he found himself again stricken with cancer. The old symptoms recurred. The cancer in his stomach grew larger; the pain increased. He rushed to a hospital in Tashkent specially equipped to take care of cancer patients. "He was treated with hormones and X-rays. After roughly a dozen of the latter treatments, the tormenting pains of the past months disappeared."[19] The story of *Cancer Ward*, which opens with a scene in the Tashkent hospital, covers a period of four months in 1955.

17. *Ibid.,* p. 259.
18. *Ibid.,* p. 430.
19. David Burg and George Feifer, *Solzhenitsyn (New York: Stein and Day, 1972), p. 124.*

Solzhenitsyn passed through this terrifying experience with unabated courage. He was now able to sleep; his appetite returned. As his body recovered its strength, he was able to resume his creative work with renewed energy. *Cancer Ward* tells the story of his struggle against death, as viewed through the sensibility of Oleg Kostoglotov. Solzhenitsyn describes how the patients in this oncological hosptial were forced by their disease and their encounter with death to reexamine their lives, but this does not constitute the heart of the novel. Solzhenitsyn is more interested in looking into their political past, to determine the degree to which they were corrupted by the Stalinist regime. Lukács, in his book on Solzhenitsyn, is prompted to ask whether such works as *The First Circle* and *Cancer Ward* are political novels. He remarks:

> According to the new current in the Stalinist period, the political character of literature became manifest in its obligation to provide definite and concrete guidelines for the solution of certain current political problems; its value or lack of value depended upon whether and to what extent these solutions were able to pave the way for correct political decisions in practical life.[20]

20. Lukács, *Solzhenitsyn*, p. 77. Not until Stalin died did Lukács speak out frankly on this controversial issue. As far back as 1923, Trotsky pointed out: "Our Marxist conception of the objective social dependence and social utility of art, does not at all mean a desire to dominate art by means of decrees and orders" (Leon Trotsky, *Literature and Revolution* [New York: Russell & Russell, 1957], p. 170). He also dwells on the important fact that Marxist categories are not capable of determining what is or is not art. "A work of art should, in the first place, be judged by its own laws, that is, by the law of art" (*ibid.*, p. 178). Trotsky was forced to go into exile and was finally murdered by a hired assassin. How was it that a prolific critic like Lukács managed to survive? Lukács defends himself against the charge that he was a servile echo of the Party line during the period of Stalin's dictatorship. In his preface to a collection of essays published in Moscow and Budapest during the thirties and forties, he states that "the main direction of these essays was in opposition to the dominant literary theory of the time. Stalin and his followers demanded that literature provide tactical support to their current political policies. Accordingly, all art was to be subordinated, both in the positive and negative sense, to these needs. . . . As everyone knows, no open polemics were possible during that period. Yet I did protest consistently against such a conception of literature" (Georg Lukács, *Writer & Critic and Other Essays*, ed. and trans. Arthur D. Kahn [New York: Grosset & Dunlap, 1970], p. 7). Aczel and Meray, in reviewing Lukács' career, report that he was respected for his vast erudition, his remarkable capacity for work, and his uncanny ability to survive. He yielded on points of ideological orthodoxy in order to be able to go ahead with his work as a critic. "After World War II, he returned to Hungary as the exponent—in fact, almost the Pope—of Communist literary policies" (Tamas Aczel and Tibor Meray, *The Revolt of the Mind* [New York: Frederick A. Praeger, 1959], p. 59).

In the lecture Solzhenitsyn could not deliver in person but that the Nobel Foundation published in its yearbook, he spoke out in the accents of a Hebrew prophet denouncing the forces of evil that were rampant in his land. He referred bitterly to the prison camps where many gifted writers were incarcerated, most of whom never came out alive. "A whole national literature is there, buried without a coffin, without even underwear, naked, a number tagged on its toe."[21] What did these lost souls wish to cry out before they were cast into oblivion? He refers to the fact that in the Soviet Union men are sentenced to prison terms of twenty-five years, "solitary confinement in cells with ice-covered walls and prisoners stripped to their underclothing, insane asylums for healthy men. . . ."[22] The writer today lives in a brutal age, amoral in its crazed lust for power. Force, not justice, is the arbiter of destiny. In such a cruel world, what is the role of the writer? Solzhenitsyn carries on the humanistic tradition of the writer as the voice of social conscience. The writer is under a moral obligation to reveal the truth and report the evil that walks the earth. Proclaiming his faith in the mission of world literature[23], he calls upon writers of all nationalities to bear their share of responsibility for the unhappy condition of the world today.

The furore generated by his acceptance of the Nobel Award had hardly died down when Solzhenitsyn once more aroused the wrath of the Soviet leaders. His decision to publish *The Gulag Archipelago* abroad was a provocation not to be borne. Solzhenitsyn knew that the publication of this book in Paris would earn him the implacable enmity of the Kremlin. The Soviet security police had been trying to find out what Solzhenitsyn was up to in his writing. One woman to whom he had given a copy of *The Gulag Archipelago* so that she could hide it, was arrested and subjected to a sadistic third-degree inquisition. She broke down and disclosed the hiding place of the manuscript. After being released, she committed suicide. Solzhenitsyn had prudently not entrusted this woman with the whole body of his manuscript. Now he had to make haste and bring this book before the public. He had devised

21. Alexander Solzhenitsyn, *Nobel Lecture*, trans. F. D. Reeve (New York: Farrar, Straus and Giroux, 1972), p. 9.
22. *Ibid.*, pp. 15-16.
23. *Ibid.*, p. 30.

the one method that would deter the police and his enemies in the Soviet Union from killing him. One copy of the manuscript was kept in Europe, with explicit instruction that it be published at once in the event of his death or imprisonment.

This book was a thorn in the flesh of the Soviet authorities, for it described in detail the methods used by the secret police, the kind of life the inmates led in prison or concentration camp, the effectiveness of the spy system Stalin had organized, the devious methods employed to terrorize the entire populace. In this massive, painstakingly documented study, which contains the story of Solzhenitsyn's own experience in a concentration camp and the material contributed by about two hundred collaborators, everything is based on fact. Solzhenitsyn defends the thesis that the campaign of terror, lawless arrests, wholesale imprisonment, and ruthless liquidation of "the class enemy," were not the work of the arch-villain, Stalin; they began with the seizure of power on November 7, 1917. Lenin had actively supported such drastic measures. Lenin established the precedent for ignoring or overriding the strict letter of the law; he approved the use of terror; indeed, he was instrumental in creating the secret police. Stalin undertook the task of perfecting this nefarious system.

The Gulag Archipelago shows us why Solzhenitsyn gradually lost his faith in Communism and ceased to idealize the figure of Lenin. Why, he asks, were the Moscow trials regarded as a "mystery" during the thirties? The accused were promised that their lives or the lives of their family would be spared if they publicly confessed their "crimes." They could easily have been killed and no one would know what became of them. If they cooperated with the interrogator and played their part well in the courtroom drama, then their trial would have a salutary effect on the people in the Soviet Union.

The Gulag Archipelago is an epoch-making work. It consists of two parts and forms the first volume of a monumental tripartite investigation. It presents in great detail the deadly evidence that will necessitate a drastic revision of life in Russia after the October Revolution. Solzhenitsyn emphasizes that he has invented nothing: the cases and the statistics he cites are factually correct. Solzhenitsyn is that rare type of writer who cannot rest until he has ferreted out the truth and brought it to the attention of the world. He knew that he was risking his life in daring to reveal these ghastly secrets of the past. When the leaders of the Soviet Union learned that this "slanderous" book was to be published abroad, they decided to act at once. But what could they do? It would be politically unwise to try him in open court. Solzhenitsyn, they felt, could not be tortured to a point where he would break down. He was a world-renowned novelist who would, if imprisoned and punished, be canonized as a martyr by public opinion. Hence, what was done was to force him into exile. He decided to settle with his family in Zurich. By uprooting him from his native land, the Russian leaders felt that he would be hindered in his "seditious" activities and no longer be able to stand forth as the peerless champion of the right to dissent.

Why does Solzhenitsyn call *The Gulag Archipelago* "an experiment in literary investigation"? What is "literary" about this copiously documented investigation? Solzhenitsyn devised a method that lifted his mass of material above the pedestrian level of mere factuality. He illuminates his narrative by refracting it through the prism of his imagination. He portrays with empathy the fate of the victims, the suffering they had to endure, the fiendish tortures to which they were subjected. He does not hesitate to pass judgment on these monstrous crimes committed against humanity. Why did all this happen? Why were the chosen victims so apathetic, so submissive, waiting patiently for the knock on the door in the middle of the night? Why did they not unite their forces agsint the imprisonment of innocent people? Solzhenitsyn blames them for putting up no resistance.

This literary enhancement of his tale of woe does not depend on the dubious technique of "fictionalizing" the historical events he relates. In 1929-30, millions of the dispossessed "kulaks" were forced to migrate. Since there were too many of these "kulaks" to be accommodated in the available space in the Soviet prisons where interrogations were held, they were sent to the Gulag territory. Solzhenitsyn branded this forced resettlement of a whole people "an ethnic catastrophe."[24] There were few kulaks among these farmers and peasants who were deprived of their land and driven like cat-

---

24. Aleksandr I. Solzhenitsyn, *The Gulag Archipelago 1918-1956: An Experiment in Literary Investigation,* trans. Thomas P. Whitney. (New York: Harper & Row, 1974), p. 54.

tle to the concentration camps established in the icy terrain where few inmates could survive. The epithet "kulak" was used as a means to besmirch their character, cast aspersions on their loyalty to the Soviet Union, and thus justify the decision to destroy them. Article 58 covered all contingencies of crime, actual or potential, proved or suspected. As Solzhenitsyn made clear in *The First Circle,* Article 58 could be invoked to punish any act the arrested person was accused of; it could also be employed to punish those who failed to act in a given situation. They were considered guilty if they betrayed an *intention* to work against the Revolution.

In this intensive paranoid hunt for "traitors," "saboteurs," and "spies," informers could single out anyone they pleased as an "enemy" and report his alleged misdeeds to the secret police. Students, actuated by patriotic motives, informed against professors who, while quoting lavishly from the writings of Marx and Lenin, never referred to the published works and oracular utterances of Stalin. Guilt and innocence were terms stripped of any precise substantive meaning. Solzhenitsyn describes what took place at the so-called interrogations, when inhuman methods of torture sooner or later induced the prisoner to "confess." For these victoms were completely alone; they were led to believe that their family and friends were under arrest. They were told that abundant proof of their guilt had been turned in. In 1937, however, the jails were so badly overcrowded that the prisoners tightly packed in a cell could find no space to move in. Solzhenitsyn seeks to determine who was responsible for this state of affairs. Stalin was absolutely necessary in order to carry out a purge on such a gigantic scale, but the Communist Party cannot be cleared of blame; they were guilty of complicity in these crimes. The great majority of those in power were extremely zealous in apprehending others, working without a qualm to destroy the career and end the life of Bolsheviks who had been their friends or comrade-in-arms. They obeyed with alacrity the orders emanating from above, never pausing to question the truth of the charges brought against these doomed men. They were willing to cooperate fully with the authorities—until the time came when they were arrested and thrust into a prison cell. No one protested against this monstrous perversion of justice. The leading Bolsheviks, when caught in the net, were contemptible in their craven submission. Their ideology did not give them the moral strength to bear up under these cruel blows of adversity. The mass arrests during 1937 and 1938, the staged trials in which the accused publicly confessed the atrocious crimes they had planned and committed against the Soviet Union—if all this material is examined in detail, "the principal revulsion you feel is not against Stalin and his accomplices, but against the humilatingly repulisve defendants. . ." (p. 130).

Why were the Russian so easily corrupted—and rendered silent? Why did they lack the moral stamina to resist? Man is so constituted, Solzhenitsyn maintains, that he requires some principle of justification for his evil deeds. The Russian masses and their unscrupulous leaders found casuistic support for their evildoing in ideology, which Solzhenitsyn shrewdly defines as the social doctrine that enables the transgressor to regard his acts as good in his own estimation and in that of others, "so that he won't hear reproaches and curses but will receive praise and honor" (p. 174). Then Solzhenitsyn goes on to say that it was because of ideology that "the twentieth century was fated to experience evildoing on a scale calculated in the millions. . . . Without evildoers there would have been no Archipelago" (p. 174). Here at last is a writer who refuses to be taken in by the smokescreen of ideology or by the semantics of moral relativism. He identifies evil as evil. Throughout life man is engaged in a Manichaean battle between the forces of good and evil. Solzhenitsyn believes that man seeks the good but he is tempted and falls into evil ways. Up to a certain point he is still capable of being redeemed. If in his unbridled lust for power he goes beyond that point, he forfeits his humanity and turns into a ravening beast.

Though the hideous crimes of the past have finally been brought to light, the cult of evil that perpetrated these crimes is not publicly condemned. The killers are exonerated on the ground that it was not the fault of anyone in particular. If the accuser dwells on the atrocities committed by Stalin and his band of professional torturers and assassins, he is reproached for opening old wounds. The arch-criminals, when confronted with their dastardly misdeeds, see no good reason why they should be punished. All that belongs to the dead past. Why is this horrendous debt of guilt not paid by these criminals who scoff at all vapid talk about justice? Why have they not been tracked down and brought to trial? They betray no sign of wrongdoing, no hint of remorse. Solzhenitsyn then forthrightly announces what these evil men must do as a form of penance. He does not propose that they be shot or tortured by the fiendish methods the secret police under Stalin employed. What he demands is that all these men be brought to trial so that the world will know the nature of their crimes. Each one must be compelled to confess in a loud voice: "Yes, I was an executioner and a murderer" (p. 177).

A man of indomitable faith, Solzhenitsyn has carried out his self-appointed task of making the truth about Gulag known to the world. He wanted the Russian people in particular to hear, in his documentary report, the rhythm of the slave transports, the cattle cars rolling through the peaceful countryside with their tightly packed cargo of victims. He wanted his fellow men in the Soviet Union to hear the piercing cries of these sufferers, "the complaints of those who have been plundered, raped, beaten to within an inch of their lives" (p. 586). This experiment in literary investigation endeavored to convey to an unsuspecting and incredulous world the meaning and the truth of the Stalinist reign of terror. "In the deep, deaf stillness of midnight, the doors of the death cells are being swung open—and great-souled people are being dragged out to be shot" (p. 591).

Critics abroad are puzzled by Solzhenitsyn's career: his acclaim in the West, the furious attacks on his work in the Soviet Union. A staunch Socialist like Raymond Williams in inclined at first to be suspicious of this writer: does Solzhenitsyn have clean hands? Is he for or against Communism? Are his books designed to aid and comfort the anti-Communists in the West? Williams clears him of all blame and looks upon him not only as a genuinely Russian writer but also as a social realist, a humanist. He finds that Solzhenitsyn, in his "interests, his values and his methods is in some very important ways an identifiably Soviet writer. . . ."[25] Williams asserts that Solzhenitsyn has been profoundly influenced by the experience of the October Revolution, and this influence is present in his work. Thus he finally gives the Russian novelist a clean bill of health.

25. Raymond Williams, "On Solzhenitsyn," in *Literature in Revolution*, ed. George Abbot White and Charles Newman (New York and Chicago: Holt, Rinehart and Winston, 1972), p. 321.

At the other extreme is Geoffrey Clive, who denies that Solzhenitsyn, despite his persistent concern with the frightful evils of Stalinist misrule, is basically interested in developing the political theme. Like Tolstoy, Clive tells us, Solzhenitsyn is engaged chiefly in exploring metaphysical issues, the sphere of the spiritual, the effort of the inner man to achieve authenticity of being.

> The major theme of Solzhenitsyn's fiction is the inconsequence of politics. This judgment may at first strike the reader as perverse, considering Solzhenitsyn's repeated and impassioned preoccupation with the theory and practice of Communism in the Soveit Union. Nevertheless, not unlike Turgenev in his chronicle of events in Russia, from serfdom in *Sportsman's Sketches* to the analysis of the "back to the people" movement in *Virgin Soil*, Solzhenitsyn, though intensely absorbed with the Soviet political scene in general and Stalin's machinations in particular, focuses his attention on the perennial dilemmas of human existence."[26]

If Solzhenitsyn resembles Turgenev in some respects (he lacks the latter's tragic sense of life, his melancholy, his lifelong obsession with the finality of death), he has a closer tie to Tolstoy.

Clive's contention that Solzhenitsyn is fundamentally an existential novelist would be more convincing if Solzhenitsyn had been portrayed as in conflict with himself and his age. Thrust by the vicissitudes of the historical situation into a country ruled by a paranoiac dictator in the name of Communism, Solzhenitsyn absorbed the ideologies of his age. He believed in Communism and he venerated the figures who had been responsible for the triumph of the Revolution. His arrest and imprisonment, the years he spent in a concentration camp, his exile, the knowledge he gained of what was taking place in the Soviet Union—all this forced him to tackle the political theme, though at bottom he was not a believer in dialectical materialism. Though he has painted an unsparing picture of the beast in man, he has not fallen into despair. He has rejoiced in the power of the few who will not under any circumstances betray their faith. Character can overcome the pressure of adverse circumstances. As he indicated in *The*

26. Geoffrey Clive, *The Broken Icon: Intuitive Existentialism in Classical Russian Fiction* (New York: The Macmillan Company, 1972), pp. 129-30.

First Circle, some men, even under inhuman conditions, manage to preserve their integrity and self-respect. Had Solzhenitsyn not been a victim of the Soviet system, he would surely have dwelt at greater length and with greater insight on those aspects of human existence that transcend the plane of economic determinism. He is aware of the meaninglessness of death but fails to grasp its tragic impact on the life of man.

Part VI
CONCLUSION

23
Conclusion

The modern artist who longs impotently for a time when he can be released from interior struggle in order to take his values outwardly from external society only reveals his own inner bankruptcy.[1]

The revolutionary writer must reason as follows: "Today, we are working at our typewriters, but we ought to be aware that, tomorrow, these machines may be replaced by machine guns. Today, we are soldiers whose only weapon is the pen; tomorrow, or the day after tomorrow, we shall be fighting with guns."[2]

The actual fact was that Russia had become in the Stalin period a powerful, industrialized country with an enslaved, miserable, poverty-stricken population, with an economy best described as state-monopoly capitalism, and with a political system of führerist police-state variety; and the empire was an extension of all this to captive peoples abroad. In the official illusion, however, the U.S.S.R. appeared as the realization of man's dream of social utopia, a land of progress and prosperity, where all the economic problems were solved or in process of solution, where culture was in flower, where freedom and justice prevailed, where nearly everybody was happy.[3]

In the end every attempt to place literature under the aegis of politics is a mistake.[4]

1. D. S. Sarage, *The Personal Principle* (London: Routledge, 1944), p. 112.
2. Paul Nizan, *The Watchdogs: Philosophers and the Established Order,* trans. Paul Fittingoff (New York and London: Monthly Review Press, 1971), p. 127.
3. Robert C. Tucker, *The Soviet Political Mind* (New York and London: Frederick A. Praeger, 1963), p. 174.
4. Albert William Levi, *Humanism and Politics* (Bloomington and London: Indiana University Press, 1969), p. 346.

Communism, if seen as the most radical expression of a utopian society, permeates all contemporary literature.[5]

1. Recapitulation

Considerations of space compel me to call a halt to the critical examination of literature on the international scene and its connection with politics. I have therefore had to omit a discussion of the problem of literary commitment in Hungary, Poland, West Germany, East Germany, and the United States. Enough material bearing on this topic has been presented to warrant the conclusions I have drawn.

We have seen that the development of twentieth-century literature in Europe, the United States, and Russia was overshadowed by the political obsession. Today this obsession seems to have reached its peak. It is taken for granted that everything in the world is today influenced by the power of politics. Books are published with such unlikely but impressive titles as: *The Politics of Heroin, The Politics of Ecstasy, The Politics of Religion, The Politics of Sex*, and so on.[6] Every aspect of experience is affected by the ubiquitous, if at times hidden, influence of politics.[7]

In conducting this inquiry into the meaning of "commitment" as applied to the imaginative writer and his work, I have pointed out that this comprehensive term is instinct with ambiguity. The Marxist critics assume that they have established the unitary and unequivocal meaning of "commitment," and they never let up in their drumbeat of insistence

5. Jürgen Rühle, *Literature and Revolution,* trans. Jean Steinberg (New York and London: Fredrick A. Praeger, 1969), p. 314.
6. "Everything, in a way, is political, and a book with the title of 'Politics and Film' must, like books on politics and poetry, politics and art, or politics and religion, be marked by the writer's personal inclination." Leif Furhammar and Folke Isaksson, *Politics and Film,* trans. Kersti French (New York and Washington: Praeger, 1971), p. 6.
7. It is interesting to note that whereas English writers in the nineteenth century were formerly regarded as unconcerned about the business of politics, books of late have begun to appear that demonstrate that this interpretation was mistaken. In his introduction to *Literature and Politics in the Nineteenth Century,* the editor states that the assumption that guided him and the other contributors was "the very obvious one, that nearly all the great nineteenth-century writers, and many of the minor ones, at one time or another in their careers chose to confront political issues in their work" *(Literature and Politics in the Nineteenth Century,* ed. John Lucas [London: Methuen & Co., 1971], p. 1).

on the necessity and desirability of such a form of commitment. Nizan declares: "Indeed, impartiality and indifference to practical matters are decidedly partisan atittudes."[8] Like Sartre, he contends that it is impossible not to choose. Even abstention or professed neutrality betrays our preference. Sartre, who is one of the leading exponents of the ethic of commitment, means by it a quasi-religious dedication to the revolutionary cause. To be modern is to be an advocate of revolution, and in democratic countries the ideology of revolution can be preached with comparative safety.

> Revolution is the daily fare of our affluent consumer society, the minimal requirement of any citizen wishing to share in society. Whoever is not a revolutionist in current French society (and, I venture, throughout the world) is feeble-minded, reactionary, egotistical, and exploitative—damned both morally and intellectually as a worthless idiot.[9]

Art, in our time of trouble, is expected to adopt a revolutionary stance. The art of painting, the novel, poetry, the drama, films, "happenings" are all required to be revolutionary in content.

But the rise of "politicized" literature in the modern age seems to bear out the point stressed throughout this study that the proliferation of political themes, the attempt to create "proletarian" literature, the overall strategy of commitment, and the use of Communist symbols did not result in the production of "great" works of art. The cult of Socialist realism gave birth to no novels that could compare with the fiction of Dostoevski or Turgenev, no plays that could possibly rival the dramatic heritage bequeathed by a Chekhov, a Strindberg, or an Ibsen. What does all this indicate?

It does not "prove" that the writer should heed the lesson of the past and refuse to lend his talent to a political party or a political cause. He is free to decide what he should do with his life. In this respect, no one can restrict his freedom of choice. In the end he discovers that he cannot with impunity run counter to the prompting of his conscience. He is the one who in the final analysis must pass judgment on himself. In this existential crisis, no Father Confessor can grant him

8. Nizan, *The Watchdogs*, p. 43.
9. Jacquest Ellul, *Autopsy of Revolution*, trans. Patricia Wolf (New York: Alfred A. Knopf, 1971), p. 174.

absolution. He must absolve himself, if he can. Perhaps the finest comment on Ezra Pound, the confused man of politics and superbly gifted but irascible poet, is the one made by E. E. Cummings. Cummings knew that every artist is driven to explore a country that is without limits: the inner self. If he betrays that country, he has in effect committed suicide. But if, throughout all the temptations that beset him, he remains true to himself, he achieves "immortality."[10]

There is, to be sure, a connection between literature and politics. Greek drama—for example, *The Trojan Women* and *Antigone*—was often political in content. Aristophanes used his comedies as a medium of propaganda for the cause of peace. After his period of exile in Siberia was over, Dostoevski attacked the beliefs of the revolutionaries. He had become converted to Christianity. He developed into a mystic, a rabid reactionary. Thomas Mann, who early in his career published a book affirming his unpolitical stand, was forced to take up the political struggle when the Nazis seized power in Germany.

It is difficult to recapture the climate of thought during the thirties that induced many intellectuals to support Communism or join the Communist Party. Writers like Koestler, Malraux, and Spender saw Communism as the only positive force that could defeat Fascism. What drew them to Communism was the vision it held up of an ideal commonwealth that did not transform the individual into a robot. They were convinced that in the classless society of the future the State would disappear, the Party would cease to exist. The new mán, released from all external restraints, will inherit the earth. But the neo-Pavlovian version of man denied the reality of his inner decisions. "Man is 'hollow.' He has no wishes, instincts, emotions, drives, or impulses, no reservoir of energies emanating from the environment and the person's reflex response."[11]

But Communism, as practiced in the Soviet Union, constituted a flagrant violation of the humanist ideal formulated in Marx's *Economic and Philosophical Manuscripts.* The intellectuals in the West were disillusioned by what they learned of conditions in the Soviet Union: the censorship of literature, the arrest and imprisonment of dissident writers, the purges,

10. Quoted in *The New York Times,* November 2, 1972.
11. Tucker, *The Soviet Political Mind,* p. 109.

the Moscow Trials, the Doctors' Plot. When the Stalin-Hitler
pact was signed, a number of writers resigned from the
Communist Party. They rejected the double-dealing abstractions that dialectical materialism had fed them. They questioned the underlying meaning of the Marxist thesis that the
recognition of necessity represents the fullest manifestation
of human freedom. According to the Marxist lexicon, freedom means "being conscious of necessity."[12] The intellectuals
knew at first hand the difference between the freedom that
the democracies in the West granted its citizens[13] and the
measure of freedom Stalin allowed the Russian people.[14]

From their failures, their disillusionments, their defeats
and betrayals, the intellectuals on the Left learned to be less
credulous and more critical in their attitude toward Communism. Methodological doubt saved them from yielding to
the spellbinding appeal of the Marxist faith and the total
political commitment to which this led. They gave up their
naive admiration of the professional Communist, who is sure
of his purpose in life and who makes the confused bourgeois
liberal seem small by comparison. The Communist knows
what he wants to achieve in his stay on earth and forges

12. George Plekhanov, *The Role of the Individual in History* (New York: International Publishers, 1940), p. 16.
13. Popper points out that the Marxists speak slightingly, even contemptuously, of
the liberal's adherence to the cause of "formal" freedom, yet this disparaged
formal freedom is essential to the life of the democratic state; it implies that
the electorate have the power to protect themselves against bad laws and to
oust the regime that does not truly represent them. This is one important
check on the abuse of political power. As Popper says: "And since political
power can control economic power, political democracy is also the only means
for the control of economic power by the ruled." K. R. Popper, *The Open Society and Its Enemies* (London: Routledge and Kegan Paul, 1945), 2: 119.
14. Observe how Christopher Caudwell interprets the idea of freedom and free
will. "To have become a dialectical materialist is to have been subject to
exploitation, want, anxiety, insecurity; to have had one's barest human needs
denied or one's loved ones tormented or killed in the name of bourgeois liberty, and to have found that one's 'free will' alone can do nothing at all, because one is more bound and crippled in bourgeois economy than a prisoner
in a dungeon." Trapped in this hopeless condition he comes to realize that
the only way in which he can improve his lot is by cooperating with those of
his fellow men who are confined in the same dungeon: the proletariat of the
world. By means of this cooperation he discovers the laws that are drawn
from the nature of society. Then one has thrown off the role of bourgeois
philosopher and become a *bona fide* dialectical materialist. "One has seen how
men can leave the realm of necessity for that of freedom, not by becoming
blind to necessity, or by denying its existence, but by becoming conscious of
it." Christopher Caudwell, *Further Studies in a Dying Culture,* ed. Edgell
Rickword (London: The Bodley Head, 1949), p. 256.

straight ahead. Fanatical in his devotion to the Revolution, he plunges fearlessly into battle. He gives himself wholly to the mystique of action and is deterred by no introspective nonsense. For him the main thing is to succeed, without regard for scruples of conscience. His devotion to the Party supersedes all other considerations. History, he is certain, is on his side.[15]

The ex-Communists had to vindicate themselves, though it was painful for them to confess the whole truth about their experiences in the past and the series of events that made them leave the Party. The fellow travelers had considerably less difficulty in breaking away. Gide aroused a storm of controversy when he published his report of conditions in the Soviet Union. The Communists felt that he had dealt the cause a treacherous blow. Malraux, whom the Communists had admired greatly for his novels, severely criticized the foreign policy of the Party. André Breton exposed the crimes of the Stalinist dictatorship.

Unlike Sartre, Camus in *The Rebel* refused to serve the Communist cause. He questioned its messianic, utopian vision of the future, its faith in the necessity for revolutionary violence, its mystical exaltation of the character of the proletariat, and its casuistic justification of all forms of action, however illegal or immoral, that lead to the ultimate triumph of the Revolution. Camus charges that the Soviet Union, in its concerted drive to achieve technological supremacy, speeded up the process of production and reduced the workers on the assembly line to animated robots.[16] The revolution

15. See Joseph Needham, *History Is on Our Side* (New York: The Macmillan Company, 1947). Daniel Bell remarks: "It is this commitment to the 'absolute' that gives Bolshevism its religious strength. It is this commitment which sustains one of the great political myths of the century, the myth of the iron-willed Bolshevik. Selfless, devoted, resourceful, a man with a cause, he is the modern Hero." Daniel Bell, *The End of Ideology* (Glencoe, Ill.: The Free Press, 1960), p. 281.

16. In the strenuous campaign to fulfill the Five-Year Plan, the Communist Party in Russia expected writers to turn out material that would stimulate industrial production. "Special writers' brigades were mobilized and given such assignments as describing conditions in Siberian manufacturing plants or in the Donbas coal mines" (Marc Slonim, *Soviet Russian Literature* [New York: Oxford University Press, 1964], p. 157). The industrial process was lyrically glorified in fiction, which consisted chiefly of reportage. *Cement* (1925), by Gladkov, represents a model of Communist ideology parading as a novel. Pilnyak's *The Volga Flows into the Caspian Sea* (1930) describes the building of a dam. Kataev's *Time, Forward!* introduces the technological theme into the Russian novel. Whereas much of modern literature in the West protested bitterly

that was supposed to usher in a golden age of brotherhood, equality and justice culminated in a despotic empire governed by fear, suspicion, paranoia and the terrors of hell. Camus rightly observed that this apocalyptic revolutionary struggle resulted in the tragedy of nihilism. Unlike the committed revolutionary, the rebebel is not the slave of absolutes. He sets himself limited aims and strives for what is humanly possible. At the very end of *The Rebel*, Camus affirms that, despite the man-wrought disasters of history, all of us "are preparing a renaissance beyond the limits of nihilism."[17]

The writer in the Soviet Union, as the historical record shows, was worse off than his counterpart in the West. After an early period of largely unhampered freedom in the practice of the seven arts, painters as well as novelists had to conform to a body of externally imposed standards. The ideology that informs a work was said to constitute its most essential element. In *Art and Revolution*, John Berger distinguishes between those works which are meant to produce an immediate short-range effect and those works which are meant to endure.[18] Art that is intended to last does not serve as a guide or spur to political action; it is not a vehicle for propaganda. In order to protect Russia against its treacherous enemies within its borders and in the hostile world outside, Stalin kept a vigilant, inquisitorial eye on the activity of writers, artists, and intellectuals. From the time of Lenin on, the leaders of the Russian Communist Party were not so naive as to grant the "enemy" (and he was always at work underground, deadly in his machinations) freedom to overthrow the Communist State. The only freedom they recognized was "proletarian" freedom.[19] All writings that disputed or deviated from the ideology of Marx, Engels, Lenin, and (for thirty years) Stalin were banned, and the disseminators of such seditious ideas severely punished. The first five years or so after the October Revolution had witnessed a feverish burst of experimentation in literature, but then the period of repression began. Heretical writers were denied the right to

against the increasing mechanization of life, Soviet writers enthusiastically blessed the fruitful marriage of man and the machine.

17. Albert Camus, *The Rebel*, trans. Anthony Bower (New York: Alfred A. Knopf, 1961), p. 305.
18. John Berger, *Art and Revolution: Ernst Neizvestny and the Role of the Artist* (New York: Pantheon Books, 1969), p. 54.
19. See nn. 12, 13, and 14 in this chapter.

publish their work. Many were arrested, imprisoned, tortured, and put to death. The brutal censorship exercised by Stalin's secret police and their army of anonymous informers surpassed anything the Spanish Inquisition ever attempted.

I have listed some of the victims of the campaign, which began under Lenin, to root out counterrevolutionary conspiracies. Mayakovsky, who could not be indicted on this score, committed suicide when he incurred the hostility of the Party leaders and of the fickle public whom they had turned against him. Mandelstam, because of his satire of Stalin, was put out of the way. Those writers who violated the canons of revolutionary orthodoxy were, like Olesha, forced to do penance in public. Those writers who were lavishly praised for their delineation of life in the Fatherland of the Proletariat had to fulfill all the doctrinaire requirements included in the cult of Socialist realism.

2. Gorky and the Conflict between Art and Politics

The harsh repressive measures Stalin forced upon the cultural life of the Russian people were not without precedent. They merely carried to a psychopathological extreme the paranoia of persecution that seems to be inherent in the ideology of Communism when it has gained control of the State. Lenin himself set the pattern by establishing the dictatorship of the Communist Party over the Russian people. The clash between Gorky and Lenin over the question of the freedom of art and the imposition of censorship foreshadowed on a small scale the cruel methods of totalitarian control Stalin would use in destroying all sources of opposition.

How did this conflict between Gorky and Lenin arise? For Gorky has not been considered a dissident. He has been fulsomely eulogized as "the first practicing Socialist realist."[20] This enthusiastic critic points out that for Gorky, unlike Tolstoy, the goal of Socialist humanism could be reached only by means of proletarian revolution. For Gorky the only basis for the regeneration of mankind was "the dictatorship of the proletariat."[21] The literature of Socialist realism is not

20. A. Lavretsky, "Gorky on Socialist Realism," *International Literature,* no. 4 (April 1937), p. 87.
21. *Ibid.,* p. 97.

infected with the spirit of pessimism; it is not decadent in content or nihilistic in outlook. It glorifies the contribution of labor, it supports the Stakhanov movement. Gorky demanded that the writer portray man not only as he is but as he should be.[22]

Early in his career as a writer, Gorky dedicated himself to the revolutionary ideal. He believed that Lenin, a born leader, would inspire the working class to rise up and defeat the ruling class and firmly seize the reins of power. Then the new man, liberated from ignorance, superstition, and economic slavery, would emerge. Gorky believed that the Revolution would effect this profound moral transformation in the life of man. Lenin, he found, judged every problem that came up solely in the light of politics. The Bolsheviks expected Gorky to create a work of fiction that would be truly revolutionary in content. They wished to enlist the aid of the writer in enlightening the masses and imbuing them with revolutionary courage. Gorky wrote *Mother* (1907-8), which he wrote, according to an American scholar, "as the conscious voice of the revolutionary proletariat. . . ."[23] The leading

22. A. Fadeyev at one point defined Socialist realism as follows: "it ought to show people not as they are but as they ought to be" (Ilya Ehrenburg, *Post-War Years 1945-1954*, trans. Tatiana Shebunina [Cleveland and New York: The World Publishing Company, 1967], pp. 164-65). Fadeyev was a loyal supporter of Stalin's policy, never pausing to question whether it was just. Ehrenburg pens this curious defense of Fadeyev's relentless persecution of Russian writers whom Stalin had singled out as "enemies" of the Revolution. "Undoubtedly Fadeyev knew that Babel was no 'spy', that Zoshchenko was no 'enemy', that Stalin's dislike of Platonov and Grossman was unfounded, but he also knew that for many millions of courageous and self-sacrificing people Stalin's word was law" (*ibid.*, p. 165).

23. Irving Weil, *Gorky* (New York: Random House, 1966), p. 17. Weil calls *Mother* "that paragon of Socialist Realism and *bête noire* of most of Gorky's non-Communist critics" (*ibid.*, p. 54). He adds these remarks: "A whole Marxist generation found inspiration and encouragement in Gorky's whole-hearted and vigorous espousal of revolutionary doctrine. The expression of faith, uncomplicated by psychological complexities, does not necessarily make a bad work of art. . . . And *Mother* is nothing if not a depiction of the lives of revolutionary saints and martyrs" (*ibid.*, p. 54). A close reading of *Mother* does not lend support to Weil's perfervid overestimation of this tendentious novel. It is a roman à thèse, a doctrinaire prototype of what later was labeled "the proletarian novel." It is an edifying moral tale with idealized working-class characters while those who belong to or defend the ruling hierarchy—the factory owners, the police, the members of the middle class—are portrayed as blackguards, heartless, rapacious, unconscionably cruel in their treatment of those workers who protest against conditions as they exist. Pavel, the son, assures his mother that all workers are comrades, dedicated to the task of creating a new and better world. "We are all children of one mother—the great, invincible idea of the brotherhood of the workers of all countries over all the

spirits of the revolutionary underground felt that he was the ideal candidate for becoming the founding father of proletarian literature. He had achieved some fame in the middle nineties as the creator of superb stories about down-and-out characters. He had risen from "the lower depths" and had lived the kind of life these tramps and outcasts led. Lenin in 1910 praised Gorky as the most talented representative of proletarian art.

The revolutionaries did not know the character of this man. He did not, as an artist, fit the conception they had of him. He was not convinced that art is class-born and class-conditioned. His dramatis personae in the short stories consisted of vagabonds, pariahs, beggars, derelicts, the dregs of society; he understood these rootless creatures and what motivated their hankering after "freedom," even if it meant they would have to endure hardships and privations of the worst kind. In *Foma Gordeyev* (1900), he portrayed the nihilistic impulse that takes possession of a merchant's son. The protagonist seeks to subdue his restless, questioning intellect; he tries to overcome his fear of sickness, old age, and death by giving free rein to his sexual appetite, by wallowing in drunkenness, by committing reckless deeds. Those around him can not understand what ailed him. He is fed up with the paltry business of making money. What does he want money for? He has inherited more than he needs. He cries out in anguish: "My soul aches because it's not willing to accept things. It's got to know the answers. How to live? To what purpose?"[24] He cannot bear this life he is leading. He searches for a meaning that will justify his life but cannot find it. "Can it be that a man is born just to work, to make money, build a house, breed children, and die? I don't believe it; there must be some meaning to life. A man's born,

earth." (Maxim Gorky, *Mother*, trans. Isidore Schneider [Secaucus, N. J.: The Citadel Press, 1972], p. 38.) The mother is gradually converted to the faith in Communism and becomes the saintly, martyred heroine. At the end, when she is caught carrying illegal pamphlets, she cries out: "Arise you working people! you are the masters of life!" (*ibid.*, p. 399). Gorky has produced a didactic tract. Alexander Kaun points out that "Gorky has come to agree with most of his critics, namely, that the novel suffers from weakness of characterization and too obvious didacticism" (Alexander Kaun, *Maxim Gorky* [New York: Jonathan Cape & Harrison Smith, 1931], pp. 556-57). The dramatization of Gorky's novel by Brecht was first produced in Berlin in 1932. (See Bertolt Brecht, *The Mother*, trans. Lee Baxandall [New York: Grove Press, 1965].)

24. Maxim Gorky, *Foma Gordeyev* (London: Lawrence & Wishart, 1956), p. 172.

lives, and dies. What for? We've got to find out what we live for."[25] His metaphysical quest ends in failure.

It is significant that Gorky's first novel tackles the theme that appears so often in nineteenth-century Russian fiction, the utter meaninglessness of life. Foma Gordeyev is not simply the victim of socioeconomic forces; the universe of being seals his doom. The mechanistic view of life deprives him of the will to live. His paralysis of will "derives from a vision of biological evolution overlaid with a heavy Schopenhauerian color."[26] In this unequal contest, Nature is inevitably the victor and sentences the individual to death. Man is a predestined victim of the biological will, for life is devoid of purpose. Such a plumbing of the depths by Gorky, his awareness of the alienation of man in the cosmos, would seem to indicate that he was not the kind of writer who would readily accept and act upon the simplistic imperatives of proletarian fiction. Gorky was by no means the pillar of ideological rectitude that he has been credited with being or the pioneer who prepared the way for the fulfillment of Socialist realism.

Though he was a friend of Lenin and recognized his genius, they were at odds on a number of important issues. They entertained surprisingly different conceptions of the nature of man. They differed, too, "in attitude toward the autonomy of the artist in relation to classes, parties, and organs of censorship and control; in their views of the role literature and art should play in the informing and shaping of life. . . ."[27] Gorky felt a deep and abiding aversion for politics whereas for Lenin it was the very breath of life. The dedicated artist was bound to come into conflict with the dedicated politician.[28] Gorky listened sympathetically to the complaints of artists and writers who turned to him for help. Gorky, who was inclined to give in too quickly to his moods, followed no clearly defined political course. He had ventured to criticize Lenin. Though he was a loyal Communist, he held

25. *Ibid.,* p. 233.
26. Sherman H. Eoff, *The Modern Spanish Novel* (New York: New York University Press, 1961), p. 161.
27. Bertram D. Wolfe, *The Bridge and the Abyss: The Troubled Friendship of Maxim Gorky and V. I. Lenin* (New York and London: Frederick A. Praeger, 1967), p. 3.
28. "Lenin believed in classes, class struggle, dictatorship, the Party, and himself as the maker and mover of history. Gorky believed in Man, in freedom, in the redeeming power of art and science, in the sacredness of the individual person." *Ibid.,* pp. 3-4.

that writers should be free to write in accordance with their convictions. "Contrary to official legend, he was a consistent opponent of party control of literature, detesting the idea that party or government bureaucracy—or official critics— should tell a writer what to write."[29] Or *how* to write. In particular, he vehemently blames Lenin, Trotsky, and their associates for having become intoxicated with the sense of power. They ignore the cry for freedom of speech and "the rights" of the individual. The road to revolution had led "to anarchy, to the destruction of the proletariat and of the revolution."[30]

When the Bolsheviks seized power on November 7, 1917, and dismissed the Constituent Assembly, Gorky assailed the move since it might lead to civil war. Lenin would not listen to reason. A fanatical ideologist, Lenin was determined to insure the success of the Revolution. A humanitarian at heart, Gorky was not the type of revolutionist who, when the Bolsheviks were guilty of acts of terrorism, glibly quoted the adage that one cannot make an omelette without breaking eggs. Such superficial rationalizations found no favor in Gorky's scornful and censorious eyes. A compassionate, warm-hearted man, he emphasized the necessity for enlightening the masses and urged the intellectuals of his country to put an end to these senseless assassinations. In the articles he wrote from May 1917 to July 1918 for the newspaper *Novava Zhim* (New Life), he protested against the utter disregard of democratic safeguards by the Bolsheviks, the rise of anti-Semitism, and especially the bigotry that identified most Bolsheviks as Jews. He blamed Lenin for these unfortunate developments. *Pravda* brought Gorky's newspaper under fire. Lenin finally gave orders that it be suppressed.

Nor would Gorky write novels that faithfully endorsed or echoed the "truths" of a given political doctrine. He was not afraid to speak out on controversial matters, though after 1930 he made his peace with the Stalinist regime. When Lenin assumed dictatorial powers, Gorky took it upon himself to defend the cause of the workers. He had to be silenced. Lenin was not troubled by doubts as to the rightness of his

29. *Ibid.*, p. 23.
30. Maxim Gorky, *Untimely Thoughts: Essays on Revolution, Culture and the Bolsheviks 1917-1918*, trans. Herman Ermolaev (New York: Paul S. Eriksson, 1968), p. 85.

political decisions. "Who is not with us," he proclaimed, "is against us."[31] Now that a ruthless class war was being waged, Gorky feared that the cultural heritage of the country was in danger of being wantonly destroyed. The old intellectuals, born of bourgeois parents, all those who did not accept the dictatorship of the proleariat, as it was euphemistically called, were put out of the way. Artists, scholars, poets, and composers were forced to do their share of manual labor.[32]

Gorky could not check the irresponsible outburst of revolutionary extremism. During Stalin's despotic reign, repression became a fiendishly efficient method for keeping the Russian populace fearful and submissive. Those who were suspected of disaffection—and who could be looked upon as completely innocent?—were "taken care of." The Russian poet Joseph Brodsky, who is now Poet-in-Residence at the University of Michigan, describes the hellish conditions that existed in the Soviet Union while Stalin was dictator of the land. For almost a third of a century this man exercised absolute power over two hundred million people. He launched a campaign of wholesale murder unparalleled in the history of mankind. He surpassed Hitler in his paranoiac fury, in his ferocious need for victims. He spared no one. His purges and liquidations resulted finally in genocide.[33]

After Stalin died, the thaw set in: writers were allowed considerably more leeway in criticizing "the cult of personality." But Khrushchev drew the line at what he branded as treason: slanders directed at the Soviet Union, "collaboration" (and this covered a multitude of ideological sins of commission) with the capitalist West, and the abominations of "formalism." Sinyavsky and Daniel were penalized for "the crime" of publishing their work abroad. Solzhenitsyn was expelled from the Writers' Union and was prevented from getting his novels into print inside the Soviet Union. He was accused of smuggling *The First Circle* and *Cancer Ward* out of

31. Wolfe, *The Bridge and the Abyss*, p. 75.
32. Weil argues that he does not agree with "the common critical assertion in the West that Gorky's writing suffered from his deep involvement with revolutionary politics or his deep dependence on Lenin's approval. Just the contrary is true: Gorky apparently needed the kind of guidance and direction that he found in Lenin's personality and program. . . . Deep political engagement was requisite to the way he wanted to write; without it, he would have been a far less interesting and productive literary personality." Weil, *Gorky*, pp. 19-20.
33. Joseph Brodsky, "Reflections on a Spawn of Hell,": *The New York Times Magazine*, March 4, 1973.

the country in order to spread his anti-Soviet propaganda in the West. Though Stalin was gone, life in the Soviet Union had not improved much in the last twenty years.[34]

3. The Challenge of Commitment

We come back, finally, to the troublesome question of commitment. The term, as I indicated at the beginning of this study, is not only ambiguous but misleading. It is assigned a bewildering variety of meanings, and these are often in conflict. Victor Nekrasov, in *On Both Sides of the Ocean,* points out that in the Russian language the meaning of the term "commitment" is perfectly clear: "Has a particular writer joined a particular camp, what idea does his work embody, what course is he following and exactly what form does he use?"[35] In the Soviet Union, literature is, of course, wedded to the Marxist-Leninist ideology, which offers the writer, through the mediation of the Party, a revelation of the Way and the Truth. And Marxist critics have taken up this cry: they believe in the redemptive power of this doctrine. Lukács, for example, affirms with plenary conviction that Marxism is the only aesthetic that consistently emphasizes the need for the truthful delineation of reality. "Thus, *any* accurate account of reality is a contribution—whatever the author's subjective intention—to the Marxist critique of capitalism, and is a blow in the cause of socialism."[36] While Lukács stresses the inherent superiority of Socialist realism to the type of realism that is practiced in the West, he realizes the enormous complexity of the problem the writer faces.[37] "If a writer feels obliged, like an agitator, to supply ready solutions to all the political problems of the day, his work will suffer."[38]

34. Robert C. Tucker reports that the events of the past twenty years, after the death of Stalin, have made it clear that the influence of Stalinism cannot be easily removed from the bureaucratic and authoritarian structure of the Soviet Union. The purges that Stalin and his henchmen carried out, the reign of terror he instituted, resulted in the survival of the mediocre. See Robert C. Tucker, "Russia in the 20 Years Since Stalin's Death," *The New Republic,* March 10, 1973, p. 13.
35. Patricia Blake and Max Hayward, eds., *Half-Way to the Moon* (New York and Chicago: Holt, Rinehart and Winston, 1964), p. 225.
36. Georg Lukács, *The Meaning of Contemporary Realism,* trans. John and Necke Mander (London: Merlin Press, 1962), p. 101.
37. See n 1 in chap. 21.
38. Lukács, *The Meaning of Contemporary Realism,* p. 122.

The writer in the open society of the West is inclined to be more skeptical, not at all convinced that he must support some ideological or political cause. His role as an artist is not to change society.[39] His creative work springs out of a vision that is not only iconoclastic but truly "revolutionary" in its confrontation of the self and the world. This deliberate repudiation of political responsibility meant a break with the traditional conception of the avant garde, which has been essentially a movement in revolt. Originally, the avant-garde image "remained subordinate, even within the sphere of art, to the ideals of a radicalism which was not cultural but political."[40] In its early stages, avant-gardism represented a strong and steadfast commitment to the Left. The alliance of artistic and poltiical radicalism lasted for some time, but the partnership could not last. The artists could not be kept in line. The expression "avant garde" was divorced from its political context. The art of the avant garde was "revolutionary" in a new sense: it fought against the dead weight of tradition and was nonconformist on principle. Bohemians, in their rejection of society, frequently emulate the life of the outlaw, but without becoming criminals. "Bohemia . . . despite all of the burning bitterness of its anti-social feeling was almost by definition, politically powerless."[41] This, as I have said, was perfectly true of the beat generation. Nor is it to be assumed that the life-style of the avant garde is necessarily bohemian in character. "It possesses no built-in political posture and its only consistent social demand is freedom of creativity."[42]

Hesse, for example, did not believe that the writer should respond to the call for commitment. The occasional articles he wrote for the press in times of crisis were, he maintains, far removed from politics. "An Attempt at Justification" is his

39. In 1970, a symposium was held at Cambridge University in England, the subject of which was "The role of the artist is to change the world." One of the speakers was Michael Kustov, director of London's Institute of Contemporary Arts. As reported in *The New York Times,* this is part of what he said on that occasion. He developed the theme that works of art are impotent to prevent war or end unemployment. A work of art that aims to transmit a message or that seeks to tell us directly how to behave or what to believe arouses our resistance, for it denies us the right to think for ourselves. See *The New York Times,* August 3, 1970.
40. Renato Poggioli, *The Theory of the Avant-Garde,* trans. Gerald Fitzgerald (Cambridge, Mass.: Harvard University Press, 1968), p. 9.
41. César Graña, *Bohemia versus Bourgeois* (New York and London: Basic Books, 1964), p. 78.
42. David Caute, *The Illusion: An Essay on Politics, Theatre and the Novel* (New York: Harper & Row, 1971), p. 134.

reply to Max Brod's letter asking Hesse to speak out on the issue of Palestine. Hesse refused to intervene. He did not believe that he had the power to affect the outcome. The kingdom of the writer, he tells Brod, is not of this world.

> We cannot expect to exert the least influence through our fame or through the concerted action of our fellows. In the long view, to be sure, we shall always be the winners, something of us will remain when all the ministers and generals are forgotten. But in the short view, in the here and now, we are poor devils, and the world wouldn't dream of letting us join in its games. If we poets and thinkers are of any importance, it is solely because we have hearts and minds and a brotherly understanding that is natural and organic.[43]

Though Hesse did not shirk his social responsibility when the occasion required him to act, he set strict limits to such activities and involvements. He did not dwell in an ivory tower, there to devote himself to the cultivation of his garden. He never, he confided to Brod, "attempted to exert an influence on policy . . . never set hand to any of the hundreds of solemn but fruitless proclamations, protests, and cries of warning that our intellectuals keep issuing to the detriment of the humanitarian cause."[44]

"Commitment" is a multivalent term that can be applied to a wide assortment of uses, spritual and religious, philosophical and political. William Warren Bartley III, in *The Retreat to Commitment,* cogently analyzes the problem of religious commitment. In the sphere of literature, it all depends on what the writer is committed to. Alfred Jarry was "committed" to the 'pataphysics of the absurd. Ezra Pound was committed to the creative life and the difficult art of poetry. But the social-minded literary critics pay no attention to these semantic distinctions. For them, commitment refers to only one meaning: the politics of radicalism, the Marxist eschatology, the revolutionary dream that the proletariat will bring to fruition in the fullness of time.[45] It is important to deter-

---

43. Hermann Hesse, *If the War Goes On. . . ,* trans. Ralph Manheim (New York: Farrar, Straus and Giroux, 1971), p. 182.
44. *Ibid.,* pp. 183-84.
45. Eric Bentley, in *The Theatre of Commitment and Other Essays,* says: "Relative to the general social situation, the literature of Commitment is radical. It is a literature of protest, not approval, of outrage, not tribulation." Eric Bentley, *The Theatre of Commitment and Other Essays* (New York: Atheneum, 1967), p. 197.

mine, in context, the kind of commitment that characterizes a writer and his work. Günter Grass is an excellent example of a writer who is "committed," but not to the political dogmas of the Left.

He participates conscientiously in the political campaigns and conflicts of West Germany. He freely speaks his mind as a citizen. He does not don the mantle of a prophet. He recalls the period in his youth when he was deceived by Nazi propaganda and acknowledges his share of guilt for the inhuman crimes committed under Hitler. He defends his right to plunge into the melee of politics even though he is by profession a novelist. The man who is a storyteller, is he sustained by a political program? Does he probe social reality to the lowest depths and reveal what goes on behind the scenes? Is he the Grand Master who pulls the wires of this puppet show? Günter Grass wants to know why the writer must dabble in politics. Why doesn't he leave the "science" or "art" of politics to the politicians? "Politics is not an occult science. . . . Even a storyteller knows that. True, he doesn't know as much as he should about the labor laws or about rent reform, but he knows aspects of society that are not dreamt of in your statistics. He is able to single out the individual from the mass and give him a name."[46]

Grass does not regret the time and energy he spent in writing polemics and delivering speeches in behalf of parliamentary democracy in Western Germany. He does not ask that he be granted special privileges nor assume that his work as a novelist endows him with superior wisdom in the world of politics. Grass cleverly ridicules the writer who publicly announces that he is "committed."

> From the start, before even inserting his paper into the typewriter, the committed writer writes, not novels, poems or comedies, but "committed literature." When a body of literature is thus plainly stamped, the obvious implication is that all other literature is "uncommitted." Everything else, which takes in a good deal, is disparaged as art for art's sake.[47]

But the mistaken notion still persists that writers, "speaking as writers . . . should protest, condemn war, praise peace and

46. Günter Grass, *Speak Out!* trans. Ralph Manheim (New York: Harcourt, Brace & World, 1968), pp. 10-11.
47. *Ibid.*, p. 50.

display noble sentiments."[48] In the course of this study I have referred to various attempts that have been made to rebuild the foundations of literary Marxism. In the chapter on Bertolt Brecht I discussed his efforts to create epic drama, based on dialectical materialism, that would revolutionize the consciousness of the audience, but his practice was often not in agreement with his theory.[49] The forces of the New Left, under the leadership of Herbert Marcuse, are making themselves heard on the contemporary scene, but their energy is spent chiefly in composing diatribes.[50]

In the West, the fever of commitment has abated. Unpolitical writers like Genet, Beckett, and Ionesco are opposed to the dramaturgy of Brecht. Novelists like Moravia and Robbe-Grillet are not tempted by the eschatological promise of Communism. The history of radicalism during the past fifty years has disillusioned them with the categorical imperative of Marxism. They are not fired by the militant faith in the Revolution that made Nizan feel that "tomorrow, or the day after tomorrow, we shall be fighting with guns."[51] Ironic in their interpretation of the human condition, they broadcast no message of social redemption. Friedrich Dürrenmatt, for example, has no solution to offer. Indeed, he seems convinced that the evils that afflict mankind are incurable. His exposure of the limitations of the human animal—his absurd egotism, his blindness, his chronic seizures of irrationality—is designed to demonstrate his point, namely, that the modern drama must dispense with the hero.

For the art of our time, if it hopes to communicate its vis-

48. *Ibid.*, p. 53.
49. "Brecht is consistent only when he incorporates into his dramaturgy that *Weltanschauung*, the communist philosophy, to which he—so he seems to think—is committed; but in doing so he often cuts off his own nose" (Friedrich Dürrenmatt, "Problems of the Theatre," in *Four Plays: 1957-1962*, trans. Gerhard Nellhaus [London: Jonathan Cape, 1964], p. 13).
50. The New Left attracted a large number of supporters because it permitted different ways of interpreting the Marxist synthesis. The New Left came into being—an amalgam of anarchism, Socialism of the utopian variety, Bohemianism, existentialism, nihilism, populism, and even black nationalism. Artists were drawn to this eclectic and libertarian movement because it left them free to formulate their own aesthetic theories and experiment to their heart's content. No Commissar—a Zhdanov or a Fadeyev—could say them nay. They could thumb their noses at those who demanded that they adopt the principles of Socialist realism and conform to ideological orthodoxy. Many who decided to join the New Left were influenced to take this step by their reading of Sartre's work, his philosophy of existentialism.
51. See n2 above.

Conclusion 423

ion to men, must center its attention on the victims. Statistics, Dürrenmatt tells us, are the measure of our fate. Power is incarnate in the lethal explosion of the atomic bomb. And it is man who has created this monstrous weapon of mass destruction.[52] In confronting such a chaotic and catastrophic world, a world in which man is restrained by no sense of moral responsibility, tragedy cannot emerge. For the concept of guilt is abolished. If the sense of guilt is eliminated, then no one can be singled out as the culprit, and the tragic hero is banished from the modern stage. Comedy is our appropriate genre. Dürrenmatt avoids facile generalizations. Though he is sustained as a writer by his social conscience, he refuses to be politically committed. If he were to yield to this temptation, he would be burdened and harassed by demands that are alien to his art. The writer in the democratic world is able to enjoy the benefits of "the open society" and therefore does not become the victim of a political mystique. Committed to the perfection of the work, such a writer has learned that it is a ruinous mistake for him to become involved in the ephemeral politics of his time. After the Second World War, the poets looked back on their past devotion to the Left and felt the ignominious humiliation of their betrayal.

> Poet after poet suddenly saw the true mechanism of ideologies, most of them fool-driven and therefore collapsible. And if once he had acted as a naive believer, an intimidated convert, or a bought propagandist, the action itself gave him a feeling of nausea. All over Eastern Europe after Stalin's death those who had been activists of literature vomited their disgust with words into more words.[53]

The writers of our time who are still tempted to justify their calling by producing literature that is "engaged" would do well to heed the seasoned words of wisdom of Wilhelm Emil Mühlmann, who writes from West Germany:

> revolutionary voluntarism is doomed to failure even in literature. The itch for self-involvement at short range—further coupled with the vanity of writers that leads them to believe that they must copy the political "man of action"—puts them on the wrong track. . . . Art can only present the problems and go on question-

52. Dürrenmatt, "Problems of the Theatre," p. 13.
53. Jerzy Peterkiewicz, *The Other Side of Silence* (London: Oxford University Press, 1970), p. 40.

ing. Writers do not transform the world. . . . Anyone who feels with Marx that he wishes to transform rather than grasp the world need not be surprised when he fails and, in the end, stands with empty hands.[54]

54. Wilhelm Emil Mühlmann, "Tradition and Revolution in Literature," in *Literary Criticism and Sociology,* Yearbook of Comparative Criticism, vol. 5, trans. Gerhard Nellhaus and ed. Joseph P. Strelka (University Park: Pennsylvania State University Park, 1973), p. 167.

Appendix

Merleau-Ponty Attacks *Darkness at Noon* and Defends the Moscow Trials

During the turbulent postwar period, the political situation in France was in a confused state. Party allegiances were abruptly canceled. Writers shifted from the Left to the Right. Anti-Communist sentiment was on the rise. Merleau-Ponty endeavored to combat the campaign against Communism that the extreme Right was waging. He composed a series of articles for *Les Temps Modernes* (they ran from November 1946 through July 1947) that critically examined *Darkness at Noon* and the interpretation Koestler gave of the Moscow Trials. Later in 1947 he incorporated this material in his book *Humanisme et terreur*. Merleau-Ponty analyzes the contrast Koestler draws between the yogi, the spiritual man who relies primarily on the truths intuitively disclosed to his inner being, and the commissar, the hard-boiled revolutionary who believes that the universe functions like a machine and that the Revolution won by the heroic efforts of the proletariat will reconcile the needs of history with those of the machine. The commissar is the realist, the man of action, who has no faith in the mystique of vertical transcendence. He is, moreover, not too scrupulous about the means he employs to gain his ends. Rubashov, in *Darkness at Noon,* is the commissar who, while waiting to be liquidated, catches a glimpse of the vision that the eye of the yogi beholds, but he is unable to unite the two conflicting outlooks in a synthesis his mind will approve. Since the decisions of the Party incarnate the immanent will of history, Rubashov is forced to conclude that he is a significant force in life only as a part of the ongoing historical process. The "I," the ego-identity to which he clings, is but a grammatical fiction. Nothing must be allowed to stand between him and his loyalty to the Party. But after his imprisonment, he begins to wonder whether the motives that governed his actions in the past were truly valid. He perceives that the masses have lost their faith in the Party. Finally, he is convinced that his "confession" will perform a useful service for the Party and he signs it, despite his knowledge that Stalin has ordered his death and will now be in a position to assure his complete monopoly of power.

Merleau-Ponty maintains that the Moscow Trials must be understood in relation to the times in which they were held. For the revolutionary, the future is the arbiter of destiny, the supreme court of justice. Subjective intentions are of no avail and in the final analysis they do not count. The accused must be judged solely by the degree to which he contributed to or hindered the development of the Revolution. His intentions, subjectively considered, may have been ideologically pure, blameless, but he is nonetheless responsible, from an "objective" point of view, for the consequences his action brought about. In brief, if he bet on the wrong horse, if he aligned himself with the faction that was defeated and expelled from the Party or exiled, he is guilty. Once Stalin took over the reins of leadership, those who had dared to criticize him or his program were called deviationists. Bukharin's confession of "objective" guilt meant that his failure to obey Stalin's implicit commands constituted an act of treason. "The real situation is that Bukharin capitulated because he saw that history had proved him wrong."[1] The category of "objective" guilt simply formulates the pragmatic lesson that history is always right. The winner takes all. As Auden says in his poem "Spain 1937": history may deplore the plight of the defeated but it cannot help or pardon.

1. Albert Rabil, Jr., *Merleau-Ponty: Existentialist of the Social World* (New York and London: Columbia University Press, 1967), p. 99.

In *Humanism and Terror,* Merleau-Ponty raises the question whether revolutionary violence is justified. The professional Communist is usually pictured as a political realist who is ruthless in pursuit of the revolutionary goal, whereas the liberal, by contrast, is unwilling to use immoral or illegal methods. Unfortunately, liberalism cannot be taken at face value. Its leading ideas constitute a grandiose cult of mystification. Merleau-Ponty pens this paradoxical statement: "A regime which is nominally liberal can be oppressive in reality. A regime which acknowledges its violence might have in it more genuine humanity."[2] In short, Marxism cannot be refuted by setting it in opposition to a body of ethical principles.

Merleau-Ponty then argues that *Darkness at Noon* is not grounded in historical fact, though Merleau-Ponty himself in 1946-47 had no knowledge of the true facts in the case. He cannot accept Koestler's account of the trial. "Rubashov is in the opposition because he does not support the Party's new policy or its inhuman discipline. But inasmuch as this involves an ethical revolt and his ethics have always been to obey the Party he ends by capitulating unconditionally" (pp. xv-xvi). Bukharin, on the other hand, made no issue of the ethical problem.

Merleau-Ponty readily concedes that Marxist politics is "formally dictatorial and totalitarian" (p. xix). He is aware, too, that the bureaucratic hierarchy is in command. Dissenters are treated as if they were criminals at heart. There is no indication that Communism in Russia is heading toward the withering away of the State or that the dictatorship of the proletariat will be lifted in the foreseeable future. Merleau-Ponty is under no illusion as to the kind of behavior that now prevails in the Soviet Union; cunning is a valued trait, distrust is widespread, and people are swayed for the most part by selfishness and unmitigated cynicism. The spirit of proletarian solidarity and revolutionary idealism has practically vanished.

These negative features exist, but they do not invalidate the Marxist analysis of capitalism nor do they justify the hysterical anti-Soviet campaign unleashed by the West. He realizes that the Revolution has ceased to be a living force in the Soviet Union; the reality of the Stalinist dictatorship

2. Maurice Merleau-Ponty, *Humanism and Terror: An Essay on the Communist Problem,* trans. John O'Neill (Boston: Beacon Press, 1969), p. xv.

makes a mockery of the power of the proletariat. In these circumstances he announces that "it is impossible to be an anti-Communist and it is not possible to be a Communist" (p. xxi). He reminds us, as Sartre does in his play *Dirty Hands,* that political action is "of its nature impure" (p. xxxii).

Merleau-Ponty admits that *Darkness at Noon* confronts the crucial problem of our time, though he criticizes Koestler severely for not stating the problem properly. He also calls attention to the contradictions that are to be found in the character of Rubashov, the revolutionary who broods in his cell on the meaning of historical necessity. Such a man is not affrighted by the thought of death, for he knows that the Revolution will forge ahead without him. Rubashov does not trust his sensibility, "the reasons" of the heart; his rational mind, which has shut off the flow of feeling, is always in control. He obeys, without ever pausing to question, the instructions of the Party. He is not interested in such toplofty abstractions as honor, justice, fidelity. "There is only *objective* treason and *objective* merit. The traitor is he who in fact deserts the country of the Revolution as it stands.... All the rest is psychology" (p. 4).

Rubashov asks himself why he should die in silence, a victim of the Stalinist purge. What purpose would his death then serve? Yet he cannot get himself to denounce the regime. Despite everything he has been made to suffer, he is unwilling to repudiate his revolutionary past. The Revolution had to take place; even if he had known in advance that the Revolution would later culminate in this mindless purge, he would have participated in the struggle and rejoiced in the triumph of the proletariat. Had his actions, in effect, been counterrevolutionary? At the end he signs the damning confession of guilt that Gletkin had prepared for him. Merleau-Ponty, who was himself an intellectual, a professor of history, furnishes this facile explanation of Rubashov's fall from grace. In thus accounting for Rubashov's errors, Merleau-Ponty runs counter to the portrait in depth that Koestler painted. Merleau-Ponty declares that

> Rubashov belongs to a generation which believed it could restrict violence to the enemies of the proletariat, treat the proletariat and its representatives humanely, and save one's personal honor through devotion to the Revolution. That is because he and his comrades were intellectuals born in comfortable circumstances and brought up in a prerevolutionary culture (p. 9).

Because he is "objectively" out of step with his Party, he is guilty of treason.

Though Rubashov was a disciplined Bolshevik, he could not shut out the outraged cries of his conscience. He was no traitor. It was a profound impulse of moral indignation against the cruelties visited upon the masses in capitalist society that had made him join the Communist Party. Had he kept faith with this humanistic vision of a classless commonwealth that gave to each in accordance with his need and took from each in accordance with his ability? Had he, perhaps, been the dupe of logic? Merleau-Ponty complains that there is "very little Marxism in *Darkness at Noon*" (p. 13). The Marxist affirms that the individual has a part to play in the making of the Revolution. "Marxism rested on the profound idea that human perspectives, however relative, are absolute because there is nothing else. . ." (p. 18). The individual is not helpless in relation to the march of history; he can do his share in helping to change the world.[3]

The Moscow Trials raised serious doubts about the alleged guilt of the accused. What could possibly have motivated these old and revered Bolsheviks to engage in sabotage and espionage? Their confessions contained no concrete incriminating evidence, only general statements about their culpable attitude toward Stalinism. No proof was cited that they were in

3. In Marxist discussions of the role of the individual in history, it is history that is represented as the dominant and determining power; the responsibility of the socially awakened individual is to move along with it. George Plekhanov, in *The Role of the Individual in History*, contends that the opportunity on the part of the individual to exercise an influence on the historic process depends on the structure of the society of which he is an integral part. The talented individual, the charismatic leader must to some degree conform to the pressing needs of his epoch, and second, the social order must provide opportunities for the demonstration of this exceptional capacity for political leadership. History is made "by the *social man*, who is its *sole 'factor'* " (George Plekhanov, *The Role of the Individual in History* [New York: International Publishers, 1940], p. 60). The individual can influence the process of change if he is endowed with the vision to anticipate the direction in which society is moving.

Fromm denies that Marx underestimated or minimized the importance of the individual. Marx is not the opponent of human freedom. He never envisaged a Communist social order in which equality of income would be granted while the workers would be reduced to the status and fuction of robots. This version of Marxism is essentially false. "Marx's aim was that of the spiritual emancipation of man, of his liberation from the chains of economic determination, of restituting him in his human wholeness, of enabling him to find unity and harmony with his fellow man and with nature" (Erich Fromm, *Marx's Concept of Man*. [New York: Frederick Ungar Publishing Co., 1961], p. 3). Fromm bases his reinterpretation of Marxism on his close reading of the *Economic and Philosophical Manuscripts* by Marx.

league with foreign powers or that they functioned as a conspirational force against the Revolution. The Moscow Trials failed to establish their guilt once and for all. Merleau-Ponty argues that these men were being tried for their views about the future. If the future-become-present has discredited their present ideological position, then they were "objectively" guilty of belonging to the opposition and deserved to die. Merleau-Ponty insists

> that in history there is no absolute neutrality or objectivity, that the apparent innocence which states a probability in reality states what is possible, and that every existential judgment is a value judgment; even *laissez-faire* involves a commitment.[4]

The revolutionary invests heavily in the future; indeed, he stakes his life on the outcome of the struggle, but the future, when all is said and done, remains contingent. He is convinced that he is making the right decision, that history is on his side. Then, to his dismay, he is betrayed by the fickle Muse of history. To run counter to the government in power—which in this case meant Stalin, who controlled the Party apparatus—is, Louis Aragon fulminated, to lend support to the Fascist cause. Bukharin, Merleau-Ponty speculates, capitulated because he realized that history had proved him wrong. Recent research discloses that he gave in because his jailers promised to spare the lives of his wife and young son.[5]

What caused Merleau-Ponty to draw back from his com-

4. Merleau-Ponty, *Humanism and Terror,* p. 39.
5. The fate that befell the versatile Karl Radek throws some light on the Bukharin case. Radek committed the "objective" error of siding with Trotsky and advocating a policy of internationalism. Unfortunately, Stalin succeeded in defeating his opponents and became the supreme leader of the Soviet Union. His doctrine of building socialism in one country became the official ideology. Radek was shrewd enough to realize that he had made a blunder that might cost him his life and from that time on he never felt safe. He must ally himself with Stalin or be pushed into political oblivion. He did not rule out the possibility that he might be liquidated. Radek was chosen to address the First Writers' Congress and promulgate the principles of Socialist realism. He seemed to be on the road to political rehabilitation when the blow struck. In 1936 he was put into prison. Why did Radek's scheme to save his life miscarry? Stalin had made up his mind in 1934 "to purge the Bolshevik Party and to eliminate anyone who owed the smallest amount of loyalty elsewhere . . ." (Warren Lerner, *Karl Radek* [Stanford, Calif.: Stanford University Press, 1970], p. 162). Radek's trial took place in 1937. He was induced to confess his "crime." He was assured that the death sentence would not be imposed in his case. In reciting his list of political sins, he implicated Bukharin.

mitment to the Left? Sartre says that it was probably the Moscow Trials.[6]

Solzhenitsyn saw no mystery or contradiction in the strange behavior of the accused during the Moscow Trials. Once arrested, there was no question as to their guilt. Had they not confessed their crimes? The prosecutors selected those who betrayed the greatest weakness of will. But torture alone could not have forced these men to confess. They finally gave in because they were assured that they would not be put to death or that their children would not be harmed. Solzhenitsyn concludes that the man who seems "to have embodied the highest and brightest intelligence of all the disgraced and executed leaders . . . was N. I. Bukharin. Stalin saw through him, too, at that lowest stratum at which the human being unites with the earth."[7]

After the murder of Kirov, when Kamenev and Zinoviev were brought to trial, Bukharin felt that they were indeed capable of committing such acts of treason. They would not have been arrested without cause. The man who reasoned in this casuistic manner was "the leading theoretician of the Party."[8] When Kamanev and Zinoviev were sentenced to death, Bukharin uttered no word of protest. He begged for the opportunity to confront these traitors and prove his innocence. He wrote numerous letters to Stalin, seeking to regain his favor. For Bukharin, the worst form of punishment, the supreme tragedy of life, was to be expelled from the Party. Stalin assured him that he would not be driven out of the Party, but Kaganovich and Molotov preferred charges against him, calling him a Fascist, and demanded that he be shot. Bukharin was not afraid to die, but he had no faith to sustain him during this ordeal, no point of view that he could call his own. He was abject in his capitulation.

6. See "Merleau-Ponty," by Jean-Paul Sartre, in Jean Paul Sartre, *Situations*, trans. Benita Eisler (Greenwich, Conn.: Fawcett Publications, 1965), pp. 156-226.
7. Aleksandr I. Solzhenitsyn, *The Gulag Archipelago 1918-1956: An Experiment in Literary Investigation. I-II*. Trans. Thomas P. Whitney (New York and London: Harper & Row, 1974), p. 412.
8. *Ibid.*

Selected Bibliography

Aczel, Tamas and Meray, Tiber. *The Revolt of the Mind.* New York: Frederick A. Praeger, 1959.

Adereth, M. *Commitment in Modern French Literature: Politics and Society in Péguy, Arrabal, and Sartre.* New York: Schocken Books, 1968.

Alexandrova, Vera. *A History of Soviet Literature.* Translated by Mirra Ginsburg. New York: Doubleday & Company, 1963.

Alvarez, A. *The Savage God: A Study of Suicide.* New York: Random House, 1972.

Anders, Gunther. *Kafka.* Translated by A. Steer and A. K. Thorlby. London: Bowes & Bowes, 1960.

Andrews, Wayne. *Siegfried's Curse.* New York: Atheneum, 1972.

Ardagh, John. *The New French Revolution.* New York and Evanston: Harper & Row, 1969.

Arendt, Hannah. *The Origins of Totalitarianism.* New York: Harcourt, Brace and Company, 1951.

———. *Men in Dark Times.* New York: Harcourt, Brace & World, 1968.

———. *The Human Condition.* Chicago and London: University of Chicago Press, 1959.

Aron, Raymond. *The Opium of the Intellectuals.* Translated by Terence Kilmartin. Garden City, N.Y.: Doubleday & Company, 1957.

———. *Marxism and the Existentialists.* New York and London: Harper & Row, 1969.

433

Arp, Jean. *Arp on Arp: Poems, Essays, Memories.* Edited by Joachim Neugroschel. New York: The Viking Press, 1972.

Arvon, Henri. *Marxist Esthetics.* Translated by Helen R. Lane. Ithaca, N.Y.: Cornell University Press, 1973.

Auden, W.H. *Collected Longer Poems.* New York: Random House, 1969.

――――. *Spain.* London: Faber and Faber, 1937.

―――― and Isherwood, Christopher. *Two Great Plays: The Dog Beneath the Skin* and *The Ascent of F 6.* New York: Vintage Books, 1962.

―――― and Isherwood, Christopher. *The Dance of Death.* London: Faber and Faber, 1933.

―――― and Isherwood, Christopher. *Two Great Plays.* New York: Vintage Books, 1962.

―――― and Isherwood, Christopher. *Journey to a War.* New York: Random House, 1939.

―――― and MacNeice, Louis. *Letters from Iceland.* New York: Random House, 1937.

Auerbach, Erich. *Mimesis.* Translated by Willard R. Trask. Princeton, N.J.: Princeton University Press, 1953.

Ayer, Alfred J. *Language, Truth and Logic.* New York: Oxford University Press, 1936.

Balakian, Anna. *Surrealism.* New York: The Noonday Press, 1959.

――――. *André Breton.* New York: Oxford University Press, 1971.

Balzac, Honoré de. *Lost Illusions.* Translated by Kathleen Raine. New York: The Modern Library, 1967.

Barnes, Hazel E. *Humanistic Existentialism: The Literature of Possibility.* Lincoln, Neb.: University of Nebraska Press, 1962.

Barthes, Roland. *Critical Essays.* Translated by Richard Howard. Evanston, Ill.: Northwestern University Press, 1972.

Bartley, William Warren III. *The Retreat to Commitment.* New York: Alfred A. Knopf, 1962.

Bauer, George. *Sartre and the Artist.* Chicago and London: The University of Chicago Press, 1969.

Bauer, Raymond A. *The New Man in Soviet Psychology.* Cambridge, Mass.: Harvard University Press, 1952.

Beach, Joseph Warren. *The Making of the Auden Canon.* Minneapolis, Minn.: The University of Minnesota Press, 1957.

Beauvoir, Simone de. *The Prime of Life.* Translated by Peter Green. Cleveland and New York: The World Publishing Company, 1962.

———. *Force of Circumstance.* Translated by Richard Howard. New York: G. P. Putnam's Sons, 1965.

Bell, Daniel. *The End of Ideology.* Glencoe, Ill.: The Free Press, 1960.

Bentley, Eric. *The Theatre of Commitment and Other Essays on Drama in Our Society.* New York: Atheneum, 1967.

Berger, John. *Art and Revolution: Ernst Neizvestny and the Role of the Artist.* New York: Pantheon Books, 1969.

Bigsby, C. W. E. *Confrontation and Commitment: A Study of Contemporary Drama, 1959-66.* Columbia, Mo.: University of Missouri Press, 1968.

———. *Dada & Surrealism.* London: Methuen & Co., 1972.

Binswanger, Ludwig. *Being-in-the-World.* Translated by Jacob Needleman. New York and London: Basic Books, 1963.

Blackmur, Richard P. *Anni Mirabilis 1921-1925: Reason in the Madness of Letters.* Washington, D.C.: The Library of Congress, 1956.

Boak, Denis. *André Malraux.* London: Oxford University Press, 1968.

Bonnefoy, Claude. *Conversations with Ionesco.* Translated by Jan Dawson. New York and Chicago: Holt, Rinehart and Winston, 1971.

Borkenau, Franz. *The Communist International.* London: Faber and Faber, 1938.

Bowra, C. M. *Poetry and Politics.* Cambridge: At the University Press, 1966.

Bradbury, Malcolm. *The Social Context of Modern English Literature.* New York: Schocken Books, 1974.

Brecht, Bertolt. *Brecht on Theatre.* Translated and edited by John Willett. New York: Hill and Wang, 1964.

———. *Threepenny Novel.* Translated by Desmond I. Vesey. Verse translated by Christopher Isherwood. New York: Grove Press, 1956.

———. *The Mother.* Translated by Lee Baxandall. New York: Grove Press, 1965.

Brée, Germaine. *Camus and Sartre: Crisis and Commitment.* New

York: Dell Publishing Co., 1972.
Breton, André. *What Is Surrealism?* Translated by David Gas-
coyne. London: Faber, 1936.
————. *Manifestoes of Surrealism.* Translated by Richard Sea-
ver and Helen R. Lane. Ann Arbor, Mich.: The Uni-
versity of Michigan Press, 1969.
Briefs, Goetz. *The Proletariat: A Challenge to Western Civiliza-
tion.* New York and London: McGraw-Hill Book
Company, 1937.
Brombert, Victor. *The Intellectual Hero: Studies in the French
Novel.* Philadelphia, Pa.: Lippincott, 1961.
Browder, Clifford. *André Breton.* Geneva, Switzerland: Lib-
rairie Droz, 1967.
Brown, Clarence. *Mandelstam.* Cambridge: Cambridge Uni-
versity Press, 1973.
Brown, Edward J. *Mayakovsky: A Poet in the Revolution.* Prince-
ton, N.J.: Princeton University Press, 1973.
Brustein, Robert. *Revolution as Theater.* New York: Liveright,
1971.
————. *The Theatre of Revolt.* Boston: Little, Brown and Com-
pany, 1964.
Buell, Frederick. *W. H. Auden As a Social Poet.* Ithaca, N.Y.:
Cornell University Press, 1973.
Burg, David and Feifer, George. eds. *Solzhenitsyn.* New York:
Stein and Day, 1972.
Burnier, Michel-Antoine. *Choice of Action: The French Existen-
tialists on the Political Front Line.* Translated by Bernard
Murchland. New York: Vintage Books, 1969.
Burns, Elizabeth and Tom, eds. *Sociology of Literature and
Drama.* Harmondsworth, Middlesex, England: Pen-
guin Books, 1973.
Burroughs, William S. *Naked Lunch.* New York: Grove Press,
1966.
————. *Nova Express.* New Yorkj; Grove Press, 1964.
Camus, Albert. *Notebooks 1935-1942.* Translated by Philip
Thody. New York: Alfred A. Knopf, 1963.
————. *Notebooks 1942-1951.* Translated by Justin O'Brien.
New York: Alfred A. Knopf, 1965.
————. *Lyrical and Critical Essays.* Edited by Philip Thody.
Translated by Conroy Kennedy. New York: Alfred A.
Knopf, 1969.
————. *The Rebel* Translated by Anthony Bower. New York:

Alfred A. Knopf, 1961.

────. *Resistance, Rebellion and Death*. Translated by Justin O'Brien. New York: Alfred A. Knopf,1966.

Caudwell, Christopher. *Illusion and Reality*. New York: International Publishers, 1947.

────. *Further Studies in a Dying Culture*. Edited by Edgell Rickword. London: The Bodley Head, 1949.

Caute, David. *Communism and the French Intellectuals 1914-1960*. New York: The Macmillan Company, 1964.

────. *The Illusion: An Essay on Politics, Theatre and the Novel*. New York and London: Harper & Row, 1971.

────. *The Fellow-Travellers: Postscript to the Enlightenment*. New York: The Macmillan Company, 1973.

Céline, Louis-Ferdinand. *Journey to the End of the Night*. Translated by John H. Marks. New York: New Directions, 1960.

────. *Death on the Installment Plan*. Translated by John H. Marks. New York: New Directions, 1938.

────. *Guignol's Band*. Translated by Bernard Frechtman and Jack T. Nile. Norfolk, Conn.: New Directions, 1954.

Chace, William M. *The Political Identities of Ezra Pound & T. S. Eliot*. Stanford, Calif,; Stanford University Press, 1973.

Chiari, Joseph. *Symbolism from Poe to Mallarmé*. New York: Gordian Press, 1970.

Clive, Geoffrey. *The Broken Icon: Intuitive Existentialism in Classical Russian Fiction*. New York: The Macmillan Company, 1972.

Coffin, Arthur B. *Robinson Jeffers: Poet of Inhumanism*. Madison and London: University of Wisconsin Press, 1971.

Cohen, Stephen F. *Bukharin and the Bolshevik Revolution: A Political Biography, 1889-1938*. New York: Alfred A. Knopf, 1973.

Collingwood, R. G. *The Principles of Art*. Oxford: Clarendon Press, 1938.

Connolly, Cyril. *Enemies of Promise*. Boston: Little, Brown and Company, 1939.

────. *The Unquiet Grave*. New York and London: Harper & Brothers, 1945.

Crossman, Richard, ed. *The God That Failed*. New York: Bantam Books, 1951.

Cruickshank, John. *Albert Camus and the Literature of Revolt*.

London: Oxford University Press, 1959.

Demetz, Peter, ed. *Brecht.* Englewood Cliffs, N. J.: Prentice-Hall, 1962.

Desan, Wilfrid. *The Marxism of Jean-Paul Sartre.* Garden City, N. Y.: Doubleday & Company, 1965.

Dorfles, Gillo. *Kitsch.* New York: University Books, 1969.

Dostoevsky, Fedor Mikhailovich. *Notes from Underground.* In *Short Novels of the Masters.* Edited by Charles Neider. New York: Rinehart & Company, 1948.

Duchene, François. *The Case of the Helmeted Airman: A Study of W. H. Auden.* Totowa, N. J.: Rowan and Littlefield, 1973.

Duplessis, Yves. *Surrealism.* Translated by Paul Capon. New York: Walker and Company, 1962.

Dürrenmatt, Friedrich. *Four Plays: 1957-62.* London: Jonathan Cape, 1964.

Egbert, Donald Drew. *Social Radicalism and the Arts.* New York: Alfred A. Knopf, 1970.

Ehrenburg, Ilya. *Post-War Years 1945-1954.* Translated by Tatiana Shebunina. Cleveland and New York: The World Publishing Company, 1967.

Elliott, George P. *Conversions.* New York: E. P. Dutton & Co., 1973.

Ellul, Jacques. *Autopsy of Revolution.* Translated by Patricia Wolf. New York: Alfred A. Knopf, 1971.

———. *A Critique of the New Commonplaces.* Translated by Helen Weaver. New York: Alfred A. Knopf, 1968.

Emrich, Wilhelm. *Franz Kafka.* Translated by Sheema Zeben Buehne. New York: Frederick Ungar Publishing Company, 1968.

———. *The Literary Revolution and Modern Society and Other Essays.* Translated by Alexander and Elizabeth Henderson. New York: Frederick Ungar Publishing Co., 1971.

Esslin, Martin. *Reflections: Essays on Modern Theatre.* Garden City, N. Y.: Doubleday & Company, 1969.

Fast, Howard. *Literature and Reality.* New York: International Publishers, 1950.

Feldman, Gene and Gartenberg, Max, eds. *The Beat Generation and the Angry Young Men.* New York: Dell Publishing Co., 1958.

Forster, E. M. *A Passage to India.* New York: Harcourt, Brace

& Company, 1924.

Foucault, Michel. *Madness and Civilization*. Translated by Richard Howard. New York: Random House, 1965.

Freedman, Ralph. *The Lyrical Novel*. Princeton, N.J.: Princeton University Press, 1963.

Freeman, E. *The Theatre of Albert Camus: A Critical Study*. London: Meuen & Co., 1971.

Freud, Sigmund. *Civilization and Its Discontents*. Translated by James Strachey. New York: W. W. Norton & Company, 1961.

Frohock, W. M. *André Malraux and the Tragic Imagination*. Stanford, Calif.: Stanford University Press, 1952.

Fromm, Erich. *Marx's Concept of Man*. New York: Frederick Ungar Publishing Co., 1961.

Furhammar, Leif and Isaksson, Folke. *Politics and Film*. Translated by Kersti French. New York and Washington: Praeger Publishers, 1971.

Galante, Pierre. *Malraux*. Translated by Haakon Chevalier. New York: Cowles Book Company, 1971.

Garaudy, Roger. *The Literature of the Graveyard*. Translated by Joseph Bernstein. New York: International Publishers, 1948.

———. *Marxism in the Twentieth Century*. Translated by René Hague. New York: Charles Scribner's Sons, 1970.

Garten, H. F. *Modern German Drama*. London: Methuen & Co., 1959.

Gass, William H. *Fiction and the Forms of Life*. New York: Alfred A. Knopf, 1970.

Gershman, Herbert S. *The Surrealist Revolution*. Ann Arbor, Mich.: The University of Michigan Pres, 1969.

Gide, André. *The Journals of André Gide*. vol. 2. Translated by Justin O'Brien. New York: Alfred A. Knopf, 1952.

———. *The Journals of André Gide*. vol. 3. Translated by Justin O'Brien. New York: Alfred A. Knopf, 1949.

———. *The Journals of André Gide*. vol. 4. Translated by Justin O'Brien. Alfred A. Knopf, 1951.

Ginzburg, Eugenia Semyonovna. *Journey into the Whirlwind*. Translated by Paul Stevenson and Max Hayward. New York: Harcourt, Brace & World, 1969.

Glicksberg, Charles I. *The Self in Modern Literature*. University Park, Pa.: The Pennsylvania State University Press, 1963.

————. *Modern Literary Perspectivism.* Dallas, Tex.: Southern Methodist University Press, 1973.

Gorky, Maxim. *Mother.* Translated by Isidore Schneider. Secaucus, N.J.: The Citadel Press, 1972

————. *Foma Gordeyev,* London: Lawrence & Wishart, 1956.

————. *Untimely Thoughts: Essays on Revolution, Culture and the Bolsheviks 1917-1918.* Translated by Herman Ermolaev. New York: Paul S. Eriksson, 1968.

Graña, César. *Bohemian versus Bourgeois.* New York and London: Basic Books, 1964.

Grass, Günter. *Speak Out!* Translated by Ralph Manheim. New York: Harcourt, Brace & World, 1968.

Grazzini, Giovanni. *Solzhenitsyn.* London: Michael Joseph, 1973.

Greene, Norman N. *Jean-Paul Sartre: The Existentialist Ethic.* Ann Arbor, Mich.: The University of Michigan Press, 1960.

Griffiths, Richard. *The Reactionary Revolution: The Catholic Revival in French Literature 1870-1914.* New York: Frederick Ungar Publishing Co., 1965.

Gross, Miriam, ed. *The World of George Orwell.* New York: Simon and Schuster, 1971.

Grossman, Manuel L. *Dada.* New York: Pegasus, 1971.

Guicharnaud, Jacques. *Modern French Theatre.* New Haven, Conn.: Yale University Press, 1961.

Haas, Willy. *Bert Brecht.* Translated by Max Knight and Joseph Fabry. New York: Frederick Ungar Publishing Co., 1970.

Hamburger, Michael. *The Truth of Poetry.* New York: Harcourt, Brace & World, 1969.

Hamsun, Knut. *On Overgrown Paths.* Translated by Carl I. Andersen. New York: Paul S. Erisson, 1947.

Harrington, Alan. *Psychopaths.* New York: Simon and Schuster, 1972.

Harris, Frederick John. *André Gide and Romain Rolland.* New Brunswick, N.J.: Rutgers University Press, 1973.

Harrison, John R. *The Reactionaries: A Study of the Anti-Democratic Intelligentsia.* New York: Schocken Books, 1967.

Harrison, O. B., Jr., ed. *Modern Literary Criticism.* New York: Appleton-Century-Crofts, 1962.

Hassan, Ihab. *The Dismemberment of Orpheus: Toward a Post-*

modern Literature. New York: Oxford University Press, 1971.

————, ed. *Liberations.* Middletown, Conn.: Wesleyan University Press, 1971.

Hawthorn, Jeremy. *Identity and Relationship: A Contribution to a Marxist Theory of Literary Criticism.* London: Lawrence & Wishart, 1973.

Hay, Eloise Knapp. *The Political Novels of Joseph Conrad.* Chicago and London: The University of Chicago Press, 1963.

Hayman, I. Ronald. *Samuel Beckett.* New York: Frederick Ungar Publishing Co., 1973.

Hayward, Max, ed. and trans. *On Trial: The Soviet State vs. "Abraham Tertz" and "Nikolai Arzhak."* New York: Harper & Row, 1966.

———— and Crowley, Edward L., eds. *Soviet Literature of the Sixties.* New York: Frederick A. Praeger, 1964.

———— and Labedz, Leopold. *Literature and Revolution in Soviet Russia, 1917-1962.* New York and London: Oxford University Press, 1963.

Heller, Erich. *The Ironic German.* Boston and Toronto: Little, Brown and Company, 1958.

————. "Literature and Political Responsibility: Apropos the "Letters of Thomas Mann." *Commentary* 52 (July 1971): 47-54.

Heppenstall, Rayner. *Four Absentees.* London: Barie & Rockliff, 1960.

Hesse, Hermann. *If the War Goes On. . .* Translated by Ralph Manheim. New York: Farrar, Straus and Giroux, 1971.

Hindus, Milton. *The Crippled Giant: A Bizarre Adventure in Contemporary Letters.* New York: Boar's Head Books, 1950.

Hoffman, Frederick J. *The Mortal No: Death and the Modern Imagination.* ·Princeton, N. J.: Princeton University Press, 1964.

Hofstadter, Richard. *Anti-intellectualism in American Life.* New York: Alfred A. Knopf, 1963.

Hoggart, Richard. *Auden: An Introductory Essay.* New Haven, Conn.: Yale University Press, 1951.

Holmes, John Clellon. *Nothing More to Declare.* New York: E. P. Dutton & Co., 1967.

Hoskins, Katharine Bail. *Today the Struggle.* Austin and London: University of Texas Press, 1969.

Howard, David; Lucas, John; and Goode, John, eds. *Tradition and Tolerance in Nineteenth-Century Fiction.* New York: Meridian Books, 1957.

Huyghe, René. *Art and the Spirit of Man.* Translated by Norbert Guterman. New York: Harry N. Abrams, 1962.

Huysmans. Joris Karl. *A Rebours.* London: The Fortune Press, n.d.

———. *Against the Grain.* Translated by John Howard. New York: Albert and Charles Boni, 1930.

Ibsen, Henrik, *When We Dead Awaken.* vol. 11. In *The Collected Works of Henrik Ibsen.* London: William Heinemann, 1929.

Ionesco, Eugène. *Notes and Counter Notes.* Translated by Donald Watson. New York: Grove Press, 1964.

———. *Present Past, Past Present.* Translated by Helen R. Lane. New York: Grove Press, 1971.

Ionesco. Edited by Rosetta C. Lamont. Englewood Cliffs, N.J.: Prentice-Hall, 1973.

Isherwood, Christopher. *Lions and Shadows.* Norfolk, Conn.: New Directions, 1947.

Jameson, Frederick. *Marxism and Form.* Princeton, N.J.: Princeton University Press, 1971.

Jeffers, Robinson. *Solstice and Other Poems.* New York: Random House, 1935.

———. *Such Counsel You Gave to Me and Other Poems.* New York: Random House, 1937.

Jefferson, Carter. *Anatole France: The Politics of Skepticism.* New Brusnwick, N.J.: Rutgers University Press, 1965.

Johnson, Priscilla. *Khrushchev and the Arts.* Edited by Priscilla Johnson and Leopold Labedz. Cambridge, Mass.: The M.I.T. Press, 1965.

Jolas, Eugene, ed. *Transition Workshop.* New York: The Viking Press, 1949.

Joll, James. *Three Intellectuals in Politics.* New York: Pantheon Books, 1960.

Jones, LeRoi. *Home.* New York: William Morrow & Co., 1966.

Josephson, Matthew. *Life Among the Surrealists.* New York: Holt, Rinehart and Winston, 1962.

Kaelin, Eugene. *An Existentialist Aesthetic.* Madison, Wis.: The University of Wisconsin Press, 1962.

Kahler, Erich. *Man the Measure: A New Approach to History.*

New York: Pantheon Books, 1943.

Kamenka, Eugene. *The Ethical Foundations of Marxism.* New York: Frederick A. Praeger, 1962.

Kampf, Louis and Lauter, Paul, eds. *The Politics of Literature: Dissenting Essays on the Teaching of Literature.* New York: Pantheon Books, 1972.

Katbe, George. *Utopia and Its Enemies.* New York: The Free Press of Glencoe, 1963.

Kaun, Alexander. *Maxim Gorky and His Russia.* New York: Jonathan Cape & Harrison Smith, 1931.

———. *Soviet Poets and Poetry.* Berkeley and Los Angeles: University of California Press, 1971.

Kerouac, Jack. *On the Road.* New York: The Viking Press, 1959.

Knight, Everett W. *Literature Considered as Philosophy.* London: Routledge & Kegan Paul, 1957.

Koestler, Arthur. *The Gladiators.* New York: The Macmillan Company, 1939.

———. *Darkness at Noon.* Translated by Daphne Hardy. New York: The New American Library, 1948.

———. *Invisible Writing.* New York: The Macmillan Company, 1954.

———. *Scum of the Earth.* New York: The Macmillan Company, 1948.

———. *Arrow in the Blue.* New York: The Macmillan Company, 1952.

———. *The Age of Longing.* New York: The Macmillan Company, 1951.

Kubal, David L. *Outside the Whale: George Orwell's Art and Politics.* Notre Dame and London: Notre Dame University Press, 1972.

Labedz, Leopold, ed. *Solzhenitsyn: A Documentary Record.* New York and London: Harper & Row, 1971.

Laing, R. D. *The Politics of Experience.* New York: Ballantine Books, 1971.

——— and Cooper, D. G. *Reason & Violence: A Decade of Sartre's Philosophy 1950-1960.* New York: Pantheon Books, 1971.

Langer, Susanne K. *Philosophy in a New Key.* New York: Penguin Books, 1948.

Langlois, Walter. *André Malraux: The Indochina Adventure.* New York and London: Frederick A Praeger, 1966.

Laquer, Walter and Mosse, George L. *The Left-Wing Intellectuals Between the Wars, 1919-1939.* New York: Harper & Row, 1966.

Last, R. W. *Hans Arp: The Poet of Dadaism.* Chester Springs, Pa.: Dufour Editions, 1969.

Laurenson, Diana T. and Swingewood, Alan. *The Sociology of Literature.* New York: Schocken Books, 1972.

Laver, James. *The First Decadent.* New York: The Citadel Press, 1955.

Leary, Timothy. *The Politics of Ecstasy.* New York: G. P. Putnam's Sons, 1968.

———. *High Priest.* New York: College Notes & Texts, 1968.

Lebel, Robert. *Marcel Duchamp.* Translated by George Heard Hamilton. New York: Grove Press, 1959.

Lehmann-Haupt, Hellmut. *Art Under a Dictatorship.* New York: Oxford University Press, 1954.

Lemaitre, Georges E. *From Cubism to Surrealism in French Literature.* Cambridge, Mass.: Harvard University Press, 1941.

Lerner, Warren. *Karl Radek.* Stanford, Calif.: Stanford University Press, 1970.

LeRoy, Gaylord and Beitz, Ursula, eds. *Preserve and Create: Essays in Marxist Literary Criticism.* New York: Humanities Press, 1973.

Levi, Albert William. *Humanism and Politics.* Bloomington and London: Indiana University Press, 1969.

Levin, Harry. *The Gates of Horn.* New York: Oxford University Press, 1963.

Lewis, C. Day. *The Buried Life.* London: Chatto and Windus, 1960.

———. *Collected Poems.* London: Jonathan Cape, 1954.

———. *A Time to Dance.* New York: Random House, 1936.

Lewis, R. W. B. *The Picaresque Saint: Representative Figures in Contemporary Fiction.* Philadelphia, Pa.: J. B. Lippincott, 1959.

———, ed. *Malraux.* Englewood Cliffs, N. J.: Prentice-Hall, 1952.

Lewis, Wyndham. *Rude Assignment.* London and New York: Hutchinson & Co., 1951.

———. *Apes of God.* Baltimore, Md.: Penguin Books, 1965.

———. *Self Condemned.* Chicago, Ill.: Henry Regnery Company, 1955.

——. *The Doom of Youth*. New York: Robert M. McBride, 1932.

——. *The Art of Being Ruled*. London: Chatto and Windus, 1926.

——. *Time and Western Man*. New York: Harcourt, Brace and Company, 1928.

——. *Paleface*. London: Chatto and Windus, 1929.

——. *Hitler*. London: Chatto and Windus, 1931.

——. *Blasting and Bombardiering*. London: Eyre and Spottiswoode, 1937.

——. *The Diabolical Principle and the Dithyrambic Spectator*. London: Chatto and Windus, 1931.

——. *Left Wings Over Europe, or, How to Make a War About Nothing*. London: Chatto and Windus, 1936.

——. *The Writer and the Absolute*. London, Methuen & Co., 1952.

Ley-Piscator, Maria. *The Piscator Experiment: The Political Theatre*. New York: James H. Heinemann, 1967.

Lichtheim, George. *Marxism in Modern France*. New York and London: Columbia University Press, 1966.

Lief, Ruth Ann. *Homage to Oceania*. Columbus, Ohio: Ohio State University Press, 1969.

Lipton, Lawrence. *The Holy Barbarians*. New York: Julian Messner, 1959.

Lodge, David. *Language of Fiction*. London: Routledge and Kegan Paul, 1966.

Louria. Donald B. *The Drug Scene*. New York and London: McGraw-Hill Book Company, 1968.

Lukács, Georg. *Writer & Critic and Other Essays*. Edited and translated by Arthur D. Kahn. New York: Grosset & Dunlap, 1970.

——. *The Meaning of Contemporary Realism*. Translated by John and Necke Mander. London: Merlin Press, 1962.

——. *Solzhenitsyn.* Translated by William David Graf. Cambridge, Mass.: The M.I.T. Press, 1971.

McMahon, Joseph H. *Human Beings: The World of Jean-Paul Sartre*. Chicago and London: The Universtiy of Chicago Press, 1971.

Malraux, André. *The Temptation of the West*. Translated by Robert Hollander. New York: Vintage Books, 1961.

Mandelstam, Nadezhda. *Hope Against Hope*. Translated by Max Hayward. New York: Atheneum, 1970.

————. *Hope Abandoned.* Translated by Max Hayward. New York: Atheneum, 1974.

Man, Henry de. *The Psychology of Socialism.* New York: Henry Holt & Co., 1927.

Mann, Thomas. *Letters of Thomas Mann.* Translated by Richard and Clara Winston. New York: Alfred A. Knopf, 1971.

Mannheim, Karl. *Essays in the Sociology of Culture.* Edited by Ernest Manheim and Paul Kecskemeti. New York: Oxford University Press, 1956.

Manser, Anthony. *Sartre.* London: The Athlone Press, 1966.

Margolies, David N. *The Function of Literature: A Study of Christopher Caudwell's Aesthetic.* New York: International Publishers, 1969.

Matthews, J. H. *An Introduction to Surrealism.* University Park, Pa.: The Pennsylvania State University Press, 1965.

————. *Theatre in Dada and Surrealism.* Syracuse, N. Y.: Syracuse University Press, 1974.

May, Rollo; Angel, Ernest; and Ellenberg, Henri F., eds. *Existence.* New York: Basic Books, 1958.

Medvedev, Roy. *Let History Judge.* Translated by Colleen Taylor. Edited by David Joravsky and Georges Haupt. New York: Alfred A. Knopf, 1971.

Medvedev, Zhores A. *Ten Years After Ivan Denisovich.* Translated by Hilary Sternberg. New York: Alfred A. Knopf, 1973.

Melville, Keith. *Communes in the Counter-Culture.* New York: William Morrow & Company, 1972.

Memmi, Albert. *The Colonizer and the Colonized.* Translated by Howard Greenfield. New York: The Orion Press, 1965.

Merleau-Ponty, Maurice. *Sense and Non-Sense.* Translated by Hubert L. Dreyfus and Patricia Allen Dreyfus. Evanston, Ill.: Northwestern University Press, 1964.

Meyerhold, V. E. *Meyerhold on Theatre.* Translated and edited by Edward Braun. New York: Hill and Wang, 1969.

Mihajlov, Mihajlo. *Russian Themes.* Translated by Marija Mihajlov. New York: Farrar, Straus and Giroux, 1968.

Money-Kyrle, R. E. *Psychoanalysis and Politics: A Contribution to the Psychology of Politics and Morals.* New York: W. W. Norton & Company, 1951.

Monod, Jacques. *Chance and Necessity.* Translated by Austryn

Wainhouse. New York: Alfred A. Knopf, 1971.

Moravia, Alberto. *Man as an End.* Translated by Bernard Wall. New York: Farrar, Straus and Giroux, 1965.

Mossop, D. J. *Pure Poetry: Studies in French Poetic Theory 1740-1945.* Oxford: At the Clarendon Press, 1971.

Motherwell, Robert. *The Dada Painters and Poets.* New York: Wittenborn, Schultz, 1951.

Mullins, Eustace. *The Difficult Individual, Ezra Pound.* New York: Fleet Publishing Corporation, 1961.

Nadeau, Maurice. *The History of Surrealism.* Translated by Richard Howard. New York: The Macmillan Company, 1965.

Needham, Joseph. *History Is on Our Side.* New York: The Macmillan Company, 1947.

Nizan, Paul. *The Watchdogs: Philosophers and the Established Order.* Translated by Paul Fittingoff. New York and London: Monthly Review Press, 1971.

Norman, Charles. *Ezra Pound.* New York: The Macmillan Company, 1960.

O'Brien, Conor Cruise. *Writers and Politics.* New York: Pantheon Books, 1965.

Odajnyk, Walter. *Marxism and Existentialism.* Garden City, N. Y.: Doubleday & Company, 1965.

Odier, Daniel. *The Job: Interviews with William S. Burroughs.* New York: Grove Press, 1970.

Olesha, Yuri. *Envy and Other Works.* Translated by Andrew MacAndrew. Garden City, N. Y.: Doubleday & Company, 1967.

Ortega, José y Gasset. *The Dehumanization of Art* and *Notes on the Novel.* New York: Peter Smith, 1951.

Orwell, George. *Burmese Days.* New York and London: Harcourt, Brace and Company, 1950.

———. *Keep the Aspidistra Flying.* New York: Harcourt, Brace and Company, 1956.

———. *Coming Up for Air.* New York: Harcourt, Brace and Company, 1950.

———. *Nineteen Eighty-Four.* New York: The New American Library, 1950.

———. *Shooting An Elephant.* New York: Harcourt, Brace and Company, 1950.

———. *An Age Like This. The Collected Essays, Journalism and Letters of George Orwell.* vol. 1. Edited by Sonia Orwell and Ian Angus. New York: Harcourt, Brace and World, 1968.

————. *My Country Right or Left. 1940-1943. The Collected Essays, Journalism and Letters of George Orwell.* vol 2. Edited by Sonia Orwell and Ian Angus. New York: Harcourt, Brace and World, 1968.

————. *In Front of Your Nose. The Collected Essays, Journalism and Letters of George Orwell.* vol. 4. Edited by Sonia Orwell and Ian Angus. New York: Harcourt, Brace & World, 1968.

————. *Dickens, Dali and Others.* New York: Harcourt, Brace and Company, 1946.

————. *Homage to Catalonia.* New York: Harcourt, Brace & World, 1952.

————. *Such, Such Were the Joys.* New York: Harcourt, Brace & Company, 1953.

Ostrovsky, Erika. *Céline and His Vision.* New York: New York Universtiy Press, 1967.

————. *Voyeur Voyant.* New York: Random House, 1971.

Ostow, Mortimer and Scharfstein, Ben-Ami. *The Need to Believe.* New York: International University Press, 1969.

Oxley, B. T. *George Orwell.* New York: Arco Publishing Company, 1969.

Panichas, George, ed. *The Politics of Twentieth-Century Novelists.* New York: Hawthorn Books, 1971.

Peckham, Morse. *Man's Rage for Chaos.* Philadelphia and New York: Chilton Books, 1965.

————. *Beyond the Tragic Vision: The Quest for Identity in the Nineteenth Century.* New York: George Braziller, 1962.

————. *Victorian Revolutionaries.* New York: George Braziller, 1970.

Pelles, Geraldine. *Art, Artists and Society.* Englewood Cliffs, N. J.: Prentice-Hall, 1963.

Peterkiewicz, Jerzy. *The Other Side of Silence.* London: Oxford University Press, 1970.

Peterson, Elmer. *Tristan Tzara.* New Brunswick, N. J.: Rutgers University Press, 1971.

Peyre, Henri. *Literature and Sincerity.* New Haven and London: Yale University Press, 1963.

Plekhanov, George. *The Role of the Individual in History.* New York: International Publishers, 1940.

Poe, Edgar Allan. *The Complete Poems and Stories of Edgar Allan*

Poe. New York: Alfred A. Knopf, 1951.

Poggioli, Renato. *The Theory of the Avant-Garde.* Translated by Gerald Fitzgerald. Cambridge, Mass.: Harvard University Press, 1968.

Poirier, Richard. *The Performing Self.* New York: Oxford University Press, 1971.

Pollman, Leo. *Sartre and Camus.* Translated by Helen and Gregor Sebba. New York: Frederick Ungar Publishing Co., 1970.

Popper, Karl. *The Open Society and Its Enemies.* 2 vols. London: Routledge and Kegan Paul, 1945.

Pound, Ezra. *Jefferson and/or Mussolini.* New York: Liveright, 1936.

Praz, Mario. *The Romantic Agony.* Translated by Angus Davidson. New York: Meridian Books, 1956.

Pronko, Leonard. *Ionesco.* New York and London: Columbia University Press, 1965.

Putnam, Samuel, ed. *The European Caravan.* New York: Harcourt, Brace and Company, 1931.

Quilliot, Roger. *The Sea and Prisons: A Commentary on the Life and Thought of Albert Camus.* Translated by Emmett Parker. University, Ala.: The University of Alabama Press, 1970.

Rabil, Albert Jr. *Merleau-Ponty: Existentialist of the Social World.* New York and London: Columbia University Press, 1967.

Raskin, Jonah. *The Mythology of Imperialism.* New York: Random House, 1971.

Ray, Paul C. *The Surrealist Movement in England.* Ithaca, N. Y.: Cornell University Press, 1971.

Read, Herbert. *The Grass Roots of Art.* New York: Wittenborn, 1947.

Reck, Rima Drell. *Literature and Responsibility: The French Novelist in the Twentieth Century.* Baton Rouge, La.: Louisiana State University Press, 1969.

Reddaway, Peter. *Uncensored Russia: Protest and Dissent in the Soviet Union.* Edited and translated by Peter Reddaway. New York: American Heritage Press, 1972.

Redfern, W. D. *Paul Nizan: Committed Literature in a Conspiratorial World.* Princeton, N. J.: Princeton University Press, 1972.

Richter, Hans. *Dada: Art and Anti-Art.* New York and Toronto: McGraw-Hill Book Company, n. d.

Righter, William. *The Rhetorical Hero.* London: Routledge and Kegan Paul, 1964.

Rothberg, Abraham. *Alexander Solzhenitsyn: The Major Novels.* Ithaca and London: Cornell University Press, 1971.

————. *The Heirs of Stalin: Dissidence and the Soviet Regime.* Ithaca, N. Y.: Cornell University Press, 1972.

Rühle, Jürgen. *Literature and Revolution.* Translated by Jean Steinberg. New York and London: Frederick A. Praeger, 1969.

Russell, Bertrand. *A History of Western Philosophy.* New York: Simon and Schuster, 1945.

Sachs, Hanns. *The Creative Unconscious.* Cambridge, Mass.: Sci-Art, 1942.

Sartre, Jean-Paul. *Situations.* Translated by Benita Eisler. Greenwich, Conn.: Fawcett Publications, 1966.

————. *The Age of Reason.* Translated by Eric Sutton. New York: Alfred A. Knopf, 1948.

————. *The Communists and Peace.* Translated by Martha H. Fletcher. New York: George Braziller, 1968.

————. *Being and Nothingness.* Translated by Hazel E. Barnes. New York: Philosophical Library, 1956.

————. *Search for a Method.* Translated by Hazel E. Barnes. New York: Alfred A. Knopf, 1963.

————. *What Is Literature?* Translated by Bernard Frechtman. New York: Philosophical Library, 1949.

Saunders, J. W. *The Profession of Letters.* London: Routledge & Kegan Paul, 1964.

Savage, Catherine. *Malraux, Sartre, and Aragon.* University of Florida Monographs. Humanities no. 17, 1964. Gainesville, Fla.: University of Florida Press, 1965.

Savage, D. S. *The Personal Principle.* London: Routledge, 1944.

Scarfe, Francis. *Auden and After.* London: Routledge, 1947.

Schaff, Adam. *A Philosophy of Man.* New York: Monthly Review Press, 1963.

Schalk, David L. *Roger Martin du Gard.* Ithaca, N. Y.: Cornell University Press, 1967.

Schopenhauer, Arthur. *The World as Will and Idea.* Translated by R. B. Haldane and J. Kemp. vol. 1. London: Kegan Paul, Trench, Trübner and Co., 1906.

————. *The World as Will and Idea.* Translated by R. B. Haldane and J. Kemp. vol. 2. London: Routledge & Kegan Paul, 1948.

————. *The World as Will and Idea*. Translated by R. B. Haldane and J. Kemp. vol. 3. London: Routledge & Kegan Paul, 1948.

Shapiro, Karl. *In Defense of Ignorance*. New York: Random House, 1960.

Sheridan, James F. *Sartre: The Radical Conversion*. Athens, Ohio: Ohio University Press, 1969.

Shlovsky, Viktor. *Mayakovsky and His Circle*. Edited and translated by Lily Feiler. New York: Dodd, Mead & Company, 1972.

Silone, Ignazio. *Emergency Exit*. Translated by Harvey Fergusson II. New York and London: Harper & Row, 1968.

Sinyavsky, Andrei. *For Freedom of Imagination*. Translated by Laszlo Tikos and Murray Peppard. New York and Chicago: Holt, Rinehart and Winston, 1971.

Slonim, Marc. *Soviet Russian Literature*. New York: Oxford University Press, 1964.

Smith, David E. and Luce, John. *Love Needs Care*. Boston and Toronto: Little, Brown and Company, 1971.

Sokel, Walter H. *The Writer in Extremis*. Stanford, Calif.: Stanford University Press, 1959.

Solzhenitsyn, Alexander. *Stories and Prose Poems*. Translated by Michael Glenny. New York: Farrar, Straus and Giroux, 1971.

————. *The First Circle*. Translated by Thomas P. Whitney. New York and Evanston: Harper & Row, 1971.

————. *Nobel Lecture*. Translated by F. D. Reeve. New York: Farrar, Straus and Giroux, 1972.

————. *The Gulag Archipelago: An Experiment in Literary Investigation*. 1-2. Translated by Thomas P. Whitney. New York and London: Harper & Row, 1974.

Spears, Monroe K. *The Poetry of W. H. Auden*. New York: Oxford University Press, 1963.

Spender, Stephen. *Collected Poems*. New York: Random House, 1955.

————. *World Within World*. London: Hamish Hamilton, 1951.

————. *The Destructive Element*. London: Jonathan Cape, 1935.

————. *Forward from Liberalism*. London: Victor Gollancz, 1937.

Stansky, Peter and Abrams, William. *Journey to the Frontier*. Boston: Little, Brown and Company, 1966.

————. *The Unknown Orwell*. New York: Alfred A. Knopf, 1972.

Steiner, George. *Language and Silence*. New York: Atheneum, 1967.

Stendahl (Marie Henri Beyle). *The Charterhouse of Parma*. Translated by C. K. Scott-Moncrief. New York: Liveright Publishing Corporation, 1944.

Stock, Noel. *The Life of Ezra Pound*. New York: Pantheon Books, 1970.

————. *Poet in Exile*. Manchester, England: Manchester University Press, 1964.

Symons, James M. *Meyerhold's Theatre of the Grotesque: The Post-Revolutionary Productions, 1920-1932*. Coral Gables, Fla.: University of Miami Press, 1971.

Symons, Julian. *The Thirties*. London: Cresset Press, 1960.

Tertz, Abram. *On Socialist Realism*. Translated by George Dennis. New York: Pantheon Books, 1960.

Thiher, Allen. *Céline: The Novel as Delirium*. New Brunswick, N. J.: Rutgers University Press, 1972.

Thomson, George. *Aeschylus and Athens*. London: Lawrence & Wishart, 1941.

Trilling, Lionel. *Sincerity and Authenticity*. Cambridge, Mass.: Harvard University Press, 1972.

Trotsky, Leon. *Literature and Revolution*. New York: Russell & Russell, 1957.

Tucker, Robert C. *The Soviet Political Mind*. New York and London: Frederick A. Praeger, 1963.

Tynan, Kenneth. *Tynan Right and Left*. New York: Atheneum, 1967.

Tzara, Tristan. *"Approximate Man" and Other Writings*. Translated by Mary Ann Caws. Detroit, Mich.: Wayne State University Press, 1973.

Uitti, Karl D. *The Concept of the Self in the Symbolist Novel*. 'S-Gravenhage: Mouton & Co., 1961.

Valéry, Paul. *The Outlook for Inteligence*. Translated by Denise Folliot and Jackson Mathews, edited by Jackson Mathews. New York and Evanston: Harper & Row, 1962.

Venable, Vernon. *Human Nature: The Marxian View*. New York: Alfred A. Knopf, 1946.

Vernon, John. *The Garden and the Map: Schizophrenia in Twentieth-Century Literature* and *Culture*. Urbana, Ill.: University of Illinois Press, 1973.

Villiers de l'Isle-Adam. *Axel*. Translated by Marilyn Gaddis Rose. Dublin: Dolmen Press, 1970.

Villiers, Marjorie. *Charles Péguy*. New York: Harper & Row, 1965.

Voorhees, Richard Jr. *The Paradox of George Orwell*. Purdue University Studies. Humanities Series (1961).

Wain, John, ed. *Literary Annual*. no. 1. New York: Criterion Books, 1959.

Waldberg, Patrick. *Surrealism*. Translated by Stuart Gilbert. Geneva, Switzerland: Albert Skirra, 1962.

Wasserstrom, William, ed. *Civil Liberties and the Arts*. Syracuse, N. Y.: Syracuse University Press, 1964.

Weidell, Walter. *The Art of Bertolt Brecht*. Translated by Daniel Russell. New York: New York University Press, 1963.

Weill, Irving. *Gorky*. New York: Random House, 1966.

Wellwarth, George. *The Theater of Protest and Paradox*. New York: New York University Press, 1964.

White, George Abbott and Newman, Charles, eds. *Literature in Revolution*. New York: Holt, Rinehart and Winston, 1972.

Wilkinson, David. *Malraux: An Essay in Political Criticism*. Cambridge, Mass.: Harvard University Press, 1967.

Willener, Alfred. *The Action–Image of Society*. Translated by A.M. Sheridan. New York: Pantheon Books, 1970.

Willhoite, Fred H. Jr. *Beyond Nihilism: Albert Camus's Contribution to Political Theory*. Baton Rouge, La.: Louisiana State University Press, 1968.

Williams. Raymond. *The Long Revolution*. New York: Columbia University Press, 1961.

———. *Culture and Society*. New York: Harper & Row, 1958.

Wilson, Edmund. *Axel's Castle*. New York: Charles Scribner's Sons, 1931.

Wood, Neal. *Communism and British Intellectuals*. New York: Columbia University Press, 1959.

Woodcock, George. *The Crystal Spirit: A Study of George Orwell*. New York: Minerva Press, 1966.

Wolfe, Bertram D. *The Bridge and the Abyss: The Troubled*

Friendship of Maxim Gorky and V. I. Lenin. New York and London: Frederick A. Praeger, 1967.

Woroszylski, Wiktor. *The Life of Mayakovsky.* Translated by Boleslaw Taborski. New York: The Orion Press, 1970.

Yablonsky, Lewis. *The Hippie Trip.* New York: Pegasus, 1968.

Zamayatin, Yevgeny. *A Soviet Heretic.* Edited and translated by Mirra Ginsburg. Chicago and London: The University of Chicago Press, 1970.

Zhdanov, Andrei A. *Literature, Philosophy, and Music.* New York: International Publishers, 1950.

Zolla, Elémire, *The Eclipse of the Intellectual.* Translated by Raymond Rosenthal. New York: Funk & Wagnalls, 1968.

Index